The Spirituality of Cornelia Connelly:
In God, For God, With God

The Spirituality of Cornelia Connelly: In God, For God, With God

Caritas McCarthy SHCJ

Studies in Women and Religion
Volume 19

The Edwin Mellen Press
Lewiston and Queenston

Library of Congress Cataloging-in-Publication Data

McCarthy, Caritas.
  The spirituality of Cornelia Connelly.

  (Studies in women and religion ; v. 19)
  Bibliography: p.
  Includes index.
  1. Connelly, Cornelia Augustus Peacock, 1809-1879. 2. Nuns--Biography. 3. Society of the Holy Child Jesus--History. I. Title. II. Series.
  BX4527.Z8M33   1986   271'.97[B]   86-21718
  ISBN 0-88946-530-4

This is volume 19 in the continuing series
Studies in Women and Religion
Volume 19 ISBN 0-88946-530-4
SWR Series ISBN 0-88946-549-5

All rights reserved. For more information contact

The Edwin Mellen Press
P. O. Box 450
Lewiston, New York
USA 14092

The Edwin Mellen Press
P. O. Box 67
Queenston, Ontario
CANADA L0S 1L0

Printed in the United States of America

To Elinor McCarthy and Mary Anthony Weinig, SHCJ

Acknowledgements

Heartfelt thanks are given to many Sisters of the Holy Child Jesus, too numerous to name, whose labors in researching, cataloging and interpreting sources on Cornelia Connelly have made this study possible. Special mention should be given to Srs. Mary Evangelist Stewart, Marie Madeleine Amy, Mary Clara Eales, Ursula Blake, Annette Dawson, Therese McSorley, Mary Conneely, Mary Anthony Weinig and Helen Logan. The last two gave editorial assistance and encouragement and Sr. Helen typed the manuscript.

Thanks are due also to Frs. James Walsh, SJ, Paul Molinari, SJ, and Leonard Whatmore for research on and interpretation of sources on Cornelia Connelly; and to my mother, Elinor McCarthy, for her research and her encouragement of my work. Thanks are due in a special way to Fr. Gervais Dumeige, SJ, former director of the Institute of Spirituality of the Pontifical Gregorian University for direction of this study as a dissertation, and to him and Sr. Mary Milligan, RSHM, also of the Gregorian University faculty, for enlightenment and constant encouragement.

Gratitude is also due to the American Philosophy Society and the American Association for State and Local History for research grants in 1965 and 1966; to Virginia Mahinske, and to the Connelly Fund of Rosemont College for financial assistance in publishing this work; also to Dr. Herbert Richardson of the Edwin Mellen Press for assistance in publication. Finally, thanks are due to my religious superiors for support of this work, and to Dr. Dorothy Brown, President of Rosemont College for academic leave, Spring semester, 1980.

Table of Contents

Abbreviations Used	xi
Introduction	xiii

Part One
"The Spirit Blows Where It Will"   1

1   The Charismatic Dimension of the Church   3
The Primitive Church and the Charismatic Dimension   5
Vatican II and the Charismatic Dimension   8
Current Studies on the Charism of the Founder   10
The Spirit of the Founder and of the Institute   16

2   Family Heritage and Early Life of Cornelia: 1732-1832   24
Maternal and Paternal Roots   25
Happy Family Life   27
Good Education   27
Protestant Religious Affiliations   28
Marriage to Pierce Connelly   30

3   Through Successive Calls to Ultimate Vocation: 1832-1852   35
Married to an Episcopalian Priest   36
Called to Roman Catholicism   37
Providential Role of Joseph Nicollet   40
Implication of Conversion: Pierce a Catholic Priest?   43
Cornelia's Reception into the Church   46
Holding Their Marriage Together   47
Introduction to the Spiritual Exercises of St. Ignatius   52
Cornelia's Offering of Her Son and Husband   53
Discerning Her Own Call to Religious Life   56
Papal Support of Pierce's Priestly Vocation   58
Cornelia as Quasi-Postulant and Mother   59
To Return to Married Life?   64
"I have given him to God"   65
Vocation to be a Founder   65
Testing of Vocation:
    Pierce's Deterioration and Cornelia's Growth   68
Wife and Children as Property   73
Marriage, Celibacy and "Perfection"   75
Pierce a "big catch"   80

Part Two
Embodiment of the Inspiration 89

4   The Primitive Society: 1846-54 92
    Mission and Ministry 92
    Cornelia as Exemplar 98
    The Founder Developing the Constitutions 106
    The Original Inspiration Expressed in the Constitutions of 1850 108
    The Original Inspiration Expressed in the Constitutions of 1854 111

5   Years of Fruition: 1854-69 121
    Spiritual Formation and Government 122
        The Original Inspiration Developed in Auxiliaries
            to the Constitutions 122
        Constitutions and Government 128
        Use of the Constitutions of Other Orders 133
        The Spiritual Exercises as the Means to the
            "True Spirit of the Constitutions" 136
        The Spiritual Tradition from which Cornelia Drew 143
    Ministry 149
        The Single End 149
        Breadth and Depth 151
        The Teacher Training College 153
        The Book of the Order of Studies 155
        Holy Child Schools 158
        The Restoration of Mayfield 161
        Mission to America 162

6   Years of Purification: 1869-79 172
    Evolution of Apostolic Poverty, Chastity, Obedience 172
        Poverty 172
        Chastity 174
        Obedience 176
    Purification 181
    Cornelia's Last Years and Death 195

Conclusion
    In God, For God, With God 203

Appendices
A   **The Writings of Cornelia Connelly: Survey and Analysis** 209
B   **Schematic Outline of SHCJ Constitutional History:**
    1854-1986 216

Sources and Select Bibliography 218

Index 246

Abbreviations Used

For Sources

Bellasis	Life of the Mother Foundress of the SHCJ by Mother Mary Francis Bellasis. Documentation presented by the Historical Commission for the Beatification and Canonization of the Servant of God, Cornelia Connelly, Foundress of the Society of the Holy Child Jesus, vols. 72-75 (cited as D).
Buckle	Materials Collected for a Life of Cornelia Connelly by Mother Maria Joseph Buckle. Documentation presented by the Historical Commission for the Beatification and Canonization of the Servant of God, Cornelia Connelly, Foundress of the Society of the Holy Child Jesus, vols. 63-67. (cited as D).
CC	The Writings of the Servant of God, Cornelia Connelly, Foundress of the Society of the Holy Child Jesus [compiled for] Beatification and Canonization, 58 vols.
Const	Constitutions of the Society of the Holy Child Jesus. Documentation Presented by the Historical Comission for the Beatification and Canonization of the Servant of God, Cornelia Connelly, Foundress of the Society of the Holy Child Jesus, vols. 46-53, compiled in *Source* 4.
Const SJ	Constitutions of the Society of Jesus. Varying editions are cited in footnotes and Bibliography.
D	Documentation Presented by the Historical Comission for the Beatification and Canonization of the Servant of God, Cornelia Connelly, Foundress of the Society of the Holy Child Jesus. 85 vols.
Ex	Spiritual Exercises of St. Ignatius of Loyola.
GA	*God Alone*. An Anthology of the Spiritual Writings of

xii   *The Spirituality of Cornelia Connelly*

                       Cornelia Connelly, ed. J. Walsh and C. Sullivan, London, 1959.
RSCJ   Religieuses du Sacré Coeur de Jésus.
Rules SHCJ   Rules of the Society of the Holy Child Jesus, compiled/composed by Cornelia Connelly with the aid of J. Grassi, SJ, and Pierce Connelly, Rome 1845-46; MS in SHCJ Archives, Rome.
SHCJ   Society of the Holy Child Jesus, or Sister of the Holy Child Jesus.

                       For Documents of Vatican II

AA   *Apostolicam Actuositatem*, Decree on the Apostolate of the Laity.
AG   *Ad Gentes*, Decree on the Church's Missionary Activity.
GS   *Gaudium et Spes*, Pastoral Constitution on the Church in the Modern World.
LG   *Lumen Gentium*, Dogmatic Constitution on the Church.
PC   *Perfectae Caritatis*, Decree on the Appropriate Renewal of Religous Life.

                       For Other Works Consulted

CIS   *Centrum Ignatianum Spiritualitatis*
DBT   *Dictionary of Biblical Theology*
DS   *Dictionaire de spiritualité ascétique et mystique*
DTC   *Dictionaire de théologie catholique*
NCE   *New Catholic Encyclopedia*
Prog. Sp. Ex.   *Program to Adapt the Spiritual Exercises*
SM   *Sacramentum Mundi: An Encylopedia of Theology*
Studies SJ   *Studies in the Spirituality of the Jesuits*
Way Supp   *Supplement to the Way*

Introduction

To study Cornelia Connelly's spiritual itinerary is to take religion out of books and theories and to see it tested in the most fundamental and varied, complex and challenging of woman's life experiences. In her native America, 1831-43, she was wife/helpmate to her Episcopalian priest-husband, and with him, a convert to Roman Catholicism; she was mother of five children and teacher in a pioneer Catholic mission school in Louisiana. In Rome, 1844, she separated from her husband that he might become a Roman Catholic priest. Finally in England, 1846-79, she became founder[1] of an apostolic congregation of sisters in which she was both spiritual and educational leader.

Role changes made their demands on Cornelia within five years of marriage. Her husband, Pierce, having renounced his Episcopalian ministry, asked, when he was received in the Roman Catholic Church, to continue the priesthood to which he had been ordained eight years earlier in the Protestant Episcopal Church. Rome's rule of clerical celibacy made Cornelia's role uncertain, even anguishing. At first, Roman authorities supported what Cornelia believed in—continuance of the sacramental union which bound husband as well as wife to each other, and together to the nurture of their children. Rome counseled Pierce toward lay ministry which Cornelia warmly supported and in which she was an able collaborator. However, when her husband renewed his request for ordination, Cornelia, after eight years of discerning, gave her consent to a Roman decree of separation that allowed Pierce to become a priest the following year, 1845. Her spiritual notes through this difficult period reveal a profound spiritual life marked by a steady growth in union with God that included a sense of her own identity and worth. She recognized her own God-given call to celibate community life, and even to the founding of a new congregation of sisters when the pressing needs of English and American Catholic women and children were presented to her. Like Elizabeth Seton before her, she believed she could, as founder, care for her children within the context of her convent life.

Scarcely had Cornelia launched her congregation than her husband, manifesting severe emotional illness, used anti-feminist British marriage law, the anti-Catholic British press, and even, in 1848, the kidnapping of their children to force her to return to married life. She refused, citing the injustice of his demands and the irrevocability of the new commitments each had made, an irrevocability she had warned him of. She remained faithful until her death thirty years later to what she believed to be her ultimate calling from God, even though this meant years of fruitless, painful struggle to regain her children. Because her husband had posed as founder of her congregation, the shadow of his apostasy hung over it for as long as she lived. Yet she grew increasingly effective as leader in spiritual formation and education that affirmed women as full persons in their relationships with God and the human community.

This first documented study to be published will deal more directly than have biographies with the misogynist elements in her milieu and will include new source materials which show how severely these elements constrained her, limiting her options in the difficult moral decisions she had to make. The injustices imposed on women by nineteenth-century British marriage law were not the only source of her suffering. In a more subtle way her spirit was tested by the lack of a positive affirmation within the Catholic Church of the fullness of holiness to be found in fulfilling the vocation to marriage. And finally, as she lived out her celibate vocation, she and her religious sisters were constrained by cloister laws for women which conflicted with the demands for active service to which the Church and world called them. They also found themselves hampered by clerical interference in matters where authority was rightfully theirs.

Feminist consciousness today highlights the centrality of women's issues in Cornelia Connelly's story. Insights from contemporary women's studies will be utilized in this book. But it is not written from a specifically feminist viewpoint because feminism was not the focal, integrating factor in Cornelia's life nor did she utilize feminist rhetoric. Clearly, the focus of her life was the profound inner journey she traversed to always deeper union with her God through his gifting and her free response. This book centers on her spirituality, and, within that, her evident spiritual gift for leadership in the service of others to which St. Paul gave the enduring name "charism." Among the more striking expressions Cornelia gave to her awareness of her charism was her reminder to her sisters: "in God, for God, and with God you can do all things."[2] From her expression is drawn the title of this book.

The concept of charism we are utilizing for this study demands that we research beyond the religious vocation of the person with a charism-for-founding to the early and successive manifestations of the Spirit's providential grace in the person's youth. Laurentin has noted recently that charism as "supernatural" does not mean "super-added to nature, like a kind of super-structure." Rather, "the charism sets free natural gifts according to the diversity of people and of the human communities . . . .

Charisms touch the whole of human reality, individually and collectively."³ We believe with Dumeige that a founder may "utilize all that he [or she] is for God and for men," to "realize his [or her] vocation as founder."⁴ Therefore we have dealt with Cornelia's Protestant Philadelphia family origins and youth, and with her married life in Mississippi, Louisiana, Rome, noting her growth in feminine as well as Christian identity. If her Protestant beginnings and her marriage seem unlikely backgrounds for the emergence of a founder of a Roman Catholic sisterhood, they can serve to deepen our understanding of the Holy Spirit's infinite freedom in bestowing his charisms "creatively and unexpectedly." Joannine theology tells us "the Spirit blows where it will" (Jn. 3:8); we have used this for the title of Part One of this book.

Since our understanding of charism of foundation includes not only an evangelical inspiration capable of attracting followers, but also the ability of the founder, in union with her followers, to give institutional form to the mission inherent in her inspiration, we have devoted Part Two, "Embodiment of the Inspiration," to the last thirty-three years of Cornelia's life as superior of the Society of the Holy Child Jesus. There she gave expression to her ideal of psycho-spiritual maturity for women. We have traced her manifest efforts to inculcate, and the efforts of her followers to develop, a "spirit" proper to the original inspiration. Under the themes of spiritual formation, constitutions, government, and ministry we have traced her initial responses to the needs especially of the women and children of the English Catholic Revival; her missionary expansion to central and northern England, the United States, France; and her successful struggles, in the last decade of her life, to hold together a divided membership.

Extended, documented treatment of the theology of charisms, of SHCJ constitutional development, of Cornelia's spiritual themes, of the spiritual tradition from which she drew, and the nature of her writings has been given not only as a base for further studies of her and her congregation, but also as an aid to research on other nineteenth-century Catholic women's congregations. Their archives are important for feminine and American spirituality. The women of these congregations shared many religious ideas as well as problems in common, and perhaps more with Protestant and Jewish women than has been demonstrated.

Several reasons make it appropriate to focus this first documented, full-length study of Cornelia's spirituality through her charism. It is a focus which underscores the continuity between the first and second halves of her life, between her vocation to marriage and to celibate community life. It is a focus which links, as she consistently did, her inner journey to her outer one, with an awareness that the events of her life were the God-given circumstances in which her unique spiritual identity would be forged.

The abundant sources available for the study of Cornelia's spirituality lend themselves to a study of her charism. It was the recognition of her special gifting for mission by the Spirit that caused many sisters of her congregation and several members of her family to preserve her writings—both printed ones, and manuscript notes, jottings, letters. It was a renewed recognition of her charism and of the possibility of the Catholic Church's accepting her as a candidate for sainthood that spurred the sisters of her congregation in the last forty years to recover many additional source materials to be used in her Cause for Beatification and Canonization. The wealth of source materials now available have been used for this study. They shed new light on certain aspects of her life; nevertheless, this study does not supersede published biographies which continue to contribute to an understanding of this American woman whose cause for canonization is currently under consideration in the Catholic Church.

As an American woman, Cornelia adds an important chapter to emerging studies of American spirituality. Her story raises the question as to whether she was the first Catholic woman missionary *from* the "New World" *to* the "Old." Cornelia's spiritual journey supplies an enlightening chapter in the currently developing field of charismatic theology, that study of the dynamic element in the Church which reminds us that our God is present to us in the reality of our on-going historical development, both individual and communal. Hopefully her spiritual journey helps us to understand more clearly not only the nature of the charism for celibate communal life, but also encourages us to explore more deeply that charism for Matrimony shared by husband and wife.

Cornelia Connelly is an exemplar and witness to a universal call to holiness. She seems to have perceived life itself as calling from God. Through response to successive calls, she grew ever more sensitive to the *One* who called, to his fundamental call to share his life in holiness. Her spiritual notes take us to the roots of vocation itself as she adhered to her God in the midst of insoluble problems and found him faithful.

Notes

1. Throughout this book the one term "founder" is used to designate both founders (male) and foundresses (female).
2. Bellasis D 74:362.
3. R. Laurentin, "Charisms: Terminological Precision," *Charisms in the Church*, Concilium, 109 (1978), 7.
4. G. Dumeige, "Ignace de Loyola. Experience et doctrine spirituelle," *DS* 7 (1976).

The Spirituality of Cornelia Connelly:
In God, For God, With God

Cornelia Connelly

Part One

"The Spirit Blows Where It Will"[1]

Chapter 1

The Charismatic Dimension of the Church

Renewed awareness since Vatican II of the enduring charismatic element in the Church and increasing emphasis in theological reflection on the active role of the Holy Spirit in all phases of Christian life have enhanced appreciation of the creative richness of that life and have contributed to contemporary spiritual renewal. Karl Rahner had been concerned, even before Vatican II, to insure that the charismatic dimension would become central to ongoing theological studies. Recently he reiterated his concern:

> The charismatic dimension is as necessary and permanent a part of the life of the Church as are offices and sacraments. Charisms were not given simply to help the Church in its beginnings, but it is of the nature of charisms as an essential feature of the Church that they should appear in constantly new forms and therefore constantly have to be rediscovered (in contrast to ministries and their transmission.) This characteristic of charisms is also the explicit teaching of the Church (D 2288; Pius XII, *Mystici Corporis* [AAS 35 (1943) 200 f]; Vat. II *De Eccl.* 15; *De Oec.* 3). Such charisms may be equally regarded as assistance to ministries in the Church without which they cannot be properly performed, as a promise to the ministries for which their holders have a duty to remain ready, and (when already present) as a sign of suitability for ministry.[2]

Although the foregoing statement is clear and emphatic, especially in points that relate to the subject of this thesis—the charism of a founder of a religious congregation—one cannot say that great theological precision has been achieved in all phases of study of the charismatic dimension. Rahner has underlined this last point, noting that "the history of the theology of the charismatic movement in the Church and in the service of the Church is still to be written." This is because, he says, the theology of the movement "has remained relatively undeveloped."[3] Current studies on the charisms of religious founders, emanating as much from Vatican II's call to renewal of religious life as from academic theological considerations, can contribute to charismatic theology and its history insofar as they utilize sound theological and historical methodology. Essential to this is the dispassionate scholarship which allows the evidence of the gifting of the Spirit to emerge in all the originality of the particular evangelical vision and institutional form for which he empowered each founder. This applies to the limitations as well as the strengths of each founder's vision and enduring works, and to the contexts, edifying or questionable, in which the Spirit of God chose to work powerfully within receptive men or women for the upbuilding of the Church. Teresa Ledochowska, after studying deeply the sources on her founder, Angela Merici, was able to report some aspects with great clarity: "Her life of prayer and service makes one think of an arrow shot at a single target with the dynamic force of love." But regarding the question as to what direction Angela thought her company should go, what part it was to play in the Church in order to comply with God's plan, Ledochowska answers honestly: "we do not know."[4] In respecting the sources she shows respect for the limited role this particular founder was to play in institutionalizing her original inspiration, and what was left to those who had identified with and developed her spirit. For the study of the founder under consideration in this thesis, Cornelia Connelly, the demands for fidelity to truth are of another sort. There is first of all the need to accept the burden of sifting through the very rich sources on her eventful life and on the central role she played in gathering a community and shaping an institution for mission in the Church according to her original inspiration. There is also the need, if one is to grasp the depth of the Spirit's action in her, to accept as she did the scandal of the Cross in the flawed human context in which God allowed her original inspiration and her Society of the Holy Child Jesus to develop. Only with this acceptance can we see the validity of her vocation and charism, and appreciate the depth of her insight into the Paschal character of the humble and hidden life of the Holy Child Jesus, and of the redemptive nature of accepted suffering.

In the treatment of charisms, in general and in particular, it is both difficult and important to set limits to the scope of any one study. The very aspect of charismatic theology which is clearest to the theologians—that the Spirit is infinitely free and creative, inspiring those who are receptive to him with divine adaptability to make salvation history out of most mundane or most tortured human history—makes the charismatic dimension broad and diverse. It would be too broad a base for this study to utilize Rahner's "Charisms may be present in all Christians, and are present in germ in all who are justified and are therefore members of the body of Christ each with his own functions." As a beginning of limitation we accept here the distinction, which Rahner himself suggests, between charisms and the hidden, individual, though often heroic practice of the Christian virtues: ". . . that charisms give additional prominence to the social, public, witnessing and missionary character which always accompanies Christian virtues in the Church, though in varying degrees."[5] This distinction seems to express rather neatly what emerges when one studies the lives of at least those charismatics who were founders—that there is manifest a mysterious and powerful *enabling*, which either stimulates or assists them to give public, witnessing, missionary and above all communitarian form to their evangelical endeavors.

We shall also refrain here from a particular exposition of the charisms of the hierarchy for their offices, as belonging to another order, while having a role complementary to the non-offical charisms. The former are gifts of the Spirit for the good of the Church, but they are already assured to the hierarchy through the promise of Christ, to his apostles and their successors, of the abiding gift of the Spirit to his Church. What we are concerned with here are those charisms by which the Spirit certainly gifts the Church, but in gratuitous, unpredictable and adaptive ways which must be recognized, discerned, and ultimately accepted, even welcomed by the hierarchical Church for the continued growth of the whole body of Christ. A valuable distinction which has been made concerning the charismatic in this latter sense, is that in this instance the personal grace *precedes* the institutional embodiment which, in fact, owes its existence to that personal grace.[6] This notion becomes important in understanding the nature and extent of a charism of foundation.

It should be noted here that in distinguishing between official and non-official charisms we do not in any way suggest a fundamental dichotomy. We reject the Sohm vs. Rome theory,[7] in favor of the obvious fundamental unity of the two kinds of charisms emanating from the one Spirit of God for the one end—the upbuilding of the Church. But if the dichotomy should be rejected, the distinction should be maintained as clarifying the complementarity which should exist between the two. The more stable form of charismatic endowment is needed both to facilitate the emergence of always new charismatic manifestations relevant to succeeding stages in the pilgrimage of the People of God, and to test and channel the new gifts for the common good. This complementarity was already evident in the charismatic experience of New Testament times where distinctions were barely evident, where the prevailing note was the unity of purpose in the Spirit's gifting—the service of the Body of the Risen Lord.[8]

The Primitive Church and the Charismatic Dimension

It is to the New Testament and especially to the Pauline letters that exegetes and theologians look for the seed of contemporary charismatic theology. It was Paul who first employed the term "charism" in reflecting with his early Christian community of Corinth on their experience of the Spirit of the Risen Lord.[9] He can assure them that they are "not lacking in any charism" while they wait for the "day of our Lord Jesus Christ"[10]; that "Each has his own charism from God, one of one kind, one of another."[11] In twelve additional passages in his letters to his communities, Paul refers to their charisms[12] and four times he lists with somewhat overlapping content, kinds of charisms,[13] e.g., in 1 Co 12:28 ff., a list which includes the hierarchical charism: "first apostles, second prophets, third teachers, then miracle-workers, healers, assistants, administrators and those who speak in tongues." But we are not to think that Paul "gives us an organized and orderly theology of the charismatic gifts" any more than we are to think of him in a highly structured Church. Rather, "he attempts to express in a sometimes imprecise vocabulary the rich experience of the Spirit of which he was aware in the early Church." To explore fully Paul's connotations for charism we would have to refer to other terms by which he expresses the uniqueness of the Christian experience after Pentecost:

> Not only does he use four different terms to express this reality, but he freely intermingles what later tradition distinguishes as ordinary and extraordinary gifts, gifts of office and non-official gifts, transitory and "stable" gifts. The terms "spiritual gifts" ($\chi\alpha\rho\iota\zeta\mu\alpha\tau\alpha$ and $\pi\nu\epsilon\upsilon\mu\alpha\tau\iota\chi\alpha$), "ministries" or "services" ($\delta\iota\alpha\chi\omicron\nu\iota\alpha\iota$) and "workings" or "operations" ($\epsilon\nu\epsilon\rho\gamma\eta\mu\alpha\tau\alpha$) cover a wide spectrum of manifestations of the Spirit—from wisdom and leadership to healing and speaking in tongues.[14]

If Paul gives only rich seeds for a later more precise theology which has been slow to develop (does the charismatic dimension resist precision?), he does establish clearly the enduring theological tradition that charisms are for the service of the Body of Christ.[15] Käsemann has picked this up in our own time to note that "service is not merely the consequence but the outward form and realization of the charism."[16] In a further synthesis of what endures from Paul to our own time, Schürmann finds in the primitive Church an "essential archetype" for the development of the life of the Church. On the basis of the four terms used by Paul he finds four elements common to all the spiritual phenomena described as charisms:

1) they are "spiritual" in their origin and manifestation ($\pi\nu\epsilon\upsilon\mu\alpha\tau\iota\chi\alpha$);
2) they evidence the powerful "working" of God ($\epsilon\nu\epsilon\rho\gamma\eta\mu\alpha\tau\alpha$);
3) they "serve" to edify the community ($\delta\iota\alpha\chi\omicron\nu\iota\alpha\iota$);
4) they are "gifts of divine grace," that is, totally gratuitous ($\chi\alpha\rho\iota\zeta\mu\alpha\tau\alpha$).[17]

Commentators on Paul's use of charism in Romans 5 and 6 find their particular emphasis on the powerful "working" of God coupled with the paradox of the essential freedom the Spirit leaves to the potential charismatic. A commentator on Rom 5:16: "but the charisma following many trespasses brought justification," notes "for the first time we find it [charisma] used in a total sense, i.e., as the 'energizing' which is poured out through the Spirit on all who pass by faith from the death dimension of the first (disobedient) Adam to the life dimension of the second (obedient) Adam."[18] Commenting on Rom 6:23: "The wages of sin is death, but the charisma of God is eternal life in Christ Jesus our Lord," Milne Home continues: "The gift is free, but he [Paul] asks us to realize that our choice is also free, for it is open to us to give our service where we will . . . ." She notes the "urgency" of Paul's exhortations throughout Romans 6 that "each one make an active response to the *challenge* of the gift."[19] She concurs with Käsemann who comments on Romans 5 and 6: "eternal life does not encourage sleeping partners or uninvested capital;" . . . "there is no passive membership in the body of Christ."[20] Milne Home sees in Paul a "conviction that there is a human and 'free' side to the divine 'energizing.' Even if we are receptive to it, it does not simply stream through to us; we make it our own with all the resources of our personal make-up and abilities."[21]

For understanding charism of foundation we want to recall both poles of the paradox manifest in the primitive church—of divine respect for the freedom of the individual, yet *divinely* powerful working of God the Holy Spirit. We want to grow in the awareness in which the early Christians grew—that the spirit of God was working among them not only through the sensational and miraculous, but through the power to practice truly Christian virtue.[22] The public, witnessing character of the Spirit's "working" was especially manifest in sustained heroic virtue. Thus martyrdom, and very soon, virginity and asceticism as ways of life, came to be recognized as charisms, that is, as human actions or courses of action not possible by purely human power, indicative of the direct, divinely powerful and sustained intervention of God. It is such a gift that seems to be manifest in the lives of many founders currently under study as charismatics.

Such gifts have indeed been recognized and affirmed throughout the twenty centuries of the Church's history, but, as we have noted, the theology of the charismatic dimension of the Church has never been fully developed from its New Testament and Patristic roots. Patristic writings, especially those of the early Fathers, e.g., Clement of Rome, Ignatius of Antioch, and the compilers of the *Didache* and the *Apostolic Constitutions* continue the Pauline teaching and terminology on the charisms of the Holy Spirit within the growing Church. The *Apostolic Constitutions* "clearly suppose that they [charisms] will continue in the Church."[23] Their continuance is recognized in the High Middle Ages by St. Thomas' definition of "freely bestowed grace." He distinguished "gratia gratis data" from "sanctifying grace"—"gratia gratum faciens." Although "freely bestowed grace" is, like "sanctifying grace," "beyond the capacity of [man's] nature, and beyond his personal merit, . . . it is not given that a man might himself be justified by it, but rather so that he might cooperate in the justification of someone else."[24] Thus Thomistic teaching picks up the Pauline emphasis on charisms for the service of the Church.

But even the Thomistic treatment of charisms, and the recognition given throughout the medieval and post-Reformation centuries to founders and leaders of religious orders and congregations, to saintly and effective theologians and preachers, to ministers to the poor, sick and oppressed, to mystics and miracle-workers, has not given to the Church a full elaboration of the theology of its charismatic dimension. A more insistent search for that elaboration emerged in our century in the course of the Second Vatican Council.

Vatican II and the Charismatic Dimension

The Bishops of the world who assembled in Rome for Vatican II manifested a sense of urgency to respond to the ever-present energizing action of the Spirit in the life of the Church. In view of this, they sought a base for theological renewal in the Church of the New Testament and the early Fathers. One result of their return to the sources of Christianity has been a renewed emphasis on pneumatic theology and on charismatic contributions to the development of the Church. Although Rahner rightly reminds us that the base for this renewal was laid as early as 1943 in Pius XII's *Mystici Corporis*[25] (and, one might add, in his 1950 address to the first international congress of religious),[26] it was not until Vatican II that the renewal movement gained momentum. In this movement religious have gained a new sense of their identity and the importance of their mission in the Church and a new recognition of the meaning of the charismatic role of their founders.

In *Lumen Gentium*, Vatican II draws attention to its charismatic dimension in its initial statement on the Church's mission: the Father sends the Son; the Father and Son send the Spirit; the Spirit, "sent into the hearts of the faithful . . . guides the Church into the fullness of truth . . . He furnishes and directs her with various gifts both hierarchical and charismatic . . ." Here, as in the primitive Church we find a recognition of the unity of the hierarchical and charismatic in one source, the Spirit: "Thus the Church shines forth as a people made one with the unity of the Father, the Son and the Holy Spirit."[27]

References to the Holy Spirit's abiding and enabling presence pervade *Lumen Gentium*. Section 12 provides a brief but rich synthesis of Pauline teachings on charism which have continued to be developed by theologians since the Council.

> It is not only through the sacraments and Church ministries that the same Holy Spirit sanctifies and leads the People of God and enriches it with virtues. Allotting His gifts "to everyone according as he will" (1 Co 12:11), He distributes special graces among the faithful of every rank. By these gifts He makes them fit and ready to undertake the various tasks or offices advantageous for the renewal and upbuilding of the Church, according to the words of the Apostle: "The manifestation of the Spirit is given to everyone for profit" (1 Co 12:7). These charismatic gifts, whether they be the most outstanding or the more simple and widely diffused, are to be received with thanksgiving and consolation, for they are exceedingly suitable and useful for the needs of the Church.

Still, extraordinary gifts are not to be rashly sought after, nor are the fruits of apostolic labor to be presumptuously expected from them. In any case, judgment as to their genuineness and proper use belongs to those who preside over the church, and to whose special competence it belongs, not indeed to extinguish the Spirit, but to test all things and hold fast to that which is good (cf. I Th. 5:12, 19-21).[28]

One of the major contributions of Vatican II has been to give explicit recognition to the charisms of the laity and, especially among these, of married people.[29] It also gave renewed recognition to religious as belonging expressly to the charismatic dimension of the Church. We read in *Ad Gentes*:

. . . the Holy Spirit, who shares His gifts as He wills for the common good (cf. 1 Co 12:11), implants in the hearts of individuals a missionary vocation and at the same time raises up institutes in the Church who take on the duty of evangelization, which pertains to the whole Church, and make it as it were their own special task.[30]

It was especially through *Perfectae Caritatis* that Vatican II turned the attention of religious to the charisms of their founders, laying a foundation for a future theology of the charism of foundation. The decree noted that:

under the influence of the Holy Spirit many [of those practicing the evangelical counsels] pursued a solitary life, or founded religious families to which the Church willingly gave the welcome and approval of her authority. And so it happened by divine plan that a wonderful variety of religious communities grew up. This variety contributed mightily toward making the Church experienced in every good deed (cf. 2 Tim 3:17) and ready for a ministry of service in building up Christ's body (cf. Eph 4:12.)[31]

Thus Vatican II defines the work of founding a religious community in the Pauline tradition: Charism is seen as a free gift of the Holy Spirit for the edification of the Church, a gift characterized by the Spirit's creative originality, a gift that bears testing by the hierarchy.

In directing the orders and congregations toward their renewal, the Council singles out perhaps three elements associated with the Spirit's gift enabling a founder to found:

The appropriate renewal . . . involves . . . a continuous return to the original inspiration behind a given community . . . . It serves the best interests of the Church for communities to have their own special character and purpose. Therefore loyal recognition and safe-keeping should be accorded to the spirit of founders, as also to all the particular goals and wholesome traditions which constitute the heritage of each community.[32]

It would seem from the above 1) that the Holy Spirit gifts the founder with an original inspiration; 2) that he/she develops his/her own spirit; and 3) gives as a heritage to his/her community, this spirit, and the special character, purpose and wholesome traditions of that community.

Current Studies on the Charism of the Founder

Working from the base given here, religious were noteworthy in the decade following Vatican II for their efforts to renew in the spirit of the founders for the upbuilding of the Church in the twentieth century. The first enthusiasm yielded gradually to the sober realization that great labor, skill and grace are needed to renew according to the charism of the founder.[33] Some congregations have had to research a group of founders, and some have had to trace a process of refoundation. These are important aspects for consideration, but we have limited ourselves here to the study of the charism of a single founder whose Institute has endured to the present. Many articles have offered insight on the process; one book-length study and a follow-up article seem to offer sufficiently comprehensive framework and methodology to be used as a base for this study.[34] The framework and methodology have been useful not only for direct application, but also as a testing ground against which the circumstances unique to the evolution and fulfillment of Cornelia Connelly's charism of foundation stand out more clearly and indicate the need for adapting and supplementing.

In her study of Jean Gailhac, founder of the Religious of the Sacred Heart of Mary, M. Milligan identified charism in its most fundamental sense as an "evident gift given to an individual by the Holy Spirit for the good of the Church."[35] Gailhac's charism for founding, as well as that of the subject of this study, Cornelia Connelly, and an impressive number of other founders of the last two centuries, have been tested and approved by the hierarchical Church as evidencing the direct action of the Spirit for the needs of the Church. Thus M. Milligan began her study, as we do here, with the fact of a charism, the fact of the existence of a very rich and tested experience of the Spirit within the Church. Proceeding from this she utilized, as we do here, the methodology of St. Paul and of Vatican II, to "attempt to describe it, to circumscribe it in various ways." This method has been underscored by Futtrell: "The founder's charism . . . is a *mystery* . . . It cannot be defined. it can only be described, as we describe those presently visible characteristics of a living human being, . . . character and personality, and history and body . . . ."[36]

But even the process of describing needs a structure, and this Milligan provides. She distinguishes three "moments," not necessarily chronological, in the process of founding a religious congregation under the inspiration of the Holy Spirit; 1) the *original inspiration*, "expressed externally by the founder in word or deed, in some way;" 2) the *gathering of a community* in true spiritual kinship; and 3) *institutionalization*, "that is, the articulation of goals, values and means in a stable form." Directing attention to the person the Spirit inspired to found, she distinguishes three further elements: 1) a *particular synthesis of the Gospel*— or a *faith-vision*; 2) a *sensitivity to the needs* of the People of God; and 3) a *dynamic charity* or *holiness*.[37] In delineating these two triads, Mary Milligan has indicated the extensive and complex nature of the grace which is currently termed "charism of the founder" or "charism of foundation." They have been used to focus research on the life and writings of Cornelia Connelly. But they cannot be, nor were they intended to be used as neat little compartments which, when filled with descriptive materials, constitute an exposition of charism foundation. Rather, what we are concerned with is tracing a process, a providential flow of graces, a "complex of graces,"[38] given to a human collaborator responding sensitively to the Spirit within his concrete life situations. Laurentin has recently warned us of the error of reifying the notion of charism and detaching the supernatural vivification by the Spirit from the living human person who is transformed from within by grace. Laurentin writes:

> If charisms may be said to be 'supernatural' in the sense that they are free gifts of the Spirit, it is only on condition that 'supernatural' is not understood as superadded to nature, like a kind of superstructure, a metal crown on a bodily head. The charism sets free natural gifts according to the diversity of people and of the human communities. Hence, charisms touch the whole of human reality, individually and collectively, the body and physical features, according to the diversity of commitment or involvement.[39]

We have found the notion of a Spirit-guided *process*, gradually but powerfully developing within the whole life of the founder, to be indispensable in interpreting what sources show on Cornelia's charism of foundation. We recall Gervais Dumeige on Ignatius: "It is in utilizing all that he is for God and for men that Ignatius realizes his vocation as founder."[40] From an historical perspective we see the gratuitous *energizing* power of the Spirit especially manifest in the *light* he gave Cornelia to see more and more how she could use her life experiences and her gifts for the edification of the Church, and in the *conviction* and *strength* he gave her to found and develop her Society in the face of obstacles.

Because the manifestations of the charismatic power given to Cornelia are so deeply embedded in the varied and demanding events of her life, and because Cornelia responded with increasing sensitivity to the light the Spirit shed through the Gospel on those events, it has been necessary, in the forthcoming chapters, to deal extensively with the events of her life. Therefore it will be valuable here to treat briefly in analytical form the theology of charism of foundation sketched by Mary Milligan, and to indicate where and how they are exemplified in the narration to follow. She directs us first, as did Vatican II, to the *original inspiration*, analyzing it, as has been noted, under the three-fold concept of a *faith-vision*, a *sensitivity to needs*, and the *dynamism* of *charity*. We can utilize these distinctions in understanding Cornelia Connelly if we do not lose sight of their essential interrelationship in an always evolving process.

When we speak of the first aspect of the original inspiration, of Cornelia's *faith-vision*, of a "personal synthesis of the Word which is both meaningful and motivating, having certain accents and emphases," providing "a unity and a 'hierarchy' to all elements of . . . experience," we are speaking of a "seeing" and a "knowing" that involves immediately for Cornelia response and relationship. It is more appropriate to speak of Cornelia's "experience" of the Gospel than of her Gospel "vision" because her way of knowing tended to be experiential, that is, characterized by a knowing-process and its end result "which of necessity involve the whole person."[41] Her experience of the reality of her relationship with the Triune God through Jesus Christ, and the light which Scripture continually shed on this, continued to grow in intensity and depth to the end of her life. Because, like many of the nineteenth-century women founders, Cornelia had little formal academic theological training, she tended less to explain God, than to witness in word and deed to the reality of his Presence, and of his incorporation of her and her followers into his life and mission. She taught a *way* to live this incorporation. She taught and guided others out of her own experience, always subjecting it to the spiritual direction of the Church, and always clarifying and deepening it by doctrinal and devotional reading.

The Spiritual Exercises of St. Ignatius of Loyola played a decisive role at a crucial stage in Cornelia's life, in bringing her to profound awareness of her own insertion in the Paschal Mystery; they provided her with an instrument which throughout her life clarified and confirmed her grasp of Revelation, and nurtured her in the way in which God was leading her. The Exercises also became for her an instrument by which she could aid others, especially her religious sisters, to hear the Paschal message of the Gospel and respond as individuals to their own Christian vocation to live the mystery. It is apparent that in Cornelia's case the Spiritual Exercises were intrinsic to the Spirit's gift to her for the whole process of founding.[42]

It was within this total vision of the Paschal mystery continued in the Church, and it was especially in "contemplating the Eternal Wisdom"[43] in the mysteries of his earthly life vis à vis the events of her own life, that Cornelia received her inspiration for the Society of the Holy Child Jesus. She came gradually to see, by the integral association of contemplation with personal experience, that the mystery of the "humble and hidden life"[44] of God upon earth contained the whole Paschal dynamism and formed the base for a consecrated life of service within the Church. There had occured for her what Mary Milligan describes as the "intersection of the Word and the world," a situation in which "grace acted at the point of intersection of the Word and the world in a person's life, and that grace, freely responded to, moved the founding person to act."[45] Chapter III is concerned with Cornelia's initial response to this grace, and Chapters IV, V and VI with her evolution and institutionalization of her inspiration through its embodiment in the Society of the Holy Child Jesus.

Historical studies have sometimes revealed questionable elements in the circumstances in which some congregations originated. Mary

Milligan's observation that the Spirit worked *through* those very circumstances rather than despite them, seems appropriate to the scriptural and theological assertion that the Spirit is infinitely free and divinely powerful in the distribution of his charisms.[46] In Cornelia's own time and in our time, questions have been raised regarding the circumstances which led her to found the Society of the Holy Child Jesus. Unless we accept the validity of these questions, pointing as they do to spiritual, ecclesiastical, civil and cultural defects which helped to shape the very circumstances in which the Society originated, we miss a vital aspect. It was precisely the Divine Spirit of the Risen Lord who gave Cornelia light and love to bring a great good for the Church out of a complex and flawed human situation. It was her faith and maturity in these situations which enabled Cornelia to develop a meaningful doctrine of "spiritual crucifixion" and "accepted suffering."[47] Chapter III, indicating the circumstances in which her inspiration for the Society originated, is as necessary as Chapters IV, V, and VI where its institutionalization is traced.

We concur with Mary Milligan's observations that *sensitivity to the needs* of the Christian community has been marked in those charismatics gifted to serve the Church through their institutions. We also concur in noting the appropriateness to their original gospel inspiration, of the services rendered by many religious congregations, at least in their beginnings.[48] It will be evident in Chapters IV, V and VI, that Cornelia, and the approximately two hundred Holy Child sisters who associated themselves with her in her lifetime, clearly derived inspiration for their ministries of education for children, and for the spiritual and cultural development of the women of their time from "the humbled God" who in Nazareth "progressed steadily in wisdom and age and grace before God and men."[49]

Throughout Cornelia's life we find evidence of a Providence shaping her to meet the needs she would encounter as founder. She was able, as Ignatius had been, to utilize all that she was for God and for his people "to realize her vocation as founder."[50] In ensuing Chapters we shall see that the excellence of her own education and cultural advantages prepared her to share these with less fortunate women and children, and that her maternal experiences gave spiritual and psychological insight and warmth, breadth and depth to her educational endeavors. Her Protestant family background and that of her husband imbued both from childhood with that sense of mission for the spread of Christianity which was America's Protestant heritage from its founding.

In common with many founders, Cornelia had a deep sensitivity not just to concrete spiritual, social, cultural and physical needs, but also the perennial *need* of the People of God for the witness to holiness, to the sign in the Church of eschatological fulfillment already begun in this world. Rahner's exposition of the role in the Church proper to those who are publicly vowed to the evangelical counsels explains how the founders ministered to this perennial need. He notes that while Christians in all walks of life are "living their faith to the full," are striving for perfect holiness, it is only in the renunciation entailed by the evangelical counsels, "and this *alone*," that the eschatological witness "is made *explicit*." He adds that the sign "of the fact that in her eschatological faith, she [the Church] is reaching for a goal that lies beyond the present world" is essential for the upbuilding of the faith of all the members of the Church, is a permanent service to all the members of the Christian community, all of whom are called to holiness.[51] The renunciation Cornelia was called upon to make was, for those who understood it, a striking eschatological sign, an embodiment of her faith.

The last of the three aspects which Mary Milligan finds characteristic of the person who founds is *holiness* or the *dynamism* of *charity*. As one who collaborates with the Holy Spirit in establishing an enduring mode of life which by its very nature "tends to the perfection of charity," the founder seems to need, and the lives of many founders witness to, an eminent supernatural love of God and of neighbor.[52] This exemplary charity, completing our description of the charismatic who has a divine inspiration to found, leads us to a consideration of the second element in the whole process of founding, that of the *gathering* of a *community*. It is by the exemplary quality of this charity or holiness, informing a particularly vital insight into a way of living the evangelical life, that the Spirit enables the founder to gather a community. This latter has been termed "the proper object of the charism of foundation."[53] Mary Milligan observes that the founder's life, words and work are privileged in the sense that they resound in other persons with a force which motivates them to leave all and follow Christ in this particular form of life and service . . . . There is a real spiritual affinity among those who participate in the founder's charism, a real bond of fraternity."[54] G. Lafont notes that others gather round the founder because they encounter in her/him "the external expression of their own personal and intimate grace." They find communion "in the same spiritual experience and share the same evangelical sensitivity . . . . By what she/he said and did, the founder liberated in them certain dynamic forces, showed them the real goal of their spiritual search."[55] M. Olphe-Galliard, in noting the enduring as well as the attracting quality of the charism of foundation, speaks of it as "a grace pregnant with lasting effects, since it is the source of a spiritual animation destined to last."[56]

Recollections of Cornelia's early companions, some of which are cited in Chapter IV, verify the reflections noted above, especially in terms of her ability to "liberate in them certain dynamic forces," to show them "the real goal of their spiritual search." And sources on the early days of the Society verify the implication contained in Olphe-Galliard's note that the very gathering of a community through a spiritual inspiration is already the beginning of its *institutionalization*, or the enduring embodiment of the inspiration. Cornelia had a particular gift for institutionalizing, for transforming ideal to act. This is shown through the whole of Chapters IV, V and VI.

The Charismatic Dimension of the Church

It seems to be of the essence of charism that it be specified in the *creation* of an *institution*, the institution being "the external form of a gift and not just its consequence. This institution is designed to protect and transmit the founder's charism within a living tradition."[57] The institution becomes the means by which the Spirit continues a vitalizing, healing, strengthening action in the Church beyond the earthly life of the founder. The institution, supplying a firm, stable and enduring embodiment of the founder's graced way of life, is in turn kept vital and relevant by the original inspiration.[58]

In her first steps toward institutionalization, Cornelia gave personal expression to her original inspiration in the Constitutions she composed/compiled throughout the first eight years of her congregation's existence. Her personal composition was incorporated at the express request of her sisters. These constitutions, headed by her own expression of the Spirit of the Society of the Holy Child Jesus were one of the principal means by which the sisters felt they had both firm and enduring foundations and potential for growth. The Constitutions were supplemented by auxiliaries such as general letters in which Cornelia had greater freedom of expression. Above all, they rested on "the bulwark" of the Spiritual Exercises which Cornelia counted on as the "groundwork of the spiritual life" of her Society. The Exercises had made of Cornelia a spiritual guide who assisted "them to advance in their way, and thence to the spirit of the Society."[59] and who formed Superiors and Novice Mistresses to do the same.

For Cornelia, immediate service in and the setting up of structures for ministry, especially for education, was integral to the very life of the Society which had for its single end the glory and service of God *in* the salvation of souls—those of its members and of their neighbors. From the beginning she shared generously her own exceptional talents for school administration and for teaching both teachers and students. She so incorporated her young sisters into the process of developing a philosophy and system of education that she was able to publish a manual for Holy Child education that was the treasured fruit of their cooperative endeavor and served the Society's schools for over one hundred years.[60] Always, and especially in the earliest days Cornelia undergirded the institutionalization of consecrated life for ministry with her own exemplary role. In Chapter IV the force of this role is indicated.

J. F. Gilmont gathers up the elements of charism of foundation—from original inspiration, through gathering a community, to institutionalization— in a synthetic and concrete fashion. Using texts which span the whole theological tradition of religious life from the fourth to the twentieth century, he examines the founder's charism under the aspects of grace of paternity (or parenthood) in the mission of Christ. By the grace of paternity (or parenthood), the founders engenders a new family *within* the larger Christian family of the baptized. By the grace of mediation the founder is enabled to image or model Christ effectively in those particular aspects of the whole mystery of the Incarnation to which the new religous family is especially called by their founder's inspiration.[61] We find the notion of parenthood, family, and role-model appropriate to what Cornelia manifests of her grace as founder, if these notions are not applied with sentimental or with psychoanalytic overtones. The power of grace seems to have manifested itself especially in her transcending these latter limitations to reach a real spiritual maternity and role-modelling. What Gilmont finds at the base of both these notions accords with Cornelia's experience of her charism—a call to deeper participation in the mission of Christ.[62]

As each individual Christian contributes a unique element to the building up of the body of Christ, so, in Gilmont's view, does each religious community, given its own character through the charism of its founder, contribute uniquely to the Church. *Perfectae Caritatis* underlined this noting that the providential variety of religious communities "contributed mightily toward making the Church experienced in every good deed (cf. 2 Tm. 3:17) and ready for a ministry of service in building up Christ's body (cf. Eph 4:12)."[63]

The Spirit of the Founder and of the Institute

If the charism of the founder is to be of enduring service to the Church, it seems that her/his congregation must develop and preserve an appropriate spirit. Vatican II called upon religious congregations to renew their original inspiration and to recognize and preserve the spirit of their founders.[64] M.Milligan has, we think, identified the relationship of the founder's "spirit" to her/his charism for foundation: The grace to gather an enduring community for the service of the Church, in other words, the charism of foundation, is the founder's *own* grace. The Holy Spirit relates to individuals as individual. The founder, gifted by the Spirit to live her/his way of holiness or faith-vision, and her/his mission or service to the church, communicates a "spirit" with which the members of the congregation can identify, and which they can live out. They can identify, in the consistent spirit of the founder, a fulfillment of the ideal to which they responded in their first attraction to the founder's witness. Each member of the congregation then develops a spirit similar to the founder by sharing the same faith-vision. By living according to a like spirit (each maintaining her unique identity before the Lord), the members participate in the charism of the founder and together they develop a "collective mentality" through which they ensure that the gift given for the Church endures. It is through the members that the institution, which is the "external form" of the charism, becomes informed by the founder's spirit through their "dynamic memory of his life and words," expressive of his original inspiration.[65] Thus the formation of a "spirit" of the congregation in an essential aspect of the founder's charismatic efforts because it is through this "spirit" that the congregation remains faithful to the Holy Spirit in its service of the Church.

But what is this "spirit"? The "spirit of the Society of the Holy Child Jesus" was a term Cornelia and her sisters used frequently to epitomize their thoughts on the essence of vocation to their Society.[66] First of all, it should be noted that, in spiritual literature from at least the seventeenth to the nineteenth century, the term "spirit" is used so frequently, often loosely and generally, that to some extent it has lost its force.[67] M. Milligan attempts to give it some precision with respect to the founder or an individual member of the congregation: "The spirit of a person is that reality, very difficult to describe, which gives a person a particular sensitivity and capacity to perceive reality, and to act in accord with that perception." She continues: "Louis Cognet has called it 'one's interior attitude in regard to God, to the Church, and to other members of the congregation.'"[68] M. Milligan adds to this definition, "the adjective 'fundamental,' as 'spirit' seems to her to be situated at a level much deeper than the word 'attitude' is usually understood as implying." Each individual member of a community is called to share this spirit, this interior attitude. Sharing in the same spirit created what Louis Cognet calls a "collective mentality." Mary Milligan goes on to say that the shared attitude, the "collective mentality" is expressed in shared vision and shared values, in the quality of relationships both within and without the community. "For Father Gailhac, the 'spirit' of a congregation was incarnated in a community. It consisted in a network of relationships consequent on sharing the same faith-vision."[69]

Sources on Cornelia and the SHCJ do indicate that their spirit was related to interior attitudes and relationships especially as they stemmed from the original inspiration and were expressed in shared vision, values and relationships. But Cornelia and, gradually, her sisters had their own way of understanding the origin, nature, and means of development of the spirit of their congregation. She was most explicit in her constitutional texts and especially in the First Chapter she composed when preparing to present her Constitutions for pontifical approbation in 1854. Her sisters recognized the importance of the First Chapter for its instruction on their spirit.[70] Near the end of her life they worked together with her to restore this First Chapter to alien constitutions imposed on them in 1874, and they added texts to reinforce their emphasis on their proper spirit.[71] We give a synthesis here of what emerges from their sources on this all-important aspect which enables a congregation to preserve its charismatic nature. This synthesis will be more fully understood when Cornelia's teachings, especially in her Constitutions, have been analyzed more fully in Chapters IV, V and VI.

The SHCJ understood the spirit of the members of a religious congregation—a group sharing the same evangelical vision and lifestyle—to be the grace of transformation into the likeness of Christ through contemplating Him in a given mystery or mysteries, a transformation manifested in the consistent practice of those virtues of Christ especially revealed in the mysteries contemplated. Thus the spirit with which a religious is graced is a supernatural reality, as is the charism of the founder; it requires, as does the charism of the founder, a free collaboration with the Holy Spirit.

This understanding of the "spirit" of the Society of the Holy Child Jesus is supported by current theological teaching on the charism of the founder. According to this teaching the members of an institute are drawn to associate with a founder with whom they "commune in the same spiritual experience and share in the same evangelical sensitivity."[72] They have an affinity with her which is truly "spiritual," that is, created by gifting of the Holy Spirit who also gifted the founder. P. Molinari explains: "It is as if the Holy Spirit sent a ray of light which filled the soul of the founder. This ray continues on, through the founder, until it reaches the souls of those who are called to a certain religious family. It is a ray of light which has its own particular characteristics and limitations. It is thus that institutes receive a specific mission from the Holy Spirit."[73] The common spirit of the members of a congregation grows through their contemplative emphasis on the same mystery and their sharing a life appropriate to it. The freedom of the members to develop and preserve (or not to) the spirit of the institute, is seen in their willingness to accept their call to contemplation with the asceticism entailed, and their fidelity in practicing the virtues to which their contemplation orients them.

At the head of her Constitutions of 1854, Cornelia stated clearly that the spirit of the Society was drawn from contemplation of Jesus in "his humble and hidden life"—that life in which the Society's life was rooted: "In the humble and hidden life of the Holy Child Jesus we find mysteries of the most sublime teaching . . . we find our Divine Master, our Model and our Spouse; and from the living wells of His perfect humility, His divine charity and His absolute obedience, we are to receive the Spirit of the Society of the Holy Child Jesus."[74] One cannot fail to note here in constitutional texts what is found also in Cornelia's more informal writings—the immediate reduction from the abstract to the concrete in terms of virtues as they are manifest in the living human person of Jesus.[75] She frequently recalled to herself and to her sisters that they were living "in Christ Jesus," and must manifest that reality in the practice of his "interior and exterior virtues."[76]

After twenty years of living by their Constitutions of 1854, the SHCJ were required by their Ordinary, Bishop Danell, to accept his Constitutions. This occasioned urgent representations from them regarding the necessity of maintaining their own proper spirit. The trials to which they were subject had at least the merit of enhancing their awareness of the spirit appropriate to their particular congregation:

> The Spirit [of] the New Rule [Bishop Danell's] is not of the religious tone inculcated in the Old Rule of [approved by] Card. Wiseman [included in Constitutions of 1854.]

The great grievance is that while our conscience holds to the Rule upon which we made our vows, a fresh one is imposed upon us of quite a different spirit involving difficulties with which we cannot cope.[77]

It was in the midst of this crisis that, attempting to revise the Bishop's constitutions in the direction of their own, Cornelia and her sisters inserted a definition of spirit given by the Jesuit Pierre Cotel in a Scheme of Constitutions he had set forth for a congregation he had helped to reorganize:

The Spirit of a Religious Institute is that interior principle of life which gave it birth, and with which all its members ought to be penetrated, so that every individual in particular, and the body in general, may be maintained in its primitive fervour.

The general definition was followed by a specific application to the virtues by which Cornelia had characterized the spirit of the Society in 1854. It was then further specifically applied to the practice of zeal, an addition which the SHCJ saw as a particularly appropriate expression of the spirit by which they were living:

The Spirit of this Institute, being that of the Holy Child Jesus, is a spirit of simplicity, humility, obedience and charity, together with a spirit of affectionate devotion to the works of zeal and charity undertaken by its members. This Spirit embraces in a very special manner the virtue of zeal, because its chief end is our own sanctification and the salvation of souls . . . .

The particular means by which the Sisters who are engaged in the great work of training children may acquire and preserve the true spirit of the Institute will be to cultivate assiduously a loving devotion to the Holy Child Jesus . . .[78]

Jean Gailhac, whose concept of the spirit of a congregation M. Milligan studied, makes the same reduction from the abstract term "spirit" to the more concrete virtues by which the reality of the spirit of the congregation can be verified. In a letter to the Religious of the Sacred Heart of Mary which he founded, he wrote:

Put on the spirit of Jesus Christ; in a special way it is the spirit of our Institute. The spirit of Jesus Christ is a spirit of humility, of renunciation, of dedication, of sacrifice.[79]

In a constitutional text he wrote:

The spirit of the Institute is, in fact, the spirit of our Lord Jesus Christ and consequently a spirit of faith. The sisters . . . to be images of their Model . . . will direct all their efforts toward the practice of humility, simplicity, detachment from the world.[80]

It is worth noting that Gailhac, too, found the virtue of zeal central to the expression of the spirit of his congregation, M. Milligan wrote: "The accent which he puts on zeal in his writings to the congregation is extraordinary. He does not hesitate to call zeal 'the principle mark of your vocation,' for it is the end of your institute."[81]

It is probable that an examination of seventeenth to nineteenth-century spiritual literature would reveal a common practice of associating the concrete virtues communicated effectively by Christ in his human life, with the more abstract reference to the "spirit" of the persons or institutes imitating Christ in one or other of his mysteries. But even if this is a stereotype, it expresses a reality.[82] "Spirit" would seem to be that grace, that real share in the life of Christ, that likeness to him which is the fruit of true contemplative identification with him through his living Word of Scripture, identification expressed in the faithful practice of virtue. Those whose contemplation of Christ is focused through the accents of a particular mystery—for Cornelia, "the humble and hidden life"—will, if faithful to grace, develop the attitudes and the virtues Jesus especially manifested in the particular mystery.

When the spirit of a congregation is understood to include the reality of concrete, faithful practice of virtue, it becomes clearer how the spirit ensures the endurance of the congregation as the Spirit's gift to the Church. Divine grace—the charism of foundation, the graces that develop a spirit, are not magic. They require the free collaboration that the acquisition and practice of virtue entails.

Notes

1. Jn 3:8.
2. K. Rahner, "Charism," *Encyclopedia of Theology* (N.Y., 1975), p. 184. For Rahner's pre-Vatican II treatment of the charismatic dimension, see *The Dynamic Element in the Church*, published in English in 1964 (London), but composed of three essays first published in 1956 and 1957 in: *Wort und Wahrheit*, 12 (1957); *Stimmen der Zeit*, 160 (1957); Fritz Wulf, *Ignatius von Loyola, Seine geistige Gestalt und sein Vermächtnis* (Würzburg, 1956).
3. Rahner, "Charism," p. 185.
4. T. Ledochowska, *In Search of the Charism of the Institute*. Trans. M. Lawrence and M. Bellasis (Rome, 1976), p. 37.
5. Rahner, "Charism," p. 185.
6. M. Milligan, *That They May Have Life*, A Study of the Spirit-Charism of Father Jean Gailhac, Founder (Rome, 1975), p. 23. (Hereafter cited as *Gailhac*.)
7. J. Milne Home, "What is Charisma? Part I," *Source* 8 (1978), 51-3, citing W. Lowrie, *Interpretation of Sohm's Kirchenrecht* (London, 1904); and E. Schweitzer, *Church Order in the New Testament* (London, 1961), p. 230.
8. 1 Co 12:4ff.; 1 Pt 4:10; also A. George and P. Grelot, "Charisms," *DBT* (N.Y., 1967), p. 56; Rahner, *Dynamic Element* pp. 42-83, especially pp. 47-48.
9. Milligan, *Gailhac*, p. 16.
10. 1 Co 1:7.
11. 1 Co 7:7.
12. 1 Co 1:7, 7:7, 12:4, 9, 28, 30, 31; 2 Co 1:11; Rm 1:11; 5:15, 16; 6:23; 11:29; 12:6; 1 Tm 4:14; 2 Tm 1:6.
13. 1 Co 12:7-10; 1 Co 12:28-30; Rom 12:6-8; Eph 4:11-12.
14. Milligan, "Charism," p. 185.

15. 1 Co. 12:4-31; v. also George and Grelot, p. 56; Milligan, *Gailhac*, pp. 21-3; Rahner, "Charism," p. 185.
16. E. Käsemann, "Ministry and Community in the New Testament," *Essay on New Testament Themes* (London, 1964), p. 65.
17. H. Schürmann, "Les charismes spirituels," *L'Eglise de Vatican II*, Collection Unam Sanctam 51b (1966), 547 cited by Milligan, *Gailhac*, p. 17.
18. J. Milne Home, "What is Charisma? Part II," *Source*, 9 (1979), 29.
19. Milne Home, p. 31.
20. Käsemann, pp. 65, 73; Milne Home, p. 31.
21. Milne Home, pp. 32-3.
22. George and Grelot, pp. 55-7; Rahner, "Charism," pp. 185-6.
23. J.H. Crehan, "Charisms," *Catholic Dictionary of Theology*, 2 (967), 21; Crehan, pp. 19-22, discusses patristic, medieval and modern references to charisms in the context of the recurrent question as to whether they are meant to continue in the Church. Rahner, "Charisms," pp. 185-86, notes inadequacies in the development of the theology of charisms. G. W. Lampe, ed., in *Patristic Greek Lexicon* (Oxford, 1961), pp. 1518-19, gives numerous citations for both official and non-official charisms. The following references are pertinent to references in this thesis: 1 *Clem* 38.1; *Did* 1.5; Ign. *Eph* 17.2; *Const. App.* 8.3 1-2; 8.1.9..2; Greg Naz. *or* 41.16; Chrys. *hom.* 86.3 *in Jo.*
24. Thomas Aquinas, *Summa Theologiae*, ed. C. Ernst, 30 (1a 2ae, 111), (1967), 125-19.
25. *AAS*, 35 (1943), 200 ff.; CTS translation, *The Mystical Body of Jesus Christ* (London), pp. 13-1, 23-24, Pius XII wrote: "But it must not be supposed that this coordinated, or organic structure of the Body of the Church is confined exclusively to the grades of the hierarchy, or—as contrary opinion holds—that it consists only of 'charismatics,' . . . though these, be it said, will never be lacking in the Church . . . . But when the Fathers of the Church mention the ministries of this Body . . . they rightly have in mind not only persons in sacred orders, but also all those who have embraced the evangelical counsels . . . ; also those who, though living in the world, actively devote themselves to spiritual and corporal works of mercy; and also those who are joined in chaste wedlock . . . . also Rahner, *Dynamic Element* pp. 51-2.
26. In his letter to Cardinal Micara on the "Adaptation of Religious to Contemporary Conditions" (*AAS* 43 [1951], 24-26), Pius XII wrote: "What in fact is necessary is so to recreate and renew minds and wills, with the aid of the grace of the Holy Spirit, that as far as possible the new fashions of our time and the spiritual destitution of our age will be met . . . . Complete reform of oneself and one's possessions . . . means striving by every means that the holy laws of one's institute will not appear as a collection of exterior and useless regulations, 'whose letter,' in the absence of the spirit, 'kills' (2 Co 3:6); but that these laws will really be so many instruments of heavenly virtue, . . . that those who are bound to obey them will be enabled to . . . spend all their powers . . . in securing the salvation of their brethren."
27. *LG*, 2-4. All documents of Vatican II are cited from the English translation, *The Documents of Vatican II*, ed. W. Abbott, (N.Y., 1966).
28. *LG*, 12.
29. *AA*, 2, 4, 11; *LG*, 41.
30. *AG*, 23.
31. *PC*, 1.
32. *PC*, 2.
33. J. Walsh, "The Difficulties of Revision," *Way Supp*, 36 (1979), 13-15.
34. Milligan, *Gailhac*; also Milligan, "Charism and Constitutions," *Way Supp*, 36 (1979), 45-57.

35. Milligan, *Gailhac*, p. 21.
36. Milligan, *Gailhac*, p. 23 and J. C. Futtrell, "Discovering the Founder's Charism," *Way Supp*, 14 (1971), 65.
38. Milligan, "Charism," pp. 46-57.
38. Walsh, "Difficulties," pp. 14-15.
39. Laurentin, p. 7.
40. "Ignace de Loyola," *DS*, col. 1302.
41. For faith-vision, see Milligan, "Charism," pp. 46-47; for experience, see B. O'Leary, *The Discernment of Spirits in the Memoriale of Blessed Peter Favre, Way Supp*, 35 (1979), 42. O'Leary's treatment of "Favre's Reflections on Experience," pp. 42-55, has been especially helpful; so also as R. Haughton's *Theology of Experience* (N.Y., 1972) in which she singles out Cornelia Connelly as an exponent of "theology of experience," pp. 157-59.
42. Cornelia's extensive use of the Spiritual Exercises is treated in Chapters III, IV and V. Her notes on and references to the Exercises are too numerous to catalog.
43. Const. 1854, *Source* 4:78.
44. Const. 1854, *Source* 4:77.
45. Milligan, "Charism," pp. 45-46, 48.
46. J. Guillet, "Spirit of God," DBT, p. 500.
47. On "spiritual crucifixion" CC 21:52; Const. 1850, *Source* 4:52-53; CC 7:104; reference to "accepted suffering"; for the latter, also CC 6:57; CC 15:44; CC 27:9.
48. Milligan, *Gailhac*, p. 27; "Charism," pp. 46-48.
49. Lk. 2:6-7, 52.
50. Dumeige, "Ignace," *DS*, col. 1302.
51. K. Rahner, "On the Evangelical Counsels," *Theological Investigations*, 8 (1971), 162 and 164; cf. Rahner's whole exposition, pp. 159-67.
52. Milligan, *Gailhac*, p. 27.
53. G. Lafont, "L'esprit-saint et le droit dans l'institution religieuse," *Supplément de la vie spirituelle*, 20 (Sept. 1967), 484.
54. Milligan, *Gailhac*, pp. 29, 30.
55. Lafont, p. 486.
56. M. Olphe-Galliard, "Charisme des fondateurs religieux," *Vie consacrée*, 39 (Nov. Dec., 1967), 343-44.
57. Milligan, *Gailhac*, p. 29; also Rahner, "Charism," p. 185.
58. Milligan, *Gailhac*, p. 25.
59. Spiritual Exercises as "bulwark," CC 27:3, as "groundwork," CC 6:75a; as means to "advance in their way," CC 54:85.
60. *The Book of the Order of Studies in Schools of the Society of the Holy Child Jesus*, 1863. For the cooperative endeavor which produced it, see *Source*, 4:148:49.
61. J. F. Gilmont, "Paternité et médiation du Fondateur d'Ordre," *Revue d'ascétique et de mystique*, 40 (1964), 393-426, especially pp. 408-09, 416-19, 424-26.
62. Gilmont, pp. 408-09, 423-25.
63. *PC*, 1.
64. *PC*, 2.
65. Milligan, *Gailhac*, p. 33-36, 25-29.
66. Const. 1854, *Source*, 4:78; Const. 1877, 1880, *Source*, 4, pp. 138-39.
67. L. Cognet, "Esprit," *DS*, 4 (1961), 1234-6.
68. L. Cognet, unpublished conference, "Qu'est-ce que l'esprit d'une congrégation?" Sessions des Supérieures Générales, Mont Saint-Odile, France (May, 1966), p. 6, cited by Milligan, *Gailhac*, p. 33).
69. Milligan, *Gailhac*, pp. 33-35, 56.

70. *Source*, 4:11-12, 77-80.
71. *Source*, 4:21-23, 138-39.
72. Lafont, p. 486.
73. P. Molinari, "Renewal of Religious Life according to the Founder's Spirit," *Review for Religious*, 27 (1968), 799; also Milligan, *Gailhac*, pp. 29-30.
74. *Source*, 4:77-78.
75. This is especially true in Cornelia's letters; see, e.g., general letters: CC 8:86-87, 88, 89-90, 91-92, 93-4, 95-96, etc.
76. "In Christ Jesus": see CC 21:80, CC 22:26, CC 8:96; "interior and exterior virtues," *Source*, 4:78-79.
77. CC 45:19, 21.
78. Source 4:21-23, 138-39; P. Cotel had worked with Mère de Faudoas to reorganize the Dames de S. Maur; see Chap. VI, notes 100, 101, and 103-05.
79. Milligan, *Gailhac*, p. 183.
80. Milligan, *Gailhac*, p. 184.
81. Milligan, *Gailhac*, p. 172.
82. P. Pourrat, *Christian Spirituality*, 4 (Westminster, Md., 1955), 314, noted that John Baptist de la Salle was influenced by the "Bérullian devotion to the mysteries of Christ." He cites a passage in which de la Salle clearly associates Gospel mysteries, spirit, and virtues in a manner similar to the one we have been considering. De la Salle wrote in *Explication de la méthode d'oraision*, p. 70:
> "It is needful to have an inward desire to profit [by the mysteries] and to receive the spirit, the grace, and the fruit that our Lord wants us to draw from them. For He wrought these divine mysteries of our holy religion not simply in order to redeem us but also to instruct us and by His example to move us to the practice in the sacred mysteries which He wrought: this is what is called the Spirit of the Mysteries. Each one of them has a spirit of its own, because in each our Lord displays certain virtues, and these impress us very deeply when we seriously study the mystery. Our Lord practiced those virtues to give us an example of them and to induce us to practice them too in imitation of Him, helped by the grace which He has merited for us and which is associated with the mystery as part of its spirit and reality."

There is no evidence of direct influence of de la Salle or Bérulle on Cornelia Connelly, but doubtless they influence some of the authors she used.

Chapter 2

Family Heritage and Early Life of Cornelia: 1732-1832.

Since a charism for founding a religious institute points to a providential flow of graces within the whole life of a person, records of Cornelia's family origins and early life have been examined for this study. Meager as these are they yield a fascinating picture of a Protestant American family whose youngest daughter Cornelia imbibed the spirit of enterprise and initiative that characterized the young Republic her family had helped to shape. That this seems unlikely background for the emergence of a founder of a Roman Catholic sisterhood serves to underline the theme that fits much of Cornelia's story: the Spirit acts freely and creatively in bestowing charisms, "blowing where it will" (Jn 3:8). Much of her early life experience is providential for later life, especially the good education that Philadelphia, with its Quaker influence, provided for women in the early nineteenth century. Remarkably, her educational leadership was accepted in mid-nineteenth century England at a time when Englishmen were rejecting the possibility of a truly cultivated person's emerging from their former colonies.

Recognition of the extent of Cornelia's ministry in England in the second half of her life, coupled with the recognition of the depths of her American roots in the first half has caused us to ask whether she is not the first Catholic woman missionary *from* the *New* World *to* the Old. Perhaps the Catholic newspapers of her time were pointing to this in hailing her as the "Mother Seaton [sic] of England."[1]

Her Protestant roots and upbringing raise another question for the history of spirituality: How did one formed exclusively in an American Protestant environment up to the very moment of her abjuration, move into the Roman Catholic communion with the conviction, ease, even familiarity she evidenced at the time of conversion and throughout her life? The bishop who received her wrote: "Nothing could have been easier than to prepare her to enter the Church."[2] Her spiritual notes and teachings show her "at home" within the central Christocentric, sacramental tradition of Catholic spirituality as it developed from the Middle Ages through the Counter-Reformation and through the mystical and devotional movements of the seventeenth to nineteenth centuries. The meagerness of records of Cornelia's Protestant years prevent us from giving full answer to this question, but her transition challenges facile "Protestant"-"Catholic" stereotypes.

This chapter presents a mosaic of the meager records of Cornelia's family heritage, drawn from a wide variety of historical sources, as well as from "flashbacks" in the letters she and her family wrote in adult life. The letters show strong bonds and vital relationships in the large, loving, enterprising American family which nurtured her.

Maternal and Paternal Roots

Cornelia's maternal roots were sunk deep in the "American Experiment," and more particularly in William Penn's "Holy Experiment." Her maternal great-grandparents, Daniel Steinmetz and Anna Maria Schryer, came from the Palatine in 1732 to Penn's Colony—a post-Reformation commonwealth almost unique in its genuine religious toleration—during the second wave of immigration after the founder's death.[3] Large numbers of sturdy immigrants who followed the first mass migration of Quakers were Germans, many religiously akin to the Quakers through various forms of Pietism: others were adherents of the German Reformed Church, who, like the Pietists, were accorded freedom of worship neither in the Lutheran nor Catholic states of Germany.[4] Daniel Steinmetz had so identified his family with the German Reformed Church in Philadelphia that his daughter Suzanna, and her daughter, Mary Swope—Cornelia's grandmother and mother—were married by the same German Reformed pastor, Casper Weyburg, in his church in Philadelphia eighteen years apart, 1768-1786.

Cornelia's mother was first married to a Jamaica planter, John Bowen.[5] After he died, she married Cornelia's father, Ralph Peacock, a recent immigrant.[6] The latter came to America in 1794 or 1795 from a family of tenant farmers of Nunnington, Yorkshire, England. He had been baptized in the Anglican Church in Nunnington.[7] He was naturalized as an American citizen the year before he married Mary Swope Bowen in 1798.[8] Cornelia hardly knew his family most of whom remained in England. Since he died when she was only nine, and since she was raised from the age of fourteen by her Bowen half-sister, her father and his family had less influence on her than her mother's family. The latter seem to have given her effective feminine role models.

Cornelia's great-grandfather, Daniel Steinmetz, prospered so well in America by the mid-eighteenth century that his family was still profiting in her time by the Philadelphia property he bequeathed to them. His son John was so well established that he joined leading merchants in fostering the opposition to British taxation that became the American Revolution.[9] His daughter married a surgeon who ministered to the American colonial troops in the Revolution against Britian.[10] Thus Cornelia's family entered her country's National Period in which she was born, with a strong stake in the "American Experiment." Her mother, through her first marriage in 1786 to the wealthy Jamaica planter, John Bowen, not only attained lasting economic security but also had her cultural experience broadened beyond the considerable sophistication of eighteenth-century Philadelphia. She had a daughter Isabella and a son John by her first marriage. By her marriage to Ralph Peacock she had seven children of whom Cornelia Augusta was the youngest. Six of these grew to maturity.[11] Although Cornelia's father had not the business acumen that Cornelia's mother's family had—nor, perhaps were his times so propitious for making fortunes[12]—her mother preserved her inheritance of Bowen Hall, Jamaica for her two Bowen children and, through them, her Peacock children. Her eldest daughter, Isabella, who married Austin Montgomery, seems to have inherited her mother's practical business sense.[13] It was this half-sister who became Cornelia's foster-mother when the latter was fourteen, her father, Ralph having died in 1818 and her mother in 1823.[14] What emerges from these details is that Cornelia, who much later became the mainstay of her own family when her husband could not fully support them between 1838-1843,[15] Cornelia who later managed the financial affairs of her impoverished young congregation with uncommon effectiveness,[16] seems to have acquired this skill so needed for her ministry, as part of her family inheritance. She grew up with women who exercised responsibility and skill in the management of household and business affairs.

If Cornelia learned to be responsible in economic matters and to have them serve her higher purposes, there is no indication that she clung to material wealth for happiness in adult life. Her husband, disconsolate at the poverty to which he was reduced by the Panic of 1837 reported that "Cornelia is as gay as a bird."[17] The Sisters who gathered round her in the Society of the Holy Child Jesus reported frequently on the vitality of her faith amid material privations and financial worries; more than one was aware that Cornelia had been used to every comfort in her youth.[18]

From both the men and women in her family, colonists and builders of a new nation, Cornelia seems to have imbibed a spirit of initiative, enterprise and resourcefulness that served her well both in the demands of her marriage and the yet more arduous demands of her religious congregation. These qualities she continued to associate with her American heritage, writing, when she was sixty-six: "I wonder if our dear boys [her nephews] have the American spirit and energy to stir up for the new countries . . . all the splendid country between the Mississippi and the Pacific? . . . If I were with you, I should rouse up from Texas and not get swamped there."[19]

Happy Family Life

The enterprise and family solidarity of Cornelia's forbears gave her a fairly secure childhood. This was a good foundation for sound religious development. Cornelia seems to have had both economic and emotional security. Even though her father died when she was nine, her eldest brother when she was thirteen, and her mother when she was fourteen, her brothers and sisters in the united Bowen and Peacock families cherished and supported her. Though the beautiful and vivacious little girl must have suffered deeply from three bereavements in five years, she had the support of a community in which the inevitability of death and the sureness of heaven were everyday realities. She had the security of a family where the older members welcomed their role of surrogate parents.

The mature and aging Cornelia recollected fondly that she had been the family's cherished "Nelie" and "little Ne."[20] To the end of her life they and she corresponded frankly, vigorously and lovingly from the far-flung homes they had established on both sides of the Atlantic. "The older I grow the more I love you all"[21] — this in one of her last family letters, speaks volumes about the vital, enduring family relationships which had begun in her Philadelphia childhood. From the correspondence and from reminiscences we get tiny vignettes of her happy family life: Cornelia's being saved by her sister from an irascible bull on their father's farm;[22] Cornelia's brother priming a canvas for her to try oil painting at thirteen years of age;[23] she and her sister attending the theater.[24]

Her sister saved four poems she wrote at nineteen, too sentimental and stereotyped for literary consideration, but useful to remind us that the strong woman of faith who founded the Society of the Holy Child Jesus had passed through the sentimentality of adolescence to reach the maturity which made her an able collaborator with the Holy Spirit. One poem is a sentimental tribute to the purity of her sister Mary, two years her senior and the companion of her childhood.[25] The other three poems reveal, in the sentimental images of her time, a hurt with which Cornelia was wrestling.[26]

Good Education

Of great significance for Cornelia's destiny in the Church, was the excellent education and the positive attitude toward education for women that her family and her city gave her. She proved, in mature life, to be a gifted educator, creative and realistic, confident in her understanding of theory and practice, enthusiastic in her application of them; confident also in her ability to train teachers. She left her city with this confidence. More than once in her early years of marriage, she proposed to her husband that they should set up a school.[27] She taught with notable success from 1834-43 in the Sacred Heart School in Grand Coteau, Louisiana, and from 1844-46 at the Trinita in Rome.[28] Although she undoubtedly learned much from the Religious of the Sacred Heart who had raised the level of education for girls in their time, evidence still points to the education of her youth in Phildelphia as a foundation for her adult ministry. The very attitude with which she approached the cultural opportunities of a stay in Rome: ". . . seeing it won't do—it must be studied"; her taking music, painting, Italian and French lessons there—[29] indicates the receptivity to learning engendered by her Philadelphia education. The city which nurtured Cornelia had been at the time of her parents' marriage the second largest English-speaking city in the world. In the half-century before her birth it had been the cultural capital of the American colonies, and the seat of the American Enlightenment. In her time it still offered the educational advantages accruing from its position.[30] The Quakers especially, and some of the German religious groups, were in advance of their time in providing schools for girls, and, by the nineteenth century, Philadelphia and its environs had over thirty schools to which girls were admitted, some with very promising curriculum, including such subjects as English, French, Italian, Music, Painting, Arithmetic, Sacred, Ancient, and Modern History, Geography, Rhetoric, Moral Philosophy, Botany and Astronomy.[31] Cornelia left a record that her half-sister Isabella obtained excellent tutors for her.[32] It was not uncommon in early nineteenth-century Philadelphia to supplement schooling with advanced tutoring. Though we do not know what school she attended, we can surmise that learning must have been a pleasant and meaningful experience for her. We find her continuing her education throughout her life, whether it was to "write a short French exercise every day"[33] in Rome, or, years later as administrator, teacher, planner of Holy Child Schools, to learn a new method for grammar.[34] Even as a young married woman she had been singled out as a "woman of much intelligence cultivated by a careful education."[35] as "Mr. Connelly's talented little wife."[36] The Society of the Holy Child Jesus became her means to share the humanism which had formed her. God gifted her for ministry. She would do more. Education deep and broad, pursued with enthusiasm and openness, holding out high goals of mature accomplishment, especially for women, became for her, as she said, a ministry of "spiritual mercy,"[37] a means of drawing others to the Eternal Wisdom in the lowliness of His Humanity.[38]

Protestant Religious Affiliations

It is highly probable in her youth Cornelia attended Presbyterian and perhaps Episcopalian Sunday schools, although we have no record of this. What records we do have of her family's religious history and that of her husband, Pierce Connelly, will be sifted here for the light they throw on Cornelia's religious development. Her mother's family had been, as noted, members of the German Reformed Church. Though her mother married her second husband, Ralph Peacock, in the Episcopalian Christ Church, she and her husband rented pews for most of their married life in the

Second Presbyterian Church. Mary Peacock continued to be a member of this Church for the five years she outlived her husband, that is, to Cornelia's fourteenth year, in 1823.[39] Although no record exists of the Presbyterian baptisms of the Peacock children, indirect evidence points to this possibility.[40] Cornelia's mother's shift from the German Reformed Church to the Presbyterian is probably explained by a trend, at the end of the eighteenth century among German (also Swedish and Dutch) congregations in America to transfer to English-speaking congregations doctrinally akin, when the original group insisted on maintaining the German language in its liturgy and catechesis.[41]

Mary Bowen Peacock, twice married to men of British origin and deeply committed to the English-speaking nation her family had fought for, had good reason to choose church services in English. Perhaps she sent her children to English-speaking Presbyterian Sunday schools.

A single reminiscence of Cornelia when she was preparing to become a Roman Catholic perhaps relates to her Presbyterian upbringing. She had been exposed to the religious polemic flooding the United States, and Philadelphia in particular, in her late teens. She recalled to her sister Adeline Peacock Duval in 1835 "all my prejudices and the horrors which I have nurtured for the Catholic faith;" she added further:

> You must remember, dearest Addie, I once thought all Catholic priests instruments of the devil, if not the devil himself and believed all Hume's falsehoods about monastic ignorance and superstition and entertained a thousand other prejudices.[42]

Adeline replied:

> I never entertained the violent prejudices against Catholic priests that you did — but I am very far from having the same respect for them that I do for our own clergy.[43]

This interchange between the two sisters shows that the youthful Cornelia had been independent enough to hold religious views different from those of her favorite older sister, Adeline. Perhaps they had been influenced by the views of Isabella, who seems to have been nominally Presbyterian, but whom Cornelia referred to in later life as religiously "indifferent."[44] Most of the brothers and sisters of the Peacock, Duval and Connelly families, however, were far from indifferent in religious affairs. This is evident from their lively correspondence, reflecting their religious convictions and providing commentary on the contemporary religious scene.[45]

Adeline's reference above to "our clergy" refers to Episcopalian clergy. She attended the Episcopal Church from at least 1823, soon after her marriage to the well-to-do Lewis Duval. Eventually, with profound consequences for the whole course of her life, Cornelia, too, joined Adeline's Episcopalian parish, St. Stephen's, Philadelphia. The very year Cornelia moved into the home of her sister, Isabella Montgomery,

Isabella's saintly brother-in-law, the Episcopalian priest James Montgomery, founded St. Stephen's Episcopal parish near the Montgomery and Duval homes. James Montgomery was a disciple of Bishop William Henry Hobart of New York, the American High Churchman who was in contact with the Oxford movement. St. Stephen's was more "High Church" than Philadelphia's Christ Church under the distinguished and beloved William White. James Montgomery's more "catholic" tendencies in no way prevented full communion with this bishop who dedicated St. Stephen's in 1823. Nor did it prevent close family relationships, as evidenced by James' marriage to the bishop's granddaughter Mary in 1827.[46] St. Stephen's records show that the families of Adeline Duval and of John Bowen, (Cornelia's half-brother), became active members of the parish from its beginnings. On what date, between the ages of fourteen and twenty-two, Cornelia became a member of the parish is not known. What is recorded in St. Stephen's parish Register is her baptism by James Montgomery on February 25, 1831.[47]

Cornelia's Episcopalian pastor and relative, James Montgomery, was well endowed to present to her the spiritual depths of Episcopalianism. His message went to the core of Revelation—Redemption through the death of God's only begotten Son, "the just for the unjust." What he had been preaching throughout his life, he summed up in his last sermon before his untimely death from tuberculosis in 1834. He chose for his text what would, in ensuing decades become Cornelia's most profound expression of the meaning of her life. Entitling the sermon, "The Spiritual Crucifixion and the Spiritual Life," he commenced with the words: "I am crucified with Christ, nevertheless I live, yet not I but Christ liveth in me." (Gal 2:20).[48]

Marriage to Pierce Connelly

The next all-important Church record we have concerning Cornelia is that of her marriage on December 1, 1831, to the Episcopalian priest, Pierce Connelly. His bishop, William White, officiated at the marriage ceremony and recorded it at Christ Church, Philadelphia. The marriage took place at the home of Cornelia's sister, Adeline Peacock Duval, since Isabella Montgomery strongly objected to her half-sister's marriage to Pierce.[49] One of Adeline Duval's daughters, Adeline Duval Mack, recalled in her old age what she had known of the courtship and marriage of her surprisingly independent young aunt. She referred to Pierce: "He was an assistant clergyman in one of the Episcopal Churches—was very handsome, fascinating—a number of the young ladies, friends of Cornelia Peacock, were vying with each other for the attentions of the young minister." Adeline Mack then recalled how the romantic element in this courtship increased:

Family Heritage and Early Life of Cornelia 31

When Mrs. Montgomery, half-sister of Rev. Mother Cornelia Peacock, discovered the growing attachment of Cornelia, she was much displeased, as she had great ambitions that her beautiful and accomplished sister would make a better match. The young minister was poor and his family had not the social standing of the Peacocks and Montgomerys, young Pierce's father being in trade, furniture business, I believe.

Mrs. Montgomery forbid him the house. He must discontinue his visits. I think Cornelia—Rev. M.[other]—sang in his church. She had a beautiful and highly cultivated soprano voice.

Cornelia—Rev. Mother—always possessed of strong will power, appealed to her eldest sister (Adeline—Mrs. Louis Duval) and arranged to visit her and be married from her house . . . the handsome residence of my mother.[50]

With her independent choice of marriage to an Episcopalian priest in reduced social and financial circumstances, Cornelia began a decisive phase of her life, rich in joy and sorrow, a phase in which she responded with courage and generosity to the demands that marriage and motherhood made. She came to know what depths of sacrifice could be contained within the humble and hidden life of a nineteenth-century wife and mother. It was in this context that she began to grasp the meaning of the ineffable mystery of God's "humble and hidden life" on earth and to respond to the Holy Spirit as he shed light on her through the Gospel. It was this "humble hidden life" that became her vision for the Society of the Holy Child Jesus.

This was to be her future. But meanwhile what did the present hold for Pierce and Cornelia in 1831? At the time she married him, he was about to leave St. James Episcopal Church near Philadelphia, where he had been curate,[51] to assume the rectorship of Holy Trinity Church, Natchez, Mississippi. Their coming together was somehow set within their Episcopalian connections, probably St. Stephen's. It is probable that the prospect of becoming the wife of an Episcopalian priest had something to do with Cornelia's baptism in the Episcopalian Church nine months before the wedding.

What more can we know of Pierce Connelly? A whole book could be written on this enigmatic, intelligent, vocal, zealous clergyman who became Cornelia's husband and who eventually succumbed to mental illness. He has left many writings behind him. Some of the deepest aspects of her graces and responses cannot be presented without including Pierce's part, and, thus, this study will not ignore him. But the focus will be maintained on Cornelia because our study must be kept within manageable limits. This will leave the reader with tantalizing questions which may now be answered in a documented study of him.[52] A desideratum for the future is a study of the two as a couple beginning a joint spiritual quest at the outset of their marriage. This book will indicate the potential which the archives of the Society of the Holy Child Jesus hold for an exposition of a married couple whose intertwined lives gradually diverging—Cornelia's into manifest holiness and constructive ministry, and Pierce's into deterioration and tragedy.

Pierce Connelly came from a family as rooted in the "American Experiment" and in Philadelphia history as was Cornelia's. His father, Henry Connelly, rose from "obscure beginnings" as a cabinet maker to rank with Duncan Phyfe and to count among his customers Philadelphia "men of affairs." He may have added to his income by cotton milling. Recent researches do not indicate that he was poor, but as a self-made man he probably had no family inheritance to give his Episcopalian priest-son whom Adeline Mack classified as "poor." And according to her, his "trade" made him socially inferior to the Peacocks and Montgomerys. Despite this, two of his sons, Pierce and George attended the University of Pennsylvania. Here strong Episcopalian influence won the allegiance of Pierce, who had been baptized as a child in the First Presbyterian Church where his father worshipped, and where his uncle was an elder. Pierce received a master's degree from the University of Pennsylvania in 1824 and was received as a candidate for the ministry at the Episcopal Convention of September 1825. He placed himself, according to prevailing custom, under the direction of an ordained clergyman, for theological training, and in 1826 the Convention accepted him as a candidate for holy Orders; in June of 1827 he was ordained a deacon in Christ Church by Bishop White and served at Old Trinity, Wilmington, Delaware, till 1828. On October 11th he was ordained a priest of the Protestant Episcopal Church at St. James Church, Kingsessing, now within the city limits of Philadelphia. It was here he served as a curate until, a month after his marriage in December, 1831, he assumed the rectorship of Holy Trinity Episcopal Church, Natchez, Mississippi, and took his beautiful bride to their mission in the elegant little city built by the plantation owners on America's frontier.[53] The Connellys began their life in Natchez exactly one hundred years after Cornelia's great-grandparents had begun their life in the New World.

The young couple's letters written from Natchez show that both began their married life with a keen sense of mission — a sense of being sent by God to do his work in the world through his church. Their American Protestant heritage had given them a strong sense of mission; they brought it with them into the Catholic Church to which they were to turn in the Mississippi Valley.[54]

Notes

1. D 10:29; citations are given frequently in this form. The numbers refer to the vol. and p. or pp. of the Documentation (D) in which sources by or relating to Cornelia Connelly and the SHCJ are filed in typescript or photocopy in the SHCJ Archives. Contents of D vols. are listed at the end of this book under "Sources."
2. D 85:9; translated from the French for this thesis.
3. *Publications of the Genealogical Society of Pennsylvania*, 9 (1924) 51-53; also R.B. Strassburger, *Pennsylvania German Pioneers*: A Publication of the

Family Heritage and Early Life of Cornelia

Original List of Arrivals in the Port of Philadelphia from 1727-1828, ed. W. J. Hinke in Publications of the German Society of Pennsylvania, vol. 6 No. 3 (1934). For this research and for much on the family history of Cornelia and Pierce Connelly in this chapter, we are indebted to Elinor McCarthy, whose work is summarized by C. McCarthy in "Cornelia and Pierce Connelly: New Perspectives on Their Early Lives," Records of the American Catholic Historical Society of Philadelphia 71 (1961), 93-105. In a letter of April 13, 1980, a descendant of Cornelia's brother Ralph Peacock—Mary Ann Guerra—asserted that her branch of the family claims Jewish as well as German blood for the Steinmetzes and Schryers. Research has turned up no records for this claim.

4. J. P. Garber, The Valley of the Delaware and its Place in American History (Phila., 1934), pp. 88-89, 339, 350-52. G. Weigel, Churches in North America (Baltimore, 1961), pp. 37-40.
5. Publications of the Genealogical Society, 9, 52: First Reformed Church of Phila., Pa., Marriages, III, 2108, 2169, 2087.
6. Records of Christ Church, Phila., vol. 7, Marriage, 1789-1800, p. 4565. The marriage was celebrated Feb. 22, 1798.
7. Records of the Church of St. James and All Saints, Nunnington, Yorkshire: Ralph, son of Thomas Peacock, 2 July, 1768.
8. Naturalization Record of Ralph Peacock, No. 108, Records Room 2040, Federal Court Building, Phila.
9. Publications of the Genealogical Society, 9, 52.
10. Pennsylvania Archives, 5th series, III, 747, Jacob Swope is listed on Jan. 15, 1777 as a surgeon in Col. Thos. Hartley's regiment.
11. D 2:xxxix.
12. D 2:22-24.
13. D 9:94-97.
14. Bellasis, D 72:3, M.M.T. Bisgood, Cornelia Connelly, (Westminster, Md. 1963), pp. 4-5.
15. D 4:129, 73.
16. See e.g. Cornelia's letters to business and professional men, CC 3 and 4, to educational authorities, CC 5; to Bishop Grant, CC 11-15. The numbers given here refer to the vol. and pp. of the Writings of Cornelia Connelly (CC) which are filed in typescript or photocopy in the SHCJ Archives. Contents of the CC vols. are listed at the end of this book under "Sources."
17. D 4:21.
18. Buckle, D 63: 27-28; D 72: 2-3, 10.
19. CC 1:114a. Cornelia wrote this in 1875.
20. CC 1:45, 118, 120; also CC 1:74, 77, 81, 104, 112; D 2:66, 68, 69, 72.
21. CC 1:112.
22. Bellasis D 72:3-4.
23. D 9:8.
24. CC 1:65.
25. CC 57:48.
26. CC 57:49.
27. CC 1:4; D 4:4-5.
28. D 4:57-58, 37, 45; letter of J. deCoriolis RSCJ to S. Barat, Mar. 1844, RSCJ Archives, Rome.
29. CC 1:65.
30. R. Nye. The Cultural Life of the New Nation, (N.Y., 1963), pp. 125-28.
31. H. G. Good, History of American Education (N.Y., 1964), p. 113; M. B. Schiffer, Historical Needlework of Pennsylvania (N.Y., 1968), pp. 12-84 passim, presents details from sources of education for girls in Pennsylvania in Cornelia's

time; also R. Wood, ed. *The Pennsylvania Germans* (Princeton, 1942), pp. 109-14.
32. Bellasis, D 72:3.
33. CC 1:65.
34. CC 7:14.
35. D 85:6; Archives of the Oeuvres Pontificales Missionaires, Lyons, 1836, App. vol. 9.
36. D 3:134.
37. CC 1:70.
38. Const. 1854, Source 4, 78-79.
39. Records of the Second Presbyterian Church, Phila., Pewholders, vols. 10 and 11.
40. Letter of M. Garvey, RSCJ to the Superior General of the SHCJ, October 22, 1929, in Archives, SHCJ, Rome. M. Garvey notes that M. Peacock, RSCJ, Cornelia's older sister by two years, had been baptized a Lutheran or Presbyterian [M. Garvey could not remember which] "in childhood." Mary's childhood baptism gives a presumption in favor of Cornelia's also in the Presbyterian Church.
41. R. Wood, ed. *The Pennsylvania Germans* (Princeton, 1942), pp. 88-91.
42. CC 1:40-41.
43. D 2: 67-68.
44. CC 1:56.
45. CC 1:1-13, 35-104, passim.
46. S. Hotchkins, *Memoir of the Rev. James Montgomery, D.D.* (Phila. 1889), pp. 5-6.
47. Parish Register, St. Stephen's Episcopal Church, Phila., vol. 1, 1823-65.
48. Hotchkins, 10-11; see also C. McCarthy, "Introducing the Rev. James Montgomery," *Pylon*, 27, no. 2 (1965), 4-7; for Cornelia and the "true way," see CC 1:63.
49. Records of Christ Church, Phila., vol. 8, Marriages, 1800-1900, p. 4847; *National Gazette*, Dec. 2, 1831; *Daily Chronicle*, Dec. 3, 1831; in his testimony in Connelly vs. Connelly, Pierce told of the marriage taking place in Adeline's home, Case A, D 7:18.
50. SHCJ Archives, Rome: N.S. Cat., Family Affairs IV, D 9: a646, 18. The Montgomerys did become reconciled to the Connellys, at least by 1842 when Pierce recorded a touching visit to them in Philadelphia: "there is a good deal they would like to make up for . . ." : D 4:172-73; v. also McCarthy, "New Perspectives," pp. 99-100.
51. *Philadelphia Recorder*, vol. vi, Nov. 1, 1828; also *Journal and Biography of Nicholas Collin*, 1746-1831. (Phila., 1936), p. 50.
52. D. Paz, *The Priesthoods and Apostasies of Pierce Connelly*. (Lewiston: Edwin Mellen Press, 1986).
53. McCarthy, "New Perspectives," pp. 100-05; the citation given above from Adeline Mack (n. 50) corrects the assertion made in "New Perspectives" that the Connellys had the same social standing as the Montgomerys. Despite their achievements, apparently they did not.
54. CC1:1-12; 35-42; D 3:2-18; E. Gaustad, *A Religious History of America* (N.Y., 1966), pp. 47, 154.

Chapter 3

Through Successive Calls to Ultimate Vocation: 1832-1852.

Cornelia's life from 1832 to 1852 was extraordinarily eventful outwardly, even more so inwardly. During these twenty years she was twice involved in the cotton-rich society of Natchez, Mississippi, twice crossed the Atlantic and traveled through Europe, twice resided in papal Rome, taught for five years on the frontier in Louisiana, and finally became an integral part of the Catholic Revival in Victorian England. She was Episcopalian, then Roman Catholic. She was cherished wife; supportive wife; separated wife; and finally, celibate Roman Catholic sister. She bore and nurtured five children, suffered the death of two in infancy, and the loss of the other three at the ages of 16, 13, and 8, when her emotionally disturbed husband forcibly removed them from her care. She became meanwhile responsible for the education of several hundred children in the schools of her newfound congregation.

Significantly, through these twenty eventful years, Cornelia grew in contemplative prayer, asceticism, discernment, in a profound interior friendship with God which gave meaning and purpose to her life in the midst of flawed human circumstances. Significantly, too, she responded to the misogynist elements in her environment with a growth in an inner sense of self-worth and spiritual freedom. As she pursued her spiritual journey, letting the Gospel shed its light on her life, she developed an inspiration for a way of life which she later embodied in the Society of the Holy Child Jesus.

In this chapter we shall allow Cornelia's story to unfold through the sources and accompanying narrative. We shall conclude the chapter with details on the legal/social, theological/pastoral, and political/religious environments surrounding her which necessarily influenced the course of her decisions and actions. By looking at these external factors we see more clearly what decisions were possible for Cornelia within the limited options available to her. With a clearer view of the flawed human context within which the Holy Spirit chose to gift her for founding, we appreciate the mystery of "the Spirit blowing were it will." (Jn 3:8) We also appreciate the grace by which Cornelia accepted the contexts of her successive calls as the crucible of suffering in which the Father formed her to the likeness of his Son for mission.

Married to an Episcopalian Priest

The newly-wed Cornelia began home-making in the elegant, prosperous Natchez, Mississippi, amid the white-pillared homes of the wealthy cotton planters, keenly aware that she was married to "a priest in Holy Orders of the Protestant Episcopal Church of the United States."[1] Beautiful, talented, sociable, vivacious, she assumed with ease and grace that role of helpmate for which nineteenth century society had a particularly esteemed pattern.[2] She took as seriously as her husband Pierce his grave responsibility for those he "received . . . at these sacred rails;" those whom he taught, to whom he preached, who gave him their confidence; those with whom he "knelt beside the bed and stood around the grave"—all those for whom he was rector at Holy Trinity Church, Natchez, and for two mission parishes thirty and fifty miles south and east.[3]

With the graciousness and lively sociability that would always be marked in her, she became friends with her husband's parishioners, many of them the wealthy plantation owners, and shared their concerns.[4] She was, of course, among the many communicants he added to Trinity's lists, as, with High Church zeal for which he was known, he restored to his parish the eighty-eight days of Communion proper to the true Anglican ritual.[5] Above all, she was the devoted, concerned, busy little mother of Mercer, whom she bore at the end of their first year of marriage, and of Adeline born three years later in 1835.

Cornelia knew well how to be tender, supportive, and appreciative of Pierce as well as of her children. He, volatile, vocal, assertive, given to extremes of moods and reactions to people and events, seemed to need and to thrive on her assurance and praise.[6] A long letter to him during a few weeks absence shows her warm supportive relationship. Writing about his mother's criticism of him she says: "if she can be the mother of such a mind as yours, I think we can indulge strong hopes for Mercer." Writing of parishioners' attitudes: "Mrs. C. told me that he told Major C. that though he had always had a high opinion of you, that it was still higher now." Writing of herself and their children: "Oh my love, haste back. It seems a year that you have been gone . . . Mercer sends you love and kisses and expects you to bring him some candy."[7]

Deeply conscious of his superior education and advanced religious and cultural views, Pierce seems to have shared much with the wife of whom he was increasingly proud, whom a bishop would describe as a "woman of great intelligence and spirit developed by a carefully planned education."[8] Pierce referred to her as "my fair amanuensis."[9] When he was away Cornelia wrote "My own dear life, it seems almost as if you were with me again to send me your 'thoughts.' " In his absence she energetically took hold of parish business. One gets a hint, in her letter to her pastor-husband, of the initiative which was native to her, and of her talent for administration, all of which for thirteen years of married life she would keep within the bounds of nineteenth-century wifehood.

> Dear love, my more than life . . . your long and anxiously looked for letter I received about an hour since . . . . You have a letter from the Rev. C. Newell respecting the Woodville parish . . . . A Roman Missal was sent to you the day you left us with an excellent letter from a pious Catholic lady who had heard you preach on Sunday . . . . Dr. Mercer stopped . . . I showed him one of the letters I received for you. It was from Mr. Biddle and on church affairs . . . . If I did wrong you must never allow me to open your letters again, but I think and hope, love, that you will say it is all right.[10]

In the years 1832-35, with his gracious and admiring Cornelia at his side, Pierce was notably successful in the Episcopal ministry, was chosen chairman of the Episcopal Convention of the Southwest early in 1835, and believed he had some hope of a bishopric.[11] As she responded to the duties and opportunities of a helpmate in the Episcopal ministry, Cornelia's future seemed promising and peaceful.

Called to Roman Catholicism

However, into the relatively peaceful religious atmosphere of Natchez in the early 1830's burst the floods of polemical religious literature spawned by the Native American Movement which had germinated rapidly in the cities of eastern United States at the time of Pierce and Cornelia's courtship and marriage. Catholic Emancipation in England, a rapidly rising tide of largely Catholic immigrants to the United States, a resurgence of effective Catholic missionaries, especially Jesuits, and an increasing number of religious sisters — all these caused the predominantly Protestant descendents of the original American settlers to fear that their young nation was threatened by what they believed to be Europe's curse, Papal domination. As fears mounted, so did fantasies, and Protestant leaders thought they divined a plot by which Papal armies would conquer America from the West—that is, from the Mississippi Valley. The flood of pamphlets, newspapers and tracts which inundated Natchez at least as early as 1834 prepared for a "Crusade to save the West from the Pope."[12]

In the case of the Connellys the crusade was to backfire, and both were to be received into the Roman Catholic Church by March of 1836. Cornelia described the backfire to her sister:

> Dearest Addie, . . .
> Pierce has resigned his parish—he has laid aside the active duties of his ministry to examine at leisure and with care the distinctive doctrines of the Roman Catholic religon. The attacks upon the Catholics have led him

into a laborious study of the controversy and he begins to doubt whether they are not more near the truth than we . . . . Against all my prejudices and the horrors I have nurtured for the Catholic faith, I am ready at once to submit to whatever my loved husband believes to be the path of duty.[13]

At great cost to both of them, Pierce addressed a letter of resignation to his Episcopalian bishop on August 26, 1835:

> The attacks from every quarter upon the Roman Catholic Church have forced me into a laborious study of the controversy, and I confess, my faith is shaken in the Protestant religion.[14]

He preached his Farewell Sermon on September 5, 1835, explaining to his beloved congregation:

> The increased interest which the Protestant Church in Great Britain and in this country has lately taken in the Roman Catholic question, turned my studies in that direction; and a sense of honor and indeed of duty, now leads me to lay aside the active functions of the ministry while I further and more fully prosecute these studies.[15]

The beleaguered missionary bishops of the Mississippi Valley, to whom the Connellys soon applied for instruction, rejoiced to see the enemy fire turned upon itself through the overtures of Pierce Connelly. Bishop Rosati of St. Louis, rejoicing in Pierce's rejection of Protestantism, revealed how keenly he had felt the Protestant attack:

> An Episcopalian minister resident for some years in Natchez . . . had always shown little satisfaction with the war that all the Protestant sects in the United States had so boldly declared and had so powerfully pursued for some years against the Catholic religion, whether it was from the pulpit by their sermons filled with invective, or from their newspapers and their pamphlets (which they call in English *Tracts*) which swarm like ants throughout the country, and are distributed by persons of all ages and of both sexes in the cities and in the country with an unbelievable zeal, and with enormous financial outlay which is amply supplied by powerful societies multiplied to the infinite. Deceiving tales, occurrences invented or badly represented, calumnies, false interpretations of Catholic doctrine, fanatical and incendiary declamations all are put to work to denigrate our holy Church, vilify her ministers, and to turn away the faithful . . . . One would wish to be able to increase freedom of discussion in religous matters here: Yes, our enemies have the freedom to say and to publish everywhere all that they wish against us, but the columns of their newspapers, open to Protestants, are in general, and with very little exception, closed to Catholics. Thus everybody can read what they advance against us, but nobody reads our responses which appear only in Catholic newspapers which the Protestants don't want to read.[16]

It should be noted that in all of the source material on the conversion of the Connellys, preserved because of the great stir it caused, Pierce is obviously "center stage;" he is much more vocal regarding his religious beliefs and spiritual itinerary than Cornelia. She tended to describe his itinerary to her family rather than her own. One reason was that it involved not just

Pierce's personal but also his public, professional witness: "he is bound to cease preaching the moment he doubts."[17] It was also integrally tied to his way of supporting his family. And it was Pierce who was leading Cornelia to examine the Roman Catholic Church. At this stage of her life, her thinking is often revealed through records which center on him.

But we can pick out some of the major elements of Cornelia's own itinerary. There is no doubt that the impetus to "a laborious study of the controversy," an openness to "whether they [Catholics] are not more near the truth than we."[18] came initially from Pierce. Cornelia followed him in thought, prayer, action:

> I have perfect confidence in the piety, integrity and learning of my dear husband. . . . I am ready to submit at once to whatever my loved husband believes to be the path of duty.[19]

But Cornelia's conversion was more than an act of wifely submission, as her abjuration made independently two months before Pierce's, was to witness. This witness continued in abundant testimonies through the ensuing forty-four years of her life, testimony to her "joy of feeling yourself in the true way." Once Pierce had opened the search, Cornelia joined him, earnestly questing for the truth, the "true way."[20]

> May God bless you, dear Addie, and lead us all into the truth for his dear Son's sake . . . . You ask . . . why he meddled with controversy. To find out the truth—the blessed truth, and as one who professes to teach nothing but the truth, he is bound to cease preaching the moment he doubts. That faith which cannot stand the test of controversy cannot be a true one . . . .
> . . . act upon your own upright principles, and in faith and charity and trust upon One who looks into the hearts of men, and governs all things.[21]

Cornelia, like Pierce, sought to find true religious authority supporting that unity Christ had proclaimed, the unity Protestantism appeared to be destroying. She spoke of this with strong personal feeling:

> . . . independent of the authority of the Church I cannot see how all these denominations compose the Church of Christ with Christ at the head, and yet opposed to each other as they are, can that be one Church which does not hold the unity of the faith in the bond of peace: Can that be one army whose branches fight against each other rather than the world?[22]

Pierce was very much concerned with the false and abusive forms of religious authority Protestantism presented—the Establishment in England; in America, he judged fanatical "Religious Associations and the stipendiary [polemical] press" to be fostering a false intellectual superiority, knowledge for its own sake. He thought the Protestant Churches had lost the true sense of authority and subordination: "I have no faith in private inspiration . . . an individual infallibility, or any absolute personal independence." He saw the validity of Peter's role. He was deeply grieved that even his own Episcopal church had betrayed her own sacramental theology: "Our Church is not the mistress of herself, nor of her clergy . . . even in the most sacred things."[23]

Significantly for the future course of her own spiritual journey, Cornelia's mind and heart reached beyond the polemics concerning external structure and form which preoccupied Pierce, to the core of Christian reality and the effective sign of the Church: Christ crucified and continuing his Paschal mystery in his faithful disciples:

> Look at the attacks upon the Catholics, the oldest and most numerous which is now *preaching Christ crucified* — and whose faithful followers are now *suffering martyrdom* in Asia as the early Christians did — the only Church which *our blessed Lord* left upon earth and the only one which he sustained and made use of to propagate Gospel truth unto salvation.[24] (emphasis added)

There is continuity and unity in the revelation of himself crucified, and risen and living in his followers which Christ gave Cornelia, and to which she responded with steadily increasing sensitivity and fervor. Through the particular evolution of her husband's vocational convictions and emotional disturbances, conversion to Catholicism would, in the ensuing years, initiate a long martyrdom of heart for her. She would call it a "crucifixion of heart." It would also lead her to the founding of a congregation whose services she would offer to propagate the Gospel in Asia and Australia, recalling "the burning of one's early fervor."[25]

Her prayer for her family had been that God would lead them all to the truth "for His dear Son's sake."[26] Her reminder to her family of Pierce's dedication seems to come from the fullness of her own heart: "Was it to his own honor and glory that Pierce vowed to devote his life or was it to the Church of Christ?"[27]

The Providential Role of Joseph Nicollet

Recently discovered manuscripts reveal that there was a third person intimately involved in the Connellys' conversion — the lay French explorer, geographer, mathematician, Joseph Nicholas Nicollet. Because his involvement, and the contacts he introduced, are evidence of that Divine Providence so clearly active in Cornelia's life; because it was partly owing to him that conversion lifted Cornelia forever out of her American domestic orbit into the wider, less secure orbit of the missionary Church with its international complexities; because French spirituality, especially in its mystical orientations was to be important throughout the development of Cornelia's Catholic life, some details of his involvement with the Connellys from 1834 to the end of 1835 belong here. A full account would require a separate study.

Born a Savoyard peasant, Nicollet had risen by 1830 to be a distinguished scientist in the Bureau des Longitudes in Paris. Having become an expatriate because of financial ruin in the stock market crash at the time of the Revolution of 1830 in France, Nicollet secured a commission from the United States government, which he fulfilled with eminent success—to survey and map the Mississippi River and environs.[28] Amongst the thousands of scientific records, descriptions, maps which cover the pages of his extant manuscripts, one finds hints of the profound interior life of this French scientist who had been led to fervent Catholicism by the Abbé Bautain.

> It is in the solitudes that one discovers the smallness of the earth and the grandeurs of the heavens, the shortness of time and length of eternity. Have there ever been atheists other than in large cities?

And

> Who knows, however forsaken or bereaved below, that he can never be alone and never be deserted—that above him is the protection of eternal power, and the mercy of eternal love![29]

Nicollet's manuscripts also show that he stopped several times in the hospitable Natchez on its bluff above the Mississippi. There he stepped into the middle of those religious discussions of the Connellys which the flood of Nativist literature had provoked. He became the catalyst by which religious questions were raised closer to that transcendent plane on which their true significance could be discerned. That he played a crucial role in the conversion of the Connellys is evident from their writings and those of the missionary Bishop Rosati of St. Louis to whom he led Pierce; that this role was the product of his personal religious fervor is evident from his own writings. Since, as has been noted, Pierce's thinking is central in all the extant sources on the conversion, we have a clearer idea of his relationship with Nicollet than Cornelia's. Yet evidence shows that she shared intimately in the communications of the two men. When Pierce wrote to Nicollet as early as January, 1835: "opinions which I honestly and deliberately hold, can, for the present be communicated only confidentially," Cornelia was his "fair amanuensis" who "made you the copy you requested."[30] A year later on hearing of Nicollet's illness, Pierce assured him that "no one . . . would more cheerfully or more carefully have been your Sister and your nurse than chérie Nelie."[31] Her most fervent message to Pierce when he went to St. Louis in September, 1835 to initiate their study of Catholicism was: "Give the warmest remembrances from me to our great and good friend Mr. Nicollet whom I pray to God may be with you."[32]

Pierce's trip to St. Louis to confer with Nicollet, Bishop Rosati, and Fr. Verhaegen, S.J., president of St. Louis University, was decisive for the Connellys and headed them toward Rome both geographically and spiritually. Cornelia became a Catholic in New Orleans in December, 1835 before the family set sail for Rome; Pierce became a Catholic in Rome in March 1836. Two months later, Pierce, reflecting on his conversion for the

Dublin Review, singled out his acquaintance with Nicollet as the most providential of the occurrences leading to his conversion:

> In looking back upon the course and progress of my *ébranlement*, next to the most unmerited favour of that grace which with the deepest humility and most fervent thanksgiving I acknowledge and adore, what most amazes me is the confidence and boldness with which I took the first decided step in writing and printing my letter to the bishop. So far as human reasons can account for it, I must in a great degree attribute that confidence to my acquaintance with a distinguished foreigner in the winter of thirty-three and thirty-four. The Chevalier N. [Nicollet] then on a scientific tour through North America, was a man of extensive and profound philosophy as well as science, of a reputation already established, and of an exactness of mind and largeness of comprehension, as well as a sincerity of purpose, altogether remarkable. He had already travelled for two years in the United States; and I could not but be amazed as well as delighted at the attention which, in the midst of his more professional labours, he had paid to all the religious and political institutions of the country. The amount of information, the facts, the documents he had collected, were truly wonderful. As the natural result of our intimacy, he applied upon a variety of subjects to my experience as a clergyman and as a citizen, and our intercourse by degrees assumed an interest of the highest, and I need not hesitate to say of the purest kind. It never indeed turned upon differences of religious faith, much less partook of the nature of controversy. It was more about systems of philosophy and politics, a comparison of moral views and of notes already made by each.

After this admiring description of Nicollet, Pierce gave his own reaction to his new friendship. It is a moment of self-awareness of his personal need for confirmation and support from others, a confirmation and support he found in Cornelia, though at this time he was less aware of his dependence on her:

> Struck with coincidences, frequently where I least expected them, and an entire approbation of 'thoughts' which I had never ventured to utter except in the secrecy of a common-place book, I confess I felt for the first time a confidence in the opinions which I formed, and in myself, which I had never allowed myself to feel before. I had been in an agreeable and cultivated social circle, but I had been in solitude as to political, philosophical and theological associations. The men of my own profession whom I had left in the northern cities, and those near me in the south, I well knew differed from me fundamentally on many points of civil as well as ecclesiastical polity, and I required some other encouragement than that of my own mind to enable me to trust to my reasonings and to believe in the justness of them.[33]

Bishop Rosati, to whom Nicollet had led the Connellys, recorded what he had learned of the explorer's discerning commentary on the anti-Catholic literature in which Cornelia as well as Pierce had been immersed:

> Without entering into discussion on any point of controversy concerning the Catholic Religion, a distinguished French savant, member of the institute de France, who had traveled for some years in the United States

and whom I knew, expressed himself quite freely in the social circle in which Mr. Connelly found himself with many other very respectable Protestants, and he made them see the complete unworthiness of a kind of conduct which an honest man could not approve; and which a sincere religious spirit could not but condemn, since no one should have difficulty in recognizing and avowing that the end does not justify the means and those who respect the authority of Scripture are obliged to submit to this injunction which it gives us—*non sunt facienda mala ut veniunt bona*. He concluded that a Religion which used such means to sustain itself and to attack the Catholic Religion could not be animated by the Spirit of God and could not be his work. Mr. Connelly was very surprised to hear from the mouth of a foreign savant reflections which coincided so well with those which had presented themselves so many times to his own spirit, and to which he had not dared to give free rein, in some way, not trusting himself to himself. Having become more confident, he set himself to reflect with proper deliberation on the Catholic Religion . . . .[34]

One brief letter of Nicollet stands out amid all the conversion texts for its revelation of the explorer's little-known missionary zeal. It rings with the note of spiritual triumph of a journey brought to its conclusion by dispassionate guidance from without, burning zeal within. Nicollet informed Rosati by note that Pierce had arrived the morning of September 17, 1835 in the frontier city of St. Louis:

Monseigneur,

My friend had just come from Natchez. The thing is done, he has raised his standard in the Holy Cause before leaving his flock. We are very much moved and at the same time happy since we have been talking together for the last hour. I have no need to speak of the impatience which he sustains until he has the honor of being presented to you. I have sent you two copies of his declaration, not yet published, although printed. Send a copy, if you would be so kind, to our dear president of the University. Let us, all four, gather together this afternoon if possible, that I may have the joy of putting my friend in better hands than mine . . . .[35]

The Connellys were never to see Nicollet again after 1835. While they were continuing their religious explorations 1835-40, he was accomplishing his great work of mapping the sources of the Mississippi River. He died in September of 1843 before Cornelia had brought to full fruit in the Society of the Holy Child Jesus the seed of so much promise he had nurtured in Natchez in 1834-35.[36]

The Implication of Conversion: Pierce a Catholic Priest?

Back home in Natchez in September 1835, Cornelia was endeavoring by mail to keep herself abreast of Pierce in their common spiritual odyssey:

Dear love, my more than life what a baby I am. I can cry better than write—Your long and anxiously looked for letter I received about an hour since. O my love I have *wished* to be a Catholic in my acts of love but I am afraid in truth and in spirit have been but a discontented Protestant—but

> you have now taken me as far as Memphis and until I hear from or see you again I must rest satisfied with your dear letter . . . There has been a Mr. Keane out to see you; a warm Catholic; is just from N.O., has travelled considerably . . . My own dear life, it seems almost as if you were with me again to send me your "thoughts" . . . dearest, do not distress yourself about the alienation of any of your family . . . Give the warmest remembrances from me to our great and good friend Mr. Nicollet whom I pray to God may be with you—Oh my love, make haste back—It seems a year that you have been gone . . . I have written you too much—but not enough yet—my own life. Ever, forever, your devoted love. C.C.[37]

Bishop Rosati described Pierce as he knew him then, as Cornelia knew and believed in him, as many would know and believe in him in the ensuing decade. It is important to have clear evidence of the very real esteem in which Pierce was held by mature, responsible persons before, in later years, his conduct became destructive and tragic:

> . . . Faithful to the principles of his conscience, he believed he [Pierce] could not exercise his ministry without causing harm; he preached a farewell sermon to his congregation who dissolved into tears; he wrote a letter to his bishop to resign into his hands his parish, and left for St. Louis. He found there the scholar who had encouraged him in his thinking and, with him, he came to throw himself into my arms dissolved in tears. It was in our Cathedral that he assisted for the first time at the Holy Mystery which so struck him. We had long conversations together during which I saw with joy the purity of his intentions, his uprightness, his candour in the difficulties which he proposed to me. During his stay he clarified various points for himself, made provision for proper books to make known to him the basics of the Catholic religion in its dogmas and its discipline; he made the resolution to travel to Europe to proceed to draw from the Source, to live some time in the Capitol of the Christian World.[38]

Even as Cornelia wrote in September, 1835, giving herself wholeheartedly to being Pierce's spouse, being Mercer's and Adeline's mother, she was wrestling with the unthinkable, with a problem that had probably never occurred to her any more than allegiance to the Catholic Church had occurred to her in 1831 when she married an Episcopalian priest. She knew in the Fall of 1835 that Pierce was considering not only: should he give allegiance to the Church of Rome? but also: should he not also continue his priesthood? And this raised excruciating questions for her: How? What did that mean for her and her children—Mercer not yet three, Adeline eight months?

Cornelia had shared intimately with Pierce as he had prepared his letter of resignation to his Bishop dated August 26, 1835. She had heard him deliver his Farewell Sermon to his parish on September 5, 1835. In both she had recognized the strong conviction he had about the irrevocability of his commitment under Holy Orders:

> [To his Episcopalian Bishop]:
> The intention of my vows I have no doubt about; it is only, of where I

ought to pay them that I am uncertain. My allegiance as an ecclesiastic, I now fear, may have been mistaken. I will always show it was at least sincere.

[To his Episcopalian congregation:]
I therefore leave my parish; but I do not renounce my office. My course as a clergyman involves too many responsibilities to the Church and even to my family and to myself, not to be long and laboriously and devoutly weighed. But, wherever my future steps may lead me, this much at least is certain, the world of business cannot be my refuge. The intention of my vows, I never, never can forget. By my own desire, by my own consent, I was forever separated from all pursuits and occupations inconsistent with the sacred character of an ecclesiastic; and the sincere purpose of my heart, and of my act, I have no wish, no thought to change. In the great kingdom of God's church militant, I listed myself to be a soldier, and I do not waver in my allegiance. Submission always, must be what I owe, and wherever I believe my fealty due, there will I pay my loyalty.[39]

Trusting in God's kindly Providence, Cornelia had been united with Pierce in his perpetual separation "from all pursuits and occupations inconsistent with the sacred character of an ecclesiastic." She wrote to her sister:

Addie dear, he must do his duty, and I do not fear under any circumstances, that God in his kind Providence will not find a way for him to support his family without going back into the world again . . . .

Was it to his own honor and glory that Pierce vowed to devote his life, or was it to the *Church of Christ?*[40]

But Cornelia went further in her trust of God's kindly Providence: Cornelia believed in their marriage. She wrote to her family, "Pierce is not a Catholic [Oct. 1835] nor could he be a Catholic priest if he desired it while I live."[41]

For the next five years she exerted every effort of her richly endowed mind and heart to hold their marriage together in the face of the dilemma Pierce's priesthood presented to him as he recognized in an institution which permitted only celibate priests the Church of Christ he was seeking. Cornelia recognized the true Church by the presence of the crucified Christ. She responded to the first intimations of her deeper share in his Passion by a calm and equanimity of spirit inexplicable except in terms of the grace of acceptance of the cross and resurrection in her life, a trust in God's fidelity to his call to herself and to Pierce in marriage: ". . . as regards my loved husband, our blessed little ones and myself, I was never happier in my life."[42]

One finds here Cornelia's brave and necessary reassurances to her family. But her life between 1835 and 1840 will show that there is more in this statement — there is behind it the force of Cornelia's resolution, sustained and developed with generosity and fidelity for five years, to assist Pierce in finding in marriage the holiness of life to which he aspired, the apostolic outlets to which his zeal impelled him, and the support of her love of and faith in him for which he so evidently yearned.

Cornelia's Reception into the Church

1835 to 1840 was an important stage in Cornelia's ever more graced journey with Christ into the depths of the Paschal Mystery. The sources, read in the light of her underlying purpose to make their marriage work, show a continuity and unity in her spiritual life which will be equally manifest in her founding and developing the Society of the Holy Child Jesus.

Pierce returned to Cornelia from St. Louis determined to study Catholicism in Rome, to consult authorities there about his doubts. With characteristic energy and enthusiasm Cornelia applied herself to this and to all subsequent projects Pierce would pursue in his spiritual quest. It meant for her selling "White Cottage," the first home of which she had been mistress, and auctioning treasured possessions. It mean leaving a warm, concerned, generous parish community. It meant preparing somehow for an ocean voyage with a three-year-old and a nine-month-old. All this she accomplished in a little more than a month.[43] In late October or early November the Connelly family went to New Orleans to book passage for Rome. There, on November 21, 1835, Cornelia attended what may have been her first Eucharistic celebration, an inspiring one, for the consecration of Anthony Blanc as bishop of New Orleans.[44] The sermon for the occasion, by Bishop Portier of Mobile, Alabama, depicted the life of the Catholic missionaries of the Mississippi Valley in terms which, a month earlier, Cornelia had identified as the true sign of the Church expressed in the lives of Catholics: willingness to follow Christ to crucifixion for the Redemption of his People.[45]

The incredibly demanding character of Cornelia's spiritual itinerary began in marriage. Her openness to spiritual growth despite the cost, her sensitive attention to others, her trust in a loving God — all of these were part of her spirituality as a married woman. She grew in spiritual maturity by relating generously to Pierce. That intimate relationship seems to have helped her to grow in her relationship with God. It was in living out fully her relationship with Pierce with all of its joys and sacrifices, obligations and rewards that she discerned the Crucifixion and the Resurrection to which the Lord was leading her. It was not in spite of but because of her response in marriage and her fidelity to all that it entailed that Cornelia was able to discern succeeding calls from God to ever deeper union with Him.

Whatever additional events helped to confirm her belief in Catholicism, e.g., that of warm welcome by the missionary bishops of the Mississippi Valley assembled for the consecration of Blanc,[46] Cornelia must have had strong interior confirmations. She quickly made her own decision for Catholicism, sought out Bishop Rosati on her own initiative, and with

Pierce present, abjured Protestantism. Just before she and her family sailed for Europe on December 10th, she received the Sacraments of Pennance and the Eucharist. Bishop Rosati left an eloquent record of Cornelia's reception into the Church:

> Having arrived at New Orleans for the consecration of Monsignor Blanc, I had the happiness to find him [Pierce] here with his family, and more determined than ever in his resolution. Mrs. Conelly [sic], a woman of great intelligence and spirit developed by a carefully planned education, had shared the conviction of her husband; she had forestalled him! She was awaiting me to confer with me and to dispose herself to follow the movement of grace. Nothing could have been easier than to prepare her to enter the Church. I heard her Confession and during the Octave of the [Immaculate] Conception she had the happiness for which she was urgently longing, to make her first Communion. She did not want to expose herself to the danger of the sea before having professed the Catholic Religion, and tasted how sweet and good God is to those who seek him.[47]

Bishop Rosati records an expressed motive of Cornelia which impelled her to take an unaccustomed initiative—"she forestalled him"—and act swiftly and surely on her new convictions regarding Catholicism. Given those convictions, it is also possible that Cornelia saw how important it was for her marriage that she act on them. From the time that the sources allow us to enter deeply into her life, we find Cornelia earnest and practical in her religious affairs, as in life in general. The threat of Pierce's priesthood gave added cogency and significance to her own plan for a serious and now, Catholic, spiritual life. She may well have reflected that if Pierce were going to ask in Rome for ordination—which he did—she wanted the Roman hierarchy to see a *Roman Catholic wife* at his side.

Holding Their Marriage Together

The Connelly family arrived at Rome on the 25th of February after fifty-one days at sea and an enforced stop-over at Marseilles.[48] Bishop Rosati and other missionaries had given them letters of introduction which quickly provided a royal welcome to the Papal Court at Rome and to English and Americans closely associated with it.[49] As a convert minister from America where violent anti-Catholicism was currently reviving, Pierce became a sign in Rome of the triumph of the Church;[50] he began to bask in the warmth of his reception. His doubts about the Church over miracles were satisfied quickly by Anthony Kohlmann, S.J. In March Pierce applied for Baptism (conditional), Confirmation and Holy Orders. He abjured and was given conditional Baptism on March 27th in the private Chapel of Cardinal Odescalchi, Cardinal Vicar of Rome. On March 31st, he and Cornelia were confirmed together by the English Cardinal Weld.[51]

The sources say little of the Roman hierarchy's response to Pierce's request for ordination to the Roman Catholic priesthood. It seems to have been recommended to him that he discuss the possibility of his priesthood with the leaders of the Greek Uniate Church. No record has been found of his discussions—we know only that he did not pursue his priesthood in the Greek Church.[52]

We have a very valuable recollection from Cardinal McCloskey, who was, as young Father McCloskey, the sole American priest studying at the Gregorian University when the Connellys arrived in Rome. Pierce had had a discussion with him within four days of their arrival in Rome.[53] But the conversation McCloskey remembered several decades later and related to her niece, was with Cornelia:

> I can see Reverend Mother Connelly approaching me clasping her hands and her beautiful eyes uplifted to my face—"F. McCloskey, is it necessary for Pierce Connelly to make this sacrifice and sacrifice me—I love my husband and my darling children. Why must I give them up—I love my religion and why cannot we remain happy as the Earl of Shewsburys [sic] family?"[54]

Obviously this text is of great value both to show us the Passion Cornelia was suffering, *and* the direction of her efforts—to preserve the marriage she believed called to with Pierce by God. One sees the poignancy of Cornelia's dilemma—Abraham's dilemma:[55] Did God contradict himself, did he both call to life and to destruction in the same moment? Fortunately for Cornelia at that time, her discernment of God's Will received some support from the Cardinal Vicar of Rome with whom Pierce discussed his priestly vocation very soon after his arrival. The latter reported to Bishop Rosati:

> What a change has that little space ... six short months ... wrought in all my feelings, in all my principles—in my friends, in my interests, in my profession! With regard to the last, it is with sincere pleasure I communicate to you that the Cardinal Vicar thinks my prospects of usefulness in embracing the Catholic Faith will be greater as a married man than as a priest; and he wisely argues that the example of my conversion will be kept in sight longer, and more frequently remembered than if I were to take my place among the clergy and thus retire more completely from the world.[56]

Cornelia must have received some reassurance from Pierce's "sincere pleasure" that the Cardinal Vicar thought it more "useful" to the Church that he remain a married man. Perhaps Cardinal Odescalchi spoke to him about the holiness of the married state. If he did so, he was a rare voice in the Connellys' milieu. Pierce did not write of such exhortations. Instead he continued his letter with his own reflections which are less firm than the Cardinal's and surely less settled and resolute than Cornelia's "nor could he be a Catholic priest if he desired it while I live." He wrote:

> For my own part I can only say as I trust I do in humbleness & in sincerity: "Lord here I am! What wilt Thou have me to do?" & relying on his grace to help me, endeavor to make myself useful in whatever way be my voca-

tion. . . . My dear wife, your faithful penitent, sends you a short and most affectionate & respectful message . . . ."[57]

It is clear that, in 1836, Cornelia and others did not see in Pierce the "signs of serious neurosis" obvious to today's professional psychologist.[58] They were by no means obvious; in fact, quite the opposite was protested vigorously by many people throughout the years 1835-1849 until Pierce took the incredible step of instituting a suit for the restitution of those conjugal rights which he had asked Cornelia to give up. There was question of his emotional and mental stability in 1835. Pierce's family and Cornelia's had questioned whether his resignation of his Episcopalian ministry and conversion to Roman Catholicism was evidence of pathology.[59] All, including Cornelia, had satisfied themselves as to his soundness. She had written firmly to her sister in October 1836

> His mind, I thank God, is as sound as ever, and as capable as ever to support his family.[60]

From her Natchez and Roman letters one can see the resolute course Cornelia pursued in the face of threat to all she held dear: In Rome she took practical steps toward her own spiritual growth, realistically acknowledging the need for discernment: "We are neither of us blind to the many abuses which belong not to the Church but to the superstitions of the ignorant."[61] She secured for spiritual director Monsignor (later Bishop) Reisach of Propaganda Fide. Within a year he was telling her to "go to Communion when she wished"—an eloquent testimony in the nineteenth century to his esteem of her spiritual progress.[62]

She gave her love, her support, her concern, her appreciation unstintingly, tenderly, faithfully to Pierce, making him feel, through her love, his own worth. She supported and defended him to family and friends. She bent all her efforts toward helping him to find satisfying ways within marriage to live out his calling from God, adapting herself to circumstances which helped him fulfill himself. She continued to be the charming wife who helped to win him welcome in high social circles. She gave their children devoted care in their Roman apartment home.

Finally, she attended to her own growth, using all available opportunities to develop her talents. She had been the enthusiastic companion of Pierce's literary and musical evenings in Natchez; in Rome she studied voice and piano, art, French and Italian. She reveled in Rome's cultural advantages: "seeing it won't do—it must be studied, and it will take at least a year to study it . . . . At every step you see the most precious works of art."[63] She participated with ease and maturity in the elegant Roman social life to which the special circumstances of their conversion had given them entrée: "Dear Mary, you may imagine poor little American me seated at a table surrounded by Princesses, Earls and Countesses!"[64]

Pierce spent five months of 1836 in England as the guest of Lord Shrewsbury. The latter, a wealthy, generous, zealous lay English Catholic leader, befriended the Connellys with affection, hospitality, and support from their arrival in Rome till his death in 1852. In his letters to his brothers from England, Pierce began the refrain which was to run persistently through his family letters even after he had initiated the separation which would lead to his priesthood. He wrote to his brother John that he had

> . . . spent my time [in England] as delightfully as I could anywhere away from dear Nelie and the Children. You may be sure I miss them dreadfully and sometimes cannot help being quite low-spirited without them.[65]

Meanwhile Cornelia struggled to demonstrate her place within Pierce's commitment. It was to her own more general ecclesial vocation that she appealed. There is poignancy in her striving to hold together their marriage, to reconcile seemingly conflicting demands of God, to find an adequate religious mission for Pierce. She wrote to Pierce when he was exploring lay apostolates in England:

> Dearest life, I received your sweet letter from P[aris] the day before yesterday—let me kiss you for it, but at the same time give you a good scolding for being so dull. Dear love I knew it would be so—you try very hard to persuade me you are happy but all the time I know your heart is with me—but this must not be so; give it all to the Church, all, all, and then I shall have it, too, for am I not one of its children without a wish that is not connected with it? Oh, Petty, don't think about want or any affliction that it may please the Almighty God to punish us with; while we have the kingdom of heaven within us will we not be happy in spite of every earthly want, and while we have the faith will we not be able to bear all even to death? Oh love, think not of me—if I still have too much pride I deserve . . . to suffer in the *sight of our relatives* . . . but never think of this my love if your duty to God would be better fulfilled by going home—but I cannot conceive you could be more useful to going back to America . . . can it be possible that a man of your abilities would not be useful to the Catholics of England? . . . at all events, don't give way to depression—the Almighty will not forsake you after having done so much for you—he will give you faith and give you strength to go on in the good work and be useful in the world; and have you not already increased the faith of some and shaken others? . . .[66]

In the Spring of 1837 Pierce was still exploring his vocational options. Although Cornelia was pregnant she unhesitatingly agreed to travel with him and their two-year old and five-year old to Vienna where the royal family and Metternich gave ready welcome to the converts of the American mission they had been supporting through their Leopoldine Society.[67] In Vienna their family life was gladdened by the birth of John Henry; it was also disturbed by the news of an American financial panic. The threat to their economic future caused the Connellys to commence their return journey to Natchez where they arrived in January of 1838. As they passed through New Orleans Pierce was anxious over his prospect for employment but was, as usual, buoyed up by Cornelia's joyous optimism:

She is dancing with delight at the thought of soon being back in our old home . . . . She is an angel of consolation . . . . she is more rejoiced than I can say over a return to our peaceful quiet home life, though at the same time she can bravely look ahead to coming — I must not say storms — but times in which we may find ourselves without a home in which to live.[68]

The resourceful Cornelia was, as she began housekeeping in Natchez, planning to open an Academy for young ladies to supplement Pierce's earnings as a bank clerk.[69] However, they soon received a request to join a missionary venture on the frontier. The Jesuits, who had just opened a boys' school at Grand Coteau, on a great prairie of Louisiana, upon hearing of the Connellys from the American Bishops, invited Pierce to become instructor of English. The religious of the neighboring Sacred Heart School invited Cornelia to be their mistress of music. Cheerfully, she again moved her family, generously she taught twenty-three music lessons a week to support them when the Jesuits could not afford to pay Pierce; courageously she accepted the privations of home-making in a forty-foot cabin housing her husband and herself, their three children and governess, and two slaves. Pierce was inclined to discouragement but he reported that his wife was "as gay as a bird."[70]

The joy which was the fruit of the Spirit's powerful action in this "valiant woman" overflowed into the life of her family. Pierce gives us a vignette of their life on the Louisiana prairie:

> When I sit down to write to you after dinner and the more serious duties of the day are over, I do so in the parlor with all around me a set of the sweetest children but the noisiest — where blind man's buff gives place to Pont d'Avignon — Pont d'Avignon to Puss in the Corner, & fifty chances to one but their Mama lends an arm to the medley and sends all dancing or rather stamping around and round the place till some youngster screams for assistance to be further active & fairly force mine papa to be an involuntary sharer in the disturbance . . . . Here is my letter begun two nights ago in noise and merriment and a crowd — ended in silence and solemness and alone — Our litanies have been said, our sweet Ave Maris Stella sung, we have all knelt together in our little Oratory at our little altar before our little copy of blessed Angelico's saintly picture of the Annunciation and the little family have all scattered to their quiet little chambers — *respiciat humilia* . . . .[71]

One of the former children at the Academy of the Sacred Heart remembered years after how, when she was five and too young to be a regular student, she was always allowed to remain in the Connelly home:

> Such times as we had together . . . belong to the brightest, sweetest memories of my life . . . Mrs. Connelly gave piano and guitar lessons . . . Young as I then was, I can never forget her lovely face, and still lovelier manner.[72]

Cornelia's own little son, at ten, reported the same warm experience of his mother. Pierce took him to Philadelphia on their way to England in 1842 and wrote:

[a family friend] said to him, two or three days ago, "Well, Merty, mama is very beautiful, is she?" "Oh yes", said Merty, "yes, she is so" — "Well," says Mrs. Read, "you have seen a good many pretty ladies here, do you see anybody like mama?" Merty said, *"No."* 'Are none of them as pretty as your mama?" "I don't like to say that," said Merty, "but I love my mama's face better than any other lady's face."[73]

Pierce ended his account with the expression of how much Cornelia meant to him: "Is he not a dear sweet little fellow? . . . and when he smiles, the image of you, especially his side face."[74]

Cornelia had had to suffer much with her little ones of the sicknesses, frustrations and privations attendant on the frequent travelling their father's religious quest entailed. But she had much joy in nurturing and educating her children and felt quite expert in the latter. It was an immense sorrow to her that, falling ill herself after the birth of her fourth child, Mary Magdalen, she had to watch her baby die at the age of six weeks, on September 10, 1839.[75]

Introduction to the Spiritual Exercises of St. Ignatius

December of 1839 was to be as richly graced for Cornelia as December of 1835 had been, when she had been received into the Catholic Church. What she experienced at the end of 1839 is best described as a confirmation of her previous intuitive perception of God's action in her life, and a deeper clarification of his purposes as directed toward her identification with Christ in his Paschal Mystery. In addition, she was given access to an enduring method or plan by which she might in ever increasing measure become more like Christ through the power of the saving mysteries of his earthly life, and might discern ever more sensitively the particular will of his Father for her. Finally she found an instrument by which she could effectively communicate to others concerning the spiritual life and help each to find her unique place in salvation history.

The occasion of this decisive grace for Cornelia, decisive for her charismatic service to the Church through the Society of the Holy Child Jesus, was her introduction to the Spiritual Exercises of St. Ignatius of Loyola. She was given the opportunity with two married alumnae of the Sacred Heart Academy, to participate in the "first days," December 21-24 (corresponding to the First Week) of the Exercises which the Religious of the Sacred Heart followed for eight days.[76] Their director, Nicholas Point, S.J., rector of St. Charles, introduced Cornelia to the keeping of a spiritual notebook; it is principally to her notebooks that we owe our insight into her profound grasp of the dynamism of the Exercises. The notebooks show both her rich graces in subsequent retreats and her ever-growing union with God in a very active, very discerning everyday life.

In succeeding chapters we shall show how from 1839 onwards the Exercises provided her with a framework through which she could express her faith-vision, and a method by which she, and those whom she would lead, could continually deepen their participation in the Paschal Mystery. It is only the cumulative revelation in her own spiritual notes and in her effectiveness as a spiritual guide in her Society, that shows what good seed was planted when Cornelia saw the plan of the Exercises and was guided through what she called the "great first fundamentals," that is, the Principle and Foundation and the "First Week," probably including the meditation on the Kingdom. Although Fr. Point limited his married women retreatants to the "First Week," following the custom of the time, God "the Creator" (as Ignatius had noted) could "deal directly with the creature [in whatever state in life], and the creature directly with his Creator and Lord."[77] How powerfully and lovingly God dealt with Cornelia is evidenced by the intimate recollections she confided to one of her sisters that

> at her first Retreat of three days she was converted, and that she could not fancy anyone seriously making the Exercises of St. Ignatius even for three days without giving themselves wholly to God—She said that all subsequent retreats only completed this one, in which she said the sketch of her interior life was drawn.[78]

Cornelia had experienced what learned Ignatian commentators have noted, that the promise of the whole of the Exercises is contained in the Principle and Foundation.

Within a few days, she was already sharing effectively the Ignatian method in which she felt at home. Her sister Mary, "whose mind was not favorably disposed towards Catholicity," had come at Christmas 1839 for an extended visit. Cornelia remembered that she consented

> to join me privately in making short meditations on a text of Scripture, using also the book of Meditations according to the Method of St. Ignatius upon which we conversed frequently during the day. In a few weeks she determined upon seeking further instructions, and was finally received in the Church by Monseigneur Blanc, Bishop of New Orleans . . . . [Feb. 3, 1840].[79]

Clearly the clarification and confirmation of Cornelia's own spiritual experience by the Exercises was immediately helpful to her for apostolic purposes, and enabled her to begin her life-long work of introducing others to their dynamism.

Cornelia's Offering of Her Son and Husband

The providential timing of Cornelia's introduction to the Exercises was that they prepared her for her own Passion which was imminent. By the time 1840 dawned Pierce was again growing restive about his vocation and Cornelia must have realized it. On January 20, she recorded her prayer, placing before God the anguish of her heart she had revealed to Father McCloskey four years before:

> O my God, *trim* thy vine, cut it to the quick, but in Thy great mercy root it not yet up—My God help me in my great weakness—help me to serve Thee with new fervour.
>
> Jan. 20, 1840.[80]

Many years after this memorable January, Cornelia recalled for one of her intimate companions in the Society of the Holy Child Jesus a similar prayer she had offered at the time, one which seems also to envision the sacrifice of her family life to Pierce's priesthood: "Oh my God!" she is said to have prayed, "if all this happiness, is not to thy greater glory and the good of souls take it from me—I make the sacrifice."[81]

To her immense agony and grief, another sacrifice, one she could or would never have envisioned was asked of her. Her youngest son, born in Vienna, the darling of her heart, a bright and beautiful two-and one-half year old boy, was horribly burned when a large Newfoundland dog accidentally tumbled him over into a boiling sugar vat. Cornelia held him for almost two days until he died at dawn on the Feast of the Purification.[82] The brief note in her spiritual notebook, austere, transcendent, seems to hint at a profound mystical grace accorded Cornelia in her time of deepest anguish:

> Feb. 2 1840
>
> Jesus   Marie   Joseph
> I.B.H.M.L. Connelly
> Fell a victim on Friday—Suffered 43 hours & was taken "into the temple of the Lord" on the Purification.[83]

John Henry's death drew Cornelia closer and closer to the living wells, to contemplation of the earthly life of God-made-man through which we are transformed. She was growing in her understanding of the depths of mystery contained in Luke's account of Jesus' humble, hidden years. A week after her offering in the Temple she prayed:

> Feb. 9—I will ask of my God without ceasing & he will give me to drink—Oh Jesus give me the sorrow in meditating on thy blessed wounds, or some portion, at least, that thy blessed mother had—Stabat Mater Dolorosa—[84]

The next major event in Cornelia's life was also, she acknowledged years later, one of equally intense suffering. She told some of her religious that the Society of the Holy Child Jesus was founded October 13, 1840, and that it was founded on a broken heart. Pierce who had, at the same time as Cornelia, been introduced to the Exercises in 1839, accepted an invitation to make them in full with some of the Jesuits, October 9-17, 1840.[85] At the midpoint in the retreat, October 13 (the day of Election?), Pierce interrupted his solitude to tell Cornelia he was now sure God had called him to continue his priesthood in the Roman Catholic church. He asked her cooperation in his renewed investigation of the means to effect this. He also made a proposal to which Cornelia acceded and which she summarized in

1849 as follows: "that thenceforth they should live in constant and perfect chastity, abstaining from sexual intercourse with each other, in order to more fully devote themselves mutually to the service of God, and with a special view to his [Pierce's] then declared wish and intention to take Holy Orders in the Roman Catholic Church."[86]

Cornelia, who was three-and-one-half months pregnant with their fifth child, maintained that peace and balance of soul which, coupled with her vitality and buoyancy, continued throughout her life to be a sign to others of her union with God. We give her response as it was remembered many years later by the Jesuit who had been her spiritual director in 1840:

> C'est chose grave; pensez-y mûrement et à deux fois; mais si le bon Dieu demande le sacrifice, je suit prête à lui faire de grand coeur.[87]

With this response Cornelia changed decisively the central focus of her spiritual efforts even as she faced the fact that Pierce did not expect their life to change outwardly for some years, since they would have to fulfill their obligations to their children. She seems to have accepted from the beginning that this sacrifice would eventually include some sort of religious consecration for her. She knew that Pierce was considering the Jesuits for himself. It was not difficult for her to look toward the Society of the Sacred Heart with which she already had deep spiritual and professional ties. It was toward religious consecration that she began resolutely to direct her efforts while sustaining her role as mother and teacher.

She had included in her response to Pierce what she would maintain up to the irrevocable moment of his ordination and her public vow of perpetual chastity in 1845, the need for continual, faithful discernment entailing openness to further light on the true nature of God's calling: "This is a very serious matter; do consider it deeply and repeatedly." Cornelia had believed deeply enough in their mutual vocation to marriage to devote all of her human endowments and spiritual resources to the fulfillment of that vocation, and especially from 1835 to 1840. She would be mature enough to live for the next five years with the ambiguity which fidelity to God in human circumstances sometimes demands. On the one hand, she would give herself as whole-heartedly as she had given in marriage, to make it possible for Pierce to live out the priestly calling for which he had proclaimed himself "forever separated from all pursuits . . . inconsistent with the sacred character of an ecclesiastic.[88] At the same time, she would keep open the possibility she offered to Pierce in the Spring of 1845: "to resume their former mode of life."[89]

Cornelia struggled not to allow her children to feel the effects of a future family break-up. She bore her last child, Pierce Francis, on March 29, 1841, and nurtured him with the same joy and tenderness as her other children. In a letter to her brother-in-law and sister-in-law she shows her delight in her youngest son:

> You would find Frank quite a big boy and trying to say everything: with pretty curling hair and rosy cheeks and saucy chin, and altogether an envious object for you and Gecla.[90]

That she integrated her more structured spiritual program into the rhythm of her maternal role is shown in her personal spiritual notes:

> I promise to make the Exercises [in honor of St. Joseph] of the Ven. Pere Lallemant until 11 days after the baby will have been weaned.[91]

Sources through which we glimpse the family life of the Connellys show Cornelia bestowing the same joyous, caring presence to her husband and children *after* October 13, 1840, as before. Her "bright joyous spirit" which was remarked on from the beginning to the end of her life became increasingly, as her sufferings mounted, the manifest fruit of her union with the suffering Christ.[92] Recording her desolation of soul in her notes for 1844, she resolved to "give to the Holy Ghost many smiles."[93]

Discerning Her Own Call to Religious Life

Full-time homemaker and school-mistress though she was, Cornelia so disciplined herself as to make use of the opportunities Grand Coteau and later Rome (1844-46) offered for a formal spiritual program. Her three spiritual notebooks chronicle such a richly graced spiritual itinerary from 1840-46 that they cannot be treated in full here. They supply much material for future anthology of Cornelia's spiritual teachings. Cornelia has left notes of three eight-day retreats in Grand Coteau: January 1-10, 1841; September 17-26, 1841; and October 1842; and of two retreats in Rome at the Trinità dei Monti, March 4-12, and November 2-11, 1844.[94] After 1839, she was always allowed by Jesuit directors to make the Exercises in full.

Already in October, 1840, Cornelia made a brief private record of the discerning process she had begun. Even under stress she reveals her profound faith in life understood as calling from God, and her grace of wholeheartedness in response.

> Oct. 1840
>
> For P.[ierce] not to be P.[riest] or N.[elie] not to be N.[un] would be owing either to:
>
> 1. Infidelity—or
> 2. Miracle
>
> but to suppose that one will be unfaithful is to suppose one will be lost—sin of despair; to suppose or expect a miracle is to suppose more than God has promised—sin of presumption—therefore they are to be P[riest] and N[un]—and are called to work out their calling—& to aim at it with all their might—what one is called to do, she is called to do with all her might.[95]

Cornelia's spiritual program included not only eight day retreats but also daily Mass (which she and her husband had attended since 1838), daily meditation and examen, and monthly days of recollection on First Fridays. It was on First Friday in 1841, shortly before her retreat that Cornelia wrote the prayer which could be taken as the sum of her life:

> 1st Friday Sept.
> O my Good Jesus I *do* give myself all to Thee to suffer & die on the cross, poor as thou wert poor, abandoned as thou wert abandoned by all but thee, O Mary—Sub tuum.[96]

During her retreat at the end of September 1841, Cornelia wrote simply, "Ex. vocation. Decided."[97] She manifests here as she will in the future, strength and calm both in making and carrying out momentous decisions.

Pierce saved a note she wrote him on the last day of that retreat. It reveals the intimacy with which they still shared their feelings and also their spiritual experiences. It also gives us an insight into Cornelia's "familiarity with God our Lord in spiritual exercises of devotion,"[98] that true contemplative ease with which she identified with Jesus in the mysteries of his earthly life. She was completing the Exercises at the Sacred Heart Convent a half-mile from their home, while Pierce was preparing to commence them at St. Charles College.[99] She had apparently been sharing with her husband the services of Sally, their slave who had prepared dinner for him and their nine-year-old son, Mercer. She wrote to ask for Sally's services, but above all to share intimately with her husband her joy with Christ risen, even as He led her ever more deeply into the renunciation her future entailed:

> September 25, 1841
> Dearest
>
> Be sure to send Sally back at 1/2 past 2—we will be at the Ascension, and after going through the sorrows we won't give give [sic] up the right to the joys, you know. I wish you all a merry dinner as a preparation to your retreat. Father said we might relax a little today, though perhaps he did not mean quite so far as I am doing—but I am not *yet* a religious.
>
> Yrs ever in J.C.
> C.C.[100]

By May of 1842 Pierce had gone to England to become a tutor-travelling companion to a wealthy young Englishman, and to place Mercer in an English Catholic boarding school, the latter's education being Lord Shrewsbury's gift to the family.[101] As Cornelia and Pierce's directors knew, Pierce's principal object was to explore the means to his priesthood. In a little over a year he returned to the United States to take Cornelia, Adeline and Frank with him because ecclesiastical authorities had indicated that her presence was required for any plans that might be made toward his eventual ordination.[102]

Pierce's extension of their journey to Rome, including a protracted stay at Lord Shrewsbury's home in England and touring on the continent, may have caused Cornelia some anxiety about her husband's ability to face the reality he was proposing. So would have a letter to his brother, written the year previous, had she seen it. "What a delightful tour if Nelie were along," wrote her husband who was asking his wife to separate. "How much rather would I be at home with her and the little ones than anywhere else without them."[103]

Meanwhile, at home in her hidden life with her little ones, Nelie was growing in profoundly graced understanding of the revelation of the Infancy Narratives. Her inspiration for the Society of the Holy Child Jesus seems to have originated in the faith, hope and love with which, in union with the Holy Family, she responded to the demands her life as wife and mother entailed—a life appearing outwardly to be that of an ordinary wife and mother, "a humble and hidden life." As she experienced the Paschal Mystery—"crucifixion of heart"[104]—within the context of marriage, childbearing, child-rearing, she grasped the wonderful condescension of the God who had lived his Paschal Mystery with his Mother and Joseph in Bethlehem and the long self-effacing years in Nazareth;[105] she committed herself to the way of life God had revealed through his human childhood, through his "ordinary" human life.[106] She understood the "Passion" of the child, but also the joy of the never-failing miracle of human growth to which the child witnesses. She united with Mary in fostering that growth and sharing that Passion. And she chose "St. Joseph for our Protector in life and in death."[107] Though she could not as yet, in Grand Coteau, have realized her destiny to be a founder of a religious congregation, she was already prepared by the depths of her own spiritual life to share the way of life she had found revealed in the Infancy Narratives. She saw the light they shed on the sanctification of family life. She saw the light they shed on the interior life, and on the apostolate of the Father's special predilection—that of fostering the development of the child. What she was able to bring to the religious women who were later drawn to her by spiritual kinship was her profound understanding that Jesus, and thus his followers, could live the fullness of the Paschal Mystery within the humble and hidden life.[108]

Papal Support of Pierce's Priestly Vocation

The Connellys arrived in Rome in December of 1843 with a baby son not yet three, and a daughter of eight. They had left their eleven-year-old son in Oscott College in England. They expected that it would be some years before Pierce's goal was realized, if only because of the needs of their young children.[109] Yet before two years had passed Pierce was ordained a priest of the Roman Catholic Church (July 1845),[110] and before three years had passed Cornelia had founded the Society of the Holy Child Jesus in England (October 1846). What caused them to move so swiftly toward their extraordinary destinies? With what results? An indication will be given in the following chapter of how many threads of history were woven together to draw Cornelia into England's Catholic Revival in 1846. For this second phase of the Connellys' history, as in the other phases of their lives, a full-scale biography is needed to present fully the complexity of the human factors which impinged upon their lives, a complexity which Pierce tended subconsciously to encourage by his need to be caught up in a vortex of international religio-political affairs. Here only those points will be given which bear directly on Cornelia's responsibility and spiritual development from 1844 to 1846.

It seems clear now that it was the aged Pope Gregory XVI, a former monk himself, who involved himself, directly in the Connellys' affair and moved Pierce quickly to ordination. "Io farò tutto" he had said early in 1844.[111] On March 15, 1844, he agreed to a decree of separation for the Connellys, and on April 1, they signed it.[112] Pierce went to study theology at the College of Nobles while Cornelia went to live at the Sacred Heart Convent, Trinità dei Monti with her two children. Gregory XVI had intervened to make this arrangement possible for her.[113] By the Pope's leave, Pierce received Minor Orders on May 1st. Just a little over one year later, with papal approbation, he was ordained on July 6, 1845. All of Pierce's ordination ceremonies took place in the Church of the Trinità so that Cornelia and the children could participate.[114] To the festivities which took place at the Sacred Heart Convent the evening of Pierce's Minor Orders, May 1st, 1844, the genial old Pope sent a gift indicative of the reasons for his unqualified enthusiasm for and support of Pierce's priestly vocation. He had a large cart delivered holding an enormous live fish caught the previous day. Pierce was a "big catch!" The religious of the Trinità interpreted the Pope's gift as his "suggestion of what the Church was gaining that day, and of the priestly life then being embraced by a former apostle of error."[115]

Another ecclesiastic in Rome inadvertently helped to speed Pierce's ordination. Father Roothaan, general of the Society of Jesus to whom Pierce applied, withheld admission to the Society of Jesus until the latter had paid his debts. A short time later, it would seem, the general represented to him that he was seeing his wife too frequently.[116] Had Pierce entered the Jesuits after his decree of separation, he might have had an extended period of religious formation before ordination.

Cornelia as Quasi-Postulant and Mother

Pierce's rapid move toward ordination with the encouragement of Pope Gregory XVI meant that Cornelia must move more quickly than she had anticipated toward the settlement of her own future and that of their children. She had already discerned in Grand Coteau, as we have seen, that God was calling her to religious consecration. Less than a month before the couple's decree of separation was signed on April 1, 1844, and thus even before she took up residence at the Trinità, she made the Exercises for eight day of searching reflection on the consecration she intended to make at some future time. The whole orientation of her generous spirit was toward sacrifice. "*Without reserves*" — this phrase, underlined, recurs in her notes. The notes began:

> Retreat   Evening preparation
> March 5   Offer to God — make it as
> 1844   the last in one's life
> Refuse no sacrifice that would be for His greater Glory.
> *Know, Love,* Serve Gloria Patri, etc.
> Mortify nature *one day* at a *time*
> Do & *suffer, one day at a time.*   A.M.D.G.

She continued a most careful examination of what she was about to undertake:

> If our proposition is for the Glory of God then it is His will—. . . .
>
> If, O God, thou art pleased to place me in Religious life, I offer myself to thee to suffer . . . .[117]

The notes for this retreat are quite full and enable us to follow Cornelia through the Exercises. She applied herself seriously to the use of Ignatian aids to the discernment — the Two Standards, Three Classes, Three Degrees of Humility. She wrote:

> The Two Standards
>   Ever ready
>   Prête d'accomplir
> *One day at a time looking forward to the eternal reward*
> *Eternity*   *Eternity*   *Eternity*
> The three Classes:
>   detest and renounce the first:
>   pigri, pigri, pigri;
>   write myself for the third:
>   March 1844
>   C. Connelly
>
> The 3 degrees of perfection:
> 1st to avoid all mortal sin
> 2nd   any venial sin or even voluntary defect
> 3rd   to *suffer* purely to be more like our divine model.
> My offering given in the Mass . . . .
>
> A.M.D.G.
> I renounce the world the flesh and the devil and give myself all to Thee. To *know* Thee, to *Love* Thee, to *Serve* Thee.
>   Amen
>   Gloria Patri etc.

God responded to her efforts to discern:

I thank Thee o my God for all the *light* & strength thou hast given me in this retreat.
Gloria Patri etc.[118]

Then in a response of grateful love, of "deeds rather than words," Cornelia offered herself to God in the great renunciation he asked of her:

In whatever state of life thou shouldst please to place me I resolve by thy help to *reject & Renounce* all temptations to sin or that which would lead to sin, in *Vigilance, Humility & Fidelity*, by *Prayer & practice* — in *purity* of *heart* & *simplicity* of *intention*.

                                                                     Gloria Patri etc.

1. If, oh God, Thou art pleased to place me in Religious life I offer myself to Thee to suffer in my *heart with Thee* & *for Thee*, not to do my will but *Thine in the will of my Superiors*.
2. I offer myself to Thee to suffer the loss of any *esteem* whatever and to be *despised* without any *exceptions*.
3. I offer myself to Thee to suffer in my body by all my senses: by cold, by hunger, by thirst and in any manner whatever (and without *reserves*) that may the most contribute to thy Glory & the good of Souls.

Lord have mercy on us
              Christ have mercy on us
                            Lord have mercy on us
                                          Amen

Actions not Words
Gloria Patri, etc.
C. Connelly
March 1844

Result [of] examination of Vocation:
"Die to nature and save one's soul" . . . .[119]

Cornelia's final note for this retreat repeated what she was later to make the motto of her Society: *"actions not words."* Here she added "finis."[120]

In the pages of this retreat Cornelia testified to her understanding of the evangelical counsels as the profound renunciation entailed in the acceptance of Christ's "Standard," an understanding she was later to include in her constitutional expression of her inspiration for her congregation. This understanding has been well-expressed recently by K. Rahner:

The evangelical counsels . . . are renunciations of supreme benefits in human life. This renunciation or self-denial can only be achieved in its true and genuine nature provided that the 'value' of what is renounced is not falsely underestimated, provided that there is no reaction against it whether already present or artificially cultivated. Rather it must be viewed and valued as it really is. Only one who loves the richness of life, one for whom domestic blessings constitute an opportunity and a means for self-expression, only one who possesses the courage of self-responsibility, only one who is capable of genuine personal love, can have a real understanding of what is involved in the renunciation, prescribed by the evangelical counsels.[121]

On April 9, Easter Tuesday, Pierce took Cornelia to live as a quasi-postulant with three-year-old Frank and his nurse in a small cottage on the grounds of the Trinità dei Monti.[122] Adeline had been a boarder in the school of the Trinità since the previous December. Cornelia's first biographer, one of the earliest sisters, recorded a rare and poignant confidence from the founder: "She told us . . . how she felt when the gate of the Convent shut upon her . . . how she felt the loneliness and the seclusion and the enclosure as a great weight upon her spirits."[123]

Cornelia followed a demanding program at the Trinità: she took part in most community religious exercises, taught music and English and gave spiritual direction to lay women; in addition, she spent the evenings with her baby son, presumably also sometimes her daughter, and some hours each week for Pierce's weekly visits for the sake of the children.[124] She seems to have been able to give them personal care. Cornelia wrote to her brother of one of Pierce's weekly visits:

> On St. Peter's day (dear Papa's feast), she [Adeline] played a little duet on the piano with me and sang some pretty little verses . . . .and little Pierce Frank, he had three little verses that he half sang and half repeated for dear Papa who had brought him a little guitar for the occasion — In the evening Papa sent a treat of ices for all the house, and at ten o'clock . . . burst forth the Girandola, the fire works . . . .[125]

In a letter to her sister a year later Cornelia shared her ideas on raising young children and showed her continuing close involvement with young Frank's upbringing:

> And now for your dear husband and your little ones. I must have some chat about them at once, especially as Julia wants some good advice she says — and then she truly finds herself naughty? That is an excellent sign; tell her I have great hopes of her being one day very good, but this must come little by little, day by day.
>
> Now I must tell you all our dear little Frank's *practice*. It has been the greatest of his mortification *to keep still*, and this during 10 minutes of study of spelling and 10 minutes of bible story; this makes his two acts, and the third is during the repetition out of a book — to keep his toes out, heels together and hands clasped, which is the greatest help in keeping his attention fixed — Now I am sure if our dear little Julia tries this she will find out what a blessed thing it is to be able to control our will and govern our passions which we will never be able to do unless we study it in *little daily* acts of virtue.[126]

Exactly what Cornelia and Pierce had in mind for the ongoing care of their children is not perfectly clear — probably it could not have been clear to her, given the problematic nature of Pierce's spiritual and vocational quest. Their plans for their children were complicated also by the fact that they had not expected their separation and Pierce's ordination to be arranged so swiftly as they were in Rome in Spring, 1844. Certainly he, and she, too, saw boarding school as an important and, they believed, valuable part of their children's future. Their view was strongly supported and influenced by contemporary educational theory and practice. The "privileged" nineteenth-century child went to boarding school.[127] It was in this way that another American Episcopalian convert couple who became priest and nun had provided for their children two decades before the Connellys. The girls of Virgil Barber's family attended the Visitation boarding school in Washington D.C., where their mother was a nun, and the son attended Jesuit schools, his father having become a Jesuit.[128]

Cornelia seems to have envisioned that, in whatever way she was to live religious life, she would also continue to give adequate maternal care to her children. She stated most emphatically to her brother concerning the years 1846-48 when all her children were in boarding school while she was founding her Congregation: "My dear children were as much under my eyes as if I had not left the world, till their father . . . . stole them away from me."[129] While in retreat, near the end of her first year as a quasi-postulant, Cornelia wrote in her spiritual notebook:

> I am so happy the good Father de Villefort thinks Frank ought to stay with me until he is eight years old. I think so, too, but I am so much afraid of having any reserve with God . . . .[130]

Seven months later, at the time she made the public vow of perpetual chastity asked of her before Pierce's ordination, Cornelia wrote: "The dear Cardinal [Fransoni], in going away, said my duty was to take care of my children, and he said he was molto contento, which made my heart palpitate with joy."[131] By the time she wrote this Cornelia had informed the Religious of the Sacred Heart that she could not identify with their spirit and was beginning to plan for an educational institute for America.[132]

Is it possible, especially as, in one providential step after another, Cornelia's opportunity to be a founder began to open up before her, that she saw in this role enough authority and freedom to allow her to care adequately for her children? Her spiritual notes from her Grand Coteau through her Roman years, show that she found compatible her God-given maternal role and her call to a structured spiritual program. What the usually realistic Cornelia does not seem to have foreseen was the insuperable difficulty in finding acceptance of the mother/nun role in the English Catholic dioceses to which she was called. The frontier conditions at Grand Coteau, where she and her husband, admired as a devout couple, were the only other inhabitants besides a community of Sacred Heart Sisters and a community of Jesuits, were propitious for the Connellys' plan. No other environment, except that provided by Gregory XVI's patronage in Rome, would ever be so favorable again for Cornelia to care for her children. She and they were to suffer immeasurably from her and her husband's failure to foresee and ameliorate the effects on their children's lives of their new vocations. Emerging scientific studies of the history of childhood show that the Connellys were simply following a centuries-old pattern of fitting their children into parental and especially paternal plans. Nothing is more lacking in the records of the historical setting in which the Connellys moved than recognition of "rights" of children and women. Their milieu was untroubled by such considerations. To be male and clerical as was Pierce, was to have automatic right to determine the course of the lives of women and children dependent on him.[133]

To Return to Married Life?

Perhaps one reason why Cornelia could not fully plan her children's future was Pierce's increasing instability, doubtless a cause of anxiety to her. She could no longer count on the religious formation of the Jesuits to steady him. Knowing him as she did, she probably saw evidences of the instability he had revealed to his brother, even before the decree of separation:

> . . . the day of my taking minor orders is not yet named. Indeed, it is all not a little uncertain, for who can tell how long he will be faithful, and nothing but God's great grace will save one's courage from failing even at the last moment.[134]

In the ensuing year and a half leading up to her profession of a solemn vow of perpetual chastity, Cornelia became more aware of evidence that Pierce did not realise the extent of the renunciation to which he was committing himself, and that she must exercise a decisive moral responsibility regarding their future vocations. Fortunately, she has left her own clear testimony to the discerning, generous step she took:

> . . . by the month of June 1845, Connelly had completed his course of study, and was about to take holy orders in the Roman Catholic Church; it being necessary, however, according to the Canons of the Roman Catholic Church, that his wife should first bind herself by a solemn vow of perpetual chastity, she accordingly, on the 18th of that month, pronounced with the requisite formalities, and signed a solemn written vow of perpetual chastity, . . . and she did so with the full knowledge and approbation (testified by his signature at the foot of such written vow) of her husband, although she had previously warned him of the difficulties and trials of the state into which he was about to bind himself irrevocably, and offered to release him from all such difficulties and trials by returning to their previous mode of life, and thereby sacrificing any will and wish of her own.[135]

Cornelia also recorded the results of her representations, results which she accepted with the trust and generosity with which, as spouse, she had accepted all of Pierce's demanding initiatives.

> He persisted, however, notwithstanding such warnings and representations; and accordingly, on the 22nd of June, received subdeacon's orders,

and on the 29th of the same month deacon's orders, and on the 16th of July following, priest's orders, all of the Church of Rome, at the hands of the Cardinal Vicar of Rome.[136]

Could Cornelia have changed the course of Pierce's determinations? Ranged against her doubts were the convictions about the "eternal" character of his priesthood which he had continuously expressed since their marriage, and throughout the changed circumstances their conversion wrought. Ranged against her doubts were the urgings of members of the American and Roman hierarchy, and leading them all, the Pope himself. It is hard to suggest what by way of verification of her doubts Cornelia would have had to produce to change Pierce and his enthusiastic friends in Gregory XVI's Rome.

"I have given him to God"

Cornelia lived our her "fiat" in a characteristic way. She celebrated Pierce's ordination on July 6, 1845, with a joy at which others marveled.[137] It was the fruit of the Spirit of her crucified and risen Lord with whom she identified ever more deeply in this latest sacrifice. Both husband and wife stayed in Rome for another nine months, Pierce commencing his priestly ministry, and Cornelia preparing under the direction of Father John Grassi, S.J., with some collaboration of her husband, an outline of Constitutions for an apostle foundation in the United States. The fruit of her sacrifice of Pierce was her growing conviction of the Spirit's gift to her to found the Society of the Holy Child Jesus. A year later she could still write simply but sublimely to Pierce's brother: "Pierce . . . is deeply engaged in the duties of the ministry . . . . So, you see, it is not for nothing that I have given him to God." "I have given him to God" was to be the foundation on which she would build her Society, the explanation of the course to which she would hold for the remaining thirty-three years of her life. Cornelia had made a real and irrevocable sacrifice of great human goods—her husband and their marriage—and she would never take back the holocaust. She added a reflection on this sacrifice:

> . . . I have given him to God. You may be sure this thought gives me much consolation, and we ought to look for a greater share of the divine love in proportion as we are willing to sacrifice our natural happiness. A.M.D.G., and look too for even more in eternity.[138]

Vocation to Be a Founder

While it became more and more habitual for Cornelia to look toward eternity, she attended actively to God's work on earth. She had already discerned several months previous to Pierce's ordination that she was not called to the Society of the Sacred Heart whose life she had tried since 1844. Her association with this Society in Rome had coincided with the last stages of an unfortunate period of misunderstanding, division and near-schism; this necessarily had its repercussions on Cornelia's experience of the Society, one which differed from her American associations where the divisions had not cut so deeply. The essence of the Sacred Heart spirit which she had found and appreciated in America, was eventually restored to the Roman Sacred Heart convents,[139] but not before the difficulties had caused Cornelia to begin to reflect on founding her own congregation. Her brief reflections give us only hints of the continuing evolution of her inspiration for the Society of the Holy Child Jesus. To her sister Adeline she wrote towards the end of 1845 that she had been obliged nine months before to tell her Sacred Heart Superior that "I doubted very much that I should ever enter the order of the S. Heart tho I had no doubts about my vocation to a religious life." After making it clear to her sister that "The nuns here are very good and kind," Cornelia gave a brief but provocative expression of her own ideal:

> I bless our dear Lord again and again that I have been prevented so wonderfully from taking any promise or obligation upon me with respect to this *french* order, for it is not the one for our country. Our own dear country women must be led to a perfect life by meekness and sweetness and not by fear.[140]

Cornelia was to find, in her thirty-three years of governing her Society, that this was an ideal always to be striven for, never perfectly attained. Near the end of her life she expressed the hope to a Holy Child teaching sister that the children might "learn the joy of loving God who died for us, and of being happy in the Convent where He dwells in His most loving form of Holy Childhood." Then she added: "Stiffness and rigour will not bring forth love and these are not the spirit of the Holy Child."[141]

We return to her letter to Adeline at the end of 1845, and find further evidence of her preoccupation at this time with the significance of the childhood of God. She picked up a theme which had recurred in her letters since the time of her conversion, that is, to take "the words of our Savior with the humility of a little child;" to be "*willing* to be led like a little child . . . *with a spirit of humility*" (1836). In 1845, in her letter to Adeline, she repeated again: "we must all become as little children in the *practice* . . . of virtue . . . till the *reality* exists . . . ."[142] This time Cornelia extended the theme to include the revelation of the Divine Child as "key" to all the virtues "to the consummation of Charity." Though her mode of expression here is "chatty," the direction of her thought is clear in its linkage with her inspiration for the Society she was by now planning to establish:

> I hope dear Ralpho is with you and happy, tho I am sure he will never be quite happy till he finds the little *child* Jesus with his holy mother—this is the *key* to happiness, and he may just as well trust to my experience and not be trying those others on his big bunch, that will only unlock *boxes* of the vipers of pride, self complacency, false humility, and disobedience. Tell him just to examine my *pretty key* and see if he does not find en-

graved on it so beautifully *obedience*, and all the other virtues to the consummation of Charity—"and going into the house they found the Child with Mary his mother". Oh thrice blessed *key* to the palaces of eternal bliss! Gloria Patri et Filio, etc. etc.[143]

By the end of 1845, Cornelia had been the recipient of providential help toward the founding of a new apostolic congregation: Father John Grassi, SJ, Jesuit General Assistant for Italy at the time he became confessor at the Trinità in 1845, was a veteran of the American Jesuit missions.[144] He became Cornelia's spiritual director and fostered her awareness of her charism to found a congregation.[145] He helped her, with Pierce's collaboration, to formulate what Cornelia later called "a sketch or outline of a Rule" which was to be filled out and undergirded by the use of the Visitation Constitutions with the Rule of St. Augustine which prefaced the latter.[146] Father Grassi's influence is especially evident in the Ignatian elements in the outline which included borrowings from Jesuit, Sacred Heart and Visitation sources.[147] The first of these Ignatian elements was a qualification Cornelia was to repeat later in 1847 when she was actually using her outline with the Visitation Constitutions, while composing/compiling her own as quickly as possible. The qualification stated that the Visitation Constitutions were to be used "wherever they be not at variance with the double object of the Congregation" which was "the greater glory of God and the good of souls;" the sisters were to strive "not only . . . for their own sanctification and perfection" but also that of others. Clearly this is the Ignatian "single end;" here we see it included in Cornelia's first constitutional efforts. We shall see below in Chapter V that Cornelia held throughout her life to the "single end" as an important constitutional principle.[148]

Another possible Ignatian influence is seen in the *order* of the subjects outlined, beginning with noviceship, vows, admission and impediments, and moving through "school sisters" and "chapter sisters" to government. To this point the order seems influenced by the Ignatian Constitutions; the final passages depart from this order to such subjects as poverty, chastity and obedience, schools, retreats and renewal of vows.[149] Finally, Ignatian influence may be found in the dedication which places the mystery of the Holy Child within the context found in the Spiritual Exercises—that of the whole Paschal mystery:

J.M.J.
A.M.D.G.

In honor of the Holy Childhood of Our Lord Jesus Christ, in union with His sacred Passion and death, in adoration, satisfaction, thanksgiving and petition to the most Holy Trinity, we offer through the most precious Blood of the same Lord Jesus the following Constitutions, without other desires or other will than the greater glory of God and the good of souls.[150]

"*We* offer . . ." Cornelia recorded later that the outline was "drawn up by Mr. Connelly . . . on the foundation I gave him . . ." and was "inspected by Fr. Grassi."[151] Pierce's association with this outline caused Cornelia, in the light of his subsequent betrayal of her, to replace it soon after founding, with Constitutions she composed/compiled with her first companion, Sr. Emily Bowles.[152] Meanwhile, while she was still in Rome, she relied upon the continuing direction of Father Grassi to discern her next step after outlining a Rule. While both he and she had been planning for a foundation in America, they concurred in seeing the action of the Spirit in an urgent appeal from Lord Shrewsbury and Bishop Wiseman that Cornelia make her initial foundation in England in 1846 in order to aid England's burgeoning Catholic Revival.[153]

Thus it was that Cornelia left Rome on April 18, 1846, for a summer's stay in Paris while awaiting notification from Bishop Wiseman that he could provide a convent in which she might commence her spiritual works of mercy for the women and children of England, and especially for convert families. Pierce wrote of the Roman leave-taking:

> Poor little Ady went away very heartbroken, but Frank rejoiced at the idea of travelling, and seeing Merty . . . and Nelie was, as she always is, the comforter of everyone . . . . My blessed angel of a wife with her little ones, travels in the second or servants' places in the steamer . . . .[154]

In Paris, Cornelia and her children accepted the hospitality of Mère Eugénie Milleret de Brou, recent founder of the Religious of the Assumption. One of Cornelia's biographers sees a possible influence of Mère Eugénie on the educational manual the Society of the Holy Child Jesus printed in 1863.[155] But Cornelia has left no record of what must have been a valuable acquaintance for the two women who had spiritual-apostolic ideals in common. The significant comment we have from Cornelia from Paris was her re-affirmation of her conviction that she was not called to the Religious of the Sacred Heart, saying, "there is something more to be done for the glory of God."[156]

Testing of Vocation: Pierce's Deterioration and Cornelia's Growth

Having given herself and Pierce to God, Cornelia was free to give herself to the People of God. She left Paris in August, 1846, in response to Bishop Wiseman's final summons to her mission to the English Church. Part Two, following this chapter, will detail her efforts through thirty-three years to give institutional form to that inspiration with which the Holy Spirit had gifted her in most unusual circumstances. But before commencing Part Two, we must trace briefly her final suffering years of direct involvement with Pierce. In these years, coinciding with the primitive stage of her Society, she gave extraordinary witness to her conviction of her charism to found the Society amid the most painful and humiliating testing of her spirit.

She was to discover, soon after 1846, that her "Passion" was not over the year she gave Pierce to God. She suffered immeasurably when, between

1848 and 1851, Pierce betrayed her by kidnapping their children from their schools, attempting to gain control over her and her Society—a sort of "claiming" of her charism—and finally by instituting a suit for the restitution of those conjugal rights he had asked her to sacrifice.

What led to Pierce's deterioration? We return to summer 1846 for indications. Bishop Wiseman had already begun, before Cornelia set foot in England, to change her plan of having her children in her own convent and school, and of continuing the weekly visits allowed to Pierce by Roman ecclesiastics for the benefit of their children.[157] Emily Bowles, Cornelia's first companion, was a zealous promoter of Wiseman's restrictions on the couple's plans for the children, and Cornelia was faced, unexpectedly, with the possibility of harm to her children from an atmosphere of rejection—"Emily is rather too anxious not to have him" [Frank]. With Pierce's full concurrence, she allowed Frank and Adeline to be sent to boarding school, deploring openly to Pierce the insensitivity of the English to her children's needs.[158]

With their children in boarding school, the couple had no need to meet—for Pierce, no excuse. Cornelia began her year of noviceship in December 1846 (even as she continued as superior), and Wiseman considered it unfitting that they meet. But Pierce had not calculated how much he needed Cornelia and her support. Only three months into her noviceship he appeared, unannounced, to see her. She and Emily remonstrated and Pierce was offended. Cornelia wrote him a letter, immensely revealing of all that her marriage had meant to her and of the depth of sacrifice she had made:

> I have been so looking and hoping for a letter from you this morning; your letter had just come, and makes me cry so that I can scarcely see what I write. Forget your visit to Derby. I never told you, nor meant to tell you, that I assumed that excitement to hide nature, as I must do sometimes. No! you have not the violent temptations that I have in thinking of the little Bethlehem room . . . [a reference to their former home, "Gracemere"] nor have you perhaps, gone through the struggles of a woman's heart. No! you never have.[159]

Pierce began gradually to reveal how emotionally disturbed he was by making contradictory demands, first that she make her vows immediately; then, near the end of 1847, that she refrain from making them lest he be responsible for her debts. He began to express his resentment of and jealousy towards Wiseman.[160]

What happened from this point on Cornelia, Wiseman, Shrewsbury and others were to characterize as unforeseen and inexplicable.[161] No one it seems had discerned the depths of Pierce's pathology, nor the weight of the strain he had put upon himself by separating from Cornelia, nor had they calculated how much exterior events, movements, and ideas drew him like a ship into a vortex.

On January 11th and 12th, Pierce kidnapped their children from their schools, keeping the news of their whereabouts from Cornelia, writing that this was "the only way to get hold of her through them."[162] She was clear on what this meant: ". . . their father broke his word and his promises, and stole them away from me in a moment of excitement and unjust anger, may God forgive him."[163]

What pain this betrayal inflicted on Cornelia is known to God alone. It was in his strength she reposed her confidence. She made a vow lest the weight of her sufferings cloud the clarity of her perception and sway her from the stand she must take:

> In union with my crucified Lord and by His most precious blood, in adoration, satisfaction, thanksgiving and petition, I, Cornelia, vow to have no further intercourse with my children and their father beyond what is for the greater glory of God and is His manifest will, known through my director and, in case of doubt on his part, through my extraordinary.
> Gloria Patri etc.
> *Jan. 21, 1848*
> St. Mary's Convent, Derby,[164]

By April she had learned that Pierce, who had gone to Rome, had posed as founder, had presented a spurious rule for approbation at Propaganda Fide, and had obtained a blessing for her from the then-reigning Pope Pius IX. He had, in effect, tried to appropriate her charism with that misguided fervor by which he had for years thought he could lay hold of supernatural graces merely by fixing his desires on them.

Now with what must have been searing clarity she understood his pathological intent to get hold, not only of her but of her new spiritual children and their work. She wrote immediately to Cardinal Fransoni, prefect of Propaganda Fide in Rome, to repudiate Pierce's rule and claims.[165] Then she took her stand with her husband over his first act of betrayal:

> I have already told you I would see you when you bring back to my care my little girl, and *I will never* see you till then; unless God manifests his holy will through the command of the bishop.[166]

When Pierce published this letter four years later in a pamphlet, using the last part of her statement to prove Wiseman's domination, she annotated with: "Yes, this was *my* will because he had broken his promise."[167]

With the calm and decisiveness of a graced maturity, Cornelia recognized Pierce's intent, rejected it, and affirmed her own charism to Bishop Wiseman who, having helped her to found, supported her loyally through Pierce's attack in the courts:

> We have God and the truth on our side, therefore we need fear nothing. I am ready for anything that God wills. Do you not see that Mr. C. has determined to break up our order and ruin and upset the whole? He declared he would do this, and he probably hopes that I may go to another Convent to begin afresh under him! I should not be at all sur-

prised that his threats of apostatising are only to gain this point . . . . As I
never intended to give Mr. C. any authority over me or the Convent, and
never considered him in any way our Superior, I fear nothing on this
point — [168]

Calmer and more perceptive than the Shrewsburys, who were understandably humiliated as well as pained at Pierce's betrayal of their trust, she rejected their urging to flee England, and again professed her faith in her charism and her responsibility for those entrusted to her through it.

> . . . a flight like this would be an acknowledgment of some cause for flight which would be contrary to the truth — We have nothing to fear; God and the truth are on our side — I think only of the consequences . . . to our convent, a question of twenty persons who are engaged with me in the establishment of this order — You see at once that this would be an unfaithful and cowardly step on my part which would be destructive to the convent and in every sense give Mr. C. the advantage over us — *He would then have gained his point* . . . . his sole subject would be to force me to begin a new congregation under his guidance.[169]

It would be hard to imagine more painful testing of her fidelity to grace than that to which Cornelia was subject. She was attacked at the most personal and intimate level by the betrayal of her husband. She was subject to gross public humiliation. Although one Catholic newspaper perceived the truth of her situation and called her a martyr,[170] in general the press exploited and vilified her.[171] Her own writings witness to powerful graces enlightening, strengthening, confirming her; since she had given Pierce to God, his betrayal could not destroy her. She witnessed under duress not only to her faith in her charism for the Society of the Holy Child Jesus, but also to her faith in the fundamental meaning of her life as given by God. A sister in her Society remembered her "possessing her soul in all that calm dignity" while England was ringing with the most horrible slanders."[172] In a few terse responses to slanders Cornelia has left striking evidence of her growth as woman in inner freedom and personal spiritual identity. She annotated Pierce's pamphlets: In the margin beside his "why she is still kept," she wrote "Because she wishes it herself. C." Beside: "I will never see you," she wrote, "Yes, this is *my* will because he had broken his promise." And finally "But Mrs. C. knows better what she wishes for herself than the *Morning Herald* can know."[173]

By the end of 1848, the emotionally vulnerable Pierce was being supported by a fundamentalist Protestant leader of the Irvingites. In seeking to know from the Drummond's lawyer by what legal means he might "rescue" Cornelia from what he viewed as Wiseman's evil domination, he was pushed into the step which not even he had intended: a suit for restitution of conjugal rights. His lawyers had told him that English law admitted of no half-way measures.[174]

The suit, heard during a wave of anti-Catholicism in England, was decided against Cornelia in 1849, the judge rejecting the legality of the separation granted by the Roman court. Cornelia immediately appealed, and two pain-filled years later received a suspension of the sentence against her, pending further investigation of the marriage laws of Pennsylvania. Pierce, destitute, was never able to pursue his case. Instead, for several years, he carried on against the "captors" of his wife—the Roman Church and its clergy—a "trial by press." The Nativist pamphlets of his Mississippi Valley days flooded back into his sickened mind. He personalized their contents and published repeated attacks against the English and Roman hierarchy, the Jesuits, convents—the very targets at which the Nativists had aimed.[175]

Numerous humiliations were inflicted on Cornelia through the years 1849-51 when "Connelly vs Connelly" made headlines in the anti-Catholic English press. Her annotations to Pierce's writings show that when she was on the Cross under Pierce's persecution, she had, with the Son, commended her spirit to the Father, and had found peace in the midst of torment. She knew Pierce's weakness—"more a love of sentiment than of sacrifice"—she trusted in the power of divine mercy. A poignant annotation to one of his pamphlets read:

> I am persuaded that Mr. C. can never in heart cease to love the Holy Catholic Church but his love was always more a love of sentiment than of sacrifice—and therefore less to be trusted. His feelings have been wounded and his love turned to hatred for a time—When the opposite party gradually let sink into nothingness [sic] we may then hope that his eyes will be opened and his heart touched.[176]

It has frequently been asked in our own time why Cornelia did not recognize earlier the extent of Pierce's pathology. A cogent answer has been suggested by a psychologist who has ventured an assessment of Pierce's psycho-pathology after careful study of the sources. George Cruchon believes that as long as Cornelia was with Pierce, she was, in a very real sense, a healing presence for him, a check against the malignant potential of his conflicts to dominate his whole personality. Cruchon note:

> As long as he lived with his wife . . . [1831-44] she brought him peace and sustained him with her admiration. This esteem satisfied his daily ambitions, but, after their final separation, he gradually realized that his wife had found a career that in some ways provided openings greater than the potential of his own life. This could be a cause of jealousy.

Speaking of the point at which Pierce came to full awareness of their changed positions, Cruchon concludes:

> At this point the sudden lack of his wife's loving and admiring presence brought the situation into full crisis. His desire for importance took on a pace that, if not caused by dementia, showed at the very least signs of serious neurosis . . . . He could barely think of others, and sought to compensate a frustration that had become intolerable. Pierce's life had, in fact, became centripetal.[177]

A legal historian specializing in marriage cases, who made an intensive study of Connelly vs. Connelly, noted that a spouse is often one of the last to recognize pathology in the other. He added a revealing commentary on Pierce as *Victorian* husband and father which helps to explain the acceptance, even admiration Pierce received for years from the social and ecclesiastical circles in which he moved:

> The fact that he was domineering, the fact that he wanted his own way, the fact that he changed his mind and expected everyone else to change their minds with him — these were the natural attributes, the rightful attributes of the Victorian paterfamilias and there was really nothing that could be said against it.[178]

Clearly there were sociological, legal, theological/pastoral and politico-religious elements in Cornelia's nineteenth-century environment which severely constrained her, limited her options and not only shaped the character of her spirituality, but also her decisions and actions. Three sets of circumstances which impacted heavily upon her will be outlined here to shed new light on her unique spiritual journey. Rahner's observation that the Spirit bestows charisms in unexpected and creative ways in the midst of flawed human circumstances is verified as we study Cornelia against the background in which she lived.[179]

Wife and Children as Property

Cornelia Connelly's children, ages 8, 13 and 16, were permanently lost to her from January 1848 when Pierce kidnapped them from their schools. Her eldest son Mercer died of yellow fever in New Orleans in 1853 without his mother ever seeing him again. Pierce kept Adeline and Frank from her until they were adults. Their estrangement from her was never really healed. Why did Cornelia not regain her children? Was she lacking in responsibility as a parent? Researches to answer these questions have brought to light the extraordinarily misogynist character of nineteenth-century British marriage law. In the oft-repeated words of Caroline Norton, a much-suffering contemporary of Cornelia: "A married woman in England has *no legal existence*."[180] In the words of the legal historian, Bernard Hargrove:

> In the Connelly case, the parties were never on an equal footing, and the reason for this was that the whole approach of the courts at that time [mid-nineteenth-century England] to matrimonial matters was one of property and not of personality . . . . the wife as such was property . . . . it also comprised [the] children . . . . The mother had, at Common Law, virtually no position at all to protect the children against the Father.[181]

In a scholarly study of the Connelly case, Hargrove has shown that Pierce, reduced to penury through renunciation of his priesthood, held the Connelly children, hoping not only to gain control of their mother, but also of her property to which they were heirs through Cornelia. Hargrove concluded:

> What was aimed at in his [Pierce's] proceedings, in so far as they were not motivated entirely by spite, was to place himself in the advantageous position in relation to such estate as Sister Connelly had at the time of separation [granted by Rome, 1844] and would become entitled to in Common Law during the remainder of her life.[182]

Hargrove summarized the case further in terms of Cornelia's attempts to regain her children:

> You might just as well ask today, why doesn't a lunatic take certain steps—because that was the group into which she fell: bankrupts, lunatics, married women . . . ! English law regarded the child as being under the paternal care . . . . And of course, it took a great deal for the husband's piece of property A to be able to prove that she was entitled to have the custody, care and control of piece of property B, not just because of . . . the husband being, in marriage, the one "person," but also because the financial settlements were all geared to providing for the children.

In considering the question of whether Cornelia might have protested Pierce's removing their children from Catholic schools, Hargrove ventured the opinion that such a step

> would have brought before the Courts the issue of whether a child should be brought up according to the desires of the father or the mother, and this might well have meant a judgment in favor of the father which would have barred her irretrievably from the children.[183]

Despite the formidable legal obstacles to which she was subject, Cornelia continued correspondence with and about her children, and discreet attempts to provide for their welfare. She wrote to an old family friend of the Connellys, Bishop Blanc of New Orleans, when she learned that her eldest son Mercer had gone there in 1852: "I beg you to interest yourself in the spiritual welfare of my son . . . . Is there anything I can do, or any influence I could make use of to regain him to his faith and duty?"[184]

Bishop Blanc assured Cornelia that he and Mercer's Catholic uncle [Pierce's brother] would continue to do for Mercer what Cornelia could not: "your mode of action toward them is necessarily regulated by your changed external position toward your children, a position which having met with the approbation of Heaven, through the authority of its Representative on Earth, could not be altered without the imminent danger of your own salvation." Blanc went on to assure Cornelia: ". . . nothing of what has happened around you has, so far, been under your control. Your conscience must be at peace."[185]

"Nothing of what has happened around you has . . . been under your control." One asks today if there was no voice raised in Cornelia's time against the ignominy, the injustice, the oppression of such a situation for so faithful, so generous a wife. One finds such a voice in at least one nineteenth-century woman writer. Her books corroborate, with facts as well as with feelings, Hargrove's presentation of the defectiveness of English matrimonial law. The author, Caroline Norton, was a contemporary of Cornelia whose oppression under the same law had striking similarities to the latter's. Although Caroline did not become a religious sister, she was, as wife, deprived of her children for many years by an abusive husband. George Norton, like Pierce, used the children and varied misogynist legal devices to maintain his wife's property and income, she being the principal breadwinner of the family. A gifted writer, she vigorously applied her literary talents to the cause of legal rights for English married women, and is credited now with influencing the beginnings, in 1857, of the slow but steady progress toward just marriage laws in England.[186] A comparative study of the poignant stories of both women, and of what they accomplished for women is indeed a desideratum, but it is beyond the scope of this study.

A few comparisons and contrasts can be made in conclusion. The stories of both women chronicle the degrading of a relationship by a husband to the point where both women must have asked, as Caroline did publicly, if a marriage was any longer possible.[187] There is no record of Cornelia's considering returning to Pierce at the time he sued for restitution of conjugal rights, 1849-51. She had offered to return in 1845 before Pierce's ordination and her vow of chastity. After this time her testimony was always in terms of the new binding celibate commitments she and her husband had made, not only with mutual consent but at his expressed wish. Caroline, with no new vows, returned once to her abusive and unfaithful husband, but refused to do so again when he kidnapped and held their children.[188] Cornelia, unlike Caroline, chose not to expose her husband publicly, and, in 1858, paid the debt he had incurred by legal action against her.[189] Caroline, as Cornelia, bore more than her share of financial support of husband and children. While she differed from Cornelia in her public exposure of her husband, one finds in her writings more an attempt to expose and improve unjust marriage laws, than to attack personally.[190] If her eventual influence on the reform of English law came too late to help Cornelia, her writings help us immensely today to understand the impasse to which Pierce had brought Cornelia vis à vis himself and their children.

Marriage, Celibacy and "Perfection"

It was not only misogynist British marriage laws which shaped the character of spiritual and psychological demands upon Cornelia and the sufferings in which she was particularly responsive to the Spirit. The writings of her husband and of other contemporaries, juxtaposed here for the first time, reveal a whole complex of distorted teachings, attitudes, assumptions, practices regarding the interrelationship of marriage/celibacy/spiritual perfection which help to explain the development of Pierce's vocation. How much they impacted on her and her discernments can not be fully known. But a review of these writings, given below, seems indispensable for an understanding of the sensitive discernment she had continually to exercise regarding authentic calls to holiness.

We recall that in 1836 the Connellys presented themselves to the Roman hierarchy with a genuine spiritual/canonical problem: Before marriage, Pierce had been ordained a priest of the Protestant Episcopal Church, believing himself to be *"forever* separated from all pursuits . . . inconsistent with the sacred character of an ecclesiastic."[191] (emphasis added) When he became a Catholic he requested ordination in that Church which admitted only of a celibate clergy. He rejected the suggestion that he seek ordination in the Greek rite which allowed a married clergy. His report that the Cardinal Vicar of Rome "thinks my usefulness in embracing the Catholic Faith will be greater as a married man than as a priest," does not resolve all his vocational questions.[192] Cornelia, with considerable anguish, addressed herself to the heart of the spiritual problem with which the couple was wrestling: "Is it necessary for Pierce Connelly to make this sacrifice and sacrifice me—I love my husband and my darling children. Why must I give them up?—I love my religion . . ."[193] The only record of a response which goes to the depth of the questions Cornelia was asking was addressed to Pierce, not to her. The married Catholic Lord Shrewsbury is reported to have written to him:

> What! do you want to break up all the laws human and divine, give up your lovely wife and children? No such sacrifice is demanded. You are mad! By ambition the Angels fell! Stop at once and be a good Catholic husband and father.[194]

The only record we have of what Pierce's ecclesiastical guides were counselling him comes from his letter cited above. He does not reveal a painful wrestling with conflicting calls of marriage and priesthood. Rather he continues to report the Cardinal's Vicar's counsel in a somewhat detached way:

> he wisely argues that the example of my conversion will be kept in sight longer, and more frequently remembered than if I were to take my place among the clergy and thus retire more completely from the world.[195]

The *Dublin Review*, commenting in this same year, 1836, about an interview with Pierce on his conversion, "regretted" that "of necessity" his marriage precluded his "entering the sacred ministry."[196]

In 1836 Pierce seemed to sum up his vocational stance with: "Lord here I am! What wilt thou have me to do? & relying on his grace . . . endeavour to make myself useful in whatever way be my vocation."[197] For the next five years he and Cornelia lived a truly devout Catholic married life and had three more children. But toward the end of that period there begins a theme in Pierce's writings—"the Royal Road of the Master"—which recurs until it reaches a climax in 1842 in a public address. The theme reflects Pierce's decision of 1840 to strive for ordination even at the cost of marital separation. It also reflects a distortion of the doctrine of Christian perfection in relation to marriage and celibacy. What is the source of Pierce's doctrine and who concurred in it? The difficulty of answering these questions and their relevance to Cornelia's story make it vital for us to review the doctrine.

In 1839 or 1840 Pierce wrote a letter to Lord Shrewsbury describing an evening of family merriment. He closed the letter with a disquieting lack of appreciation of his vocation as husband and father:

> I . . . think how little this looks like walking the Royal Road Our Master counselled and set the example of walking. In the midst of just such a scene as this do I sit down to say to you why I think that if there were the same religious atmosphere and the same independence of human respect here as in England, the movement that has begun at Oxford would go further here than in England.[198]

The "Royal Road" seems to have become the vocation beyond Pierce's reach, the life that was being denied him. In his next letter, it seems to entail walking in the public view. What is inexplicable in this letter is "we have . . . little to suffer." Earlier that year their youngest son had burned to death. Cornelia's notes for the same period show her seeking in almost mute agony of soul, strength from Mary in her Sorrows. Pierce wrote to Lord Shrewsbury:

> . . . Here in our wilderness solitude we have still so much to enjoy and so little to do and suffer that it seems to me but little like the Royal Road Our Master walked in. But all that he asks of us is a spirit *Prest à accomplir* whatever He calls us to and whenever and wherever—while you, dear Lord Shrewsbury, are already fulfilling with generous hand and faithful heart the glorious duties that the Duke of Norfolk seems to have forfeited to you as head of the Catholic nobility of Great Britian.[199]

By the time he picked up his theme again in 1841, Pierce had asked Cornelia—at that time pregnant—to sacrifice their marriage for his priesthood. She had agreed, and they had begun to live as brother and sister.

> Here we have passed three blessed years in our little cottage . . . with every spiritual consolation we can desire—with only those whom we love most in the world coming out of it to pass a week or a month or even more with us—and its noise and its vice so far off that our little ones never hear of it . . . . The happiness, which like poor worldlings we were yearning after so eagerly when we might have been earning crowns for ourselves, by bearing our burdens joyfully for Christ's sake—this happiness, now we have got it, fills us with almost as much compunction as gratitude: for a life of quiet almost luxurious domestic happiness is not the road our Master showed us—not the road His most Blessed Mother walked in, not the road of those He called with that divine "*Even as* my father, loved me, so I love you"—not, in short, the royal Road of the Holy Cross.[200]

Less than a year after this letter Pierce left Grand Coteau to become travelling tutor to a young English gentleman. His purpose was both to try separation from his wife and to discuss again with ecclesiastical authorities how he might become a priest and a Jesuit. On the way to England in May 1842 he was asked to speak in the Cathedral in Baltimore. Here again he picked up the themes of his "Royal Road:"

> When I looked for the Catholic Church's claims to be Holy . . . I took the works of their great Council, the holy Ecumenical one of Trent, and, for the first time, I saw the Bible treated, in all its breadth, as a book of not impossible commands, and the Lord's tremendous counsels of daily martyrdom — and deliberate abandonment of wealth and honor, and the holy happiness of married life, and of the love of kindred, and of the love of life . . . . And when I sought for men, such as the Fathers of Trent had created in my imagination, I looked for them, not among the idle in the market places, . . . I looked for men who had thrown their wealth into the lap of poverty or into the treasury of the Lord, who have left their babes in their cradles, who had given the last kiss to a dear mother or a dearer wife, or who had fled from even the consecrated embraces of women that they might go with the Lamb where he goeth forever . . . . in a word I found more than ever I had hoped for. I found in thee, O Holy Church of Rome, what if I had not found in thee, I could have found nowhere.[201]

There is, in this address delivered publicly, a disturbing failure to distinguish *between* the *renunciation* of wealth, honor, the companionship of mother or kindred, *and* the *rejection* of marital obligations to wife and babes, the rejection also of a vocation to marriage as on a par with celibate renunciation. It is disturbing also that this doctrine of renunciation is proclaimed as a distinctive sign of the Catholic Church's holiness. It is important to note that no reaction to it has been found in the American or British Catholic press or correspondence. This same sermon of 1842 was republished in Britain in 1853 after Pierce's apostasy, *not* with any critique of his doctrine of marriage/celibacy/perfection, but, on the contrary, to show how emphatically he had, before apostasy, proclaimed the Church's holiness. Not even John Henry Newman who read the republication of Pierce's address critiqued this particular doctrine of holiness.[202]

The same failure to critique Pierce's doctrine of holiness can be observed in a response of the English Jesuit Provincial to Pierce's inquiries in 1842 about his possible admission to the Jesuits. Pierce wrote: "In fine, the thing is to find out what is the means and when is the soonest time that both [Pierce and Cornelia] may enter a holier state." Although Father Provincial Lythgoe did not encourage Pierce, in view of his heavy obligations to his family for the foreseeable future, neither did he, at least in his letter, raise the question with Pierce whether, in fact, his marriage might be "a holier state."[203] One wonders whether anyone might have raised this question in the nineteenth century. As late as 1891 a manual on religious life read:

"Are religious obliged to strive after perfection in a more particular way then the ordinary faithful?" The answer was: "Evidently, since they are called to a higher sanctity and since they have embraced a state of perfection by profession."[204]

In all likelihood Cornelia read at least Pierce's address of 1842. Not long after that she encountered the same kind of distorted doctrine in much longer form. One of the Shrewsbury's gave her a book entitled *The Life of the Lady Warner*. It was inscribed to Cornelia as "her most esteemed friend," with the addition "Blessed are those who forsake *all* for Christ."[205] The book was published in 1696 at the end of the first Jansenist century, the century which heard Pascal reproach his sister for caressing her children.[206] The book's full title gives some idea of its contents: *The Life of the Lady Warner in Which the Motives of her Embracing the Roman Catholic Faith, quitting her Husband and Children to become a Poor Clare at Gravling, her Rigorous Life, and Happy Death are declar'd*. Near the beginning of the biography we are told that, due to the great bereavement of her children over the loss of their mother, Lady Warner was commanded by her Abbess to give them some attention. Book III, chap. iii tells how Lady Warner complied:

> Her exact compliance with Mother Abbess' orders in taking care of her children, in which she expressed more of a careful Mistress than a tender Mother, and hereby manifested that pure obedience, the inclination of Grace; and not affection to her children, —the inclination of nature, —moved her to accept this employment.[207]

Truly the spiritual climate in which Cornelia lived demanded a continuous testing and refining of discernment. One hopes that she saw the robust affirmation of the sanctity of marriage and of her that an Episcopalian priest friend Henry Mason, sent to Pierce in 1842:

> St. Peter was married, and so more probably was St. Paul. To be married is the first law of nature and the first law of God, and who is he who shall talk of a holier state on earth than that which God had made holy, or cast the priests of God out of that state which God himself has ordained. If you are as happy in the respect referred to as you are credited to be [i.e., in marriage] your views [in becoming celibate] will perhaps undergo a change, and if not you are meritorious of a severer discipline than you are like to receive from Mrs. Connelly to whom present the kind regards of a man who feels no compunction but much self-congratulation in being a married priest.[208]

Although Cornelia affirmed and valued without equivocation her own and others' vocation to celibacy, her appreciation of marriage seems to match more closely that of Henry Masons's than that of Lady Warner's. Remarkable as it seems, given the nineteenth century influences to which she was subject, one finds no devaluing of marriage in her writings, nor attempts to authenticate her own or others' celibate vocations by a comparison negative to marriage. Evidence of her spiritual gifting lies in what she did not say as well as in what she said.

A century would pass before the Catholic Church, in Vatican II, would address itself to the distortions which prevailed in her milieu, and would enunciate the "call to all the faithful to the perfection of charity," which would include a positive theology of marriage.[209] Rahner asked, shortly after Vatican II, if the immense significance of this advance was appreciated. He wrote:

> . . . so far as the spontaneous attitude and outlook of the Church throughout almost two centuries is concerned . . . it has not been so immediately obvious that on God's side there is also a *positive* vocation and mission to marriage and to worldly calling, to earthly tasks precisely as the manner positively ordained by God for the individual concerned, in which precisely he is to attain to the fullness of his Christian existence, the maturity of baptismal grace bestowed upon him, and in which he is to bring to their fulness the fruits of the Spirit.[210]

The Council of Trent had stated, without drawing further distinctions, that it was "better and more blessed to renounce marriage" for the kingdom of heaven's sake.[211] Rahner comments that the Second Vatican Council in stating its universal call to holiness enunciated a significant distinction: that "marriage actually constitutes for the vast majority of Christians the *better* means positively offered them by God himself to attain that perfection God intends for them."[212]

It is idle to speculate how twentieth-century doctrines of perfection might have affected Pierce and Cornelia. What is important is to recognize how differently this doctrine was enunciated in their century and what sensitive discernment their vocations entailed. If the depths of Cornelia's spiritual gifting and response is seen more clearly against the complexities of their background, so, too, the depth of her compassion for Pierce becomes more understandable against this background.

Pierce a "Big Catch"

We have already seen how, when Pope Gregory XVI sent a large, just-caught fish for the festivities following Pierce's Minor Orders in 1844, the gift was interpreted as the Pope's "suggestion of what the Church was gaining that day, and of the priestly life then being embraced by a former apostle of error." We have seen how the influence of the fatherly old Pope brought Pierce to ordination in little more than a year after the Decree of Separation—far less time than either of the Connellys had anticipated for providing for their children.[213] Gregory XVI had, in fact, received the Connellys warmly since the arrival in Rome in 1836 of the "former apostle of error" with his wife and children. A scrapbook which Cornelia kept of their European visits, 1836-37 and 1843-46, show an amazing number of invitations from high-ranking ecclesiastics and aristocrats to this recently obscure young American couple.[214] Cornelia could view this and laugh:

"Dear Mary . . . imagine poor little American me . . . surrounded by Princesses, Earls and Countesses!"[215] But Pierce basked in the warmth of the flattering attention and grew to need it more and more. His brothers chided him frequently for his snobbishness and unreal pretentions.[216]

From a historical perspective we can see *now* how heavy were the religio-political pressures which weighed upon the Pope, the hierarchy, and the ultramontane aristocracy who sincerely desired to help the Connellys. Perhaps "the Church *would* gain" by the priesthood of the "former apostle of error" from America. An American missionary bishop had written of Pierce at the time of his conversion: "No one has ever before exposed with such clarity and conciseness, the falsity of Protestantism and the necessity of an infallible Church to direct us in our faith, than that great man."[217] Gregory XVI had dedicated himself to the building up of that Church in difficult times. Above all, he was *the* nineteenth century's Pope of the Missions. He and his court were vitally interested in the progress of the recently-established Propagation of the Faith and the fruits of its charity in the American missions. The Austrian monarchy and nobility, through their Leopoldine Society, had joined with the French in supporting the American missions, especially in the Mississippi Valley whence Pierce had come. They saw, in the spread of the Church in America, reparation for the humiliation of the Church from the Liberal onslaught initiated by the French Revolution, and by the still-galling humiliation of the Protestant Reformation. Metternich received Pierce when he went to Vienna in 1837. The religio-political climate was ripe for the encouragement of Pierce's admittedly extraordinary priestly vocation. Noble motives for, and far-reaching results from his priesthood could be advanced by a formidable array of high-ranking ecclesiastics and lay leaders.[218]

After Pierce's tragic apostasy there was some recognition that more discernment had been needed in Rome over the question of Pierce's Roman Catholic ordination. M.M.J. Buckle and Cornelia's niece, Adeline Mack, have left records of their knowledge of the strong support for Pierce's ordination previous to it, and regrets after his apostasy. Although they both wrote as old women, their records have a ring of truth about them. M.M.J. Buckle, speaking of the weighty influence in Rome of people of rank, wrote:

> It is a pity that the influence of these great people should have induced the authorities at Rome to make so extraordinary an exception in favor of a convert of eight years standing so as to allow him to enter the priesthood with so little preparation — His example was a lesson at Rome that will not easily be forgotten, while the scandal remains to be always deplored by all good Catholics throughout the world.[219]

We have already cited Adeline Mack's record of Cardinal McCloskey's remembrance of Cornelia's poignant questions to him in 1836: ". . . is it necessary for Pierce Connelly to make this sacrifice and sacrifice me? I love my husband and my darling children. Why must I give them up?" Mrs.

Mack recorded the Cardinal's significant conclusion to his remembrances:

> My heart was full of sympathy. I gave all the consolation in my power. I looked upon the action of the Pope as a mistake. But I could not say so. I felt the ways of God were mysterious and no doubt something great was to be accomplished; and the great results of her noble work, as foundress of the Order of the Holy Child through so many vicissitudes have proved it—But don't let us talk about it.[220]

The reminiscences of these two women provide, as have other source materials, the context against which to view Cornelia's as well as Pierce's discernment of vocation. They add to evidence already presented to show that, prior to Pierce's apostasy, the couple had very weighty assurance that they were called to their extraordinary vocations. The American missionary bishop Flaget, regarded as "a saint capable of working miracles,"[221] gave support to Pierce's priestly vocation. Cornelia was a nineteenth-century *woman, convert* and *American*, and she was receiving spiritual instruction and direction from very high-ranking authority in the Roman Catholic Church. It is a testimony to her maturity that she spent ten years of prayerful discernment over her and her husband's vocation, and offered, just before his ordination, to resume their married life if he had any doubts about his vocation to the Roman Catholic priesthood. Concerning this offer she recorded that she was "thereby sacrificing any will and wish of her own,"[222] which seems to underline what her private spiritual notes show—that she had discerned God's own call to her to religious life[223] albeit in the mysterious circumstances of the Spirit's own choosing.

Notes

1. D 7:90. This was Cornelia's testimony in her defense against Pierce's suit for restitution of conjugal rights.
2. R. Bridenthal and C. Koonz, eds., *Becoming Visible: Women in European History* (Boston, 1977), pp. 299, 303-05, 309-13; J.E. Friedman and W.G. Shade, *Our American Sisters* (Boston, 1974), pp. 1-2.
3. D 3:28; D 2:35-38; CC 1:2.
4. D 2:41-42, 45-50, 51-53, 56, 61; C. McCarthy, "The Connellys in the Church of the Mississippi Valley," *Pylon*, 29, No. 3 (1968), 10-11.
5. D 2:33; D 3:12.
6. Buckle D 63:102; G. Cruchon, "The Case of Pierce Connelly," trans. and abridged by M.E. Wilcox and U. Blake for *Source*, 5 (1976), 14-15.
7. CC 1:1-6 passim. Throughout this book the spelling and punctuation of the original MSS have been corrected wherever the errors would hamper immediate understanding of the texts cited.
8. D 85:9. "une femme de beaucoup d'esprit cultivé par une education soignée."
9. Connelly Papers, Archives of the Archdiocese of Birmingham, England.
10. CC 1:1-2, 5.
11. D 2:35-38; W.S. Perry, *The History of the American Episcopal Church*, 2 (Boston, 1885), 215.
12. R. Billington, *The Protestant Crusade, 1800-1860* (Chicago, 1938), pp. 1-45, 118-41.
13. CC 1:35-39.

14. D 3:4.
15. D 3:24.
16. D 85:6-10; trans. from the French.
17. CC 1:38.
18. CC 1:39.
19. CC 1:36, 39.
20. CC 1:63, 112.
21. CC 1:36, 38, 39.
22. CC 1:39-40; D 3:25, 16.
23. D 3:2-17 and 24-38, passim, especially pp. 4-7, 12, 27-29.
24. CC 1:40.
25. CC 14:48.
26. CC 1:36.
27. CC 1:39.
28. M. Bray, "Joseph Nicolas Nicollet, Geographer," in *Frenchman and French Ways in the Mississippi Valley*, ed. J. McDermott (Urbana, 1969), pp. 29-42.
29. Journal of J.N. Nicollet, Schoolcraft Papers, vol. 87, MS 8401, Manuscript Division of the Library of Congress, Washington, D.C., USA; trans. from the French.
30. P. Connelly to J.N. Nicollet, Jan. 19, 1835, Connelly Papers, Archives of the Archdiocese of Birmingham, England.
31. D 85:2.
32. CC 1:5.
33. D 3:125-26.
34. D 85:7-8; trans. from the French.
35. D 2:94; trans. from the French.
36. Bray, pp. 29-30, 40-42.
37. CC 1:1, 4-5.
38. D 85:7-9; trans. from the French; praises of Pierce recur from pp. 6-13; for further evidence of the esteem in which Pierce was held, see, e.g., Buckle D 63:131; D 10:59.
39. D 3:4, 24-25.
40. CC 1:35, 39.
41. CC 1:38.
42. CC 1:39.
43. D 2:51-56; CC 1:35-36.
44. D 2:80-81; *L'Abeille*, New Orleans, Tues., Nov. 24, 1835, p. 1: Archives of the Archdiocese of New Orleans,
45. *L'Abeille*, pp. 1-4; McCarthy, "Connellys in the Mississippi Valley," p. 13.
46. D 2:85; D 85:9; *L'Abeille*, p. 1; McCarthy, "Connellys in the Mississippi Valley," p. 13.
47. D 85:9; trans. from the French.
48. D 3:55-57, 65; U. Blake (pseud. L.S. Muir), "The Connelly's First Visit to Rome, Part I," *Pylon*, 23, No. 1 (1961), pp. 2-3.
49. D 2:86-88, 95; D 3:191, 69-70, 87-88, 117, 138-43; M.D. Lynch, "Connelly V. Connelly: Aftermath—Trial by Press, Part I," *Source*, 6 (1977), 16-18; D 3:191-92.
50. D 3:101; *Diario di Roma*, No. 33, 1836, p. 1.
51. D 3:82; a record in the Congregation of the Holy Office for Mar. 22, 1836: Da "Sponte comparentes" a.1836, n. 16, notes that Pierce enquired about the validity of his Anglican Orders; see also Blake, "Connellys' First Visit to Rome," pp. 2-5.
52. D 8:16; Pierce, in his *Domestic Emancipation from Roman Rule in England* (London, 1852), p. 5, stated that in 1836 he was urged to take Orders in the

Greek Rite of the Catholic Church.
53. D 3:66, 99; J. Reynolds, "McCloskey, John," *NCE*, 9 (N.Y., 1967), 6-8 J. Cardinal Farley, *The Life of John Cardinal McCloskey* (N.Y., 1918), p. 40.
54. Recollections of Adeline Duval Mack compiled Jan. and Feb., 1911, entitled "Synopsis: Life of Rev. Mother," N.S. Cat., Family Affairs IV, D9 a646, No. 18, SHCJ Archives, Rome.
55. Gn 22:1-14.
56. D 3:191-92.
57. D 3:192.
58. G. Cruchon, "The Case of Pierce Connelly," *Source* 5 (1976) 15-19.
59. D 2:70-71, 74; CC 1:38.
60. CC 1:38.
61. CC 1:65.
62. D 3:119.
63. CC 1:61.
64. CC 1:63.
65. D 3:132.
66. CC 1:6a-6b.
67. Lynch, pp. 17-20.
68. D 4:2, 85-86; Buckle D 63:108; Bisgood, p. 22.
69. D 4:1, 4, 18-19.
70. D 4:19-21.
71. D 4:41-42.
72. Gompertz, p. 18.
73. D 4:172.
74. D 4:172-73.
75. CC 21:75; D 4:32-33; Buckle D 63:110; D 64:6.
76. D 4:37: for Dec. 21, 1839, the "Journal de la Maison du Sacré Coeur," Grand Coteau, noted that the three married women "ont suivi les exercises des premiers jours, avec beaucoup de ferveur et au grand contentement de leur ame."
77. CC 21:1; Ex 15. After the first retreat of 1839, Cornelia was always allowed to make them in full.
78. Buckle D 64:37.
79. CC 2:82-83; D 9:164.
80. CC 21:12.
81. Buckle D 64:35.
82. Buckle D 64:35-36; Bellasis D 72:34-35; D 4:85-86.
83. CC 21:5.
84. CC 21:7.
85. Buckle D 64:45-45a; D 4:66, 111.
86. D 7:99.
87. Buckle D 64:18-19; also D 64:41 and D 63:22-25.
88. D 3:24-25.
89. D 7:100.
90. CC 1:90.
91. CC 21:14.
92. D 41:4, 33; Buckle D 64:112; D 68:15; Bellasis D 73:165; D 76:25, 44, 76.
93. CC 22:2.
94. CC 21:11, 14:38.
95. CC 21:6.
96. CC 21:15.
97. CC 21:15.
98. Const SJ, No. 813. This Ignatian principle was apparently communicated well to Cornelia by her Jesuit spiritual directors.

99. D 4:108.
100. CC 1:7.
101. A. Armour, *Cornelia* (N.Y., 1979), p. 21. Bishop Blanc, close friend of the Connellys, advised Pierce that Mercer was too young to be sent to boarding school, but Pierce did not heed the advice: See D 4:143.
102. Armour, p. 22.
103. D 4:192; Buckle D 63:126.
104. CC 21:52, 15, 28, 31; CC 22:16-17.
105. Mt 1 and 2; Lk 1 and 2.
106. Lk 2:39-52.
107. CC 21:10; v. also Buckle D 64:9-12.
108. CC 6:57; CC 7:22, 104; CC 15:44; CC 27:9; CC 30:12; Buckle D 64; 9-12, 35, 41, 46, 52, 63.
109. Buckle D 66:118; D 4:140, 181.
110. Armour, pp. 24-26.
111. D 5:41; also D 5:19-21.
112. D 5:9-11; the Petition for Separation was signed only by Pierce; D 5:32-34: the Deed of Separation was signed by Pierce and Cornelia.
113. D 5:7-8, 20, 39.
114. D 5:40-41, 70, 85-89, 93.
115. Journal de la Trinité du Mont, D 5:45.
116. D 5:21; D 6:156; Walsh, "Vocation of CC," p. 21.
117. CC 21:19, 28.
118. CC 21:26-27; Ex 136-57, 165-68.
119. CC 21:28-30; Ex 230-37.
120. CC 21:31.
121. Rahner, "Evangelical Counsels," pp. 151-52.
122. D 5:20, 49.
123. Buckle D 64, 122.
124. CC 1:103.
125. CC 1:103.
126. CC 1:52-53.
127. P. Aries, *Centuries of Childhood*, Trans. R. Baldick (N.Y., 1962), pp. 279-83, 413; also B. Pope, "Angels in the Devil's Workship," in *Becoming Visible*, p. 305. Armour, p. 68, shows that this was the attitude toward Cornelia's own boarding schools after she became a founder.
128. T. Meehan, "Barber Family," *Catholic Encyclopedia*, 2 (N.Y., 1907), 287; this family was guided by the same J. Grassi, SJ, who guided the Connellys in Rome, 1845-46.
129. CC 1:71.
130. CC 21:35.
131. CC 1:10.
132. CC 1:51.
133. L. de Mause, ed. *The History of Childhood* (N.Y., 1974), pp. 1-6, 51-54, and passim; B. Hargrove, "Connelly vs Connelly," *Source* 6 (1977), 7-8.
134. D 5:21.
135. D 7:91; for Cornelia's Vow of Chastity, see D 5:84.
136. D 7:91; Pierce Connelly was ordained on July 6, 1845, as is attested by records of the Vicariato di Roma, of the Trinità dei Monti, and by letters of Pierce and of a friend: see D 5:88-94; "the 16th of July" in the legal allegation cited here is an error.
137. D 5:90-91.
138. CC 1:97.
139. D 63:136, 152. M. Williams, *St. Madeleine Sophie, Her Life and Letters* (N.Y., 1965), pp. 304-36, 364. Manuscript letters of Mother Galitzin, de Lim-

minghe, and de Coriolis, 1840-44, held in the Archives of the Religious of the Sacred Heart, Rome, add greatly to the picture M. Williams gives of the troubles of the Society of the Sacred Heart in Rome, 1840-45, and show how much Cornelia was exposed to knowledge of these troubles. I am indebted to Sr. M.U. Blake for photocopies of these letters.
140. CC 1:51-52.
141. CC 8:76.
142. CC 1:6a, 6b, 46, 53, 68-69; C. McCarthy, "The Child as Key," *Source*, 3 (1972), 25-35, for a fuller account of Cornelia's development of this theme.
143. CC 1:54.
144. G. Garraghan, "John Anthony Grassi, S.J., 1775-1849," *Catholic Historical Review*, 23 (1937), 273-92; U. Blake, " 'Nothing if not Versatile'—Fr. J.A. Grassi, S.J.," *Pylon*, 25, No. 1 (1963), 34-38.
145. D 5:152; Buckle D 63:152; Blake, "Grassi, SJ," p. 38.
146. CC 49:24; Source 4:6. The outline is entitled "Rules of the Society of the Holy Child Jesus." Cornelia and her sisters later sometimes used the term "Rule" for what was, in fact, their "Constitutions," which bore that title in writing; see also Buckle D 64: 156-7.
147. M. Crook, "Cornelia's Constitutions, Part II," *Source*, 10 (1979), 42.
148. "Rules of the Society of the Holy Child Jesus," pp. 1-2, SHCJ Archives, Rome; CC 21:60 for the qualification in 1847; also "La fin unique de la compagnie de Jésus, "*Archivum Historicum Societatis Jesu*, 35 (1966), 186-211, trans. and abridged in *Way Supp*, 14 (1971), 46-61.
149. Crook, pp. 41-43; Const SJ, Examen and Parts I, II, III, IV, V, IX; C. McCarthy, "Constitutions for Apostolic Religious," *Way Supp*, 14 (1971), 39.
150. Rules SHCJ, p. 1; Ex 116.
151. CC 49:24; D 50: 79-80; *Source* 4:5-6.
152. *Source* 4:7-10.
153. D 5:115, 152.
154. D 5:115-16.
155. Bisgood, p. 70.
156. CC 1:99; D 5:124.
157. CC 1:8-11; D 5:110, 114, 115, 238-39, 241; Buckle D 63:157, 161, 163.
158. CC 1:9-11.
159. CC 1:12.
160. D 5:198-200, 222-24, 238-39; D 6:85, 155-57; D 8:14; D 10:84; D 50:57; Bellasis D 73:219.
161. Cornelia wrote (CC 9:5) that what Pierce did was "more of an enigma to me than it is even to others;" also D 6:27, 29; D 8:1-2.
162. Bisgood, p. 93.
163. CC 1:71.
164. CC 21:60a.
165. CC 19:5-6; Bisgood, p. 94.
166. CC 1:9.
167. D 8:138.
168. CC 18:40.
169. CC 2:64-65; also 72.
170. D 6:116: *The Tablet* (London), Mar. 30, 1850.
171. *The Times* (London) and the *English Churchman* were especially vocal: articles from 1850 have been collected in D 6:80-81, 97, 104-05; from 1851 in D 6:160, 207; from 1853 in D 8:50-64, 69-88.
172. D 63:172.
173. Pierce's pamphlet was the *Case of the Rev. Pierce Connelly*, 2nd ed., with Preface and Supplement, London, 1953. It has been reproduced in photocopy

in D 8:99-144, *with* Cornelia's marginal annotations. The annotations noted above are found in D 8:134 (p. 31 of the *Case*); D 8:138 (p. 35 of the *Case*); D 8:123 (p. 20 of the *Case*).
174. D 5:231-32, 235, 239; Bisgood, 101.
175. Lynch, *Source*, 6, pp. 10-23; *Source*, 7, pp. 30-50.
176. D 8:118 (*Case*, p. 15.)
177. Cruchon, pp. 14-15.
178. Tape of a Lecture on the Case of Connelly vs. Connelly by Bernard Hargrove, Senior Lecturer in Law, University College, London, Sept. 29, 1976, St. Leonards-on Sea, England; also Hargrove, "Connelly vs Connelly," p. 8.
179. *The Dynamic Element in the Church* (N.Y., 1964), p. 58.
180. C. Norton, *A Letter to the Queen* (London, 1855), p. 8.
181. Hargrove, "Connelly vs Connelly," pp. 5-7.
182. Hargrove, "Study of the Case: Connelly vs Connelly" in *Positio: A Documentary Study for the Canonization Process of the Servant of God Cornelia Connelly* (nee Peacock), 1809-79, (Rome, 1983), p. A40.
183. Hargrove, "Connelly vs Connelly," pp. 5,7; also unpublished paper on "Cause of Cornelia," (Dec., 1974), p. 3.
184. CC 18:2-3.
185. D 8:6-7.
186. C. Norton, *Separation of Mother and Child by the Law of Custody of Infants considered*. Printed privately by J. Ridgway, 1837; *A Letter to the Queen*, London, 1855; *English Laws for Women in the Nineteenth Century*. Printed privately, 1854; reprinted with introd. by J. Huddleston, as *Caroline Norton's Defense*, Chicago, 1982.
187. Norton, *English Laws*, pp. 23-44.
188. Norton, *English Laws*, pp. 38-44.
189. D 9:29-36.
190. Norton, *English Laws*, p. 23 ff.
191. D 3:24-25.
192. See nn. 51-52 of this chapter.
193. See n. 54 of this chapter.
194. Recorded in MS of Adeline Mack, cited in n. 54 of this chapter.
195. D 3:191-92.
196. D 3:129: *Dublin Review* I (May-July, 1836), xii.
197. D 3:192.
198. D 4:41-2.
199. D 4:60-61.
200. D 4:87-88.
201. D 8:175-77.
202. Pierce's "Address in the Cathedral of Baltimore," D 8:172-82; Preface published in 1853 by Shrewsbury's heir Bertram (who was "Lord Shrewsbury" after the death of John. Earl of Shrewsbury in 1852): D 8:145-82; Newman's letter to Shrewsbury D 8:187.
203. D 4:180.
204. Milligan, *Gailhac*, pp. 148-150, citing A.M. Meynard, *Réponses canoniques et pratiques sur le gouvernement et les principaux devoirs des religieuses à voeux simples* (Clermont-Ferrand, 1891), p. 71.
205. The book, published in London, 1696, can be found in the SHCJ Archives, Mayfield, England.
206. Pourrat, vol. 4, p.22.
207. *The Life of the Lady Warner*, p. 185.
208. D 4:127.
209. Marriage and family: *GS*, 47-52; *AA*, 11-12; this-worldly vocation: *GS*, 34;

AA passim; universal call to holiness: *LG*, 39-42.
210. Rahner, "Evangelical Counsels," p. 136.
211. Rahner, "Evangelical Counsels," p. 136.
212. Rahner, "Evangelical Counsels," p. 135-47.
213. CC 21:35 D 5:40, 114; D 7:53; Buckle D 63:93-4.
214. Book of European Souveniers, SHCJ Archives, Rome.
215. CC 1:63.
216. Buckle D 63:90, 100, 103, 105, 131; D 5:64-68.
217. Bishop Rezé of Detroit, Oct. 21, 1863, to the Propagation of the Faith, Lyon: D 85:15.
218. Lynch, Part I, pp. 13-20; A. Simon, "Gregory XVI, Pope," *NCE*, 6 (1967), 783-88; K.S. Latourette, *Christianity in a Revolutionary Age*, vol. I: *The Nineteenth Century in Europe* (N.Y., 1958), pp. 241, 254-66, 322, 370; T. Roemer, *The Leopoldine Foundation and the Church in the United States, 1829-39* (N.Y.l, 1933).
219. Buckle D 63:131.
220. Mack, pp. 13-14.
221. J.H. Schauinger, "Flaget, Benedict Joseph," *NCE*, 6 (1967), 957; M.J. Spalding, *Sketches of the Life, Times and Character of the Rt. Rev. Benedict Joseph Flaget* (Louisville, 1852), pp. 311-25; for his associations with the Connellys, D 3:145; D 5:41; Buckle D 63: 135, 172.
222. D 7:100.
223. CC 21:6-38.

Part Two

Embodiment of the Inspiration

The second part of this book shows Cornelia and her sisters developing an institution, striving to give tangible form to a spiritual vision. This mission occupied the second half of Cornelia's life which continued to be as eventful as was the first half. This was partly due to the lifelong effects on her and her congregation of Pierce's apostasy and the scandal he caused. It was also due to the ardor and vitality with which she and her sisters fulfilled their vocation, to their liberty of spirit and courageous initiatives, as well as to their painful mistakes.

We have tried, as far as possible, to allow the process of institutionalization to emerge from the sources, letting the topics suggest themselves. This seems an authentic way to recapture the particular means by which Cornelia, energized by the Spirit, used her unique gifts to give concrete form to her inspiration for the Society of the Holy Child Jesus. By being attentive to the sources we see how creatively she adapted when her way was blocked, how resilient and hopeful she remained in adversity, how human were her faults and mistakes.

What also emerges from the sources are three phases of Society development: 1846-54: primitive years manifesting great spiritual élan; 1854-69: years of spiritual and apostolic fruition, when numbers of sisters and schools increased rapidly and Cornelia found full scope for her gifts for spiritual direction, education, administration; 1869-79: years of near-schism for the Society which led to purifying trials and a maturing of the sisters who gradually assumed the responsibilities of their dying founder who again became an exemplar as she had been in the primitive years.

Throughout these periods of development, sources show Cornelia engaged in three major functions: spiritual formation; government—including compiling, composing, revising constitutions; and ministry. These, of course, were completely intertwined in the life experience of the Society and have not been rigidly separated topically or chronologically in this study. For example, sources from earlier times in the Society have been used in Chapter VI (covering the last decade) to show the mature stance Cornelia and her sisters had developed in their practice of Poverty, Chastity and Obedience. Cornelia fostered personal responsibility, a wholesome lifestyle, and an "independence," as one of her sisters exclaimed, "of priestly government,"[1]

Since struggles to develop Constitutions for the Society and to obtain pontifical approval involved Cornelia deeply for many years, they have had to be treated extensively in this study. At the beginning of the Society she had expected Constitutions to be a fundamental instrument for shaping its spirituality, government and ministry; she obtained episcopal approbation for a basic document in 1850. In 1854, with initiative uncommon in religious women of her time, she composed her own expression of the Society's Gospel inspiration and mission. But from that time onwards she was consistently blocked in constructive constitutional efforts by both diocesan and Roman ecclesiastical authorities, and hampered by her own lack of expertise in canon law. For over twenty years her bishop refused to use his authority to summon a Chapter, thus depriving Cornelia of an election as the basis for her authority as Superior-General. The Constitutions approved by the original band of sisters had stated the Society's mission to be pontifical and universal. The Society remained, for all of Cornelia's life, under the authority of the Bishop of Southwark, England, even though Holy Child sisters had made foundations in several other dioceses in England and America.

Constitutional anomalies which plagued the Society year after year gradually weakened the confidence of many sisters in their government which had remained in the hands of their founder. Eventually tensions and divisions brought the Society to the brink of schism in the 1870's. There was, besides rancor and bitterness, an element of maturity developing in sisters who wanted to assume more responsibility for their government. The maturing process was to continue in the midst of pain, and to unite the Society again before Cornelia died. The sufferings of the Sisters of the Holy Child Jesus were shared by women religious throughout the Church of the nineteenth century. Canon law envisioned a cloistered form of life for women. The new apostolic congregations were desired by the Church for the service they gave, but were not supported by a coherent body of the Church's canon law. Cornelia had more than her share of suffering from ecclesiastical superiors. The positions in which they placed her make it difficult to assess the extent of her own mistakes within the Society. We shall let the sources speak for themselves.

Sources show a consistent vitalty in the spiritual life and ministry of the Society. They show that Cornelia used several instruments other than Constitutions to sustain and develop her congregation. Chief among these was the spiritual instrument which had been formative for her from the time of her married life, the Spiritual Exercises of St. Ignatius. They have been treated extensively in this study because their influence was so enduring and pervasive in her own spiritual life and her guidance of others. Her reliance on the Spiritual Exercises in no way indicated a false reliance on the Jesuits. Rather they had been the instrument by which she had been confirmed in a profound experience of her identity and her unique mission with the Son in the Father's plan. They had centered her prayer and her life on the Gospel revelation of Jesus as Master, Model and Spouse. They had enabled her to discern, with increasing sensitivity, the voice of the Spirit amidst the often conflicting voices in her milieu. She utilized the Spiritual Exercises so that each Sister of the Holy Child Jesus might be led to her own graced identity and find fulfillment "in God, for God, and with God."

The Spiritual Exercises confirmed for Cornelia what her own life experiences had taught her was the meaning of the Gospel narrative of the Incarnation. Contemplatively she understood the whole Paschal mystery to be expressed in the narratives of Matthew and Luke. It was this depth of meaning she communicated in naming her Society "of the *Holy Child Jesus*." It was this depth of meaning she and her sisters endeavored to express in their lives.

SHCJ sources depict a zealous ministry. In this study we do not attempt to give the methodical history of Cornelia's foundations found in her biographies. Rather we have endeavored to present some aspects of ministry which are particularly expressive of that service to the people of God for which he had empowered Cornelia and her sisters.

Chapter 4

The Primitive Society: 1846-54

Mission and Ministry

It was as a generous, courageous response to the spiritual needs of England's "Second Spring" that the American convert, Cornelia Connelly, gathered a small community of English women around her in Derby, England, October 1846, thus "founding" the Society of the Holy Child Jesus. The previous October, John Henry Newman, who was to immortalize the Catholic Revival in England—". . . the English Church was not, and the English Church is once again . . . . It is the coming of a Second Spring . . ."[2]—had been received into Roman Catholicism. The hopes of Bishop (later Cardinal) Wiseman, and Lord Shrewsbury, both acknowledged leaders of the Catholic Revival in England, were mounting; so, too, were the needs of English Catholics—"old" (born) Catholics, converts, and ever-increasing numbers of Irish immigrants.[3]

Especially in 1845-46, Wiseman and Shrewsbury were concerned for English women converts who needed spiritual and emotional support; some aspired to vowed celibate life. Wiseman and Shrewsbury saw in Cornelia "the female counterpart of Newman and Faber,"[4] the two converts who were providing spiritual centers for male Anglican converts. They had known her since she and her Episcopalian minister-husband had come to Rome as converts in 1836. They saw her as one who could share with English women and children her familiarity with Roman ritual and devotion, and her reverence for the Holy See; they found her as an American "free from the prejudices and pre-conceptions"[5] which were keeping converts and old Catholics from uniting. They saw her as well-educated and gifted; they found in her the hope of Catholic schooling more adapted to English ways than existing schools conducted mostly by Continental religious. Their friend, Pope Gregory XVI, who had played a crucial role in the evolution of Pierce and Cornelia Connelly's extraordinary vocations to the priesthood and religious life, and Cardinal Fransoni, Prefect of Propaganda Fide, supported their call to Cornelia to found a religious congregation in England. In giving verbal sanction to the Society, the Pope had encouraged her to plan for later expansion to her native America for which both he and she were apostolically concerned. Even in the last months before his death, June 1, 1846, Gregory XVI was interested in the possibility that a revived Church in England and a rapidly maturing Church in America might repair something of the recent humiliations of the Church and Papacy on the Continent. Wiseman and Shrewsbury, as has been noted, were already experiencing signs of a resurrection of full Catholic life. All saw Cornelia as providentially prepared to collaborate in their project. Shrewsbury noted that "there is no one so capable of carrying out an Institute of this description as good Mrs. Connelly," and Pierce assured his brother that "Lord Shrewsbury so strongly argued in favor of [Cornelia's going to] England that she is now on her way there."[6]

Despite the magnitude of the problems she faced in fulfilling her vocation as founder, especially that of providing for the care of her children, Cornelia saw in the direct call of the hierarchy and the advice of her spiritual director, a further indication of the unfolding of God's mysterious plan for her. She seems to have known little of the complexity and inner divisions of the Catholic body struggling to revive in England. Her attention was caught by their needs. A month before going to Derby she summarized her motives for her brother in the United States:

> . . . our rules were at first drawn up for the United States, as I had no intention nor have I now for deserting my own dear Country, but the immense number of converts in England offered so large a field for Spiritual Mercy that it seems more in the design of God to begin here.[7]

Cornelia told her brother that her last year in Rome was spent "reflecting over the wants of the day and the means of Spiritual Mercy to be exercised," and that her "Rev. Father Director decided upon my coming to England to form an order upon the rule of St. F. de Sales." Finally, she spoke of the two, who, with her, had the most to do with the concrete circumstances of foundation:

> Since coming [to England] I have united myself with a very distinguished writer of the day, Miss Emily Bowles [convert, friend of Newman] to put our work in operation. The great and good Dr. Wiseman whose learned and interested works you may have seen, has entered warmly into our designs and we have nearly concluded upon accepting the beautiful building at Derby . . . which has been offered to us by the Parish Priest and his Lordship [Wiseman].[8]

Cornelia did, in fact, respond effectively to the needs for which she was called. Of the ten companions who had associated themselves with her by the end of the first year, six were converts.[9] Although Cornelia's inspiration for the Society was never narrowed to that of a "Society of Converts", she remained to the end of her life a sensitive, spiritual guide for those whose personal or family background included the provocative experience of conversion to Roman Catholicism. Her sisters came from all classes of

Society—the servant class, many from the middle class, and some from the aristocracy. Within three months of founding, she had arranged for a retreat at the Derby convent "to which some ladies were invited who wished to try their vocation;" she endeavored in ensuing years to see that each succeeding convent be in some way a center for various spiritual ministries.[10]

But from the very beginning, it was the need for schools and her remarkable talent for education that determined the central thrust of her Society's service to England at the time of the Catholic Revival and the Industrial Revolution, and to the United States at the time of the rapid growth of its Catholic communities. "The poor school was waiting for us to go into . . ." reported one of Cornelia's first companions who went with her to St. Mary's parish convent, Derby, on October 13, 1846; "it was being taken care of by an old-fashioned person who seemed to me to be always carrying a cane in her hand."[11] By Christmas, Cornelia had expanded the "poor school" to meet as far as possible the needs created by the appalling conditions under which the poor of England's Industrial Revolution lived. In 1846 their numbers were swelled by the destitute Irish fleeing from the Potato Famine. She began a "very crowded night school of about a hundred girls," which opened at 6 P.M. and closed at 9 P.M.[12] In a Christmas "thank you" letter to Lord Shrewsbury, Cornelia told how her ministry was further adapted to the poor:

> Sunday is a *very busy* day with two hundred girls to lead to Church for a High Mass after an hour's labour in teaching them, and from two o'clock until four in the afternoon, teaching them to read, etc., etc. Much as we deplore the state of things which renders this necessary, we cannot but acknowledge that it is the only way to get hold of the working class—the factory girls. With respect to our poor day-schools, they are going on very well, but we shall never get on without some pecuniary assistance.[13]

In a remarkable letter which Bishop Wiseman addressed to the primitive Holy Child community six days after it had been established, he showed how central education had become to his intention for inserting the new congregation into the mission of the English Church.

We give this letter in full because it recognizes in the founding of the Society those elements which the Church, since St. Paul, has associated with charism, that is: a "gratuitous" gift of the Spirit, "spiritual in both origin and manifestation," manifesting the powerful "working of God for the upbuilding of the Church."[14] Wiseman was one with Cornelia in seeing that the foundation for "these good things" which, "with God's good grace, you may hope to do for His holy Church," would be in the spiritual edifice "built up in your hearts", in a community "of but one heart and soul." The fulfillment of his hope that what was "now begun" in God's name, God would "perfect and confirm" is the subject of this chapter—that is, the development of the society of the Holy Child Jesus as an enduring institution for spiritual ministry. The "material" edifice to which he referred at the opening of his letter—a large, cold, damp, neo-Gothic convent, did not remain the permanent center for the Holy Child apostolate beyond its second year, because Wiseman could not continue to subsidize it. But the spiritual fruits—those toward which the charism is directed—were evident by the time of Cornelia's death, in the ministry of five convents with ten schools in England, three convents with five schools in America, and one convent and school in France.

St. Mary's College
Feast of St. Peter of Alcantara,
[Oct. 19], 1846.

My dear daughters in Christ Jesus,

Allow me to address you in words, and with feelings of sincere congratulations upon your entering into the house which a bountiful Providence has most singularly and almost miraculously prepared for you.

For it is impossible for you and for me, who have known all the circumstances connected with this happy result, not to see and bless in this the Hand of God, which on one side, through the zeal and generosity of a faithful servant, built up the splendid edifice wherein now you live, and on the other built up in your hearts the spiritual house, and as I humbly trust, the holy community, by their union, which is to be the soul and living principle of that material structure.

This clear disposition of His Providence inspires me with the grounded hope that what has now begun in His Name He will perfect and confirm, to your present consolation and eternal happiness, and to the comfort, salvation and sanctification of innumerable souls.

The field which you have chosen for the exercise of spiritual mercies is indeed vast and almost boundless, but it presents the richest soil, and promise of the most abundant return.

The middle classes, till now almost neglected in England, form the mass and staple of our society, are the 'higher class' of our congregations out of the capital, have to provide us with our priesthood, our confraternities, and our working religious. To train the future mothers of this class is to sanctify entire families, and sow the seeds of piety in whole congregations; it is to make friends for the poor of Christ, nurses for the sick and dying, catechists for the little ones, most useful auxiliaries in every good work.

And while you are thus indirectly providing the exercise of noblest charity in the future through others, you will be yourselves partaking in the most consoling of duties, the education in Catholic piety of the lambs of Christ's flock, His dear poor children.

Lay therefore now, deep and solid, the foundations of that religious and spiritual life in which and through which, with God's grace, you may hope to do these good things for His holy Church.

Be not discouraged by present difficulties, but courageously pursue the good course on which you have entered. Have but one heart and one soul, and let that be the Sacred Heart of Jesus, Which throbbed and bled for the saving of souls alone. Seek now in fervent prayer, in loving meditation, in affectionate communions at the foot of the Cross and before the Altar, that abundance which may enable you to communicate it to many others.

May God prosper and bless you and your work; may He fill you with His consolations, making you His faithful Handmaids for the good of His holy Church.

> I am ever sincerely and affectionately yours
> In Christ
> N. Wiseman[15]

In the Society's two years in Derby, marked by arduous labours, real poverty and eventually by difficulties with the parish priest, twenty-one novices were received.[16] In the second year Cornelia was able to establish a small boarding school. This she transferred in 1848 to what became the first permanent foundation of the Society in England, a convent and schools at St. Leonards-on-Sea. Here she soon opened poor schools and engaged in other parish ministries. The pattern for ministry, outlined in the first sketch of Constitutions she brought from Rome in 1846, was to be followed in most foundations of the Society throughout her thirty-three years as superior-general, and even after her death. We give below the statement of ministry which headed the outline of 1846:

> I. This little Congregation is intended as a safe and holy Asylum for pious females, who called by the gracious mercy of Our most dear Lord to a life of religion, desire to devote themselves not only to their own sanctification and perfection, but also to that of others, and offer themselves with great good will to the same Most Blessed Lord for little servants of the Bishops of His Holy Church to be employed under them and by them in works of Spiritual Mercy: especially
> 1. In educating females of all classses:
> 2. In receiving into houses of retreat pious ladies, catechumens, neophytes and young persons preparing for their first Communion:
> 3. In teaching the catechism to children in the Church and in preparing sick females for the Holy Sacraments at the request of the Parish clergy.[17]

Fortunately, by 1850, Cornelia had eliminated from her Consitutions "safe and holy asylum for pious females" and "little servants of the Bishops," concepts as alien to her as the language in which they were expressed.[18] For the Constitutions of 1854 she added details on the schools. Therefore the statement in the Constitutions of 1854 is truer to the Society's actual pattern for ministry, though its outline is discernible in the text of 1846.[19]

More will be said below to show how this comprehensive, practical and viable apostolic scheme flowed directly out of Cornelia's original inspiration for a life of contemplation in action as expressed in her Constitutions. But first, attention must be called to a further, far-sighted aspect of the educational apostolate, the training of teachers, which Cornelia inaugurated at Derby and developed with great success in ensuing decades. With that professional approach to ministry which she had developed in her years with Pierce and with the Religious of the Sacred Heart, she began early to collaborate with the incipient Catholic Poor School Committee. The year she founded the Society, Kay Shuttleworth had introduced the pupil-teacher system in England, a five-year course of education for girls from the age of thirteen onwards who taught in the Poor Schools while they were learning. Before she left Derby, she obtained annuities from the Poor School Committee for five pupil-teachers; she was among the first Catholic school Managers to receive such grants.[20] She continued to train pupil-teachers at St. Leonards-on-Sea where, as will be seen, she was finally able to establish what she had planned at Derby, a recognized teacher-training college. A Catholic Poor School Commissioner testified in 1848: "The Nuns at Derby have represented to the C.P.S. Committee that the training of mistresses is their chief desire, and the first object of their Institute."[21]

The way Cornelia trained her Holy Child sister-teachers shows us not only her professional skills for education, but also for building community through developing a corporate apostolic endeavor. As early as 1851, records show her guiding a collaborative work among the sisters which, by 1863, resulted in the publication of a manual spelling out the Holy Child philosophy and system of education. The corporate teacher-training endeavor of the primitive years has been summarized as follows:

> In a notebook of Cornelia can be found a series of specific questions asking a particular sister to compose a syllabus in a definite subject. These questions range over topics from opening new schools, organizing a new school, designing buildings, to a grade-by-grade analysis of the teaching of English grammar and literature. She asked each to name the best books for each subject, and also to include teacher references. She asked for evaluation of specific texts. She asked for the preparation of teaching aids, charts, maps, and instructions for the use of the materials . . . . Subjects covered by other sisters appear to be geography and history, grammar and literature, foreign language and elementary religion, especially the preparation for the sacraments.[22]

In the midst of effective and ever-expanding educational endeavors from 1846-53—including new convents and schools in London, Liverpool and Preston, Cornelia had to wrestle with the continued heart-rending personal sufferings caused by Pierce and the death of her eldest son. Her sufferings were increased by the temperamental Bishop (now Cardinal) Wiseman who was piqued with Cornelia because she could not accede to some of his inappropriate requests; he tried through an Italian Jesuit chaplain to undermine her authority in the community.[23] Yet in the midst of these sufferings, which included material poverty, Cornelia devoted herself to the molding of religious educators and environments that reflected her own graced humanism as a woman of the spirit. The 1853 report of a Poor Schools Committee inspector, on the school for one hundred five poor girls at St. Leonards-on-Sea, was eloquent witness that Cornelia and her sisters were indeed bringing to English girls a new sense of their own worth and potential.

> "Buildings excellent. Desks excellent. Furniture excellent. Playground excellent. Books abundant and good. Apparatus abundant. Organisation excellent. Methods mixed, and applied with rare skill and judgment. Discipline excellent. Instruction of the highest order.
> "It is impossible to witness without admiration the results obtained in

this very interesting school, in which consummate skill in the art of teaching, unwearied patience, and the most persuasive personal influence, have combined to accomplish all the rarest fruits of Christian instruction. The school is now one of the most perfect institutions of its class in Europe."[24]

Ministry to the poor of Derby was the first public, social witness that the English church had that the Spirit was active in their behalf through a charism for the Society of the Holy Child Jesus. For the remainder of the Chapter we shall continue to present what has been introduced here in terms of ministry, that is, an indication of the process by which Cornelia gave enduring institutional embodiment to the inspiration she had received for an apostolic religious congregation. Cornelia had a gift for administration, an insight into the service supplied by organization and planning, as her numerous notes and record books attest. She had made these a practice of virtue in her years of managing a family household, and now she was prepared for school and parish households, putting spiritual and apostolic ideals into serviceable realities. Her earliest biographer had an intuitive grasp of the interplay of the divine and human manifested by the charismatic role: "the materials of the building [of the Society] were prepared by Providence and she [Cornelia] put them together with masterly skill."[25]

Cornelia as Exemplar

Cornelia came to Derby prepared by motherhood and family life to trust the promise contained in the seed time and to know the value of fostering each sign of growth. She recorded: "The Religious of this Institute of the Holy Child Jesus . . . began the germ of their future life in . . . Derby." Significantly, she associated the Constitutions with the dynamism of the Society for growth: "Our Holy Rule . . . its germ was first planted and gradually developed in the Derby Convent."[26] Her heritage from the Religious of the Sacred Heart and, above all, from the Jesuits, had given her a strong sense of Constitutions as foundation and framework for insertion into the mission of the Church and for internal stability and growth. She reminded her Bishop that she had brought incipient Constitutions from Rome for the founding: "The Institute of the Holy Child Jesus was formed at Derby upon the sketch or outline of a Rule that was inspected by Father Grassi . . ."[27] The next section will show the significance of the Constitutions "gradually developed" in Derby and St. Leonards.

But here we must look at the chief instrument by which, in the primitive years, and to some extent, always, Cornelia developed the "germ" of the Society. The instrument was herself as exemplar. One striking feature of that exemplary role was the sight of her in the midst of the community, compiling/composing the Constitutions with one of the earliest companions, Emily Bowles. The process, made visible and shared with the community seems to have supplied an élan which the written text would supplement after 1850.²⁸

In the first decade of the Society, Holy Child sisters found in Cornelia a model of sister, mother, teacher, novice mistress, superior, animator, inspirer, friend. These were the "primitive church" years.²⁹ In his inaugural letter Bishop Wiseman had exhorted them "Be of one heart and soul." When Bishop Ullathorne, not an early supporter of the Society, made a Visitation of the Derby convent in 1848, he commended the community for "the great charity and union among the sisters."³⁰ There exists a vivid reminiscence of the beginnings at Derby, by one of the first companions, Sr. Aloysia. It is a remarkable record of her recognition of Cornelia as a charismatic whose presence manifested the power of the Spirit within the community. Cornelia's first biographer, who joined the community in its second year, attested to the insightfulness of this reminiscence written almost fifty years after the founding:

> . . . of the five first Religious only Sister Aloysia is living to give us her testimony to those early days which were the beginning of so much in after years. It reminds us of the grain of mustard springing up no one knows how.³¹

Sr. Aloysia is cited at some length because spontaneously and informally she fleshed out the theology of the charism of foundation. Uninhibited by theological terminology or the rules of composition, she reconstructed a concrete picture of one inspired by the Spirit so that her "life, words, and works were privileged in the sense that they resounded in other persons with a force which motivated them to leave all and follow Christ in this particular form of life and service."³² With ease she recalled how Cornelia, her founder, was able to manifest those virtues, — that "spirit" — to which the sisters aspired, and in which they found nurture for religious community:

> —I only relate what struck me and others at the time as being so beautiful and saint-like in her . . . . Her beautiful confidence and trust in God grew upon us so, the thought of not succeeding never entered into our minds.
> —You felt she was with our Lord all the time she was at work . . . I say work! for she did all kinds . . . .
> —She had all to do for we were such children . . . . Our dear Mother was always so encouraging . . . .
> —She thought of so many things we felt confiding and safe as little children . . . .³³

Sr. Aloysia remembered that, from the day of their arrival at Derby, Cornelia provided for basic physical, psychological and social needs, while making it plain that "the first thing" was Mass, reservation of the Blessed Sacrament, and a framework for fostering life in the Spirit.

> We went . . . to the convent [St. Mary's, Derby] which was quite empty except the Parlour & some bed steads with beds & pillows (in the dor-

mitory). A leg of mutton in the kitchen oven and some potatoes & carrots on the fire but no knifes or forkes, plates or anything else in the place . . . we . . . began buying in & furnishing the place, the airing of rooms, making of beds . . . and nobody but Rev. Mother to attend to all, for Miss E.B. [Emily Bowles, who left the Society in 1856] was sick . . .

The first thing after dinner on the day we arrived was to begin to arrange for a chapel . . . it was impossible to get an Altar till the next day, 14th, which made us to have Mass & the B. Sacrament on the 15th which was the feast of St. Theresa . . . . As soon as the B. Sacrament was in the house she wished to begin the religious life as strictly as possible with the few rules—reading, penances, conferences, instructions—everything when there were only 4 of us.

What with attending to visitors—and there were many, especially priests, attending to the trades people, furnishing the convent, attending to the front door, attending to workmen & writing letters, you can imagine how little time our Mother had for rest, for even the time of recreation which she tried always to have was a great exertion for her to try to keep us from being dull; she used to get up games, tell us tales and do everything to make the time bright and happy . . . .

Sr. Aloysia was impressed by Cornelia's ability to provide for institutional needs without losing her personal touch:

Though the convent was empty we began order & regularity as if the house was full of people; hours were written out for each one . . . You can imagine how hard our dear Mother had to work the first weeks in order to make the place comfortable and dry . . . in the distribution of offices which was done very soon [she] named herself Infirmarian, an office she fulfilled for a long time, and the care she showed each one was so like a mother . . . She thought of so many things we felt confiding and safe as little children.

. . . as soon as the first few I have named were collected together [Veronica left, but Srs. Stanislaus, Joseph and Francis Magdalen soon came] our dear Mother began . . . to teach us all about a religious life. She had to do all for we were all such children and had none to look [to] for example . . . . Our dear Mother was always so encouraging—if she saw a sister move quietly and religiously she used to make some kind remark which used to teach more than a long instruction because it came at the right moment to make an impression—speaking with calm, care in making little acts of poverty—she was always on the watch to encourage or to teach. Whenever she had to correct it was done in little sentences such as "humility is truth dear" . . . . then at recreation these virtues would be talked over . . . . Our Mother began to do the ordinary penances as soon as possible . . . We soon followed. The first time we asked to do something she was so pleased we might have conferred a favor on her, but she had to do everything first . . . .

Sr. Aloysia learned from Cornelia both how to pray and how to work:

I often think of those days when we would go to the community room when our work was done and sit with Reverend Mother to sew; every now and then she would repeat short acts of Faith, hope and charity or some other little prayer . . . loud enough for us to hear and follow in spirit . . . you felt she was with our Lord all the time she was at work—I say work!

for she did all kinds from washing dishes to staining flowers .... I can tell you how many a time she came into the kitchen to teach the cook ... the poor cook [Sr. Aloysia] was not very expert ... many a weary mess she got into ... which called forth much of our dear Mother's charity and assistance ... No one else but myself knew that when the boots she had been wearing from the beginning began to wear out. A Sister covered them with a piece of cloth put on all over to cover up the rags. Our dear Mother wore them with joy (it must be remembered she had only just left every comfort.)

Sr. Aloysia and her companions knew that with Cornelia they had been empowered by the Spirit of the Lord to do his work:

It was but a simple and poor beginning. It might have disheartened many, but our dear Mother never once showed the slightest fear but that Our Lord would watch over us, and send those whom He wanted to do His work.... I used to wonder how we should get along. I once heard her say that all her means were gone. I understood she meant she had spent all in furnishing and supporting the Convent up to that time.
... But no sight of discouragement appeared: her beautiful confidence and trust in God grew upon us; so that the thought of not succeeding never entered into our minds and all this made us very happy and cheerful ... Christmas Eve she made a pretty little crib in the corner of the room we then used as a chapel ... I think there could be a whole book of events of this kind, both happy and interesting, but, of course, she had her crosses ...[34]

Sr. Aloysia's closing note to these recollections written after Cornelia's death gives some indication of how enduring and widespread her personal influence had been among the sisters: "I fear I am repeating things you know so well ..."[35]

Varying records of a charismatic quality of early SHCJ life continued after 1846. In the winter of 1849-50, the community was severely tested by poverty to the point of hunger, and by the threat of homelessness. They had come to St. Leonards-on-Sea the year before at the invitation of Mr. Jones, an eccentric old priest, who, through a legacy, held lands and buildings to be used for Catholic charitable purposes. His intrusions and suspicions, which had repelled other congregations, and finally his niggardliness with and threats to the Holy Child sisters to change his will, caused them, by January, 1850, to wonder if he would drive them out of the only home they had. A member of that straitened community remembered how Cornelia had assembled them and shared with them that they might find themselves without shelter. "She asked pardon of us all, if the difficulties had in any way arisen through her fault, and with tears in her eyes begged of us all to join in fervent prayer to our sweet and Heavenly Mother to come to our aid in the desperate state in which we so unexpectedly found ourselves."[36] As they had no Pietà, the sisters put a black veil over their statue of the Immaculate Conception and began a novena to Our Lady of Sorrows. What happened as they prayed has prodded the faith of Holy Child sisters ever since. On the seventh morning of the novena, the old priest, who had been ailing for some time, sickened mortally, begged Cornelia's forgiveness, assured her that his will was not changed, and died! The lawyer who was to have drawn up a new will arrived later that day to find his client in no need of his services. But Sisters of the Holy Child again needed the powerful help of our Mother of Sorrows to find the will. After a further month of anxiety, it was discovered in a secret drawer of Mr. Jones' desk and the community had, indeed, a permanent home from which, for one hundred twenty years, they continued the educational and parish ministry.[37]

The evangelical élan continued to be manifest in the Society's first missionary venture, the establishment of schools for London's poorest of the poor in February 1851. The sisters shared the poverty of their people living on a "breakfast of bread and dripping and a mid-day meal of the same, varied with milk and water."[38] Cornelia accompanied the first three missionaries to the pestiferous section of London bordering Lincoln's Inn Fields where Bishop Wiseman had made available to them a tall, narrow house in which the sisters occupied the basement and attic, and used the four storeys in between for the school.[39] Writing to her community at St. Leonard's, she drew them all in spirit into this new phase of their mission, calling them to that confidence in God needed for the expansion of the Institute:

> J.M.J.
> Dieu seul.
> My dear children,
>
> One word only to say we are 69 steps high, and happy in the love of our poor and lowly Jesus. I am in penance — having been out shopping all day, and am writing this in the middle of our nice little iron 4 posts. You would be quite charmed with our attics — we shall have a Community room, and a reception room with 3 large and one small cellar, a kitchen and refectory below, and a larder or pantry big enough for 20. You will have another parting, for Sr. Stanislaus and Sr. Martha may come on Saturday! But I feel quite sure you have wiped away all naughty tears in the soul-strengthening flame of love, "Loving in strength rather than in too much sweetness." Be one in the heart of our Divine Spouse, and He will help us and do all things for us. Let us try to be great in Humility, and little in ourselves.
>
> Laus Deo & Mariae
> Yours in J.C.
> C.[40]

Vignettes could be multiplied to show the kind of spiritual community Cornelia was endeavoring to create by her role-modelling. The juridical element was minimal, and the relationships of sister-to-sister, teacher-student, mother-daughter clearly prevailed, while Cornelia carried out the full responsibilities of a superior. Although the Constitutions being compiled solemnly listed the ranks of Choir, School and House sisters, there was little or no distinction of rank in the primitive years and well beyond.[41] When, two decades later, Rome imposed discriminatory practices upon the House Sisters, they were deeply hurt and blamed Cornelia for a departure from their evangelical beginnings.[42] Sr. Aloysia's recollection—"I say work—she did all kinds!"—was supported by Sr. Austin's testimony that Cornelia "took part in all the work and menial offices . . . joyfully, choosing especially the most repulsive work."[43] It has been recorded that she allowed no special protocol for herself, and that she regularly took her share of community duties such as laundering, ironing, serving, though her health was always delicate.[44] There was consonance between the life being lived in the Society and the Constitutions being compiled. Cornelia included before 1850 a text from the Jesuit Constitutions which read:

> As the example of the aged is of great weight in animating others to advance in virtue, the Superior & the other elder sisters whom she may appoint, shall be employed in the House-work on certain days, or in serving in the Refectory or in the Infirmary (unless for the greater service of God it be necessary to avoid it.)[45]

If Ignatius' Constitutions gave Cornelia texts, it was his Spiritual Exercises which had brought her into contact with Christ modelling the role of leader, the Father as source of spiritual parenthood. In her retreats she had contemplated often and lovingly the Eternal King who asked his followers to "be willing to labor with me, that by following me in suffering, he may follow me in glory."[46] She had reflected that "love ought to manifest itself in deeds, rather than words," "that love consists in a mutual sharing of goods," and had contemplated the Father in his unending bestowal of the goods of creation and redemption upon her.[47] She had given at least one instruction on Jesus in the midst of his apostles as "one who served," who came "not to be ministered to but to minister." From the strength and light of him who was "Master, Model, Spouse" in her Society, she, too, became a model within their midst.[48]

From 1852 comes a striking example of how Cornelia identified herself with her sisters in their common dedication to glorifying the Father through their sanctification and the service of others, even to death. She had, before 1850, incorporated into her constitutions passages from Ignatius' constitutional texts on the Superior General.[49] In her first general letter to the Society on the occasion of their first renewal of vows on Epiphany, she applied these texts to all the sisters. We give it below, not just as a good example of her sister-to-sister relationship, and of the constant use she made of the writings of the saints, but above all because it reveals the doctrine of the spiritual life she was teaching her sisters, as she had learned it from her experience of the Spiritual Exercises, and her study of the Ignatian Constitutions. Italics below indicate verbal dependence on the Constitutions of the Society of Jesus, Part IX, Nos. 723-735 passim:

Jan. [1852]

Dear Children in Xt.
You have begged me to tell you what I most desire to see you grow

and excel in. This day being the feast of The Epiphany, our great Feast of the year, when we renew our vows, it may perhaps be well for me to comply with your request and give you a little remembrance for the year; but in doing so I need only make use of the Saints and apply their advice & their words to you being far above any I could give you of my own.

Certainly I most ardently desire to see you *closely united to God in prayer and in all* your *actions,* that the example of each in every virtue may assist and encourage the other, and above all I would wish to see you *excel in the perfection of Charity & true Humility: & may you be free from all inordinate affections, subdued and mortified by the Grace of God and so composed & circumspect especially in speaking, that nothing, not even a single word may be observed* in you *that would not tend to the edification* of all around you.

I would also wish you to learn *how to interchange severity and firmness with mildness and mercy, so as not to allow yourselves to be turned from what has been determined upon to be acceptable to God*: and may you *have the strength of mind* to resist the *weakness of many, not losing confidence by reason of contradictions,* not *suffering* yourselves *to be drawn by entreaties from that which reason and the service of God demand, not allowing* yourselves *to be elevated by prosperity nor dejected by adversity — being prepared,* were it necessary, *to submit even to death for the love and the service of our dear Lord and Savior J.C.*

Finally I would wish to see you most *illustrious in all the grace of virtue*; but at least do not be wanting in exemplary piety & *probity*, and a sincere *affection for the Community,* (I mean the Order) together with humility I repeat it, which is the only safeguard of all other virtues, true humility also being especially the guardian of poverty, Chastity, and Obedience. May the constant practice of this virtue grow and increase in you till it brings you to the perfection of Charity — & to the eternal enjoyment of the Beatific Vision.

Most dear Children in Xt.
Yrs. unworthily,
C.[50]

By 1852 the vocabulary and concepts of this letter would have evoked for Holy Child sisters the stages of the Spiritual Exercises which they knew well, especially what Cornelia called "the great first fundamentals,"[51] leading by grace to freedom from "inordinate affections," to a spiritual equilibrium in the use of creatures for the greater "service of Our Lord and Savior Jesus Christ."[52] The Spiritual Exercises had been the providential instrument by which God had formed Cornelia to recognize and respond to her inspiration for the Society. For her it became no less indispensable in shaping a community to give enduring institutional form to the inspiration. Although the role of the Exercises will be treated more fully in the next chronological period where sources regarding its use become superabundant, there is no doubt that from the first months of the Society it was for the founder her "groundwork for the spiritual life,"[53] the means by which "our novices will learn how deeply our life is founded on the life of our Lord and how essentially it is built on the solid rock of his pure evangelical, Holy Catholic Doctrine."[54]

One whom Cornelia formed later to be novice mistress knew that "from the first" the Exercises had been the founder's "syllabus."

From the first our Mother realized the seriousness of the responsibility of any dealing with souls, — her own individual soul, and the souls of all with whom she came in contact, whether religious or children. . . . In health or sickness, in buoyant life as in the throes of death, the soul's health and the soul's good, outweighed every other consideration. All the good instructions and the spiritual training she has received from the Fathers of the Society of Jesus at Grand Coteau, and later on in Rome, served as her religious syllabus in the training of her young Community.[55]

From the beginning, all members of the Society made annual eight-day retreats (usually preached) under a Jesuit director; some followed the Exercises in private if a Jesuit could not be secured. Very soon they began to renew the graces of their retreats in "half-yearly retreats" — usually three days in preparation for Epiphany — and in monthly days of recollection, usually on First Fridays. Mother Maria Joseph Buckle's reminiscence about her postulant and noviceship years, 1847-50, reveals that some made thirty-day retreats, admittedly not in the best Ignatian form:

> Manresa & Pergmayr [SJ], Parsons [SJ] Directory and DaPonte [SJ] carried the novices on for a month of prayer & recollection before their vows. The Higher Paths of Rigoleuc [Nepveu SJ was the author], too, furnished meditations: and although the Exercises were performed without a director, the excellent books used and the exactness with which the directions of the retreat were followed made this practice highly beneficial to those whose heads were strong enough to undergo the ordeal . . .[56]

Although the reminiscence here seems to place emphasis on the ritual aspect of the Exercises — which, with its vocabulary, served the Society well as a vehicle of communication — abundant sources testify to their deep understanding of use of the Exercises as "a way of living the Paschal Mystery."[57] And for the concrete modelling of this way they had not only and primarily Jesus, but also their founder whom many knew as a spiritual martyr. There are testimonies that she was regarded as such from the beginning to the end of her life in the Society. Sr. Aloysia had begun those recollections of the first days cited above with a testimony to Cornelia's Paschal witness which had drawn the young sister to the Society and formed her to its spirit:

> It was from there she sent her children to school. Never shall I forget the struggle of that separation. It was, I think, one of the greatest sacrifices she had to make. Still there was never seen a cloud of sadness. The generosity of her heart was marked in her countenance so that it was noticed by all around. It was at this time I first knew her, and watched her as I would a Saint. She was so patient, so gentle, calm and peaceful under so many annoying and trying circumstances. Peace seemed to be a virtue she possessed and valued very much . . . . I have heard it said that her heart was rather hard, and she did not feel like others or know what others felt. This was one of those hard bits she used to bear in silence, but God only knows how much she has had to suffer when she has been struggling for others who were to compose the Society.[58]

Throughout her thirty-three years of governing the Society, while some Sisters knew less than others of the depth of her sacrifice, all accepted a spirit of real renunciation as an exemplary grace of their founder. They saw her accept throughout her religious life the calumnies, misunderstandings and persecutions which seem to be the lot of founders, and of which she had full measure. Her successor as Superior General, who did not give full support to the preservation of Cornelia's memory after her death, nevertheless left an eloquent witness to the fruits of Cornelia's spiritual martyrdom experienced by her Society.

> Few . . . ever heard of the furnace of heart-sorrows she had to pass through . . . but no one but ourselves can say that, overwhelmed as she often was, she bore all her troubles with such a constant outward serenity and maintained to the last such a fresh bright spirit, that she managed to cast a sunshine round her which no other presence ever did or ever can create.[59]

The Founder Developing the Constitutions

If Cornelia as founder was initially a mother who gives and nurtures life within her own family rather than an authority imposing a rule from without, she was also an apostle with a mission. From the beginning she and Fr. Grassi had corresponded about her "work of God."[60] and at the end of her life when that work seemed threatened with failure, she affirmed: "The Society of the Holy Child Jesus is not my work. I have only followed the inspiration of God in obedience to *His* not *my* will."[61] Persecution and obstacles to the fulfillment of her ministry of service throughout thirty-three years, sometimes called forth, as in 1867, spontaneous expressions of her conviction of God-given inspiration for the Society:

> If I had toiled for him or any other human kind my courage would long ago have failed. As for the confirmation of our Institute we can only say that it is God's own hands and if God is with us who is against us: "Quis sicut Deus."[62]

We have seen how that conviction was tested within the first seven years of her Society by a cross hardly surpassed in the lives of founders—her husband's suit for restitution of conjugal rights and his pamphlet war in which he threatened to advocate the abolition of convents and nunneries from England.[63] The legal text of her defense in that suit begun in 1849 fortunately supplies us with one more unequivocal public statement of her acceptance of responsibility for founding and governing the "Congregation of the Holy Child Jesus" under her own Constitutions:

> 1846 . . . she . . . came to England and in the month of October . . . founded at Derby in that Country, a Community of Religious women (since removed to Hastings in Sussex and of which she afterwards became and is now [1849] the Superioress) under the title of the "Congregation of the Holy Child Jesus" . . . the said Cornelia Augusta Connelly had

brought with her to England rules for the Government of such (the intended) Community which had been submitted to and sanctioned by competent Ecclesiastical Authority before she quitted Rome.[64]

In all the relationships of the Society with the hierarchy, with the Catholic communities it served, and with the secular world, Cornelia never shirked the responsible, unifying role of founder and Superior General who represented the mission of her congregation. She obtained in 1850 the formal episcopal approbation of Cardinal Wiseman for the Constitutions she had compiled between 1846-50. Within the congregation, Cornelia was eager to make clear that her role as superior and especially as compiler/composer of the Constitution, arose out of the life which all the members of the Congregation were developing and to which all contributed. She wrote to her Ordinary shortly before taking revised and supplemented Constitutions to Rome in 1854:

> Our sisters are well acquainted with the Constitutions but they must reconsider them before I leave and give their approbation and signatures to this effect.[65]

The community annalist recorded how well Cornelia was able to draw the primitive community into the process of framing and submitting Constitutions and of establishing her role as servant of the Community:

> Before leaving St. Leonard's, Rev. Mother called the community together & read the Rule which was afterwards signed by all the Professed Choir Sisters. Then with touching Humility she knelt down and begged pardon of the Sisters for all the faults she had committed during the time she had governed the Society & commended the business on which she was going to Rome to the prayers of all.[66]

This scene of December 1853 has actually brought us up to the completion of the first two—and for Cornelia the most profitable—of many stages of compiling/composing/revising SHCJ Constitutions. Though they were then mercifully unaware, she and her Society would suffer a veritable agony and crisis of survival before Constitutions were finally approved by Rome fourteen years after her death. The crisis would highlight the constitutional weaknesses of the Society and help the founder, her sisters and ecclesiastical authorities to initiate the salutary if painful process of correcting these.

The story of the Society's Constitutions reading alternately like an adventure story, a mystery story, then a poignant tragedy before coming to a final, not fully satisfactory resolution, would truly fill a book. In that book, the exposition of the charism tied to the evolution of the Constitutions, but not ultimately dependent on it, might be lost. Here only facets of the story focusing on the central thread of her inspiration brought to institutional fulfillment will be selected. Primary among these facets was Cornelia's utilizing of the first two editions of the Constitutions to express her inspiration in her own words. As will be seen in Chapter VI, she and her sisters also added to this expression in the last two editions, 1877 and 1880, not in Cornelia's own words, but with texts appropriate to the Society's spirit from Pierre Cotel, SJ.[67] Here we shall present only brief notes on the whole content of the edition of 1850, and on the revised and supplemented edition of 1853-54. Primarily, we wish first to present and comment on those constitutional texts of 1850 and 1853 by which she showed the "humble and hidden life of Jesus" to be for her sisters, the source of life—literally "the living wells," Cornelia said.[68]

In the following chapter we shall also present texts Cornelia used consistently from what we have called "auxiliaries" to the Constitutions, such as general letters, her own prefaces to spiritual books, a customal.[69] Founders have had to expound their thoughts more fully outside the constitutional genre. A non-clerical, female, convert, nineteenth-century founder like Cornelia had to limit the scope of her personal constitutional expressions. She had to manifest very clearly her conformity to ecclesiastical norms and conventions. Besides this, Cornelia chose compilation as her primary method in constructing Constitutions. She plainly stated that she wanted her Constitutions to be drawn from the writings of the saints.[70]

By 1850 Cornelia, helped by Emily Bowles, had compiled fairly complete Constitutions, distributed in two parts, taken mostly from Jesuit Constitutions and Rules, but also from significant passages from the Visitation Constitutions by Francis de Sales and from the Rules of the Religious of the Sacred Heart.[71] The life of the apostolic religious woman vowed to chastity, poverty, and obedience was spelled out for Holy Child Sisters by the Jesuit Summary of Constitutions into which Cornelia inserted her own specification of the apostolate which we have already cited above.[72] This, with the Jesuit Common Rules and Rules of Modesty, with provision for twenty minor offices and for a local chapter, completed Part I of the Constitutions.[73] Part II spelled out Admission of Candidates, Formation, Rule for the Novice Mistress, provision for schools and above all for government under a general and her councillors, and under general chapters.[74]

The Original Inspiration Expressed in the Constitutions of 1850

Since spiritual formation was always Cornelia's major preoccupation,[75] it is not surprising that, in this first edition of her Constitutions, she used the Novice Mistress' rule to insert her first formal expression of her vision for a Society drawing its inspiration from the Holy Child Jesus. She copied the Visitation rule for novice mistress, making it the opening section of Part II of her Constitutions. She added two paragraphs at the end of this rule, providing for the novice mistress' assistant and on her spiritual reading.[76] But her most significant addition occurred near the beginnning of Francis de Sales' text where he spoke of the spiritual foundations of the Visitation Order. Cornelia departed significantly from his text. While she developed the Salesian passage har-

moniously, she clearly identified her own spiritual foundations for the
Society of the Holy Child Jesus, as the compared texts below demonstrate:

Constitutions pour les soeurs religieuses de la Visitation	*Constitutions Soc. H. Child Jesus*
XXXIII: De la Directrice	2nd Part
	Novice Mistress
. . . Or ce qu'elle tâchera	. . . what she shall endeavor prin-
le plus de leur fair conce-	cipally to make them conceive
voir et bien entendre, c'est	and well understand is
principalement l'intention	the intention they
qu'elles doivent avoir eu	should have in their
en l'élection qu'elles ont	choice of leaving
faite d'abandonner le	the world and
monde pour se retirer	entering
au Monastère qui est afin	religion, that is
de s'unir plus parfaite-	to unite themselves
mont à Dieu, mortifiant	more to God, mortifying
leurs sens extérieurs, et	their exterior senses and
encore plus leurs	still more their
passions intérieures pour	interior passions to
rappeler toutes leurs forces	devote every faculty to
au service de l'Epoux	the service of their heavenly
céleste, par une chas-	Spouse, by the purest
teté toute pure, une	chastity, a poverty stripped
pauvreté dépouillée de	of all things,
toutes choses, et par une	and by an obedience
obéissance établie en une	grounded on the
parfaite abnégation de	total renunciation of
sa propre volonté.	their own will.
Et qu'en somme cette	In short, as the Society of
Congrégation est fondés	the Holy Child Jesus is spirit-
spirituellement sur	ually founded on
le mont de Calvaire	the virtues of poverty,
pour le service de J.C.	suffering and obedience,
crucifié, à l'imitation	which our most blessed
duqel toutes les	Redeemer came down
Soeurs doivent	from heaven to practice
	in the grotto of Bethlehem,
	and thence through his whole
	life to Calvary,
	so ought all to begin
	life again with the most
	sweet and holy and loving
	Child Jesus—a
	humbled God—walking
	with him step by step
	in the ways ["simplicity" written
	above] of the child, in
crucifier leur sens,	humility and poverty,
leurs imaginations,	mortifying their senses
passions, inclinations,	their imaginations,
aversions et humeurs	passions, whims, inclina-
pour l'amour du Père	tions and aversions,
céleste.[77]	so that they may finally

> be united to our crucified Lord ["the Man God" is crossed out] and then look forward to a glorious Eternity. ["and that through His Sacrifice on Mount Calvary they may look forward to a glorious eternity" is crossed out].[78]

Cornelia's "humbled God" at the center of her passage seems to be a sort of contemplative exclamation rising from the depths of her mystical experience in which the original inspiration for the Society was born. Besides the grace of identification with "our most Blessed Redeemer" in the kenosis of his Incarnation, Cornelia finds for Sisters of the Holy Child Jesus the grace of growth—"step by step" in that eternal life begun here in time through baptism which has been radically accepted in commitment to the evangelical counsels. The theme of growth through the power of, and in the likeness to the effective model, Christ, Cornelia developed more fully the following year (and constantly thereafter) in one of the first of her auxiliaries to the Constitutions, a preface to a book of meditations she caused to be published. This was to be used by her students as well as sisters, for she believed that all to whom the Society ministered were invited to walk "step by step" with the "humbled God":

> For, my dear children, it will be of no use for you to learn a great many things and to like to hear stories about the saints and holy things, unless you practise what they practised, and what made them holy.
> You must take for your pattern, the Holy Child Jesus, not only to love Him and His Blessed Mother, but to imitate Him as He lived with Her in the house of Nazareth. You must follow Him as he worked with St. Joseph, as He went upon His many and troublesome errands, and as He helped His Blessed Mother in her household labours. You must learn, then, how He looked, how He acted and how He prayed.
> May you really so learn of the Holy Child Jesus, my dear children, growing as He grew, in stature and grace; and when you grow up may you so love and follow the Man Jesus that you may be of the number of those "little ones" whom this most Blessed Lord will bring into His everlasting kingdom[79]

The reader will have noticed that, in both texts, Cornelia sets the Infancy Narrative within the whole panorama of the Gospels, finds within it the whole Paschal Mystery, echoing the Ignatian Exercises.[80] For her, the Infancy Narratives were a "little Gospel." This is, of course, the full meaning which exegetes have restored to us today in showing the intentions of Matthew and Luke to introduce their respective theologies through presenting the essential Gospel story in miniature.[81]

The constitutional text we have been reviewing can serve finally as a revelation of Cornelia's personal spiritual experience. It is probably her first public expression of the significant way she named the evangelical counsels: "poverty, *suffering* and obedience."[82] This seems a powerful witness to the goodness of the marital life and love she had renounced, a poignant admission of the pain and sacrifice of her renunciation of a supreme benefit in human life.

The Original Inspiration Expressed in the Constitution of 1854

Cornelia's significant commentary on the "humbled God" which we have just reviewed was, during her lifetime, communicated to her sisters chiefly through the notes she compiled for her Novice Mistresses in which this constitutional text was included. The second part of the Constitutions where it originated was held back from wide circulation in the Society by Rome's long delay in approving the Constitutions. It was only when the Society's original Constitutions were researched and reconstituted a century later — 1968-76, that this text was recovered as a significant expression of the founder on her charism.[83] Her emphasis on the dynamism of growth, however, continued to be known through the prefaces of the spiritual books she caused to be published,[84] through the Society's manual for its philosophy and system of education,[85] and through her letters.[86]

We must now return briefly to constitutional development in order to understand the context in which Cornelia wrote the longest, most powerful, central and influential expression of her original inspiration and the Society spirit deriving from it. The context is as follows: To the Constitutions presented to him in 1850, Bishop Wiseman gave willing approbation in June of that year.[87] But Cornelia and her sisters rightly understood their mission to be pontifical. They were perhaps, the first women's congregation founded in England with this understanding. Their Constitutions opened with a passage adapted from the Jesuit Summary: "It is essential to our vocation to be ready to go wherever the great service of God and the good of souls in educating females may be looked for."[88] Cornelia had been sent to England in 1846 with a mandate from Propaganda Fide sanctioned by Pope Gregory XVI.[89] Thus from 1850, she and her sisters looked forward to eventual Pontifical approval.

Suddenly, in 1853, a summons came to her to present her Constitutions to Rome. Although she rightly judged the summons to be not only premature for her Society, but also simply a ruse "to get me out of England because of the noise of Mr.C.,"[90] she went to Rome early in 1854 in the hopes of forwarding a primary goal of her Society—recognition of their pontifical character and approbation of a universal mission. Amidst the adverse circumstances of unfair pressure upon her, and multiple family troubles in the Fall of 1853, Cornelia was inspired (the word is not too strong) to respond to the request of her sisters to head their Constitutions with her own expression of the Society's original inspiration and mission. As the context of this, she prefaced the Constitutions of 1850 with an adaption of an early *Plan Abrégé de l'Institut* drawn up by Fr. Varin and Madeleine Sophie Barat for the Society of the Sacred Heart in 1805. Cornelia retained most of the short articles 4-22 of this Abrégé which provided a sort of framework for an apostolic congregation.[91] At the request of M.M.J. Buckle, she included the Abrégé's provision for a "fourth Vow of Charity," by which the sisters "consecrated themselves to the education of youth" to be made after "last Vows."[92] With her own characteristic warmth of expression she strengthened a rather conventional expression on the interior life in the *Agrégé* to read: "*Above all things* it is necessary to maintain an interior spirit, which is the *life* and soul of our vocation" (emphasis added).[93]

But the truly significant adaptation she made of this *Abrégé* was to substitute her own original articles 1-3 for the short articles of the Abrégé focused on the Sacred Heart. These articles, shot through with the overtones of a contemplative utterance, became known and remained the treasured "First Chapter" of the Constitutions of the Society of the Holy Child Jesus. Because of their enduring influence in shaping the spirit of the Society, the text is given here in full on the following pages accompanied by a brief analysis.[94]

It is essential to understand at the outset (as Roman authorities on constitutions did *not* understand in 1886),[95] that the First Chapter given below is one integral organic unit. It represents an unbroken flow of thought, hierarchically and harmoniously ordered from call to contemplation, through interior response, to exterior apostolic response in service. In these same passages where order and logic is evident, the style is, at the same time, dense and circular, relying much on imagery and experience to convey the ineffable, mystical reality which had been intuited. There are extant three stages of the text (shown below in chronological order), the first two spontaneously revealing the contemplative experience of Cornelia from which they sprang—we "*taste*" beside the crib of an Incarnate God;" we "*drink* the spirit of the Society." In the version printed about eight years after composition (Stage 3), the contemplative richness is tempered, e.g., "study" for "taste", "receive" for "drink." The second version (Stage 2), seems to be the most sensitive expression of Cornelia's inspiration, retaining the contemplative flavor, and also giving two meaningful additions. These additions consisted of the specification of the "mystery of the Incarnation" as the mystery of "the humble and hidden life of the Holy Child;" and the complementing of "fed in the pastures of His Divine Love" with "nourished with the waters of this heavenly fountain." The last two expressed the graces by which their Master, Model and Spouse strengthened Holy Child sisters for mission.

In the powerful flow of thought contained in her First Chapter, Cornelia leads her sisters to contemplation in action. Starting from the general call to all Christians to follow Christ revealed in the Gospel, she moves to the more particular call to religious to "seek" in these mysteries "all that can serve to their greater perfection and the good of their neighbor." Within this call she identifies the special vocation of the Sisters of the Holy

Child Jesus to find their spirit in the Mystery of the Incarnation, that is, the mystery of "the humble and hidden life of the Holy Child."

Having identified their call to contemplation, Cornelia draws them to it by sharing her experience of the inexhaustible "treasures" they will find there "manifested in a wonderful manner." In the mystery of the Incarnation, God has revealed to them "His infinite mercy," "His boundless love," "the Eternal Wisdom in the lowliness of His Humanity," "the example of a hidden God," "the crib of an Incarnate God," "the Divine Child as Master, Model, Spouse."

The sisters contemplate their "Master, Model, Spouse," "enclosed for nine months in the womb of His Mother, . . . His creature," "born for us in a stable," "exposed to suffering and poverty," "weeping for our sins," "flying into Egypt," "hidden and laboring for thirty years in a humble workshop."

Through the humble and hidden life, Sisters of the Holy Child Jesus will be led to: "the school of Divine Science," "the way that He has pointed out," "the pasture of His divine love," "the sweet yoke He offers," "the heart of an infant God as a centre of love."

Above all they will be drawn to: "the living wells—the heavenly fountain" of "His perfect humility," "His divine charity," "His absolute obedience"—in sum, the "living wells" of "His interior and exterior virtues." From these "living wells" they "drink" the "spirit of the Society of the Holy Child Jesus."

Cornelia encourages her sisters to full contemplative response, to place themselves within the mystery, to yield to the delights and the exigencies of communing with the hidden God who makes himself present to them. She urges them "to seek," to "taste," to "drink", to "feel," to "hear," to "embrace," to "labour with all their strength," to "suffer," to "die," to "rejoice."

Supported by the companionship of the "humbled God," walking with him, taught in the school of his own life, imbibing his divine wisdom, she exhorts them to purification through asceticism, and finally to total commitment to the redeeming Christ under his "Standard," his "way" of the evangelical counsels. She counsels them "to attain to the knowledge of their nothingness and misery," "to uproot the evil inclinations of their corrupt hearts," "to cultivate the germ of practical mortification," "to study the sweetness of suffering and contempt in the example of a hidden God," "to rejoice to labor and to die with Him in the constant practice of poverty, chastity and obedience."

Nourished and fed by the living God, by the assistance of his grace, the sisters are to fulfill the single end of the Society—the glory of God found in their own and their neighbor's perfection, that is, assimilation to the likeness of the redeeming Christ. Cornelia exhorts them "to run with ardor in the way He has pointed out," "to employ every effort to lead others to taste and embrace the sweet yoke He offers," "to labor with all

Stage 1 of CC's First Chapter composed in 1853	Stage 2 revised 1854 - 1861
ABRIDGMENT OF THE CONSTITUTIONS OF THE SOCIETY OF THE HOLY CHILD JESUS	
[Revisions are in CC's hand. The wording as it stands before the strike-outs and marginal additions constitute the earliest version.]	
I. As it is the duty of every Christian to follow (according to the measure of grace ~~which he has~~ received), the example which our Divine Saviour has ~~set before~~ (given) him, and as it is only in striving to imitate this great Model that ~~he can attain his~~ salvation. it is more particularly the duty of those who are called by His infinite mercy to serve Him in holy Religion, to seek in the Mysteries of the life of this Divine Head, all that can serve to their greater perfection. And what more sublime teaching can we find among these Mysteries than ~~that of the Incarnation~~? Here it is that God manifests to us in the most wonderful manner the treasures of His Mercy and His boundless Love. In that Child -- enclosed for nine months in the womb of his creature, born for us in a Stable, exposed to bitter cold and weeping for our sins, now flying into Egypt, and then ~~hidden for thirty years~~ in a carpenter's workshop -- we find our Divine Master, and from the living wells of His perfect Humility, His Divine Charity, and His absolute Obedience, we drink the Spirit of the Society of the Holy Child Jesus.	is to be obtained the humble hidden life of the Holy Child labouring are to
In this school of Divine Science, contemplating the Eternal Wisdom in the lowliness of His Humanity, we ~~may~~ attain ~~the~~ (that) knowledge of our ~~own and~~ (love and) ~~misery~~ (mercy), and of His infinite ~~mercy~~, we ~~may~~ are to learn to uproot the evil inclinations of our corrupted heart, to cultivate therein the germ of practical Mortification, & tasting beside the crib of an Incarnate God the sweetness of suffering and contempt, ~~we shall~~ (may we) rejoice to labour and to die with Him in the constant practice of Poverty, Chastity and Obedience.	are to seek to nothingness and misery studying after ~~the pattern~~ the example of a hidden God the sweetness of suffering and contempt, ~~til~~ with constancy ~~we rejoice by His~~ ~~we can rejoice~~ and thus are we to watch and to pray, rejoicing to labour and to die with Him ~~in His~~ Society, in the practice of Poverty, Chastity & Obedience.

Stage 3 further revised and printed in 1861

CONSTITUTIONS OF THE SOCIETY OF THE
HOLY CHILD JESUS
ABRIDGED

I. As it is the duty of every Christian to follow the example which our Divine Saviour has given, according to the measure of grace received, and as it is only in striving to imitate this Great Model that salvation is to be attained, so it is more particularly the duty of those who are called by His infinite mercy to serve Him in Holy Religion to seek in the mysteries of the life of this Divine Lord all that can serve to their greater perfection and to the good of their neighbour.

In the humble and hidden life of the Holy Child Jesus we find mysteries of the most sublime teaching. Here it is that God manifests to us in the most wonderful manner the treasures of His mercy and of His boundless love. In that Divine Child inclosed for nine months in the womb of His Mother, born for us in a stable, exposed to suffering and poverty, now flying into Egypt, and then hidden and labouring for thirty years in a carpenter's workshop, we find our Divine Master, our Model, and our Spouse; and from the living wells of His perfect humility, His divine charity, and His absolute obedience, we are to receive the Spirit of the Society of the Holy Child Jesus.

II. In this school of divine science, contemplating the Eternal Wisdom in the lowliness of His Humanity, we are to seek to attain the knowledge of our own nothingness and misery, and that of His infinite love and mercy; we are to learn to uproot the evil inclinations of our corrupted heart, and to cultivate therein the germ of practical mortification, studying in the example of a hidden God the sweetness of suffering and contempt, that we may thus rejoice to labour and to die with Him in the constant practice of poverty, chastity, and obedience, opposed to the three human motives, profit, pleasure, and ambition, the one being the perfection of the Gospel, and the other leading to death.

The Spirituality of Cornelia Connelly

Stage 1	Stage 2
Filled with the waters of this Heavenly Fountain, we spring from the heart of an Infant God, as from a centre of Love, to run with ardour in the way which He has pointed out. To employ every effort to bring others to taste and to embrace the sweet yoke which He offers them. To labour with all our strength to increase the love, the devotion for and the imitation of the interior virtues of the Hidden Life of our sweet Jesus,-- is the aim of this little Society. II. And it is more peculiarly necessary at this time (when all seems to tend toward relaxation & instability) to bring up & to strengthen the young in a spirit essentially opposite, offering an instruction at least equal to what is found in the Schools of Schismatics, unfolding the beauty of the morality, & the spirit of Charity & union of the Holy Roman Catholic Church, in such a manner as not only to attract & confirm (in their belief)(the children of the Faithful) but also to bring the children of indifferent and schismatic parents to appreciate & finally embrace its Divine Doctrines. III And we must observe that since the Church in her Divine Universality does not limit the researches of true Science, we may not despise the means of Education to supply the wants of the age by leading others to true piety, & to bring back wandering sheep to the fold of our Mother the Church. Thus the end of this Society is not only to provide for our own salvation & our greater perfection(but as far as possible with the assistance of Divine grace, & as far as accords with the humility of our sex,) to employ ourselves for the salvation & the perfection of our neighbour, especially: [This sentence from Rules of 1845-6] In the education of females of all classes of society. 1st In the Highest Schools 2nd In Middle Schools 3d In Charity Day-Schools & Industrial Orphanages [This sentence from Rules of 1845-6] By receiving into Houses of Retreat Pious Ladies, Catechumens, Neophytes, & young persons preparing for their First Communion. In profitable & necessary relations with Externs, especially by teaching Catechism to children, preparing sick females to receive the Sacraments at the request of the Parish Priest. Note It is understood that the second & third of these works are subordinate to the first (education) which is the primary & essential object of our vocation.	Nourished with the waters of this Heavenly fountain & fed in the pasture of His Divine Love, in union with our Incarnate God, we are to run with ardour in the way He has pointed out ...

Stage 3

Nourished from the well springs of this heavenly fountain, and fed in the pasture of His divine love, we are to run with ardour in the way that He has pointed out, and to employ every effort to bring others to taste and to embrace the sweet yoke which He offers them, labouring with all our strength to increase the love, the devotion for and imitation of the interior and exterior virtues of the hidden life of our most sweet Jesus, thus endeavoring to fulfil the end and aim of this little society.

And it is particularly necessary at this time, when all seems to tend towards relaxation and instability, to bring up and to strengthen the young in a spirit essentially opposite; and how can we better secure this great end than by vividly unfolding in the course of our education the beauty of the morality, charity and truth of the One, Apostolic, Holy, Roman Catholic Church, and this in such a manner, as not only to confirm the children of the Faithful in their belief, but also to attract and bring the children of indifferent parents to appreciate and embrace its divine doctrine?

And since the Church in her divine universality encourages the means of education best adapted for each particular state of life, we are especially bound to act in unison with her, and to meet the wants of the age, while leading our children to true piety and the practice of solid virtue.

III. Thus the end of this Society is not only to provide for our own salvation and our greater perfection, but as far as possible with the assistance of divine grace, and as far as accords with humility, to employ ourselves for the salvation and the perfection of our neighbour, especially --
1. In the education of females of all classes of society.
(a) In the highest schools
(b) In middle and training schools
(c) In charity day-schools and industrial orphanages.
2. In receiving into houses of retreat pious ladies, catechumens, neophytes and young persons preparing for their first Communion.
3. In profitable and necessary relations with externs, especially by teaching the Catechism to children, and preparing sick females to receive the Sacraments at the request of the parish priest.
Note--It is understood that the second and third of these works are subordinate to the first (education), which is the primary and essential object of our vocation.

our strength to increase love of, devotion for, and imitation of the virtues of the hidden life of Jesus."

To further specify the profound redemptive mission into which the Sisters of the Holy Child have been incorporated, Cornelia instructs them "to bring up and strengthen the young in discipline and stability;" "to lead them to true piety and solid virtue;" "to unfold for them the beauty of the morality, charity, truth and unity of the One, Holy, Roman, Apostolic Church;" "to use, in union with the Church, the means of education best adapted for each particular state of life;" "to meet the wants of the age;" "to offer instruction at least equal in quality to that of Protestants."

Finally, Cornelia specified further the details of the ministry, which was especially directed to girls and women: The ministry first of all provided for the setting up of schools for "all classes of society." This work took priority over all others: "It is understood that the second and third of these works are subordinate to the first (education), which is the primary and essential object of our vocation." The second "work" provided that the convents would be available as spiritual centers for retreats, catechetical and convert instructions. The third "work" provided for the sisters to go out to attend the sick, teach catechism and be available for apostolically "profitable and necessary relations with externs."

The original tightly-knit composition analyzed above represents Cornelia's central, most comprehensive and formal expression of the spirit and mission of the Society of the Holy Child Jesus, the spirit to which the humble, hidden God had formed her as she sought Him through the light the Gospel shed on her life, through the spirit and mission he impelled her to embody in institutional form. This text gives credence to the belief held by the sisters who lived with her, that she was indeed a mystic, albeit one who lived out her ineffable interior relationship with her Lord in dedicated, active service.

From the wealth of additional commentary which could be given upon so rich a text, we must confine ourselves to a few notes. Research on Cornelia's sources has shown her dependence on the seventeenth-century Lallemant.[96] The substantial dependence on Ignatius' Exercises that pervades not only this significant portion of Cornelia's writings but all her writings, would require a separate study for exposition. It is immediately obvious that for Cornelia as for Ignatius we enter the whole Paschal Mystery, the whole panorama of the Gospel through the "door" of the Incarnation.[97] With Ignatius, Cornelia had learned that those who wish to be with Christ in the humble and hidden life must discern and choose his "Standard," his way. And those who commit themselves to him, rejoice to labor and to die with him. They are urged forward by the *magis* (also expressed throughout Cornelia's Constitutions) to seek and labor "*more* particularly," "*as much as possible* with the assistance of Divine Grace," for "*greater* perfection."[98] As also reflecting Ignatian influence, — which extends to Cornelia's fundamental understanding of life-in-Christ as mission—we must stress again, as in our introductory note, the essential unity of Cornelia's First Chapter. It spells out a program for the active apostolic religious for whom union with Jesus finds its fulfillment in leading others to him. For Cornelia there was no dichotomy, no primary and secondary ends of the religious life: *"nourished* at the well-springs of this heavenly fountain . . . *we* are to employ every effort to *lead others* to taste . . ."[99]

We should stress another of Cornelia's clear emphases in connection with the ministry of sisters whose inspiration derives from the humble and hidden life. She leaves no doubt that they are called to maturity, to learning and culture, to highest professional excellence and relevance. The sisters are to lead the children to "solid virtue," discipline, stability; they are to "meet the wants of the age," to give an excellent education; Cornelia adds an autobiographical touch to the latter—"at least" to equal Protestants in this regard! If humiliation, poverty, hidden labor, suffering, and contempt accompany their exterior as well as their interior lives, the sisters were not, as their Constitutions stated, to be the occasion for these.[100] Rather these were to be the occasion for courageous pursuit of the mission to evangelize in the best possible way, with humble dependence on God for the means needed to do his work.

Notes

1. D 30:48.
2. J.H. Newman, *Selections from Prose Writings* (N.Y., 1906), p. 235.
3. J. Walsh, "Why an American Foundress for England in 1846?" *Pylon*, 23, No. 3 (1961-62), 3-5.
4. Walsh, "*Why*," p. 6.
5. Walsh, "*Why*," p. 6.
6. Walsh, "*Why*, p. 5; see also Armour, *Cornelia*, p. 26; Bellasis, D 72:133; D 68:5-6.
7. CC 1:69-70; for the internal divisions among Catholics, W. Ward, *The Life and Times of Cardinal Wiseman*, 1 (London, 1897), 454.
8. CC 1:70.
9. Walsh, "*Why*," p. 6.
10. Buckle, D. 65:25; for convents as spiritual centers, also D 10:3-4; 27; A Armour, "Derby: The Cradle of the Society, Part I," *Source*, 5 (1976), pp. 37, 43-44; Part II, *Source*, 6 (1977), 36-41.
11. Buckle, D 65:18.
12. Bellasis, D 73:177; D 10:110.
13. D 10:31.
14. Schürmann, p. 547.
15. D 10:25-26; Gompertz, pp. 105-06.
16. Bellasis, D 73:177-78; Armour, "Derby, Part II," pp. 38, 41-42.
17. Rules of the Society of the Holy Child Jesus, 1845-46, p. 1, SHCJ Archives, Rome.
18. Const 1850, *Source* 4:26.
19. Const 1854, *Source* 4:79-80; this text is given below in this chapter under the section "The original inspiration expressed in the Constitutions of 1854." As has been noted at the end of this book in the list of "Sources," succeeding editions of SHCJ Const. have been compiled in the 4th vol. of *Source*, a journal

printed by the SHCJ. Constitutional texts are cited throughout from this vol.
20. D 10:83; Armour, "Derby, Part II," pp. 39-41.
21. D 36:4-5.
22. I. Shields in *Source* 4:146:48; see also CC 24:16 ff.
23. Bisgood, pp. 128-35.
24. Report of T.W. Marshall, published by the Poor School Committee, 1853; cited by Gompertz, p. 300.
25. Buckle, D 65:22.
26. CC 49:24; CC 28:2.
27. CC 49:24.
28. D 58:329.
29. D 68:28.
30. D 78:8; cf. Acts 2:44.
31. Buckle, D 65:22.
32. Milligan, *Gailhac*, pp. 28-29.
33. Buckle, D 65:26, 23, 24, 20.
34. Buckle, D 65:18-27.
35. Buckle, D 65:26.
36. Bisgood, p. 124.
37. Bisgood, pp. 122-26.
38. Bisgood, p. 139.
39. Bisgood, p. 139.
40. CC 8:82-83.
41. Const. 1850, *Source* 4:26; Buckle, D 78:68-69.
42. Buckle, D 78:68-69; D 53:104-11, D 54:8-9, 36-40.
43. D 10:129.
44. D 68:15; Buckle, D 65:25.
45. Revisions of Const. of 1850 (1850-52), *Source* 4:72; Const SJ 276.
46. Ex 95.
47. Ex 230, 231.
48. CC 22:25; Const 1854, *Source* 4:78.
49. Const 1850, *Source* 4:66-67; Const SJ, 719, 723, 725-31, 735; Cornelia did not use the Ignatian texts verbatim but in abbreviated and adapted form; nevertheless, the Ignatian dependence is obvious.
50. CC 8:34-35; Const 1850, *Source* 4:66-67.
51. CC 8:106.
52. Ex 21, 23.
53. CC 6:75a.
54. CC 46B:82.
55. Bellasis, D 73:173.
56. Buckle, D 66:110.
57. I. Iparraguire, *The Paschal Mystery and the Spiritual Exercises of St. Ignatius*. Prog. Sp Ex, Jersey City, trans. of "El Misterio Pascual los Ejercicios de San Ignacio," *Sal Terrae* (1965), 145-54.
58. Buckle, D 65:17-18, 26.
59. D 76:25.
60. Blake, "Grassi SJ," p. 38.
61. Buckle, D 63:27.
62. D 18:10.
63. D 6:161-64; Lynch, Part II, pp. 30-43, especially pp. 38-41.
64. D 7:91.
65. CC 11:10; D 50:122. In this citation Cornelia refers to "Constitutions." In the citation just above (n. 64) she refers to "Rules." She and the SHCJ frequently used the term "Rule" or "our Rule" when they were referring to their Con-

stitutions or a part of the Constitutions. They used the terms somewhat interchangeably.
66. Buckle, D 65:120; D 68:64-65.
67. *Source* 4:138-40.
68. *Source* 4:77-78.
69. General letters: CC 8:8-131; Prefaces: CC 30:1, 3, 6-7; Customal: CC 54, 55.
70. CC 11:35-36; D 51:39, 91; D 52:44.
71. In *Source* 4:26-76, the dependence of each section of the Const of 1850 (including the revisions to 1853) is indicated; for description of the sources see *Source* 4:151-56 and Crook, Part I, pp. 14-20; Part II, pp. 27-33. In the Const of 1850, Cornelia also used several passages from her outline of 1845-46 (Rules SHCJ) which are also indicated in *Source* 4:26-76.
72. *Source* 4:26.
73. *Source* 4:26-50.
74. *Source* 5:51-71.
75. D 73:173.
76. *Source* 4:53 nos. 13, 14.
77. *Constitutions et Directoire pour les Soeurs religieuses de la Visitation* (Paris, 1818), pp. 216-17; the title of the volume begins with *Règles de S. Augustin*, with which Francis de Sales prefaced his Visitation Constitutions. A copy of the 1818 edition, inscribed with "C. Connelly" is in SHCJ Archives, Rome.
78. *Source* 4:51-52; for further commentary on Cornelia's use of the Visitation constitutions, v. Crook, Part II, pp. 28-32.
79. *Meditations as a Preparation for Whitsuntide*, trans. E. Bowles (London, 1851), pp. 2-3; (author unknown). Cornelia's commentary on Lk 2:40-52 accords well with scholarly exegesis: R. Brown, *The Birth of the Messias* (N.Y., 1977), 493-95.
80. Ex 111-16.
81. Brown, pp. 7-9, 37-38.
82. CC 8:90; CC 24:7; the traditional expression is: poverty, *chastity* and obedience.
83. C. McCarthy, "Key Texts from the Original Rule," *Studies in the Spirituality of the Society of the Holy Child Jesus* (1970), no. 13; (Studies . . . became "*Source*" with the second issue in 1971.)
84. See n. 79 above; also Preface to *Meditations on the Holy Childhood of Our Blessed Lord*, trans. M.M.I. Bridges (author unknown), London, 1857; and Preface to Rigoleuc, *Walking with God*, p. 5.
85. *Book of the Order of Studies in Schools of the Society of the Holy Child Jesus*, St. Leonards-on-Sea, 1863.
86. See especially CC 1, 6, 7, 8.
87. In SHCJ Archives, Rome is the manuscript copy of Constitutions of the Society of the Holy Child Jesus with the seal and text of Wiseman's approval, June 1, 1850.
88. Const 1850, *Source* 4:27; "Sommario di quelle Costituzioni," *Regole della Compagnia di Gesù* (Rome, 1834), p. 4, no. 3; Crook, Part I, pp. 11-12.
89. CC 28:2.
90. D 50:121; see also Buckle, D 65:114-15.
91. J. de Charry, *Histoire des Constitutions de la Société du Sacré Coeur*, vol. I, La Formation de l'Institut, vol. 2, Textes. Rome, 1975, *Source* 4:11-12, 154-56; D 68:64.
92. *Source* 4:80.
93. *Source* 4:81.
94. These texts, taken from original MSS and printed versions in SHCJ Archives, Rome are also reproduced in *Source* 4:77-80.

95. Through the valuable skill, concern and assistance of V. Cardella, SJ, Constitutions of the Society of the Holy Child Jesus were approved by Propaganda Fide in 1887, and definitively in 1893. (SHCJ Archives, Rome), A substantial amount of Cornelia's original Constitutions was restored, but the unity of her first Chapter was broken. The First Chapter of the 1887 text, contained only the passages of section I and the first paragraph of section II (to ". . . aim of this little Society: stage 3 in the texts following). Portions of the remaining passages were inserted 12 chapters later in a Chapter XIII: "Of the Choir Sisters." Cornelia had written *all* of her First Chapter for *all* members of the Society. For an account of the compiling of the Constitutions of 1887: M.A. Weinig, " 'The Long Desired Approval of our Rule,' " *Source*, 7 (1977), 5-29.
96. M.U. Blake, "Cornelia and Gioacchino Ventura," *Source*, 3 (1972), 36-44. For the influence of Lallemant on Cornelia, see C. McCarthy, "The Child as 'Key'," pp. 28-30.
97. Ex 116. K. Rahner, "On the Theology of the Incarnation," *Theological Investigations*, 4 (1967), 105: "The mystery of the Incarnation . . . is the very centre of the reality from which we Christians live . . . the mystery of the Divine Trinity is open to us only here . . . ."
98. Ex 137-47. For the *magis* in the Const SJ, G. Ganss, trans., *The Constitutions of the Society of Jesus* (St. Louis, 1970), pp. 8, 409; for SHCJ Const, see *Source* 4:26-82, passim.
99. F. Courel, "La fin unique de la compagnie de Jésus," *Archivum Historicum Societatis Jesu*, 35 (1966), 186-211, trans. and abridged in *Way Supp*, 14 (1971), 46-61; see "The Single End" in Chapter V following.
100. Summary of the Const SHCJ, no. 9, *Source* 4:27.

Chapter 5

Years of Fruition: 1854-69

By 1854 the Society of the Holy Child Jesus had not only presented its Constitutions to Rome for approval but had established schools from South to North in England. For the next two decades expansion continued not only in England but, after 1862, in America, and to France in 1869. Cornelia and her sisters began to see the fruits of their ministry which they adapted to the special needs of the poor, the middle class and the wealthy. They adapted, also, to the "age and stage of moral and intellectual development of those we are guiding,"[1] from infant school through teacher training college and adult parish life. The breadth and depth, and some characteristic expressions of SHCJ ministry will be presented at the end of this chapter.

Vitality and effectiveness in ministry were the outcome of the spiritual formation to which Cornelia devoted the best of herself, her experience, her prayer, her study. Thus, much of this chapter is devoted to her spiritual teachings, her methods, her means, and the sources from which she drew. Her spirituality was entirely centered on the Gospel revelation of the God who had become human—even to becoming a child. She led her sisters "to seek in the mysteries of the life of this divine Lord all that can serve to their greater perfection and the good of their neighbor."[2]

Cornelia expected that the Society's Constitutions would provide a foundation and clear framework for spiritual life, ministry and government. She expected confirmation from Rome of the Society's pontifical status and worldwide ministry soon after 1854. Her composing her own expression of the Society's inspiration and mission had been a landmark for her sisters, moving them toward consolidation and expansion. Their records show the lasting significance of the event for them. They rejoiced in the "clear decision" of their founder's style in which she expressed the "practical devotion" marked by "love of the Hidden Life at Nazareth," which would help to develop the Society's Spirit:

> The first chapter in the Rule Book in which Mother Connelly traces the Spirit of the Society and which was written by herself before the first

journey to Rome in 1854, is a very fair expression of the practical devotion our Beloved Foundress desired to see grow up and flourish in the Society . . . . The chief mark of this devotion is the love of the hidden life at Nazareth . . . . It [the First Chapter] is valuable as being a composition of Mother Connelly's, and it bears the stamp of her spirit and the clear decision of her style.[3]

The high hopes of the Society for stability, unity, and inspiration from their Constitutions were not to be fulfilled in Cornelia's lifetime, as this and the succeeding chapter will show. She and her sisters waited ten years for a response from Rome; their bishop withheld this without explanation. When Cornelia learned that the response that had been given in 1854 was negative, she redoubled her efforts at revision. Finally, in 1869, she went again to Rome, this time to secure the help of Roman canonists for her constitutions.

Though dissension and division were developing within the Society over its constitutional·problems and the consequent concentration of government in Cornelia's hands, these were not the prevailing spirit from 1854-69. Rather what the sources show is the vitality of her spiritual teachings and guidance through this period. To these we turn immediately below.

Spiritual Formation and Government

The Original Inspiration Developed in Auxiliaries to the Constitutions

Even before her constitutional expression of the spirit of the Society, and increasingly after it, Cornelia expanded her teaching on the "humble and hidden life," especially in Prefaces to spiritual literature translated by SHCJ, her Customal, and "Epiphany Letters." These last were circular letters to all her communities begun in 1852.[4] Epiphany was a feast of special significance for the Society. In her first outline of constitutions made in Rome, 1845-46, Cornelia provided that the annual renewal (of devotion) of vows should take place on Epiphany or at the close of the annual retreat of ten days.[5] She included this provision in the Constitutions she presented to Rome for approbation in 1854.[6] By 1854 the feast was known by the sisters to be "our great solemnity," to be, "second only to that of Christmas." M.M.F. Bellasis records that before Epiphany 1848, the year in which the first public renewal of vows took place, Cornelia decided that "an annual retreat of three days should be made in preparation for this renewal."[7]

Cornelia often linked the Magi offering their gifts with the offering of the three vows, commenting little on the actual Gospel scene.[8] From the seven Epiphany letters extant, and from her early companions, we gather that the feast was to be the occasion for epitomizing the spirit and mission of the Society. Her contemporaries have given different aspects of Cornelia's application of the mystery of the Epiphany to the life of the

Society. M.M.J. Buckle wrote: "Her own idea of the devotion we ought to have to the Infant Saviour was expressed by the feast she chose for our great solemnity—the Epiphany—not His Birth but His manifestation—was most suitable to the teaching vocation of the Sisters."[9] This testimony accords with Cornelia's emphasis in the Constitutions on ministry, centered on education, as integral to her charism for the Society.[10]

M.M.F. Bellasis focused on Cornelia's understanding of the act of the Magi as symbolic of the offering of self which was for the founder the fundamental stance of the religious. The feast was

> an annual call to a renewal of self-sacrifice and detachment, a day on which each sister was to give not only her all to the Holy Child, but was also to search the avenues of the heart for any stumbling block, and undue attachment.
>
> If the Mother Foundress of the Society of the Holy Child Jesus could, with any truth, be called a "severe Superior," it was on this point alone; she was not only severe, but very severe. Love and affection were with her so sacred, that every attachment had to become detachment, unless it were centred in the Eternal Love. Every affection had to be purified, sanctified, before it could be trusted, and then it would lead, and was to lead, to God. Whether the soul was to be saved in the world or in the cloister, above all things the *heart* was to be trained in the great Christian law of Charity. No one knew this better than Mother Connelly, whose loving heart, ever in the crucible, had passed through so fierce and fiery an ordeal. In every department she was vigilant.[11]

It is not surprising, in the light of her "fiery ordeal," that Cornelia identified herself and her Society with the "suffering and persecuted" Child Jesus, recognizing Matthew's intent in the whole narrative that surrounds the mystery of the Epiphany. She wrote in 1863 to the Cardinal Prefect of Propaganda Fide:

> It is true, we must not hesitate in submitting to this most unjust aspersion, for we cannot but gratefully call to mind that if our dear Lord has suffered this Institute devoted to the mysteries of His Sacred Infancy and Childhood to share in the persecutions which He therein endured, He has also, in His mercy, crowned our humble efforts for His Glory with no inconsiderable result by the growth, development, and labours of our Institute in various dioceses in this country and in America.[12]

Cornelia's Epiphany letters and one of her Prefaces expand her constitutional teaching on contemplation. She assures her sisters that they are called to contemplation, linking the call especially to their vows, always reminding them of the asceticism entailed. For Epiphany of 1857, after exhorting them to constancy till death in faith, hope and charity, she gives an oft-repeated reminder of "the beatific vision where . . . you are to be encompassed by the ecstatic delight of loving God without interruption." "Now," she says:

we must delight him by our homely actions of charity, and by our passive cooperation, not resisting the love that would fill our poor hearts. Let us not resist, my dear Sisters, for we are ourselves the only obstacle to the overflowing of His Divine Love.[13]

As in her Constitutional texts, she encourages them to full contemplative involvement in the mystery of the Incarnation, into which their vows have specially drawn them:

I need not recall to your minds the hidden treasures we are secretly to carry to our lovely Savior in his lowly Manger, nor with what floods of devotion we are willingly to offer ourselves to be possessed by Him in the sweet bonds of Poverty, Chastity and Obedience.[14]

It is in the same vein that thirteen years later she recommends to the sisters the use of the "beautiful Exercises" of St. Gertrude, who was, she says, "the Virgin of [God's] especial choice and His heart's sweet love. And a better model of acts of love it would be hard to find!" These Exercises, Cornelia says significantly, "contain the very Spirit of the Holy Child, and," she continues, in a revealing juxtaposition, "contain . . . the sentiments of the Church in the Divine Office." Characteristically she prays that "He, Himself, enrich you with a constant flow of the graces of charity, of prayer and of mortification to which your correspondence throughout the year may . . . store up for each one of you an eternity of blessedness."[15]

Cornelia's Preface to a translation of Rigoleuc's work, to which she gave the title *Walking with God, or Dwellers in the Recreation House of the Lord*, was directed to religious communities. She left no doubt of her belief in their call to mysticism. She draws on Lapuente:

Divine Providence designed that religion should be a house of recreation for God our Lord in the midst of the earth, and His Paradise of Pleasure; . . . a particular house of some especial friends and favorites with whom He might delight Himself, and who should dedicate themselves to converse familiarly with Him; . . . a place of retreat for the Heavenly King, into which He brings His beloved friends, and to them discovers His secrets.[16]

In concluding this passage Cornelia characteristically employs her own words to speak of her personal experience with an authenticity that cannot be missed. She gives here, thirteen years after founding her Society, a profound revelation of the mystical union to which God had led her through "accepted suffering." He had indeed brought her to:

that kingdom of peace within, where the soul's whisperings are answered by the King Himself, giving abundantly that jubilee of heart which had not been bargained for in this life of accepted suffering.[17]

The woman who lived thus interiorly, who called her sisters to a deep interior life, lived an extraordinarily active life of service. As Superior General she supervised daughter houses in London, Preston, Blackpool, Mayfield and later in the United States and France, most foundations having several schools attached. At St. Leonard's, which was her generalate, and where she was local superior for many years, she supervised not only schools and a noviceship, but a successful Teacher Training College. She was constantly revising and developing her Constitutions. She remained available to the sisters and children, willing to "use her gift of personal influence with the troublesome characters who defeated the efforts of the other nuns to guide them."[18] It was because she was herself a contemplative in action that she could teach this integration of the spiritual life to others. Thus she wrote for Epiphany, 1854, from Rome:

> Let all be diligent in giving proofs of love this year, and as you step on through the muddy streets, love God with your feet; and when your hands toil; and when you teach the children, love Him with His little ones; and may you be blessed in your actions and in your members with an abundance of Divine Love, and purified and prepared in this world, as far as possible, to enjoy an eternity of Love.[19]

Perhaps the most distinctive contribution Cornelia's Epiphany letters added to her sisters' understanding of their spirit was her teaching on the hidden life, especially as it entailed a habitual practice of discernment, a delicate sponsal fidelity, especially to their vows. In these letters she places her sisters with virgins who wait for their Lord and constantly exhorts them to the "Vigilance, Humility, Fidelity" which was a constant theme of her own personal spiritual notes. Her letters to the Community, 1854, from Rome developed these themes:

> [Jan., 1854]
> What better shall I say to you on Epiphany morning than the old salutation. Arise and trim your Lamps and be no longer unfaithful. St. John was asked why he always said the same thing and he repeated again the same, "love one another", and St. Francis of Sales "love God". That is how you will learn how to love Him, so I repeat to you "Be faithful, trim your lamps with the oil of fidelity especially by fidelity in little things." This is the cooperation with divine grace. This will ensure your perfection, and send you on to all that our Blessed Lord asks of you, and to the fulfillment of His designs upon each of you. Remember the work of each day: "My God to glorify, my Savior to imitate, my soul to save, eternity to prepare for."[20]

> [Apr., 1854]
> Ah my dear Sisters, how much depends on your fidelity in little things — how much — Who knows what misfortune might fall upon us by the infidelity of *one* only, in some apparently little act? Who knows? Many a time has a whole Community suffered through the infidelity of one only. Be faithful and more and more faithful — and thus more and more united to our divine Spouse. My very dear Sisters, let us try day by day to do what He would do — To speak as He would speak — To think as He would think — To desire what He desires — To love what He loves, and thus make your life one with Him, being in one continued act of love from night till night, and from year to year . . . .[21]

Especially from 1854 through 1856, and for many years thereafter, the SHCJ suffered much from a large debt which Emily Bowles, Cornelia's first companion, rashly and independently incurred in Liverpool where she had been sent as superior in 1852. She finally left the Society while Cornelia and her Council were considering her dismissal in 1856, but continued to trouble the Society by slanders.[22] This tragedy may have contributed to the continuing emphasis, in Cornelia's Epiphany letters of 1856 and 1858, on fidelity, especially to one's vows. Her thoughts on the vows lived out in the hidden life flowed readily from her pen:

> ... Poverty—Chastity—Obedience.... they embrace the whole perfection of the Gospel truths and Counsels of our Divine Lord, and are the foundation of our supernatural life ... May these blessed Counsels be *fixed* in your hearts, so that you may day by day understand them more and more brightly, and love them more intensely, and practice them more diligently, not forgetting to cultivate their handmaids and attendant "angels", our *old* friends, though ever new, Vigilance, Humility and Fidelity.
>
> These are the ever darling companions of our Religious Life, always ready to brighten the clouds of our own natural defects, turning these defects even into some hidden treasure to be stored up for Heaven, and at the same time bringing with them the strength of a hidden life in God; and it is in this obscurity from all human view that the Divine Light shines, and in this hidden life we are clothed with our coat of mail, that we may be enabled to fight spiritually in the army of God's Church Militant.
>
> When we are seeking to know more of our dear Sisters, Poverty, Chastity and Obedience in their hidden virtues, let us turn to the great Martyr St. John the Baptist and compare our very little sacrifices to his life of penance and prayer, and let us bow down our heads at even the name of sacrifice when we think of ourselves. *Whose* standard have we chosen, my dear Sisters? And whom are we following? St. John went before Him, and, after a life of penance, suffered, humanly speaking, the most ignoble of deaths! Let us never think *we* have done enough, but more and more try to imitate the faith of the great St. John.[23]

At the end of this fervent exhortation where scriptural images[24] intertwine with those of the Exercises,[25] Cornelia picks up the notion of faith and centers it directly on the special vocation of the Holy Child sisters:

> If you have faith, you will learn the value of a suffering and hidden life, and it is to this life you are especially called by the very name you bear.
> Be then, *like* the Holy Child Jesus in your thoughts, in your words and in your actions, cherishing diligence and fidelity in what is called little by daily occurrence—and be persuaded that nothing is little with God if it is in the practice of Virtue—God and I—Fidelity.[26]

Characteristically, Cornelia explicitly refers to the "practice of Virtue" when showing how the spirit of the Society of the Holy Child Jesus is best manifested.

In an Epiphany letter two years after ths meaningful commentary on "the life you are called to by the very name you bear," Cornelia again draws her sisters into the company of the virgins who through interior and exterior fidelity wait upon their Lord. It is notable, too, that, even with growth in numbers and geographical separation, she still endeavors to preserve the communal sharing of the primitive years—"this word we will talk over . . . you will give me your views." She preserves, too, her mode of spiritual formation which respects God's unique way with each person—"apply it . . . each according to her own devotional *attrait*."

> The Eleventh Anniversary of the Epiphany must not pass without a few lines to wish you every blessing with the Manifestation of our dear Lord in your hearts.
> One word only I will write to you, and the definition of this word we will *talk* over, as I expect to see you very soon, and this is *Attention*—It is a very simple word, used very often by worldlings in every class of life, perhaps more frequently than by religious, but when we apply it in a religious sense it speaks volumes and may be carried into every thought word and deed. I beg of you all, my dear Sisters, to apply it in a religious sense each according to her own devotional *attrait*, and when I am with you we shall *finish our letter*, and you will give me your views about this common little word. May our dear Lord be with you on this blessed Feast and accept the renewal of your Holy Vows by an abundant bestowal of His Grace—So that you may henceforth be so attentive to all the duties they imply that you may be at all times ready, as the wise virgins, to hear His word, and faithful in corresponding to it.[27]

For one of her community, Sr. Clare Ranger, Cornelia composed a sixteen-page booklet of instruction and prayer on devotion to the Sacred Heart and the Eucharist and to Mary. This is probably the fullest exposition we have of how the founder communicated her profound and loving devotion to Mary. She wrote, e.g., in the booklet: "Now there stood by the cross of Jesus, Mary, His Mother. May two stand by your cross—Your Mother and yourself, Mary and Clare!"[28] In the prayer she composed for the Community, she invoked Mary's intercession for sisters, students, orphans. This prayer recalls her first constitutional expression of her inspiration for the Society with its ". . . grant us, . . . remembering Thy sufferings and humiliations, Thy Incarnation, Thy Birth, Thy hidden life during thirty years, Thy labours, Thy passion, Thy death upon the cross, we may finally become *one with Thee*."[29]

Manuscripts that Cornelia called the "Customal" contained not only prescriptive but also devotional and instructive material emphasizing fidelity and the practice of virtue. M.A. Weinig, in a study of the evolution of the SHCJ Customals, notes how much they tell us of Cornelia's "lived spirituality":

> An interesting inclusion in most of the early customals, still there in some of the later printed ones, is material related specifically to the children, who in the boarding schools must have been very present—apostolate and spiritual life were intertwined as a matter of course.
> In looking over the customals and related writings one is struck again by the primacy *and* the everydayness of the spiritual in SHCJ lives, by the

delicate attention to detail not at all inconsistent with liberty of spirit, by the wholeness and the practicality of Cornelia's grasp of the human situation. "Regulations" had their place but were not retained beyond their usefulness; constant adjustment was an expected function of the general chapters. And in all, the test of quiet experience was honored. The unglamorous sojourn at Nazareth was seriously proposed as a model for a good part of our lives.[30]

Our final indication here of the scope of Cornelia's spiritual teaching comes from a proposed "Directory for the Novice Mistress." She entitled a section of the Customal thus, and into it copied, with some abbreviation and adaptation, the rule for the novice mistress from Teresa Verzeri's *Costituzioni delle Figlie del Sacro Cuore di Gesù*.[31] Cornelia was influenced from the beginning of her religious life, through Fr. Grassie, by these constitutions,[32] and reiterated several times in her own way one of the finest of Teresa's passages which she excerpted. Teresa wrote thus:

> She is not to expect that the Novices will form their spirit on her own; but she is rather to bend hers to theirs, making herself all in all to them to assist them to advance in their way. All ought to form themselves according to their vocation and thence to the Spirit of the Society. The ways of God are many and He knows how to lead to the same end by divers means. The Mistress of Novices must study the manner in which Grace tends to sanctify each one, and she must act accordingly.[33]

In her personal notes Cornelia wrote: "*Be watchful in leading each and all* according to the Divine grace bestowed upon them, and keep oneself in spirit at the feet of all."[34] In notes for those in charge of formation she wrote: "Choir Postulants . . . should be exercised on the rules of religious Modesty . . . with prudent and discreet vigilance . . . taking care not to go beyond the guidance of God, *following His grace only*," and "remember that we do not die to our *good* nature but to our bad and *sinful* nature."[35] And finally she wrote to a sister who looked to her for spiritual direction:

> Heaven must be won according to God's own way upon us in particular and on each one in particular. Now do not lose time in imagination but '*work out*' your salvation interiorly as well as exteriorly—that you may make your calling sure.[36]

Constitutions and Government

The preceding sections have shown that simply by drawing out the meaning of her original inspiration expressed in a single passage and chapter of the Constitutions, and in a few auxiliaries, Cornelia could outline a fairly comprehensive spiritual program. She could invite the sisters who "walked through the muddy streets" to their schools, to love the Lord "with your feet" and "in His little ones;" she invited those same busy apostles to keep attuned to that interior depth of spirit where the "King himself" communed with them.[37] She had counted on Constitutions to undergird ongoing spiritual instruction. What did they consist of and what use did the Sisters make of them?

From 1854 to 1874 the SHCJ Constitutions consisted of two distinct parts. From 1854 most members of the Society knew well and cherished *only* Part One of their Constitutions—what they called their "spiritual" or "ascetical" part.³⁸ This consisted of Cornelia's First Chapter, followed by articles 4-22 of the Sacred Heart Abrégé; the Jesuit Summary of Constitutions; the Jesuit Common Rules; provision for a Local Chapter, drawn from the Visitation Constitutions; the Jesuit Rules for Religious Modesty; provision for House Sisters and for Poor School Mistresses, and for sixteen minor offices drawn from Sacred Heart and Jesuit Rules. Thus Part One was largely borrowed, but with Cornelia's invariable adaptations. She left her stamp on everything she compiled.³⁹

Part Two of the SHCJ Constitutions was circulated only to Superiors, was never printed, and was not implemented fully. Nevertheless it contained the all-important framework for government and for admission and formation of candidates. Its contents were as follows: It commenced with rules for the Novice Mistress, the Bursar, the Local Assistant and the Local Councillors, all adapted from the Visitation Constitutions.⁴⁰ Then followed a rule for the Local Superior which seems to be Cornelia's own mosaic compilation. This has echoes of her own outline of 1845-46, and of the Visitation Constitutions, but it also seems to echo her wider reading, e.g. Gautrelet's *Traité de l'Etat Religieux* and Aquaviva's *Cure of the Sicknesses of the Soul.*⁴¹ The remainig sections were from the Constitutions of St. Ignatius, that is, from sections on Admission of Candidates and Noviceship, on Scholastics, on Schools, on General Government and on the Manner of Sustaining the Society. General Government included a provision for an elected General Chapter to elect a Superior General and Assistants. By 1854 Cornelia had adopted the Ignatian provision that the General be elected for life. In the 1850 Constitutions the General's term had been six years.⁴²

Why was Part Two, outlining the all-important framework of government not circulated among all the sisters? Sources reveal at least two reasons: The Constitutions enunciated the principle that those who were not superiors should not be preoccupied with matters of government.⁴³ In the 1850's and 60's Holy Child sisters seem to have accepted the principle of leaving government to superiors. A recollection of one of the sisters reveals no general dissatisfaction. She was referring to Part Two of the Constitutions when she said:

> We saw for the first time what Cardinal Wiseman had given to Mother Foundress very concisely about the election of Mother General, the Four Assistants, etc. I really do not remember what it was about. It was, I believe, some hints about the Government of the Society, etc. But as we never had the election of a Mother General nor the Four Assistants I do not think anyone took much notice about it nor were any remarks made about it. Mother Foundress in the course of time had four General Assistants & also four Local Assistants which she chose herself.⁴⁴

Nineteenth century religious were not encouraged to involve themselves in community government unless they were superiors. At least one far-seeing canon lawyer pointed to this as a defect, urging that all religious, not just superiors become knowledgeable about the laws which applied to them.[45] Although Cornelia used the manual of this canon lawyer, she does not seem to have been influenced by him on this point. She wrote as late as 1876:

> (Notes for the Sisters going to Rome in 1876) During the time we have made the trial of the New Rule we have as much as possible kept the religious in the spirit of the order and under the ascetical part of the Rule that all may not be occupied with the government of the body and but little attentive to their own perfection and salvation.[46]

But there was a second more urgent reason why Cornelia withheld Part Two—the framework of government—from general circulation. She was concerned about its lack of approbation, since it had been revised *after* Wiseman's approbation of 1850, as Part One had not been. Part Two had been revised and submitted to Rome in 1854 with, among other revisions, that of "General for life" and she was *waiting* for approbation before circulating it. M.M.J. Buckle remembered her stating this explicitly:

> The reason for not putting into practice the Rules of Government of St. Ignatius were, as she told me afterwards, because the Society was not yet approved—When it was, she said that the Government would be carried on in exact obedience to the Rule.[47]

In the years of waiting for approbation immediately after 1854, Holy Child sisters thought they were just being subjected to the traditional slowness of the Roman Curia. Cornelia does not seem to have been overconcerned with Rome's silence. At the end of 1854 in which she had written simply to her bishop: "It seems . . . better . . . at present to simply let the matter rest in the hands of God. Time will surely bring to light His will in our regard."[48] Apparently Cornelia also felt initially secure within the Society about the revision of Constitutions that provided for "General for life." She recorded: "When we held a Council on it . . . to make it more in conformity with the Rule of St. Ignatius, we *unitedly decided that the Superior General should be for life*."[49]

As the 1850's wore on, however, Cornelia became increasingly concerned with the juridical inadequacies of the Society's position and of her role as *appointed* General. She was becoming aware that not all in the Society were content with a passive role in government and her power to appoint all Superiors. She did not seem to realize that this was the maturity she might have expected from the kind of formation she had given. But she *was* aware of the sisters' right to an approved constitutional frame of government and implored her bishop's assistance in gaining Roman approbation so that all machinery of government might operate, above all, a General Chapter.

Jan. 15, 1857

I deplore our Institution not having been approved . . . . The most intelligent and clever [sisters] are the first to bring up the fact that His Holiness has not appd for us, the same rule which he had approved for others . . . . we know that we are not worthy of any favor from his Holiness, but the only question is the work of God, and the good of souls, and that we have the means of serving Him, and of maintaining a right spirit in those He has given to us, which can never be ensured with stability, until the Church blesses us by the seal of her approbation.[50]

Letters to ecclesiastical authorities like the above reveal what was Cornelia's strength through her long years of constitutional struggles — her deep awareness of her charism and her unswerving determination to be faithful to it: "the only question . . . the work of God . . . good of souls . . . means of serving Him . . . maintaining a right spirit in those He had given to us . . . stability [through] Church . . . approbation."

The ardor of her conviction of her God-given mission for the Society and her fidelity to it seems to have veiled her perception of some sisters' dissatisfaction with the Society's government being so completely under her control. She was increasingly under pressure by the difficult position in which both Rome and her bishops left her by their failure to act. In 1860 she and her superiors attested to the Bishop that their constitutions were kept in their respective convents.[51] Repeatedly she petitioned the bishop to summon a Chapter which would elect a Superior-General and Councillors. Consistently Bishop Grant failed to do this.[52]

In the early 1860's Cornelia returned to her own work on the Constitutions, possibly hoping to bolster the Society's confidence. In 1861 she printed Part One of the Constitutions for all the sisters, with additions showing increasing Jesuit influence. From a Jesuit Rule Book she added items akin to her existing auxiliaries to the Constitutions such as her Customal. She added "Collection of some of the Decrees," "General Admonitions," the Letter of St. Ignatius on Obedience, and many prayers.[53] She included her own "Community Prayer" and, at the request of her sisters, her own "Sentences in Use."[54] The first printed "Rule Book" of the Sisters of the Holy Child Jesus was devotional indeed. The sisters cherished it, and felt that, with it in their hands, they could, with Cornelia, "work on and gain our own experience."[55]

In 1862 Cornelia sent missionaries to her "own dear country" thus fulfilling the second part of the mandate the Pope had given her in 1846: "From England let your efforts in the cause of education reach America."[56] She felt more than ever the urgent need to put a settled Constitutions in the hands of the sisters. The needs of the American foundation influenced her to make significant revisions of Part Two of the Constitutions. These were completed by the beginning of 1864. She inserted the Jesuit rule for provincial superior and of a papal decree from the Constitutions of the Sisters of Our Lady of Charity of the Good Shepherd of Angers, authorizing the setting up of Provinces. Also, under the influence of the Good Shepherd Constitutions, and of mounting pressures from ecclesiastics and her own sisters, Cornelia inserted her original six-year term for the General and the mode of election prescribed by the Visitation Constitutions (used by the Good Shepherd Constitutions also). This eliminated the provision for General-for-life. With these insertions, she had the Constitutions translated into Italian and taken to Rome, but this revision did not even reach Propaganda Fide. Unaccountably they were not delivered to Propaganda Fide, but left unopened at the English College in Rome where Cornelia found them five years later![57]

In view of the complexity of the Society's constitutional history, a chart outlining this entire history is given in Appendix B. It provides assistance for sections concerned with the Constitutions in this chapter and in Chapters III, IV and VI.

If the complexity of the Society's constitutional endeavors seems difficult to comprehend, even more so are the dealings of episcopal and Roman authorities with it: Bishop Grant revealed to Cornelia, only at the end of 1864, that he had withheld from her for ten years a Roman Consultor's report of 1854 on the Constitutions she had submitted then to Propaganda Fide. The elderly Consultor had associated Cornelia's Constitutions with spurious Constitutions presented by Pierce in 1848 and had mingled indiscriminately his objections to both texts. Bishop Grant gave Cornelia his own version of the negative report, requiring changes as follows: that the General's term be for six years, that the authority of the Ordinary be stated, and that changes be made regarding the form of the vows and administration of temporalities. The bishop gave no explanation of his delaying action. Cornelia and her sisters, still prevented from holding a Chapter, worked for five years more on their Constitutions. Finally, in 1869 Cornelia won Bishop Grant's support for her going to Rome to work personally with the Consultors of Propaganda Fide.[58] The story of the Constitutions of 1869 and their aftermath will be told in Chapter VI.

But one more rather incredible fact concerning the dealings of Church authorities with Cornelia must be added here. It only came to light eight years after her death but it related to all her constitutional endeavors from 1854 onwards. It was discovered by Holy Child sisters, working in Rome in 1887 to obtain approval for their Constitutions, that "there was a private decision of the Sacred Congregation [of Propaganda Fide] to take no decisive step [to approve SHCJ Constitutions] while Mr. Connelly still lived."[59] There is no evidence that Cornelia was ever informed of Propaganda Fide's "private decision"! She had begun her Institute with the warm support of Pope Gregory XVI and the Prefect of Propaganda Fide, Cardinal Fransoni. For thirty-three years she labored over Constitutions and inaugurated ministries that bore fruit for the Church in England, America and France. Though she might not have counted on warm support after the deaths of Gregory XVI in 1846 and Fransoni in 1856, she surely expected integrity in her dealings with the latter's successors at Propaganda Fide. It would seem that, when the scandal of Pierce's apostasy became the scandal of the Cross for her, she was, like Christ deserted. (I Cor 1:18, 23, 27-28).

Throughout all of her years of governing Cornelia had to try to achieve a delicate balance. She had to be her sisters' representative to the Church authorities under whom the Society lived somewhat precariously; on the other hand she had to exercise authority over her sisters who knew little of what the relationship with the official Church entailed. Her faults, limitations and mistakes became very apparent in her endeavors to balance her difficult roles. What was also manifest was the graced resiliency, hopefulness, enthusiasm, even joy with which she governed and sustained her Society. She believed that loyalty to the Church, especially to the Holy See was integral to her spirit and mission. This she expressed and fostered magnanimously, with freedom of spirit and maturity.

Use of the Constitutions of Other Orders

Cornelia's notebooks show that she gave regular instructions on the Constitutions.[60] When one studies her constitutional endeavors one is aware from her intelligent and skillfull excerpting and adapting that she knew and understood well the Constitutions of other congregations and Orders. This understanding and knowledge must have been important factors which made her instructions on and the Society's confidence in their Constitutions sufficient to carry them through the many years of Rome's failure to give "the long desired approval of our Rule."[61]

She referred to religious Constitutions as the writings of the saints. Primary for her among these were Ignatius' Constitutions. We shall look first at other Constitutions she used or knew, and then see the considerable use she made of the Ignatian Constitutions.

At least from 1845 on Cornelia knew and excerpted from the Constitutions of the Society of the Sacred Heart for her Constitutions and her *Book of Studies*. As we have seen, she used their primitive Abrégé to great advantage.[62] From 1845 on, Cornelia knew and excerpted from Francis de Sales' Constitutions for the Visitation Order. Her Society still has the copy of these she used throughout her life.[63] She actually used these Constitutions as the "authority" on which she founded, declaring that they were in force for whatever her first outline of Constitutions did not cover, and professing her vows in 1847 "according to the rule of St. Francis de Sales." In professing her vows, however, she left herself free to change whatever was necessary to pursue the single end of an apostolic congregation. By 1850, she had made her own Constitutions more Ignatian than Salesian, and by 1853 she had increased even more the former over the latter dependence.[64]

We have already noted that Cornelia was influenced throughout most of her religious life by the Constitutions of the Figlie del Sacro Cuore di Gesù composed by their founder, Teresa Verzeri, with the help of the same Fr. Grassi who had assisted Cornelia in founding. We have also noted excerpts from Teresa in the SHCJ Customal. Further excerpts from Teresa appear in the revision of SHCJ Constitutions made in 1869.[65] Cornelia said "the spirit of the two institutes was the same," and always kept Teresa's constitutions "on the shelf" in her room, according to M.M.J. Buckle. The latter has left a striking record of the affinity which developed between the two founders through their common spiritual director, although apparently the two women never met:

> When in the year 1868 Mother Connelly went to Rome, Padre Anselmo, The Franciscan Consultore of the Rule, when he had spoken a little to Mother Connelly and looked over our Rule book, said "I think the spirit of the Society resembles that of the Figlie del Sagro Cuore—I will refer to their rule." Mother Connelly told us she was struck by this remark from a priest who knew nothing of our first institution with Father Grassi's help, but she considered it one of those providential circumstances which showed that the spirit as well as the words of the holy Director had passed into the Rule.[66]

As has been noted, Cornelia studied and excerpted from the Constitutions of Our Lady of Charity of the Good Shepherd of Angers.[67] She has left records of her study of the Rule of the Religious of Our Lady of Sion, and of the Rules and Constitutions of the Sisters of Notre Dame de Namur.[68] Though we have no record of her use of the Franciscan Rule, we know that she studied Franciscan literature to imbue her Constitutions with the spirit of Francis of Assisi to whom she had great devotion.[69] Finally, she made extensive and ingenious use of Ignatius' and other Jesuit constitutional writings, drawing from them more text and thought than from any other source. These we shall treat below but first we should note how perceptively Cornelia assembled her constitutional sources from the writings of those founders with whom she shared spiritual kinship.

She knew that her own inspiration lay within the spiritual tradition of contemplative transforming union with God-become-man, a union in salvific mission; a union in affective love. Ignatius Loyola, Francis de Sales, Madeleine Sophie Barat, Mary Euphrasia Pelletier (drawing on John Eudes), and Teresa Verzeri share with Cornelia the same spiritual tradition, though expressed with widely varying nuances. Christ's Sacred Heart is for them the most evocative symbol of the grace of his humanity. Cornelia rightly associated the Gospel revelation of the "humbled God," the "hidden God," the "living waters," with the devotion to the Sacred Heart prevailing in her time. She taught and practiced a rich devotion to the Sacred Heart as one way of responding to the "Eternal Wisdom in the lowliness of His Humanity".

Cornelia also recognized that the Constitutions and Rules of St. Ignatius supplied a sort of unifying foundation for many of the congregations arising out of the Christocentric tradition of which he was so great an exponent. She showed this recognition in a letter to her Ordinary in 1862:

> By the morning's post I sent your Lordship the printed copy of the Rules, which we had done last year for the use of the different houses and for our own convenience.
>
> Though the Rule in all essentials is the same as that of several other approved orders, such as that of the S. Cuore [T. Verzeri's] and the French S. Coeur in Paris [M.S. Barat's] and partially I think, that of the Sisters of Notre Dame [de Namur] yet it is not a *copy* of any of these Rules, being taken from the Constitutions of St. Ignatius, the source from whence all these Rules sprang; ours, like theirs, excluding all that is unfit for women, and retaining all that leads to a perfect imitation of Our Lord, and to the highest practice of religious perfection that is set forth in the Holy Gospels.[70]

Near the end of her life Cornelia gave a very strong statement on the significance of the Ignatian Constitutions and spirit for her congregation. Exhorting the recently founded community at Neuilly to obedience and reparation she added:

> The second practice I desire you to keep is *fidelity to the rule* [Constitutions] *and spirit of St. Ignatius*, than which nothing could be found more perfect for the spiritual life. In this rule and spirit we have been trained from the first; and now it is thirty-one years [1846-77] since we began the Society on these principles.[71]

Did Cornelia mean, by such a sweeping statement to appropriate another founder's Constitutions and spirit? We think it can be shown that she and her sisters did not consider themselves "lady Jesuits" but rather that they recognized an application of the Ignatian charism beyond his own Order, especially through the Spiritual Exercises. The latter will be examined after we have reviewed the remarkable knowledge Cornelia had of Ignatian and Jesuit constitutional writings and her ingenious use of them.

As a laywoman in the United States—in Grand Coteau, La.—Cornelia was shown the Jesuit Constitutions and probably the Summary.[72] At some point after 1843 when it was published, Cornelia obtained, annotated and used her own copy of an unauthorized French translation of the Jesuit Constitutions, printed to discredit the Jesuits, but usable enough for Cornelia under the direction of Father Grassi in 1845 or the English Jesuits after 1846.[73] From 1847-50, Cornelia not only obtained from J.H. Newman, an unauthorized English translation of the Jesuit Constitutions—published in 1838, also to discredit the Jesuits—but she actually used the text of this translation for the extensive excerpts from the Jesuit Constitutions by which she put together a large part of the SHCJ Constitutions approved in 1850. She excerpted even more extensively in 1852. Although this translation she used (lacking the Examen) was also, as was the French translation, published as a witness against the Jesuits, it was useful for Cornelia's purposes since it was an accurate and polished translation and served her well. Perhaps her familiarity, as a Protestant and as a convert, with publications designed to discredit Catholicism, made her a discerning user of this type of literature for her own advantage.[74] Either from Fr. Grassi in Rome, or from the English Jesuits, she obtained the Jesuit Summary and Jesuit rule for various offices and probably a translation of these, from which she excerpted for her Constitutions of 1850.[75]

But Cornelia meant even more than we have indicated above when she spoke in 1877 of her Society's "thirty-one years" of training on the Ignatian "rule and spirit." We know that at least from 1858, as she grew increasingly concerned about the Society's precarious constitutional position, she circulated to her convents *complete manuscript translations*, made by the best latinist among her sisters, of the following: the Jesuit Constitutions (with Examen), a volume of Jesuit Rules, and of Aquaviva's "Cure of the Sicknesses of the Soul," the last contained in the sixth volume of the corpus of Jesuit constitutional material made available to her. This would be hard to believe if the Society did not possess today not only her own and her translator's record of this activity but also one complete copy (and fragments of others) of these ambitious translations. Cornelia recorded in 1858:

> We are now making four copies of the Rules [Constitutions] of St. Ignatius which are again to be copied for each Community. These must serve as our guide in all things that can be embraced by women not otherwise ordered by our Constitutions.[76]

Apparently Cornelia was trying to supply a sort of base for the Society's own truncated Constitutions (as she had supplied the Visitation Constitutions as a base for her first outline of Constitutions, 1846-50), by giving the Jesuit Constitutions as "guide" for what SHCJ Constitutions lacked. The translations of Jesuit Constitutional materials were begun when, in 1855, Fr. Gallway SJ made available apparently the whole corpus, or at least six of the seven volumes, of Ignatian constitutional materials published between 1827-38 at Avignon by the revived Society of Jesus. The SHCJ manuscript translations and Cornelia's and her translator's references prove dependence on the first six of these seven volumes.[77] The translator, who was M.M.J. Buckle, left a record which shows how assiduously, in the midst of many other activities, Cornelia constantly worked to bolster, through the Jesuit Constitutions, the defective constitutional framework within which her Society lived.

The Spiritual Exercises as the Means to the "True Spirit of the Constitutions"

The title of this section is Cornelia's own expression. To understand it, we must understand the Jesuit "Summary of Constitutions." It was, with Cornelia's First Chapter, the core of the truncated version of SHCJ Constitutions which most Holy Child sisters lived by during Cornelia's life. The Summary had, in its nineteenth-century editions, a title which throws much light on the SHCJ understanding and use of it: "Summarium earum Constitutionum quae ad spiritualem nostrorum institutionem pertinent, et ab omnibus observandae sunt." M.M.J. Buckle's translation of this, though awkward, puts in clear focus the meaning and value it had for the SHCJ: "The Summary of the Constitutions which belong to the *Spiritual Institution* of our Institute, and which are to be observed by all" (emphasis added). In the 1870's and 1880's, when the Holy Child sisters fought to keep the Summary, headed by Cornelia's First Chapter, as their code of life, (government, studies and ministry being under the care of Superiors), they called it the "spiritual" or "ascetical" part of "our Rule."[78] A Jesuit commentator had indicated the contents of the Summary in somewhat the same way:

> Only those passages of the Examen and Constitutions [SJ] are inserted in the Summary that pertain to the spiritual formation of Ours; that is, passages that set forth the norms of the spiritual life which each must follow, everything referring to government, studies and ministry being omitted.[79]

This seems a good estimate of how the SHCJ understood the Summary, and of what Cornelia had desired to take from Ignatius' Constitutions: that which pertains to "spiritual formation," those norms of the spiritual life which each one must follow. Contemplative in action that she was, she would have agreed with the commentator's note that since spiritual formation involved exterior manifestations, the provisions for external discipline in the Summary are consonant with its purpose. It was for this reason she and her sisters linked closely with the Summary, the Jesuit Common Rules and Rules for Religious Modesty.

We have already noted that Cornelia's extensive study of the Ignatian Constitutions enabled her to bring to her regular instructions on the Summary a good understanding of the context of the latter. Many sisters, too, apparently could have had access to the SHCJ translation of the Ignatian Constitutions. But there was a much more important means by which Cornelia bulwarked the Society's truncated Constitutions through every form of instruction she used. An abundance of sources show unmistakably that what the SHCJ, and above all Cornelia, constantly related to the Summary was not its "parent" Constitutions themselves—the Spiritual Exercises. Cornelia and her sisters undoubtedly valued the Summary because it called them to mission, to single-mindedness, generosity, humility, renunciation through poverty, chastity and obedience under Christ's standard in his Church.[80] Cornelia tended when speaking of these and other great themes of the spiritual life to relate them directly to the text of the Exercises, rather than to the Summary or Constitutions. The Exercises were her most fundamental, comprehensive and meaningful frame of reference. Due to the negative history of SHCJ constitutions, and also to her own positive experiences of the Exercises, the latter seem to have had more influence on her mode of shaping her Society than its own Constitutions or those of any other congregation. Cornelia said as much: "As Fr. Whitty says, the retreats are beyond the Rules even in the way of God."[81] The Exercises were Cornelia's primary means of building the Society's greatest strength—its profoundly spiritual orientation. But they could not and did not supply for adequate structures of government. This the Society was to learn painfully before Cornelia's death.

But we need first to see how the Exercises contributed to the spiritual épanouissement for the Society. Cornelia repeated more than once a clear statement of their role for the members of the Society:

> We must always remember, and at all times, that the Spiritual Exercises of St. Ignatius form a sort of bulwark to the Rules and Constitutions. They are the great means we have to bring us to the true spirit of the Constitutions and to an inward correspondence with the light of God leading to the perfection of a true religious.[82]

We do not have to search far in Cornelia's writings to see how the Exercises were bulwark to the Constitutions and means to its true spirit. We have noted how, from the primitive days of the Society she had made them her "syllabus."[83] References to them are so numerous it would be tedious to catalog them. We give a few samples. We see that:

> The observance on the 1st Friday as a day of recollection may be always well employed by four meditations or by two if there is not time for four from Manresa:
> 1. End of Man
> 2. Sin or death
> 3. Kingdom of Christ
> 4. The Last Supper[84]

and regarding Holy Week:

> We are making our three days—the last of Holy Week—into a sort of retreat or recollection days, taking the End of Man, the Kingdom of Christ, the three classes of men, and the three degrees of humility, into our visits to the tomb and into the Passion of Christ—renewing old retreats, etc.[85]

The Spiritual Exercises and a generous sprinkling of Jesuit authors provided her with material for daily instruction in 1858:

> The 4th volume of Da Ponte [SJ] to be used for the Passion of Our Lord during Holy Mass and for preparation for Holy Communion: The order to be observed at the 9 o'clock Instruction:
>
> | | | |
> |---|---|---|
> | Jan. | Spirit of Holy Child Jesus Offices Exercises of St. Ignatius | |
> | Feb. and March | Spiritual Combat and Peace of Soul or Père Lallemant [SJ] | |
> | April | L'Ame Intérieure | |
> | May | L'Ame Eclairée | [all by Baudrand SJ] |
> | June | L'Ame Fidèle | Heart of Jesus [perhaps Gautrelet SJ or Borgo SJ] |
> | Jly. | Père Rigoleux [SJ] | |
> | Aug. | Père Lallemant [SJ] | |
> | Sept. | Bartoli's [SJ] Life of St. Ignatius | |
>
> General additions at all time: Meditations of DaPonte [SJ][86]

Cornelia's notes above for January 1858 illustrate an important association she made more than once: "the Spirit of the Holy Child Jesus" and "the Exercises." The latter lead not only to the "true spirit of the Constitutions" but also to the goal of the latter: "the spirit of the Holy Child Jesus." A later elliptical note not only repeats this association, but gives in capsule form, her inspiration for the Society.

> Every letter that is written (not on business) ought to bring forward the Spirit of the Exercises, the Holy Child—His passion which he had always in view—His Heart during his hidden life, always his sufferings "in conspectu"—Union in thought, word, deeds.[87]

In instructing her novice mistress, she wrote: "The little book of the Exercises is the groundwork of the spiritual life and the bulwark for its preservation."[88] Notice that what has been called a "bulwark" for Constitutions is also a "bulwark" for the spiritual life. The Exercises link the two and enable the Constitutions to foster the spiritual life. When Cornelia also calls the Exercises the "groundwork of the spiritual life," she seems to be saying that in the Paschal itinerary they chart she can identify her own faith vision. She saw her life as response to the call to "contemplate the Eternal Wisdom in the lowliness of His Humanity," in order, through discernment, to find her own role in that Paschal Mystery which shaped the earthly life of the Son of God. She also makes clear, throughout her spiritual teachings that she can identify with Ignatius in expressing her vision in terms of a "way" or "method" rather than as a systematic exposition. A recent commentary of one steeped in the Exercises, describes so well that method with which Cornelia identified, that we give his commentary here:

> Rather than content himself with speaking of the glories which comprise the divine action of God, or allowing himself to be carried away by facile enthusiasm, Ignatius points to the guideposts and indicates the concrete means . . . when St. Ignatius defines the Exercises he does not consider them as a doctrine or a spirituality, but rather as a "method." (Ex 1) . . . Ignatius does not use it to expound any dogma nor does he explain theological truths. These he takes for granted and weaves them into the fabric with which he intends to work . . . He limits himself to the essentials of those truths . . . which constitute the essential core of revelation, that is, the Paschal mystery . . . . the Paschal mystery is something objective that takes on life in each man according to the special graces he receives. He shares it personally according as God chooses and in keeping with the light which each individual possesses in order to contemplate this grandiose panorama.
>
> The mission of St. Ignatius consisted in mapping out a spiritual itinerary that would enable the soul to live this reality in its fullness . . . . preparing the soul so that it can share in the most vital and intense way possible in the paschal dynamism and thus live a "new life," dying together with Christ and rising together with Him. (R 6:3) . . . . The soul gradually discovers the motion of God through the movements which it experiences interiorly . . . . The soul situates itself in what we might call

the paschal orbit, at the exact point in the plan which enables it to proclaim publicly the mystery of salvation . . . . A salvific encounter between Christ and the soul takes place . . . in living contemplation, in smelling and tasting with the imagination the infinite fragrance and sweetness of the Divinity (Ex 124).[89]

The particular richness of Cornelia's own faith vision which drew others to associate with her was her profound identification with the Holy Child Jesus offering the Paschal Sacrifice in his humble, hidden life. Her own life experiences helped her to understand well the "passion" of infancy and childhood. The soundness of her vision is verified by current exegesis on the Infancy narratives. These, as a "little Gospel" provided her and her sisters, as the Evangelists intended, with an entrance to the full revelation of the four Gospels.[90] It was because through all instruments and methods—Constitutions, the Exercises, instructions—Cornelia fostered union with Christ revealed in the Gospels that her sisters loved and followed her as spiritual guide. She had described Part One of the SHCJ Constitutions to the bishop as:

> all that leads to a perfect imitation of our Lord and to the highest practice of religious perfection that is set forth in the Holy Gospels.[91]

She instructed her Novice Mistress that through the Spiritual Exercises

> our Novices will learn how deeply our life is founded on the life of our Lord, and how essentially it is built on the solid rock of His pure evangelical, Holy Catholic Doctrine.[92]

Basically it was the Exercises that kept the Gospel constantly before the Holy Child sisters; it was the scores of Ignatian "meditation" and devotional books that insured that their spiritual nourishment would be drawn chiefly from the stories and sayings of Christ's earthly life. And if we regret the fact that these "versions" of the Gospels were somewhat cluttered in contrast to the text of the Gospels themselves (to which the sisters had access), at least they kept the spirituality of the Holy Child sisters profoundly evangelical and Christocentric.[93]

Cornelia kept before her sisters the awareness that by the grace of the Risen Christ they were mysteriously incorporated into His very life. It was with faith in the awesome mystical reality which Paul could only describe as being "in Christ Jesus," that she spoke to them of the glorified Christ, present to them and revealing Himself and His way in the Gospels. Before founding the Society, in her years of suffering and sacrifice in Grand Coteau, she had been inspired to pray:

> Amidst the actions of the day, spiritual and corporal, O God help me to live—not, I, but Jesus in me; in His spirit of sacrifice and suffering, with only God in view, the reparation of His glory and the salvation of souls. For this end even suffering becomes sweet."

Again her personal notes reveal the same prayer:

Christ then is to live, no longer I—but Jesus; poor, obedient, suffering, each of these includes every virtue, each speaks humility—each charity.[94]

As founder and guide for her community she wrote a prayer to Mary for the same grace for her sisters:

> O Immaculate Mother, . . . obtain from the Dove, thy Spouse, that all who live in the Society of the Holy Child Jesus, may learn how to . . . despise all earthly desire and, finally, how to live "Not I, but Jesus in me."[95]

She spoke of incorporation into Christ in her letters and instructions:

> My dear Sisters we had our Conference on the perfection we are called to,—on the means of perfection,—recollection and mortification, on constancy seeking to be united to our Jesus—united in suffering, sacrifice and prayer—to be one with Him on the Cross—"No longer I—but Jesus Crucified."[96]

and

> Yes—pray—and practise mortification, that you may accomplish that which is wanting in the Passion of Jesus Christ—*your cooperation*.[97]

What she said in group instructions she reiterated in private spiritual direction:

> Again she said [to M.M.J. Buckle] "Work and prayer—prayer and work—neither are as they ought to be till God and not you work and pray—Let Him reign in your soul and and in every movement of your body—'Not I but Christ in me'.[98]

It was to "our Lord," "our dear Lord", "Our Saviour"—the Lord risen and present to her that Cornelia most commonly addressed her prayers and referred to in speaking and writing to her sisters. Her clear witness was to his presence in her daily life and in the life of the Society. By the time she was fifty she could write of an interior life the depths of which we can only glimpse. The citation below, given earlier in this chapter, is one of her most authentic expressions of mystical union:

> . . . that kingdom of peace within where the soul's whisperings are answered by the King himself, giving abundantly that jubilee of heart . . . not bargained for in this life of accepted suffering.[99]

Her profound union with her King and Lord rooted her in trust and love and gave her that "familiarity with God in spiritual exercises" which was such an attractive quality of her piety: "I never quarrel with Our Lord and Our Lady at the same time," she said, in counselling a young sister. "If I'm *out* with Our Lord, I stay in with Our Lady."[100]

Cornelia succeeded in giving her sisters a real appreciation and love for the Exercises, thus providing them with an instrument for spiritual maturity. They provided for the Society an authoritative spiritual frame of reference, a structure for the Society's "spiritual theology," which facilitated communication. Very extensive research on the numerous vital but very diffuse writings of Cornelia has shown that they have a real internal consistency when organized under the plan and the great themes of the Exercises. They fall readily under headings her own words suggest:

- "the great first fundamentals"
- "the will of my God whom I love"
- "the contemplation of the eternal wisdom in the lowliness of His Humanity"
- "the inward correspondence with the light of God leading to religious perfection"
- "to suffer and to die on the Cross, poor as Thou wert poor"
- "jubilee of heart . . . in this life of accepted suffering"
- "a love full of action"[101]

When her writings are published according to the frame of reference, the Exercises, — which throughout her life nourished and confirmed her own faith vision, they will give a valuable commentary on the Exercises. She understood and was faithful to their essential dynamic. But in adapting them for her own and her sisters' use, she gave a strong impress from her own life and graces. In the first place, she shifts from the Ignatian model of the battlefield to her own appropriate and highly articulated model. She found her symbols in the realities she knew best. She sets the spiritual life in the home where the wife awaits the Spouse and King and is lovingly attentive to him when he is present. Years before founding the Society she had exclaimed to her sister about her relationship with Pierce: "if you did but know him as I do!"[102] As foundress she communicated this sentiment to her sisters in her references to our Lord. She appropriated from St. Teresa her "garden" as the inmost recess of the spirit where the divine Spouse communes with his beloved.[103] Akin to the garden for Cornelia is Lapuente's recreation house of the Lord.[104] The Lord's presence and communication of his life through grace are symbolized by the foundation — "the living wells," and by the pastures where the Eucharistic Lord nourishes his beloved who "taste" and "drink" from his largesse. The mother in the home and the mistress of the establishment also provide symbols for the management of one's life according to the way of the Master.[105]

Cornelia also sets the spiritual life within the model of the school. Ignatius had found Manresa a school. Cornelia proposes the whole of life in her society as a "school of divine science" whose pupils, "contemplating the Eternal Wisdom in the lowliness of his humanity," "learn to uproot the evil inclinations of [their] corrupted heart, to cultivate therein the germ of practical mortification," to "grow as He grew."[106]

These models give Cornelia ample scope to develop richly her doctrine of the hidden life, the interior life, the discerning life, as learned in the home at Nazareth. Particularly noteworthy is her explicit teaching on the place of the Holy Spirit in the lives of religious and her fostering of devotion to the Holy Spirit.[107] Although the creating, provident, merciful

Father is fully present within her mystical horizon, she most frequently addresses her Lord as Jesus risen, and resplendent with the wounds of his passion, and as his enlightening, strengthening Spirit. She is, with her sisters, as we have noted, mysteriously "in Christ Jesus," and she communicates to them regarding the joys and demands of contemplative union.

Using the Exercises most frequently with those who have *made* an election, Cornelia teaches those who have committed themselves to the King in chastity, poverty and obedience, to renew frequently the entire oblation of themselves. Oblation to the Father with Jesus is Cornelia's habitual and most characteristic stance. From her earliest biographers down to her most recent, all who have studied her find her most frequently offering herself with her "humbled God," "walking with Him step by step" in an ever more delicate sponsal fidelity.[108]

The Spiritual Tradition from Which Cornelia Drew

The Spiritual Exercises having provided Cornelia with her "syllabus" for the Society's spirituality, she filled it out by wise and discerning use of the literature of western Christian spirituality. Because she was so much a compiler, and because she and her sisters left so many references to their spiritual literature, it has been possible to provide, as part of the Bibliography, a list of one-hundred-twelve authors she and her sisters are known to have used, with over one-hundred-sixty books by identified or anonymous authors. We have also provided a chart on the following pages showing the breadth of Cornelia's span of the literature of spirituality in the Christian West, and indicating the authors she cited. Her breadth of interest takes us from the Fathers of the Desert in the first Christian centuries, through the Middle Ages with Francis of Assisi and Gertrude, to the beginning of modern times with Ignatius of Loylola, and with many of his sons, down to the nineteenth century.

THE SPIRITUAL TRADITION FROM WHICH CORNELIA DREW

Below is an outline showing the *breadth* of Cornelia's appropriation of the literature of western Christian spirituality, demonstrating her perceptive choices of the exponents of the affective Christocentric tradition to which she was spiritually akin. In line with this tradition, she placed a heavy emphasis on Jesuit authors. Her use of some spiritual authors in *depth* is shown by an * before the name of her preferred authors. The works of the authors listed, used by her and the SHCJ, can be found under the name of the author in the special section of the Bibliography on her spiritual tradition. Notes indicate the few cases where dependence must be traced otherwise. This outline is not an exhaustive list of all authors used by Cornelia, but rather an illustration of the wide and discerning use she made of the western Christian spiritual tradition.[109]

Old and New Testaments, giving rise to a tradition elaborated and developed in:

Patristic Era: The Acts of the Martyrs c. 250[a]
The Fathers of the Desert c. 350[b]
St. Augustine of Hippo +430
Early Middle Ages: St. Bede OSB +735
High Middle Ages: St. Bernard of Clairvaux O. Cist. +1153[c]
*St. Francis of Assisi OFM +1226[d]
St. Bonaventure OFM +1274
St. Thomas Aquinas OP +1274[e]
*St. Gertrude of Helphta OSB +1302
St. Catherine of Siena OP +1380
*Thomas a Kempis +1471

Counter Reformation, 17th, 18th and 19th Centuries:

Jesuit Sources:	**All Other Sources:**
*St. Ignatius of Loyola 1556	Thomas of Jesus OSA + 1582
R. Parsons +1607	*St. Teresa of Avila +1582
C. Aquaviva +1615	Luis of Granada +1588
*A. Rodriguez +1616	*L. Scupoli +1610
St. R. Bellarmine +1621	*St. Francis de Sales +1622
*L. de La Puente +1624	Thomas of Jesus OCD +1627
*L. Lallemant +1635	John of Bonilla OFM + c. 1630
N. Lancicius +1636	
L. de LaPalma +1641	St. Jane Frances de Chantal VSM +1641
J.B. Saint-Jure +1657	
J. Surin +1665	
J. Mumford +1666	
*J. Rigoleuc +1669	
J. Nouet +1680	
*D. Bartoli +1685	
C. de la Colombière +1682[f]	
J. Medaille + 1689	
L. Vaubert + c. 1700	
D. Bouhours +1702	H.M. Boudon +1702
F. Nepveu +1708	Bp. J.B. Bossuet +1704
J. Dirckink +1716	Bp. F. Fénelon +1715
G. Patrignani +1733	
C. Judde +1735	
P. de Caussade +1751	
J. Pergmayr +1765	
A. Bellecius +1767	Bp. A. Butler +1773
*B. Baudrand +1787	A. Ligouri CSSR +1787
*C. Borgo +1794	
N. Grou +1805	Bp. J. Milner +1826
C. Plowden +1821	F.R. Chateaubriand +1848
M. Stone +1834	*Bl. T. Verzeri FSC +1852
J. Roothan +1853	R.F. Rohrbacher +1856
	*G. Ventura Theatine + 1861
F. Cumplido +1872	F. Faber Oratorian +1863
J.A. Fastre +1880	*M.S. Barat +1865
*P. Cotel +1883	N. Card. Wiseman +1865
P. Beckx +1887	C. de Montalembert +1870
M. de Doylesve +1892	M.T. Ratisbonne +1884
J. Morris +1893	J.H. Card. Newman Oratorian +1891
G. Tickell + 1893	Bp. J.C. Hedley OSB +1915

What authors did Cornelia use in depth? The founders, Ignatius of Loyola, Francis de Sales, Teresa Verzeri and Madeleine Sophie Barat have already been noted. Surprisingly, there is little evidence of Francis de Sales' influence beyond his constitutional writings. Cornelia expressed a deep spiritual kinship with the founders, Francis of Assisi and Teresa of Avila. She expressed the same with Gertrude of Helphta. She followed the practice of her time in her regular use of Thomas a Kempis. As the chart shows, her reliance upon Jesuit authors was heavy. She placed special emphasis on Lapuente (Da Ponte), Lallemant, Rigoleuc, Rodriguez, Bartoli, Borgo, Baudrand and Gautrelet. Cotel influenced her last revisions of her Constitutions. Her principle non-Jesuit authors were Ventura, who influenced her expression of the spirit of the Society, Fenelon whom she used for religious education,[110] and finally, Scupoli through his *Spiritual Combat*.

How Cornelia used her authors can be seen in two examples given below. These illustrate her ability to go to the heart of an author's teaching. We know from her spiritual notebooks that she had used Lallemant from the time of her stay in Grand Coteau which had proved so challenging and fruitful spiritually.[111] Her notations as a religious superior show that she used him in formulating instructions for her community.[112] What did she present of Lallemant? We have an indication from a paragraph she excerpted for her Customal from Lallemant's *Spiritual Doctrine*; she takes us to the heart of his message: "the two poles of all spirituality . . . are the cleansing of the heart and the direction of the Holy Spirit." Two recent theologians writing on Lallemant have both signaled these points as the core of Lallemant's teaching on the interior life.[113] We give below the passage she excerpted as an example of the perceptiveness with which she used her spiritual authorities:

> The two elements of the spiritual life are the cleansing of the heart and the direction of the Holy Spirit. These are the two poles of all spirituality. By these two ways we arrive at the perfection according to the degree of purity we have attained and in proportion to the fidelity with which we have cooperated with the movements of the Holy Spirit and followed His guidance. Our perfection *depends wholly* upon this fidelity, and we may say that the *sum* of the spiritual life consists in observing the ways and movements of God in our souls and in fortifying our will in the firm resolution of *following them,* employing to this purpose all the exercises of prayer, spiritual reading, Sacraments, and the daily practice of virtue *in our ordinary* and daily life.[114] (emphasis added by Cornelia).

A second example of how Cornelia used her authors is found in one of her notations in preparation for community instructions for the month of June. She gives a revealing commentary on how Gautrelet helped her to inculcate the Spirit of her Society:

> The Meditations of Gautrelet I have found of more practical use than any other book used—except the Spiritual Combat. His "New Month" [of the Sacred Heart] contains all the virtues to make a true Spouse of His Society

and an excellent religious. The devotions to the Heart of Jesus form the very life of our vocation.[115]

The works of Gautrelet and Lallemant fall into that field of religious literature with which Cornelia and her sisters were most preoccupied—devotional literature or the literature of spirituality properly speaking. In her library this field included the full range of ascetical and mystical manuals and treatises, and numerous collections paraphrasing Scripture in the form of meditations. We have a record of her use of at least one hundred or more books of this type, on some of which she relied heavily. Included in this category are books as restrained and formal as Ignatius' *Spiritual Exercises*, as diffuse and spontaneous as Teresa's *Life, Book of Foundations*, and *Interior Castle*; works as concrete as the *Fioretti* of St. Francis of Assisi, and as subjective and psychological as those of Lallemant and Surin; books as brief as Borgo's meditations for the feast of the Sacred Heart, and as lengthy as Lapuente's six volumes of *Meditations on the Mysteries of our Holy Faith*.[116]

A certain focus unites the books in this most numerous section of Cornelia's library, a focus which has been well defined by a contemporary spiritual theologian:

> In the light of Revelation and Doctrine, Spirituality reflects on the experiences the faithful may have of an intimate self-communication of God; it studies critically the records of such experiences and life praxis that guard, facilitate , foster and deepen the readiness for such experiences. Spirituality focuses on what experientially happens to a Christian who, already living in accordance with well understood doctrine and revelation, readies himself daily for the gratuitous elevation by God to a life of divine intimacy.[117]

In contrast to her extensive collection of the literature of spirituality were the relatively few books Cornelia had on liturgy. This seems to have reflected her times. Their number was in averse proportion to the importance liturgy held in the life of the Society of the Holy Child Jesus and in its ministry. For Cornelia the Sacraments, above all the Eucharist, were the vital, indispensable source of the Christian life. Sacramental life was supported by daily, weekly and monthly para-liturgical devotions. She braved criticism to warm and enliven English liturgical life by colorful processions with Puginesque banners; she fostered concern for inspiring celebration of the liturgy and enhanced it with her musical and artistic talents. The children of the Holy Child Schools had their full part in the liturgy. She supported those few of her sisters who wished to pray the Divine Office in private.[118] When the first stirrings of the liturgical renewal began about the time of her death, her sisters witnessed to her tradition by stocking their libraries with Dom Guéranger's series on the liturgical year.

Constitutional writings have already been discussed extensively as one of the categories of Cornelia's religious literature. Underlying all of her use of religious literature was her intent to grasp and follow the teachings of

Scripture, especially of the New Testament. She had described her Constitutions as "retaining all that leads to perfect imitation of Our Lord and to the highest practice of Christian perfection that is set forth in the Holy Gospels."[119] To the extent that Cornelia and her sisters followed the custom of their time, they did not always go to Scripture texts themselves, but used the paraphrases found in doctrinal and devotional books, especially those patterned on the Spiritual Exercises. The latter were a primary means for centering reading and praying on the Christ of the Gospels. However, Cornelia's plan for religious instruction in her schools points to a solid and comprehensive study of the Old and New Testaments.[120] A recent study of her use of Scripture found much significance in the number of Scriptural references and "echoes" which emerged from her writings.[121] These factors may indicate a more direct use of the Scripture text itself than was common among nineteenth century religious women. Certainly Cornelia recognized the power of the stories of the Bible.[122] It was also the power of the story in spiritual teachings that caused her to favor another type of religious literature—Church history and the lives of the saints.

There are two more types of religious writings with which we know Cornelia was familiar—the apologetical and polemical writings which flourished in the nineteenth century,[123] and the Catechism and Manuals and/or Compendiums of Christian Doctrine which also flourished. This last category Cornelia had relied on as a young convert, and later she continued to use them for the doctrinal formation of her young congregation. Her manuals of Christian doctrine ranged from catechisms covering the Trinity, Sacraments and four last things in question and answer form, and brief manuals on fundamental Christian duties, to compendiums as comprehensive as J. Guame's *Catechism of Perseverance*. This latter, used by Cornelia as a base for instruction, bore a title calculated to leave no doubt about the comprehensive and authoritative nature of the Church's teaching:

> *The Catechism of Perseverance, or an Historical, Dogmatical, Moral, Liturgical, Apologetical, Philosophical, and Social Exposition of Religion from the Beginning of the World down to our own days.*[124]

As a woman founder with no formal theological training, Cornelia was glad to cite known authors who corroborated her teachings which were rooted in her own experience reflected on in the light of the Gospel. This last use of books was an important one for her. She was not only a woman, but also a convert. If authorities, clerical and male, or, if women, from among the saints, could be invoked for her teaching, she was very willing to use their texts. Religious authors were a valued support for the orthodoxy she knew was hers. What was important to her was that Christ, His way, His Truth and His Life be communicated.

One has to read actual statements from the clerics who were her associates and ecclesiastical superiors to grasp the difficulties under which this woman, this convert, this humanist, this mystic labored as a spiritual teacher and director, and as an ecclesiastical superior. The temperamental Cardinal Wiseman who was so closely associated with Cornelia from 1846-50 as to have been almost a co-founder with her, became piqued with her in the early 1850's because she would not hand over to him a library of several thousand volumes to which her Society was entitled by the trust for Catholic education under which the SHCJ conducted schools at St. Leonards-on-Sea. Wiseman was spiteful enough to write in an official communique to Rome that "The danger of this tree of knowledge [the library] to the fragile daughters of Eve is not sufficiently realized." He continued his astounding "put-down" of the women he was only too eager to put to work in his schools, saying that the library was never intended by its original owner, Father Jones, "for the use of nuns, but for the use of the clergy and of the Bishop." He gave a clear idea of what he would exclude from the reading of nuns, saying that the library

> contains, it is true, may pious books, . . . the Fathers of the Church, theologians, . . . but, as well as these, . . . it embraces a good deal of profane literature, both classical and modern, a series of novels and dramatic compositions, comic operas, encyclopedias that deal with every subject, books of physiology and medicine, and also many English authors who are atheists and worse.[125]

Cornelia won her right with much suffering to keep Father Jones' library to which the Society was entitled. There has been no attempt here to survey its "profane literature" to which Wiseman objected. All of the books listed in the bibliography of "The Spiritual Tradition from Which Cornelia Drew" would satisfy Wiseman's requirements of "pious books" but many of them appeal to a greater spiritual maturity than Wiseman attributed to the "fragile daughters of Eve." The marvel, in view of her times and circumstances is that Cornelia used with maturity, and appropriately for her purposes, so much of the legacy of western Christian spirituality.

Cornelia's spiritual authors reflect her fidelity to the Church's magisterium, and her own emphasis on practical asceticism as purification for the comings of the Lord. Above all, they reflect her hope in that union with the Father to be attained through contemplation of "the Eternal Wisdom in the lowliness of his humanity.[126] As one reads her spiritual authors, one "hears" again the Word of God in the tones in which the Church of her time presented it to her, "sees" again the shape of the Christian message as it came to her—tones and shape whose weaknesses and inadequacies as well as strengths now appear in retrospect. Though its weakness affected her, it was particularly from its strength she drew. One of her biographers noted: "she had . . . a perfect genius for selecting the best from other people's ideas."[127] That "genius" lay in the depth of her interior communion with God, Father, Son, and Spirit. From inner spiritual experience she discerned the value of ideas and actions in the outer world. Thus she brought the light of the Spirit to that world, and contributed to the handing on of the Christian spiritual tradition which had nourished her.

Ministry

If there is any aspect of Cornelia's charism for service within the Church which has been acknowledged consistently, it has been the effective ministry of her Congregation, especially in education. This has been well-treated by her biographers. We have already indicated how much of her whole program of ministry she was able to inaugurate in the Society's primitive years. The twenty-five years from 1854 until her death were ones of continued expansion and consolidation of ministry, even in the midst of constitutional crises of the last decade of her life. Ministry was integral to the embodiment of Cornelia's inspiration.

The Single End

Giving glory to God through working for the perfection of others and oneself were, in Cornelia's faith-vision, united in a single process. We cannot find, even in the writings of her early married life, a time when this was not so. She had "married into" the ministry of her Episcopalian priest-husband and integrated this with her maternal and domestic duties. When, in Grand Coteau she entered a period of deep spiritual formation she purified and strengthened the single goal of her life, especially under the influence of Jesuit spiritual directors. As a wife and mother, following a serious daily spiritual program at the same time as she nursed and cared for her children, and taught school, she wrote in her spiritual journal:

> Purity of heart—Simplicity of intention, all actions, thoughts, words useless that do not tend to the glory of God and the salvation of souls.[128]

Having learned to live as a contemplative in action as wife and mother, she did much as a religious to shape an authentically apostolic congregation by her own unity of purpose, calm of soul and apostolic drive.

Readily and spontaneously as a religious, she could continually remind ecclesiastical superiors of the purpose of her Institute:

To her Ordinary:

> Do, my Lord, trust in God, and all will go on well and more than well—to His glory and the good of souls, which is the only worth of education.

and

> Do not be pained unnecessarily my Lord . . . How your Lordship can suppose that we can love God and not care for the souls around us, I have never understood.[129]

Her statements to Pontifical authorities, in her case to the Cardinal Prefect of Propaganda Fide, are no less clear:

> We know we are not worthy of any favour of His Holiness [approbation of Constitutions], but the only question is the work of God and the good of souls.

Another letter to Cardinal Barnabò of Propaganda Fide not only clearly repeats the single end, but also specifies its implementation in education:

> We earnestly pray . . . that the Holy Father would deign to confer upon us His Apostolic blessing and graciously confirm for us this Holy Rule and Institute. We feel we should then be renewed to fresh efforts and sacrifices to promote the glory of God in our especial work of the education of Youth; and that we should then possess the surest augury of success in striving to leaven the minds and hearts of the children of the higher and middle classes no less than the Poor with the true principles of the Holy Catholic Faith, and train them up in sentiments of devout and affectionate loyalty to the Holy See.[130]

With the Vicar General of the first American diocese in which the Holy Child sisters established schools, Cornelia was equally clear: "Our whole life is devoted to the service of God and the good of souls . . . and this life is one of no ordinary sacrifice, in which our own perfection and salvation are included."[131] And in the same vein she wrote to an English woman who was considering a benefaction to the Society: "Our aim is only the greater glory of God and the good of souls, and wherever we are the good of the mission (and of the Diocese) is one with our desires and interests in our work."[132]

Ceaselessly Cornelia reiterated the single end of their congregation to her sister apostles that each might fully integrate her own apostolic religious life. We have already seen this in the Constitutions and Epiphany letters. It is a constant theme in her letters and instructions:

> May He bless you and give you the loving meekness of His own heart and a readiness to sacrifice all your own will and desires for the sake of the perfection and sanctification of others. Fiat.[133]

and

> Be untiring in desires that all of his creatures may enjoy the same ineffable good that you enjoy, for this is true love and charity.[134]

And, in one of her inimitable "flashes," Cornelia noted: "Kindle your fires—do not stop to warm yourselves."[135]

Sometimes Cornelia used the terminology characteristic of her time which hinted at the reality of the Ignatian insight of the single end and yet recognized the current ecclesiastical preoccupation with the obligation of religious to strive for their own perfection and that of their neighbor. The term was "double end." Her compilations reflect this usage: e.g., in the Society's Customal: "Become perfect in those virtues which embrace the double end of our life, in preference to others which are of a more speculative character."[136] But no matter what terminology she used Cornelia knew that she and her sisters would give glory to the Father in laboring and dying with Christ. Frequently she suggested the concrete opportunities for integration, as in this letter to a sister preparing for a government examination for teacher certification:

You will have to give up any immediate preparation for the Examination but you will find that in following the strict order of study and explanation in the first class in the school that you will improve more rapidly than if you only studied for the preparation . . . . ask the Holy Child to help you; you will be prepared before you come down for Mid-summer. Ask Him not to let you forget anything you learn, and especially in History . . . . May God bless you, help you in every way.[137]

Breadth and Depth

The freedom that singleness of purpose gave to her and her Society—"to be ready to go wherever the greater service of God and the good of souls" demanded—gave their ministry breadth and depth. It is in terms of these two qualities that we shall see some of the major means and actions by which Cornelia developed an apostolic institution for the last twenty-five years of her life. The depth and solidity of the Society's apostolate was found in its excellent schools ranging from elementary Poor Schools to its Teacher Training College, and located from north to south in England, located across the Atlantic Ocean to Pennsylvania, and, in the last decade of Cornelia's life, in France. Depth was also achieved and assured by the Society's publication of its own manual for its philosophy and system of education evolved in its schools. Breadth was found in the Christian humanism which characterized the education given in these schools. Breadth was also found in the multiple responses Holy Child sisters gave to the needs of the people to whom they were sent. Work in the English "Poor Schools," the quality of which was described in the primitive years, expanded steadily. Cornelia was able to report to Bishop Grant in 1855:

> We are devoted to education in all classes you know, My Lord, but our poor schools greatly exceed in number the higher schools . . . . Your Lordship is aware that we have eight poor schools in London, and only 2 day schools in the Convent and seven [poor schools] in Preston, so that I think we cannot reproach ourselves upon this point.[138]

But the poor were helped in all their needs. A letter of the SHCJ community of Hadham (England) to Cornelia indicated the pastoral activity emanating from her convents:

> We owe so much to the wide and liberal spirit in the Service of God which you have always endeavored to inculcate by word and example, that we have been the means under God of effecting some conversions, amongst others, of a soldier who came to beg an alms who was struck by the sweetness and charity with which it was given, that after coming twice he expressed a desire to know something of a religion which taught so much charity to the poor. He was instructed, received into the Church . . . . With regard to Externs, their demands on our sympathy and charity have brought us into closer relations with the Poor of the neighbourhood than we ever thought could be.[139]

A poignant expostulation written by Cornelia at the time her Ordinary imposed his own Constitutions on the Society is a revelation of the pastoral work which was constantly being accomplished at St. Leonards-on-Sea in addition to the boarding school. It is also a revelation of the crisis in which the Society found itself in 1874—a subject to be treated of in the sections following:

> After being 25 years at work for the poor and keeping up the Poor School without any help from the Parish, visiting the poor weekly, feeding all the poor who come to the Convent winter and summer for soup, —and in hard weathers as many as fifty in number, protestants as well as Catholics, we are told we have done nothing—
>
> Giving instructions to Converts and sendng them to the Priest to be received—Keeping a lending library to attract Converts and to inform them etc., etc.
>
> Paying £2000 to build the Mission and agreeing to pay £30 per an. to the priest without the smallest claim either of conscience or legality—
>
> After building three churches in the Diocese of Southwark; we are told we have done nothing . . . .[140]

We shall see more of this expostulation later, but here it is valuable not only as an indication of the breadth of the Society's service, but also as a rare revelation of the powerful feelings one might expect in Cornelia but which were rarely expressed.

Visiting the sick and poor, conducting lending libraries, instructing women for the sacraments and converts were ministries Holy Child sisters performed in other parishes besides All Souls at St. Leonards-on-Sea.[141] Cornelia could have added considerably to the list: the training of governesses, the training within the convents of poor girls and orphans for domestic work, the running of an orphanage at Ore, England. She was careful to note that, besides their training for work the orphans were "thoroughly trained in the practical knowledge of their religion." She sponsored retreats for women, writing out careful directions that the sisters might provide the best possible atmosphere for the retreatants.[142]

Another even more personal text exists, revealing in its sheer spontaneity something more of the breadth and variety of Cornelia's apostolic plans all focused by the glory of God in sanctification of souls. It is an entirely private spiritual note (preserved by chance) in which she can remind St. Peter quite frankly of her impoverished congregation's need (in the 1850's) for "some rich and noble" novices. With the easy familiarity with God in prayer that was one of Cornelia's graces, she mingles huge material petitions—for four Teacher Training Colleges, two churches and several convents!—with profound spiritual desires—"to attract all hearts to the Sacred Heart and Our Lady." Finally, she allows, once again, one of those rare revelations of deep feeling: "All America for our own. Ah! St. Peter . . . take us to America . . ." Following this citation we shall see how some of her petitions were fulfilled:

For St. Peter's & Paul's
Poor beggars of the Holy Child

1. Election of our General.
2. Church built at St. Leonard's & two priests, one for the Mission, one for the Convent. Confraternities of S. Ht. & Immac. Heart of Mary—Bona Mors—a large & very pious Congregation to glorify God. All loving the Convent. One hundred young ladies—one hundred novices—some rich & noble—so that the garden may be the Quadrangle of the Convent & all built round—(no need to explain to St. Peter because he knows all about it).
3. Large College in London with beautiful Chapel & Services to attract all hearts to the Sacred Heart & Our Lady.
4. College Training School & Chapel in L'pool with 150 day scholars & 50 boarders. Lecturers & c.60 Students (Novices).
    House in the country at Gillmoss or Ince Blundell. Jesuit Chaplain & Confessor. Lamps always burning at the altars of the S. Ht. & Our Lady of Dolours.
5. Preston. Twenty nuns, all filled with fervent zeal for souls. Chapel built on to Convent or Church, where Clothings & Professions could take place.
6. Manchester. A college.
7. Edinburgh. A college.
8. All America for our own. Ah! St. Peter who walked on the waters take us to America, to California—Texas—Philadelphia—Baltimore—Charleston & Cincinnati.
9. House in Rome whenever it is time—
10. That we may have real solid virtue & sanctity with true obedience as the marks of our Society.[143]

This prayer, uttered some time in the mid 1850's shows Cornelia's preoccupation with what were to be central aspects of the Society's ministry for the next two decades, giving depth and solidity to its apostolate. These were the conducting of a Teacher Training College (1856-63), the publication of the *Book of the Order of Studies in Schools of the Society of the Holy Child Jesus* (1863), the fruitful development of these schools, and missionary expansion to America (1862).

The Teacher Training College

From 1856 to 1864 the Holy Child sisters with Cornelia as principal for all but the last year, conducted a highly commended Teacher Training College which contributed upward of a hundred teachers to serve English Catholics, especially in the Poor Schools. Government grants helped to support the students, many of whom were Holy Child sisters or who joined the congregation. This latter fact was undoubtedly one of the reasons why Cornelia worked perseveringly from the beginning of the Society to secure some government support for the establishment of the Training College. As one who saw excellence in education as one of the chief means by which her Society achieved its end, who saw the need of every child to grow as the Child Jesus grew, she had to provide training of Holy Child educators.

Thus the St. Leonards' Training College and her efforts to establish another in London were important in the institutionalization of her charism.[144] But their importance in this respect went well beyond their laudable utility in providing for the training of her own sisters. The Training College was an apostolic means to respond in terms of the *magis*, of the always greater glory of God by advancing education in the most fundamental way possible—training teachers. Cornelia explained this when, after five years of success at St. Leonards, she began to envision an American training college in the great untamed valley of the Mississippi River she had known in her years of married life.

After speaking of her hopes to make a foundation in Baltimore, she continued: "and then we should hope to form a training School out in the West which is a work most dear to us—embracing a much *larger good* than an ordinary Boarding School" (emphasis added).[145] And of the Teacher Training College at St. Leonards as she began it in 1856, she wrote: "We ought not to be satisfied with success only, but to aim at going a little *beyond what is strictly of obligation*. This is only in accordance with our religious life" (emphasis added).[146]

As Principal, Cornelia went beyond what was of obligation, planning the curriculum and timetables, supervising the lectures, and, above all, knowing and loving her students. And they responded, as this reminiscence of one in the last class shows:

> It was always a delight to us to see her at any time, but to have her all to ourselves at recreation was the next best thing to a private conference. She joined in our games, first with one set of girls, then with another. After a time we all gathered close round her. We wanted her to talk to us . . . She spoke most encouragingly and kindly, inquiring as to our intentions on leaving the College, and she showed a marked interest in each and all.[147]

Cornelia had recognized and rejoiced in the special graces that were granted to this work for the greater glory of God. She wrote to Bishop Grant that the students of the Training College "imbibe in a remarkable degree the Spirit of the Holy Child Jesus, giving us proofs of that special grace belonging to that sweet life-giving name."[148]

At the end of the second year of the school, Cornelia had explained her educational principles to the inspector for the Catholic Poor School Committee, one of her strong supporters:

> In the lectures generally we have worked upon the primary point rather than in diffuse matter. Method and means to carry out the end to be attained, cause and effect, the cultivation of the understanding and the judgment rather than the memory, have been the pivot upon which the Instructions have turned during the past two years. I do not mean to say that the memory has not been cultivated but simply that it has held a subservient position to the understanding and judgment.[149]

These principles, not common in schools for girls in the nineteenth century, proved effective, as reports of the Catholic Poor School Committee on the young graduates of the College showed in 1858:

> They are especially remarkable for the personal influence which they exert over the pupils, and the improved discipline which always . . . accompanies their presence in the school . . . . they exhibit a simplicity of character, a freedom from pride and self-complacency and a religious earnestness of motive and purpose . . . some whose abilities and attainments are only moderate, are quite as successful in the points referred to as others who have greater natural capacitiy. This . . . indicates . . . clearly the effects of the moral training they have received.[150]

But actually there was much suffering and humiliation for Cornelia in connection with the Training College. By the end of 1863, she and her sisters decided to withdraw it from government aid and inspection because of insuperable animosity and prejudice on the part of a government inspector for its last three years. Mr. Stokes was the friend of Emily Bowles and he came already prejudiced to his task of inspecting the Holy Child Training College. He capitalized on every weakness and especially those he found in Cornelia's administration. She spoke with real feeling to her bishop: "It seems to me a very dishonest and wicked thing of Mr. Stokes to represent me in this unfair way." But in the end, she could say: Where there are *many contradictions there much fruit is to be hoped for*.[151]

The Book of the Order of Studies

One of the "fruits of contradictions" was apparent the very year she had sorrowfully to close the Training College; this was the printing of the Society's *Book of Studies*.[152] We have already indicated its roots in the cooperative endeavor by which she trained her young sister-teachers in the decade before the Training College. For many decades after the College closed and the Society went on training pupil teachers, the *Book of Studies* helped to make Holy Child schools happy, productive centers of Christian development, and helped to make confident, effective educators. One who gave it much thought and study described it as follows:

> It shows at work an extremely active and comprehensive intelligence with a philosophical turn and a firm grasp of essentials. It roves over the whole field of education; every subject of the curriculum is analyzed, teaching methods at each grade are described, time-tables and textbooks indicated and a short philosophical introduction fixes the place of the individual subject in the curriculum as a whole. So practical was it in its recommendations, so effective in its results, that the pioneers sent to America were able to speak of introducing "our system" there. Its success in the parochial schools is proved by the results over the years in London and Preston and by the fact that the numbers in the boarding school at St. Leonards increased to over one hundred by 1870.[153]

Cornelia's Preface to the *Book of Studies* is one more expression of her original inspiration for the Society, her recognition of the growth in wisdom, age, and grace communicated to all who will contemplate the Divine Child of Nazareth. Here she stresses especially the human collaborative role that God asks of the sisters of the Holy Child Jesus in order to insure that the little ones of Christ will "grow as he grew." This preface, with its "step by step," echoes Cornelia's first constitutional expression of her original inspiration. The whole composition echoes and reechoes her own deep experience of motherhood. It was to a true spiritual motherhood she wished to bring Holy Child educators. She wrote to a sister:

> The children expect to find mothers in the Sisters, and we cannot expect them to be attached to the place unless they do find this motherly care.[154]

It was a sound kind of motherly care she inculcated in her *Book of Studies*:

> We have here before us the "Book of Studies," which is simply the same sort of guide as a chart is to the traveler. We must use it in the same way to assist us in the sweetly laborious duty of Education.
> Though we so well know that great things are achieved only by untiring labour and suffering, we sometimes forget that in training and teaching children it is absolutely necessary to walk step by step, to teach line by line, to practise virtue little by little in act after act, and only by such acts of virtue as are suited to the age and stage of moral and intellectual development of those we are guiding. Let us not want to "fly" by ourselves, lest we leave our pupils behind to be lost in the mist. Line by line and step by step in all learning and in all virtues form the whole educational system. See the little birds how they carry insect after insect to the nestlings, just so must we give moral and intellectual food to our dear pupils, that from this labour of love may flow the desired result. Let us remember the parable of the old man and his son in clearing the field of brambles. We are led into sin by seeking pleasure and avoiding pains and labours. Let us embrace the contrary and joyfully take pains and accept labour, piece by piece, week by week, and day by day, and thus make sure of our victory.[155]

The same principle that was used to educate the Training College students was applied in the *Book of Studies* to the young as well as to the older children in the schools, that is, "the cultivation of the understanding and the judgment." Nothing was to be memorized before it was explained. The "age and stage of moral and intellectual development" of each child was carefully provided for. The young children were not to sit still for too long but were to move about when they first begin to learn the alphabet preparatory to reading.

> They are now exercised in finding the letters among the cards. One child can print on the Demonstration Board, another places it in the letter-case, another points to it on the Reading Card. The object of this exercise is to excite interest, and thus keep up their attention by the love of activity, so natural to children.[156]

When the children were older the scope of the reading lessons was increased with their capacity.

> The object of reading is to enable the pupils to enter into the Spirit of the writer, to seize his ideas—to see his arrangement and division of the subject—as well as to test the force of his arguments, the justness of his feelings, and to enable them to place themselves in his position in order that they may speak his thoughts.[157]

Cornelia understood how easily children are crushed; she understood the need to foster and encourage creativity, to walk "step by step" with the developing child. Thus she cautioned concerning composition:

> It is well not to be too severe in the criticism and correction of the composition. We are not to expect a perfect composition from a child. "It is easy to correct redundancy, but a barren genius has no remedy."[158]

One of the sisters had a strong recollection:

> On original composition our Mother was insistent . . . : "We must encourage our children to bring out their original ideas, and put a check on this seeking to copy."[159]

All who have ever examined Cornelia's *Book of Studies* have been struck by the insight and power of her training in Art:

> Drawing a Christian Art, & c.—In our schools we are not to consider Drawing as an extra or superlative Art left to the choice of anyone to follow, or leave out, but, on the contrary, as a Christian Art and one of the most important branches of education, second only to the art of speaking and writing, and in some respects even beyond the languages, as it is in itself a universal Language, addressing itself to the ignorant as well as to the most refined. It is to be noted that drawing educates the eye in all perceptible beauty and order and that it leads to the cultivation of a habit of observation, the only habit by which knowledge generally can be obtained. Nor is it to be considered as an accomplishment, but as an Art, which has its philosophy as well as its poetry.[160]

This provocative statement is followed by fourteen pages of instruction in various aspects and techniques of the plastic arts from perspective through water colors and oils to ivory miniature painting.

Section after section of the *Book of Studies* reveals the reverence of its author/compiler for the developmental processes and human potential of the child. Nowhere does this show more than in the section on Religious Instruction in which "they must be made to feel the difference existing between this and other lessons, and remember that they are speaking of God." Cornelia adds, regarding the instruction of the youngest children, "They must be led to feel strongly their relation to God—that of a child toward a parent."[161] She cites Fénelon's emphasis on use of the stories of Old and New Testament quoting his observation that these "take away much of the dryness of catechisms, where the mystery is detached from facts."[162] Her opening remarks on the beginnings of Religious Instruction are among the most perceptive:

> The object of lessons in this grade is to consecrate to God the opening minds of the pupils by giving them a knowledge of His goodness; and their hearts, by leading them to love Him in such a manner as shall influence them in the formation of good habits and the practice of virtues suitable to their age. It seems, however it may be accounted for, an indubitable fact, that the deepest impressions are made on children's characters before they come to the use of the reason; hence it is of great consequence that the religious instruction imparted to their young minds should be suited to their age and capacity.
>
> The first lessons should be given to them in the form of simple tales—to excite their curiosity and arouse their imaginations—placing Almighty God before them in the light of a tender and loving Father—a kind and good Creator—who made us all and created everything—who has bestowed upon us all we possess, thus leading their young hearts to a sincere love of His Goodness. (They should not yet be taught to look upon God in the exercise of His power as a judge or a punisher of sin.)[163]

The *Book of Studies*, an auxiliary to the Society's Constitutions, is important as a further expression of Cornelia's inspiration for the Society. It shows us that her insight into the humble and hidden life of God upon earth leads to a profound Christian humanism. This humanism found embodiment in her schools.

Holy Child Schools

The *Book of Studies* has already introduced us to the character of Holy Child Schools. They were absolutely central to Cornelia's plan for giving enduring form to her inspiration for service in the Church. A sampling of the sources will fill out the picture of the ministry for which she and her sisters were specially gifted and which was an important means of manifesting the charism for the Society.

It is of the boarding schools, and especially of St. Leonards-on-Sea that we have the best records. Cornelia was one of the nineteenth century foundresses who did much to draw women to full maturity and to develop their intellectual potential. Her liberal, rather than specialized curriculum was an advance over the contemporary shallow and superficial curriculums for girls and included, not only literature, history, geography, mathematics and languages, but even an introduction to logic, philosophy, astronomy, geology, architecture and heraldry. Some of the oldest girls read the Gospel of St. John in Greek, Dante in Italian, before they left school; they had learned to appreciate the Church's liturgy. We have already seen the integral role art played in their curriculum.[164] A truly distinctive picture of Holy Child Schools (its distinctiveness attested to by the opposition Cornelia encountered) were the yearly dramatic productions—the "Holy Child Theatre"—for which Cornelia worked shoulder to shoulder with sisters and students, painting scenery, making costumes, directing. Although the first record of a successful dramatic performance dates from 1851 (Milton's *Comus*),[165] Cornelia was still, twenty years later, having to wrestle with Victorian suspicions against what had become a Holy Child tradition. Her jottings of a faculty meeting on this subject are revealing not only of the serious consideration she gave to the views of her fellow educators, but also of her insight into the real process of education in depth. Cornelia recorded: "The opinion of the Sisters is that the children are rather injured than improved by the plays." Then she cites their examples:

> G. Gills: Little Gertrude only a fairy full of vanity, and not attending to her lessons—full of air.
> Carry Rogan, assuming the naughty Lolo in "Beauty and the Beast"—who "cares for a snub"—what are words, etc., etc. Agnes Parker—full of conceit—full of her Beauty—Therese de Laubenque, hitherto so good, now full of her imagined beauty because she was made so by dress and paint.

Cornelia gives these representations fair consideration: "*If* the plays are sowing seeds of vanity are they to be upheld or put down?" she concludes with her own insights which, apparently accepted, contributed to the education of the sisters as well as the students:

> Again, if they [the plays] are properly used are not the children led to know their own vanity at a time when the correction can be applied, and when they are safe from the snares of the world? Again are they not thus prepared to meet the temptations of the world and to know how to conquer them? Let us examine the past effects on our children before we come to any positive decision—
> C.C. Mar 12th 1871[166]

We recognize here the method of moral/spiritual formation which had become reflexive for Cornelia—to seek and respond to God and his ways in life itself, to find in daily activities the opportunity to help children to grow as the Holy Child Jesus grew, keeping his Gospel image always before them. The children who were at boarding school, had plenty of picnics, outings and parties within the school. Their religious life was strengthened by Sodalities. They also shared rather fully, especially as Sodalists, in the convent life. A former student reminisced:

> With all this gaiety and fun, there was mingled an attractive spirit of piety. Our dear Lord and His Mother, our Guardian Angels and the Saints were mixed up with our daily life in a happy, loving spirit, which never made devotion tedious or distasteful. We were supplied with motives which raised our obedience to school regulations to a high plane.[167]

Letters of Cornelia assure us of the discerning character of religious formation in Holy Child Schools. She wrote concerning a Holy Child religion teacher in London:

> Sr. Laurenza . . . ought to keep her class for the Religious Examination and push up the children to the right mark . . . . Tell her to keep to strict doctrine and nail it in! I heard of a Sister teaching children something from Soeur Emmerich about the number of nails which fastened Our Lord to the cross!!! Piety will not supply for sound points of doctrine![168]

Her reassurance to the Bishop about religious practises was again revealing principles of Holy Child religious education:

> Regarding the Visit to the Blessed Sacrament the children are allowed to go down at 5 every day besides going after supper when Litanies are said, but they are not obliged to go. We generally find much more real piety when we do not exact practices that are not of obligation.[169]

If the Bishop could be reassured regarding Chapel visits, he was not so easily reassured regarding what he regarded as worldly, even sinful activities. He wrote to Cornelia in 1865:

> Confid.
> Enquire prudently as it is said that in one [sic] of your Houses (either St. L. or Harley St.) the pupils have been taught to waltz and dance the polka as well as to play whist.
> If you discover this to be true, stop it quietly.

We do not have her answer, but the bishop's follow-up must have been even more dismaying:

> . . . I do not think the Cards in Vacation time, provided the Sisters merely watch the game & restrict the Stakes, can be objectionable.
> But as the Archbishop of Dublin has made waltzing a reserved case in his Diocese & good Protestants refuse to waltz, make sure that it is not done in your Houses.
> Blessing all,
> + T. Grant[170]

We do not have the details of how Cornelia coped with this Jansenistic distortion of religion, but we know that she whose early history had been so profoundly affected by it, did not now capitulate to it in her schools. A delightful reminiscence of school recreations at St. Leonards-on-Sea tells us that:

> At recreation times, Mother Connelly would often come in, and if a child was at the piano playing a waltz, she would whisk one of the children round on the "light fantastic toe" regardless of her voluminous habit.[171]

It was, as we have said in our introduction, in utilizing all that she was for God and for men, that Cornelia realized her vocation as founder.[172] Much of her grace for founding was manifested in the schools where she was justifiably confident of her ability and that of her sisters to do great good for souls and so glorify God. Reminiscences multiply about the distinctive characteristics of Holy Child schools: "There was no spying on the part of the nuns, but we were greatly trusted, and trained to a high sense of honor—a method which completely achieved its end. There was a sense of freedom and broad-mindedness about the school that was delightful."[173]

If trust was a treasured recollection of many, so was relevance. Cornelia had written into her Constitutions from the beginning that Holy Child education should meet the wants of the age. A sister remembered that

> Rev. Mother Foundress was not only up-to-date in the Catholic world, but in advance of date. Higher studies, best books, needle-work, machines, even sculpturing statues.[174]

A characteristic letter of Cornelia's supports this appreciation of relevance:

> My dear Sisters,
> I wish you all to get Bromby's Grammar. It is the most useful logical little thing to be found, and has reached the 8th edition without ever coming to our notice. I think we must make it a point *of conscience* to get certain specimens of the new books of the day to send from house to house, at least for a time, and just now when the march of teaching is going on at such a rate. God grant we may march at an equal pace in the path of perfection . . . .[175]

"The path of perfection" for Holy Child sisters included a Christian humanism that turned outwards to serve the People of God. A lasting memory of this remained with one who had been a student of Holy Child schools:

> Rev. Mother Foundress was always anxious that the children should participate in the sorrows and joys of others outside, so, in 1870, on the 1st Sunday of Advent there was Exposition to beg a blessing on the passing of Forster's Education Bill, —prayers for peace during the Franco-Prussian War, and a public Te Deum after the Ecumenical Council defining the infallibility of the Pope, and again in 1872 on the recovery of the Prince of Wales.[176]

Although most of the illustrative material above has been drawn from St. Leonards-on-Sea, this material can be regarded as characteristic of Holy Child schools which were established not only from north to south in England, but which, by 1870 had been begun in America and in France. A recent study has done much to show the vitality of Holy Child Poor Schools in Preston in the second half of the nineteenth century. It documents the integral role the schools played in helping the working classes to achieve a better Christian and human life in the face of the dehumanizing conditions of the Industrial Revolution.[177]

The Restoration of Mayfield

There was one very courageous, imaginative enterprise by which Cornelia and her sisters met the needs of Catholics of nineteenth-century England. By their restoration of a ruin of England's medieval Catholic past at Mayfield, Sussex, and the setting up of a convent and school there in the early 1860's, they gave a new impetus to the English Catholic Revival. It was Cornelia who had the vision to see that the restoration of the "Old Palace" including a Synod Hall, of the medieval archbishops of Canterbury at Mayfield would be a tangible and even dramatic sign to English Catholics that the hopes voiced for England's "Second Spring" were being fulfilled. It was she, too, who was sufficiently skilled in art and architecture to collaborate with Edward Welby Pugin in the work of restoring the Synod Hall as an austere yet gracious Gothic Church. It was her fellow-country-woman, the American who became the wealthy Duchess of Leeds who, having taken a liking to Cornelia, bought and gave the ruin to the Society of the Holy Child Jesus on condition that they restore it. It was Holy Child sisters who ran bazaars and gave up their school vacations to beg successfully through England, France, Belgium, Holland, Spain and Canada for this symbolic restoration, who financed it.[178]

Cornelia' intuition proved sound. The Catholic press in England reported enthusiastically on the restoration to Catholic hands of a property whose history dated from St. Dunstan in the mid-tenth century, to St. Thomas a Becket in the twelfth, to Cranmer who handed it over to Henry VIII in the mid-sixteenth century. Cornelia won the eventual support of her cautious bishop who had at first opposed her plan. Cardinal Wiseman, who had in the 1850's cooled in his support of the Holy Child Sisters, renewed his support and encouragement in the last two years of his life, 1863-65. He rejoiced to see the Society he had helped to found for the Catholic Revival fulfilling one of his cherished plans—the restoration of the ancient shrines of England.[179]

The symbol of the Resurrection manifested in the restoration work was in itself a ministry of considerable breadth and depth, and even to this day the Church with its original medieval arches remains open to visitors from all parts of the world. Fittingly, this church houses the tomb of Cornelia Connelly who risked much to serve well the Catholic Revival in England. But Mayfield also represents to this day the ministry of the building of the living temples through the work of spiritual formation and education. For over one hundred years it was the site of the European novicehip of the Society of the Holy Child Jesus. It is still today the site of an excellent boarding school inculcating a Christian humanism that is both broad and deep.[180]

Mission to America

It was the Duchess of Leeds who helped Cornelia to fulfill the second part of the mission with which Gregory XVI had sent her from Rome: "From England let your efforts in the cause of education reach America."[181] In 1861, the Duchess gave the Society property in northern Pennsylvania for their first American mission. It was indeed the cause of education that the first Holy Child missionaries served with zeal and enthusiasm from the time they landed in America in August, 1862. They felt that they had a sort of trust to bring the benefits of "our system" and of an ardent Catholicity to a culture which they regarded as being in great need of improvement. They proved the solidity and depth of the educational training they had received. In their first foundation in Towanda—an isolated farm and forest region—they immediately set up a village school (equivalent of their English "poor schools") in a borrowed ex-carpenter shop. For their fee-paying school, by which they hoped to support themselves, they had to visit the scattered homes of the region to acquire pupils. By December the school was so well launched that the children performed a little play for the Vicar-General of the diocese of Philadelphia who visited this outpost of his diocese out of concern and admiration for the courage and zeal of the English sisters. He was so delighted with what he saw that he wrote urging Cornelia to make a second foundation in the U.S., which she did in Philadelphia in 1863. Bishop Wood of Philadelphia had approved of his new missionaries since he had met them at St. Leonards-on-Sea in England and had shared with them the sea-sickness of their Atlantic voyage.[182] He so approved their first missionary efforts, that, hearing that Cornelia was again to apply for approbation of the Society's Constitutions in 1864, he wrote a formal letter to Propaganda Fide urging the approbation. We cite his letter below as one more recognition on the part of the hierarchical church of Cornelia's charism of foundation now manifest, less than twenty years after founding, in the spirit and ministry of her congregation:

> The Bishop of Philadelphia having understood that the Religous Ladies of the Society of the Holy Child Jesus intend to apply to Rome for the approbation of their Institute, desires to give his earnest and cordial suffrage in favour of such approbation. He has two Communities now in his diocese, and from his own personal observation and most reliable information from others he feels convinced that their services will largely advance the interests of our Holy Religion especially in the thoroughly Catholic education of youth, both in the most humble and the most elevated classes of society. He therefore hopes that his memorial will meet with a most favourable reception from the Sacred Congregation of Propaganda, and that His Holiness will, in his unbounded and paternal affection, give his Apostolic Approbation to their Constitutions and Rules.
> Given at Philadelphia this 14th day of December, 1863,
> James Wood
> Bishop of Philadelphia[183]

The following year Father Carter bought and gave a farm in Sharon Hill just outside of Philadelphia to the Society. There they established a thriving boarding school and soon a thriving novitate, eventually an American provincialate from which, for over one hundred years, the Society expanded across the breadth of America from New York to Illinois to Wyoming to California. Thus, the American foundation of 1862 was an important manifestation of the solidity and depth of the Institute of apostolic religious women which Cornelia had been forming in England.

But the American mission manifested and developed something more. The zeal, courage, fortitude and sacrifice of the sisters who made this foundation in the midst of great physical hardships, showed that the Society was indeed graced with a universal "missionary" character to go — without counting the cost — "wherever the greater services of God and the good of souls demanded." What we have not yet noted is the extreme poverty the SHCJ suffered in Towanda. The unscrupulous land agent of the Duchess had allowed the house to which the sisters came to fall into decay. The sisters scrubbed, cleaned, painted, even attempted carpentry, but they were not roofers, and in the bitter winter of northern Pennsylvania the snow came in on them as they slept. "Our mattresses were so narrow that if anyone attempted to turn in bed she found herself on the floor, and the floor was each one's washstand. We could not have chairs in the dormitories when we had none in the community room." So reminisced these valiant missionaries who added that they became "well-used to being hungry," since their staple food, pea-soup, was only "greenish water with a pea or two at the bottom of the bowl."[184] Though their health was beginning to suffer badly, the missionaries did not make the extent of their destitution known to Cornelia, and she kept supporting them in their zeal to make this first American mission succeed.

But it was Father Carter who finally determined that the greater glory of God could be better served by insuring these valiant educators at least the necessities of life. His letter to Cornelia at the beginning of 1864, describing the convent at Towanda as "a miserable shanty, far inferior to your stables and cow-houses in England," made the founder see that she must allow the Towanda sisters to join the community of Fr. Carter's Assumption Parish in Philadelphia. The letter did something more for the Society as a whole: it witnessed to its early manifestation of a missionary zeal and fortitude which was, in ensuing decades of the nineteenth century to result in foundations among the Indians of Minnesota in the US; and in the twentieth century in enduring foundations in Nigeria and Ghana in Africa, and in Chile in South America. We give the letter as a record of the character and spirit the Society had developed by 1869:

> With regard to the sufferings and privations of the Sisters at Towanda during the last winter and a part of this, God knows it was worthy of the Christians of the first ages of the Church. They have borne them with patience and resignation, and never did I hear the least complaint, but they always carried cheerful and smiling countenances. I knew they could not be very flush of means, and for that reason I gave or sent them occasionally some little assistance. But it has only been within some weeks that I began to suspect that they were deficient in necessaries. When I inquired, I ascertained (not from the sisters) that some mornings when they got up they did not know where their breakfast would come from, and with regard to their bedding, they had to use their habits, cloaks, old pieces of carpet, etc. And even since, when I put the plain question on the subject, I got a smiling evasive answer. But I got sufficient, and this determined me what course to pursue.[185]

Years of Fruition: 1854-69 165

A recent writer, using Cornelia and her American missionaries as exemplars of her "theology of experience" reflected thus on their witness in Towanda:

> This kind of spiritual toughness and sense of priorities was not a matter of luck or 'breeding.' It was the direct result of the type of Christian formation which these young women had received from the foundress and that was a result of Cornelia Connelly's own growth in the experience of the Spirit.[186]

Notes

1. *Book of Studies*, Preface.
2. Const 1854, *Source* 4:77.
3. Buckle D 63:45-46; D 65:115; Laprimaudaye D 68:18.
4. Bellasis D 73:253, 295.
5. Rules SHCJ, art. 19. p. 13, SHCJ archives.
6. *Source* 4:81.
7. Bellasis D 73:295.
8. One Epiphany letter makes the direct reference: "like the Magi we are to offer the star of salvation by vigilance, humility and fidelity," CC 8:93; this letter was preserved only in a copy made by one of the sisters; we do not have the original. "Star of salvation" is puzzling, and it is possible the copyist left out a phrase between "offer" and "the star." The original could have read "offer *gifts, led by the star* . . . ."
9. Buckle D 66:58.
10. *Source* 4:78-80.
11. Bellasis D 73:252-53.
12. CC 19:32; Mt 2:1-23; Brown, pp. 231-32.
13. CC 8:94.
14. CC 8:93.
15. CC 8:105; Cornelia had great devotion to Gertrude and constantly recommended her works because "she was formed on the Liturgical Year of the Church." Buckle D 78:65.
16. Cornelia says "we have for our second title quoted the words of the Venerable Father Da Ponte . . ." (pp. 3-4). She was quoting from *Meditations on the Mysteries of our Holy Faith*, Together with a Treatise on Mental Prayer, trans. J. Heigham, 6 (London, 1854), 459. *Walking with God* was trans. by M.M. Ignatia Bridges, SHCJ, from the spiritual writings of J. Rigoleuc, first edited by P. Champion, Paris, 1686; M.M.I. Bridges probably translated from J. Rigoleuc, *Oeuvres Spirituelles*, nouvelle édition, Avignon, 1843. This latter edition was found in the SHCJ library, St. Leonards-on-Sea. For further insight into Cornelia's use of Da Ponte (Lapuente) and Rigoleuc, see an unpublished paper of M.U. Blake "A Study of Anticipated Eschatology in Walking with God," Rome, 1973; see also Buckle D 63:73, D 78:95; CC 27:2, 3, 5.
17. Preface to *Walking with God*, p. 4.
18. Gompertz, p. 304.
19. CC 8:87.
20. CC 8:86.
21. CC 8:88.
22. Bisgood, pp. 145-52.
23. CC 8:91-92.
24. "treasures stored up:" Mt 6:20-21; "hidden life in God . . . divine light: "Col

3:3; 1:11-13; "coat of mail," etc. Eph 6:10-17; 1 P 5:8 f; "John the Baptist," Lk 1:80, 3:19-20, 9:9; Mt 3:4, 14:3-12; cf. the whole passage with Col 1-3.
25. Ex 104; Ex 136-48.
26. CC 8:92.
27. CC 8:100.
28. CC 28:1-18; see especially p. 11.
29. CC 30:15; Cornelia included this in the prayers appended to the Const. printed in 1861: *Source* 4:100. Under this prayer, in a copy of the Const., one of Cornelia's early companions, M.M.I. Bridges, who was also her secretary, wrote "Composed by Our Mother one sleepless night. R.I.P."
30. M.A. Weinig, "The 1880 Chapter and the Customal," *Source*, 8 (1978), 101.
31. CC 54:84-88; CC 55:56-59; Teresa's Constitutions were approved and printed in Rome, 1847. The separate notebook mentioned above is found in SHCJ Archives, Rome. Entitled "Directions for the Novice Mistress," it shows that Cornelia also intended to include in her Directory her adaptation of the Visitation Novice Mistress' Rule included in her Const. of 1850 (*Source* 4:51-53), and to include excerpts from the Jesuit rules for those in formation (*Regulae Societatis Jesu*, Avignon, 1927, chaps. 2-6, nos. 9-87). She also composed her own notes for this Directory which are included in the Appendices.
32. Buckle D 64:157.
33. CC 54:85.
34. CC 23:24.
35. CC 24:4, 6.
36. CC 6:1.
37. CC 8:87; Preface to *Walking with God*. p. 4.
38. CC 45:1, 3, 19.
39. *Source* 4:26-50 gives text with sources indicated; pp. 8-9 gives commentary.
40. Text and source indications, *Source* 4:51-55.
41. Text and source indications, *Source* 4:56-57; Gautrelet (Lyon, 1846), passim; Aquaviva, "Industriae ad Curando Animae Morbos," in vol. 6 of the Avignon corpus of Jesuit Institute texts, (1829), pp. 336-464, passim. Buckle, in D 67:157, said Cornelia considered "Cure of the Sickness of the Soul" "invaluable for superiors."
42. Text and source indications, *Source* 4:57-76.
43. *Source* 4:66; Const. SJ, 719.
44. D 58:334; *Source* 4:14.
45. Abbé Craisson in his Preface to *Des communautés religieuses à voeux simples: législation canonique et civile* (Paris, 1869), pp. vi-viii.
46. CC 45:3.
47. Buckle D 78:65; *Source* 4:14.
48. D 50:172.
49. CC 7:99.
50. D 51:1-2; D 51:38.
51. D 51:35; *Source* 4:13.
52. D 56:76; CC 45:1.
53. *Regole della Compagnia di Gesù* (Rome, 1834), 42-80, 146-169, 179-83, SHCJ Archives, Rome. Cornelia added prayers to those she borrowed from this book. Buckle (D 78:61-2), recorded that Father Gallwey, SJ, gave Cornelia Decrees of the General Chapters of the Jesuits in 1855. For SHCJ texts: *Source* 4:83-88, 91-105.
54. *Source* 4:90-91, 100' D 68:51. Cornelia also included "Sentences" and other maxims of St. Ignatius: *Source* 4:88-91.
55. CC 45:14.
56. Armour, *Cornelia* p. 26.
57. Texts: *Source* 4: 107-08, 64-68; commentary, *Source* 4:14-15.

58. D 51:54-58; *Source* 4:16-17.
59. Bellasis D 75:588; the Spurious Constitutions which Pierce had presented to Propaganda Fide in 1848 remained, throughout Cornelia's life, a source of confusion to Roman Authorities, and an obstacle to the approbation of authentic SHCJ Constitutions, even though Cornelia wrote in 1848 to repudiate the former: D 5:195; D 10:81; D 50:2&-35, 51-96, passim; D 51-56, 59; Buckle D 65:87; Bellasis D 73:212, D 75:582. A copy of these Constitutions is held in SHCJ Archives, Rome.
60. References to these instructions abound: CC 24:8; CC 26:69-70, 72-74, 79-82, 92, 98; CC 29:28.
61. D 57:45.
62. J. de Charry, *Histoire des Constitutions de La Société du Sacré-Coeur*, Part I, La formation de l'institut, 1 (Rome, 1975), 142-205; Part II, Les Constitutions définitives et leur approbation par le Saint-Siège, 3 (Rome, 1979), 27-33, 140. *Règles des Dames due Sacré Coeur de Jésus*. Première partie (Paris, 1828), passim. *Source* 4:154-55. This Society was founded by St. Madeleine Sophie Barat at Amiens in 1800.
63. *Règles de S. Augustin, Constitutions et Directoire pour les Soeurs religieuses de la Visitation*. Paris, 1818.
64. *Source* 4:5-11.
65. Bl. Teresa Verzeri, with Canon G. Benaglio, founded the Institute of the Daughters of the Sacred Heart at Bergamo in 1831: *Annali dell'Istituto della Figlie del S. Cuore di Gesù*, vol. I, Rome, 1899. Excerpts from Teresa's Constitutions on Indifference, Spirit of the Institute, Novice Mistress, and Enclosure are incorporated in Cornelia's Customal, CC 54:65-75, 84-88; CC 55:7-11; excerpts from Teresa's rules for the General and Local Superiors are incorporated in the SHCJ Constitutions of 1869, *Source* 4:125-27, 129-30.
66. Buckle D 64:157.
67. MS copybook entitled "From the Rule of the Good Shepherd of Angers" in Cornelia's hand, SHCJ Archives, Rome; see also CC 45:20. For influence of Good Shepherd on SHCJ Const. 1864, see *Source* 4:107, 15, 156; see also *Règle de Saint Augustin et Constitutions pour les Religieuses de la Congrégation de Notre Dame de Charité du Bon Pasteur*, Rome, 1856; H. Pasquier, *Life of Mother Mary Euphrasia Pelletier*, 2 vols., trans. from the French, London, 1893.
68. *Règle de la Congrégation des Religieuses de Notre Dame de Sion* (Paris, 1863), in SHCJ Archives, Rome, has Cornelia's marginal markings; see *Source* 4:157-158.
69. Buckle and Bellasis speak frequently of the influence of Francis of Assisi on Cornelia and the SHCJ, e.g.: "We now have a good idea of the Franciscan and Jesuit element in Mother Connelly's soul.—That the devotion to the Holy Child and the poverty of the crib was inspired or borrowed from St. Francis and the interior life from the teaching of St. Ignatius," D 63:69, 55-6; see also Buckle D 64:52, 62, 64, 68, 70, 92, 135-41; D 65:56, 122; D 78:7, 80; Bellasis D 72:78, 107, 128, 129-30, 135; D 73:250; D 75:459. Cornelia used the *Little Flowers of St. Francis* for community reading—which edition is not known.
70. CC 13:13; D 51:39; also *Source* 4:149-50; Buckle D 63:20.
71. Buckle D 67:55; *G A*, p. 61.
72. Buckle D 63:152-54; Bellasis D 72:132.
73. *Les Constitutions des Jésuites*, avec les déclarations; Texte latin d'après l'édition de Prague [1757], traduction nouvelle, Paris, 1843. The discrediting of the Jesuits is in the lengthy Appendices, pp. 429-513. SHCJ Archives, Rome, contains a copy of this translation of the Const. SJ, with Cornelia's pencilled annotations.
74. D 50:99. The J.H. Newman Archives, Edgbaston Birmingham, England, con-

tains *Constitutiones Societatis Jesu*, 1558. Reprinted from the Original Edition, with an Appendix containing a translation and several important documents, London, 1838. The translation in this volume accords with the translation of the Jesuit constitutional texts Cornelia used in her Const. of 1850 and 1854: *Source* 4:57-59, 60-63, 66-71, 72-76, 9-10, 151.
75. *Regole della Compagnia di Gesù*, Rome, 1834, SHCJ Archives, Rome. It has not been possible to find a published translation of the Summary and Rules which accords with the text in the SHCJ Const. of 1850.
76. CC 27:2; Buckle was the latinist, D 78:61-62; the vols. of the Avignon corpus referred to above are 1 and 2, *Constitutiones* and *Regulae*, both published 1827, and 6 (1829), with Aquaviva's "Cure . . . ," pp. 336-464. The MS translations are in SHCJ Archives, Rome.
77. Buckle D 65:161-62; D 78:61-62.
78. *Source* 4:8.
79. A. Coemans, *A Commentary on the Rules of the Society of Jesus*, trans. M. Germing from first ed. in Latin, 1938 (El Paso, 1942), p. 51.
80. Summary SJ, Nos 2, 8-39 in SHCJ Const of 1850, these are numbered 1, and 6-37: *Source* 4:26-30.
81. CC 6:48.
82. CC 27:3; CC 41:17.
83. Bellasis D 73: 173.
84. CC 27:4.
85. CC 7:43.
86. CC 27:2.
87. CC 27:9.
88. CC 6:75a.
89. Iparraguire, pp. 2-8, passim.
90. Brown, 7-8, 37-38.
91. CC 13:13.
92. CC 46B:82.
93. See chart and bibliography of the Spiritual Tradition of the SHCJ.
94. CC 21:80, 82; CC 24:7.
95. From a prayer written in Cornelia's hand on the inside cover of a *Breviarum Romanum* (1861). The SHCJ Annals for 1858 record: "Mth Foundress composed this prayer for the Sisters on the fourth anniversary of the Proclamation of the Immaculate Conception," D 69:105-06.
96. CC 22:26.
97. CC 8:96.
98. Buckle D 63:67.
99. Preface to *Walking with God*, p. 4; CC 30:1.
100. Buckle D 63:66.
101. CC 8:106; CC 22:18; Const. 1854, *Source* 4:78; CC 27:3; CC 21:15; CC 30:1; CC 54:26.
102. CC 1:48; CC 30:1.
103. E.A. Peers, ed., *Complete Works of St. Teresa*, 1 (London, 1946), 65-68, 83-88, 100-02, 112-13, 127, 130, 134, 142; 2, p. 351. CC 22:2, 10-11; CC 27:2. Cornelia had great devotion to Teresa of Avila, read and taught from her works, D 68:21. References to Teresa are too numerous to catalog here. See chart of Cornelia's spiritual tradition in the section following.
104. Preface to *Walking with God*, pp. 3-5; CC 30:1; Cornelia held community recreations in the garden, Buckle D 78:30; D 61:22.
105. Const. 1854, *Source* 4:78-79. When Cornelia was discerning her vocation in 1844, prior to founding, she reflected, as her notes show on "Duties in marriage as wife, as mother, as head of the establishment, as Christian, as

member of society, as mother of the poor."
106. Const. 1854, *Source* 4:78-79; CC 30:7, 3; *Book of Studies*, Preface.
107. CC 22:2; CC 1:69; CC 2:34; CC 7:6; CC 8:8, 50, 66, 89; CC 20:49; G.A. pp. 47, 52; Buckle D 63:65.
108. Bellasis D 73:173.
109. Notes for Outline
    a. v. Fastre in Bibliography of the Spiritual Tradition.
    b. v. Hahn-Hahn, Biblio. Sp. Trad.
    c. Cornelia excerpted from Bernard in her spiritual notebook; his work has not been identified: v. CC 21:59.
    d. v. Bonaventure, Chalippe, and *The Little Flowers of St. Francis* Biblio. Sp. Trad.
    e. v. Bail, Biblio. Sp. Trad.
    f. Cornelia excerpted from C. de la Colombière in her spiritual notebook, CC 21:172-73; the source of the excerpt has not been identified.
110. The work or works of these authors which Cornelia and the SHCJ used have been listed in a separate section of the Bibliography and need not be repeated here.
111. CC 21:14; in Grand Coteau Cornelia was probably given an edition of the life and doctrine of Lallemant (compiled originally in 1694 by P. Champion, SJ) published in Paris in 1822.
112. CC 27:2.
113. F. Courel, *La vie et la doctrine spirituelle du Père Louis Lallemant de la Compagnie de Jésus*. Introduction et notes par F. Courel. Collection Christus 3 (Paris and Bruges, 1959), "Introduction," pp. 1-36, especially p. 23; also Courel, "Lallemant, Louis," *NCE* 8 (1967), 335-36; G. Bottereau "Lallemant, Louis," *DS* 9 (1976), 126-35.
114. CC 55:82-83, excerpted from an English translation of *La doctrine spirituelle du P. Louis Lallemant de la Compagnie de Jésus*, précédée de sa vie, ed. F. W. Faber, (London, 1855), p. 131; this passage is found on p. 169 of Courel's ed.
115. CC 27:2; also 27:1; F.X. Gautrelet SJ, *Nouveau mois du Sacré Coeur de Jésus*, ou les trente-trois années de la vie du divin Sauveur honorées pendant le mois de Juin (Paris, 1850). An English trans. by G. Tickell, SJ, was published in Phila. in 1859 (and probably previously in London) under the title *Month of the Sacred Heart*. *The Spiritual Combat* by L. Scupoli was published in an English trans. in Dublin, 1837.
116. Bibliography section: "The Spiritual Tradition from Which Cornelia Drew."
117. A. Van Kaam, *In Search of Spiritual Identity* (Denville, N.J., 1975), p. 8.
118. Buckle D 63:48-49; D 67:146-49, 154; D 68:50; D 69:103-04; D 76:130.
119. D 51:39.
120. *Book of Studies*, pp. 19-23.
121. M.W. Yore "The Influence of Scripture on the Spirituality of Cornelia Connelly," dissertation, Immaculate Heart College, Los Angeles, 1968.
122. *Book of Studies*, pp. 19-23.
123. Bibliography: "American Background: The Nativist Literature Available to the Connellys;" in Bibliography, The Spiritual Tradition: *Fifty Reasons Why the Roman Catholic Religion Ought to Be Preferred to All Others*, *The Grounds of the Catholic Doctrine*, and J. Milner, *The End of Religious Controversy*.
124. Trans. from the French, 8 vols. (N.Y., 1854); notes on Cornelia's use of Gaume for instruction are found in CC 26:40; CC 27:140; for other manuals and compendiums, see Bibliography of the Spiritual Tradition.

125. D 50:130.
126. Const. 1854, *Source* 4:78.
127. Letter of M.M. Gompertz to M.M. Amadeus Atchison, Sup. Gen., Feb. 2, 1932, SHCJ Archives, Mayfield, England; see also Gompertz, *The Life of Cornelia Connelly* (London, 1922), pp. 84-86.
128. CC 21:17-18; Courel, "The Single Aim of the Apostolic Institute," pp. 46-61.
129. CC 11:32 and D 36:28; CC 13:8.
130. D 51:2; D 51:43.
131. CC 9:10.
132. D 28:28.
133. CC 6:71.
134. CC 7:14.
135. CC 27:56.
136. CC 54:66; on the history of the problem of understanding and expressing the aim of apostolic congregations: Courel, "The Single Aim," pp. 46-61.
137. CC 6:89.
138. D 27:19.
139. D 23:137.
140. CC 45:12.
141. D 27:89; CC 19:25; D 23:21.
142. CC 4:7, also CC 18:6, 43; CC 13:95.
143. CC 22:28-29; D 68:25.
144. Bisgood, 154-70.
145. CC 1:118.
146. CC 5:31.
147. Cited by Gompertz, p. 329.
148. CC 11:106.
149. CC 5:36; cited also in Bisgood, p. 157.
150. D 37:75.
151. D 48:119; Bisgood, pp. 161-62.
152. *Book of the Order of Studies in Schools of the Society of the Holy Child Jesus* (St. Leonards-on-Sea, 1863).
153. Bisgood, p. 166; an excellent scholarly study of the sources and of the philosophy of the *Book of Studies* was published by M.M.E. Slater, "March of Teaching and March of Perfection," *Catholic Educational Review*, 60 (1962), 217-35.
154. CC 8:70.
155. *Book of Studies*, "Preface."
156. *Book of Studies*, p. 31, no. 3.
157. *Book of Studies*, p. 35.
158. *Book of Studies*, p. 53.
159. Bellasis, typescript of MS, vol. 2, p. 385.
160. *Book of Studies*, p. 53, no. 1.
161. *Book of Studies*, p. 21.
162. *Book of Studies*, p. 20; F. de S. de la M. Fénelon, *L'éducation des filles* (Paris, 1824).
163. *Book of Studies*, p. 19.
164. Bisgood, pp. 164-70; Gompertz, pp. 288-311; Slater, pp. 225-35; R. Flaxman, "Apostolate Studies: The Young Ladies' School at St. Leonard's," *Source*, 2 (1971), 31-44; *Source*, 6 and 7 (1977), 44-59, 51-57.
165. Gompertz, p. 298.
166. CC 35: Part 2: 19-20.
167. Gompertz, p. 306; Sodalities, and consequently the spiritual life of the students, flourished in Holy Child Schools. Cornelia and her sisters gave much

time and attention to Sodalities: CC 23:20, 46; CC 24:16; CC 25:19, 23; CC 27:9-12; the Sodality of the Children of Mary was established at St. Leonards at the end of May, 1852: D 42: 292; see also CC 55:3-4.
168. CC 7:58.
169. CC 12:92.
170. D 42:36-37.
171. Armour, *Cornelia*, p. 67.
172. Cf. Dumeige, Ignace, *DS*, col. 1302.
173. Gompertz, p. 306.
174. D 76:44.
175. CC 7:14; D 68:81-82.
176. D 77:41.
177. A. Armour, "Apostolate Studies: The Poor Schools in Preston," *Source*, 2 1971), 45-58.
178. Bisgood, pp. 234-41; Gompertz, pp. 356-59, 365-67.
179. Bisgood, pp. 238-40; Gompertz, pp. 359-63.
180. Bisgood, pp. 237, 243.
181. Cited by Gompertz, p. 337.
182. Gompertz, pp. 334-44; D 30:101-02.
183. Cited by Gompertz, pp. 348-49.
184. Cited by Gompertz, pp. 345, 350.
185. Cited by Gompertz, p. 349.
186. R. Haughton, *The Theology of Experience* (N.Y., 1972), p. 158.

Chapter 6

Years of Purification: 1869-79

As Cornelia began the last decade of her life in the Society, its convents and schools were flourishing on both sides of the Atlantic. But troubles within the Society were mounting to erupt with a force that would shape events of the decade until her death in 1879. Ecclesiastics who exercised or who claimed authority over the Society became deeply involved in its crises. By the time of her death the spiritual purification of accepted suffering had brought greater maturity to intra-Society relationships and to her Society's dealings with ecclesiastics. From 1874 onwards they had finally achieved an elected form of government. But all this was not accomplished without manifestation of the limitations and failures of Cornelia and her sisters. With these this chapter will be concerned.

But these are not the whole picture. Therefore, this Chapter will commence with a synthesis of sources which show the positive stance toward a more mature form of religious life for women that Cornelia and her sisters had been evolving to 1869, and which helped them through their decade of near-schism, 1869-70. SHCJ sources from at least 1860 onwards shows Cornelia's real insights into the practice of Poverty, Chastity and Obedience in the "lately approved active orders"[1] with which the Society was identified.

Evolution of Apostolic Poverty, Chastity, Obedience

Poverty

From 1854 onwards Roman and Episcopal authorities were concerned that Cornelia make her Constitutions more specific regarding provision for temporalities.[2] Bishop Grant, her Ordinary for nineteen years (1851-70) was especially timid regarding financial insecurity. When the Society became burdened with a large debt incurred through the disobedience of a member who subsequently left the Society, Bishop Grant refused from 1859 onwards to allow the SHCJ to make any but annual vows, and increased his pressure on Cornelia to require a dower—the latter a long-standing canonical requirement for cloistered nuns.³ In at least three successive representations to Bishop Grant after 1859, Cornelia pleaded a sound doctrine of "laboring for our support," of giving up the security of financial endowments—both of these in "imitation of our Blessed Lord." With equal soundness she pleaded the motive of apostolic zeal to set aside the dower. With her practical common sense she showed that professional training for the apostolate was on a par with a monetary endowment:

> [1860]
> I should be very glad if we had thirty to offer your Lordship for vows instead of three, and I should willingly take the responsibility of their old age though in all probability they would never reach it . . . . I wish you would remember, My Lord that we want only to labour for our support as mendicant orders beg, and above all as our Blessed Lord himself laboured for thirty years. If we sink into making a provision for our support, not imitating Our Blessed Lord, we shall not be blessed . . . . Now my Lord will you be generous and consent to our taking our own, considering it as a debt, which we shall pay back to the Community!⁴

> [1861]
> The responsibility of rejecting valuable vocations like these, some of which have been trained by us for seven years, is no trifle — Neither does it seem according to reason and justice — the dowered untrained vocations we have to begin to educate, while these have in themselves a rich dower — It is you my Lord who are not to fail in sustaining the good you have done and that you still have to do with us.⁵

> [1862]
> . . . . I wish with all my heart I had 500 to take over to America this year — Ah my Lord if you only knew the wants of a vast and new country your heart would warm with zeal for the souls of the poor children in utter ignorance of the true faith — There religious are valued for their works and they need no dower . . . . Do not fear the need of Dower my Lord, with those who can command none, while the missions are begging for Sisters we have none to spare.⁶

In the 1870's Cornelia continued to repeat her ideal of apostolic poverty to her new Ordinary who also pressed for dowers: "It seems to me, my Lord, that an educational order ought to meet its own expenses on the ordinary principle of justice. We have hitherto more than done so, solely by our own labours."⁷

Cornelia had stressed, in her expression of the Society's spirit, that their Master, Model, Spouse laboured "for thirty years in a carpenter's workshop." The recollections of her early companions on her practice of apostolic poverty coincided with that found above in her letters to bishops:

> We have already seen that the Society, founded in poverty, had struggled on, undertaking its liabilities with absolute trust in God's providence, the words of the sacred text being often quoted by our Mother 'For your Father in Heaven knoweth that you have need of all these things . . . . be not therefore solicitous' — and then with her common sense she would add 'God helps those who help themselves . . . .'⁸

The opening of the Society's American Mission gave her the opportunity to explain to the Vicar-General of Philadelphia how the Society's central government—for which pontifical support was being sought—offered the means to use gifts of property for the best apostolic "advantage of the province to which it belongs." She pointed out that "cloistered nuns" were obliged to seek an external authority for effecting the internal details of our ordinary duties and arrangements."[9] This obligation she hoped to avoid. She was to continue to struggle through the 1870's to establish apostolic ways of living the evangelical counsels.

Chastity

Cornelia knew well that chastity is primarily a matter of the spirit. She understood more than most the renunciation entailed in chastity and expressed this in her synonym for chastity—"suffering."[10] Her orientation toward contemplation and delicate sponsal fidelity leads one to believe she understood more than most the "jubilee of heart" found in "the kingdom of peace within where the soul's whisperings are answered by the king himself."[11] Her deepest teachings on chastity have been indicated earlier in this chapter. Here we wish to suggest that she made some contribution to apostolic chastity by not automatically adopting enclosure and Jansenist attitudes when she became a religious. We have seen how wholesome were her recreations with the students even after her bishop revealed his horror of the waltz, the polka and whist.[12] Although Cornelia and her sisters obeyed specific enclosure regulations as acts of obedience to particular requests of the bishops, they eschewed any pattern of these, as their bishops were to discover periodically. A few bits of correspondence on the subject of enclosure will show how the SHCJ under Cornelia tried to make a "dent" in the solid wall the bishops would erect around them. In the summer of 1856, Cornelia, having given her sisters a day at Fairlight, a seaside resort near St. Leonards-on-Sea, received the following from Bishop Grant:

> I am glad you have had your day at Fairlight, as I could not have agreed to it if you had asked for it. Nuns are never allowed to take amusement beyond their own walls, and altho' they may leave them to travel to other houses, for all other purposes they are always on the footing of enclosed Nuns. I am sorry that I cannot hold out any hope that the Church will relax her rules in this particular.[13]

Even if Fairlight had been declared out of the bounds of the enclosure, Holy Child sisters did not assume this about their own St. Leonards seashore, and continued to enjoy it, innocently communicating their enjoyment to their Bishop. On September 9, he imposed a sort of cloister on the community, invoking not only the authority of the Church, but of God's punishments!:

> I was so much delighted with everything yesterday that I had not the heart to mention my regret that the prohibition against leaving the Convent had been ineffectual, and that in consequence the newspapers had

described that one of the community had narrowly escaped drowning. In my time in Rome a Convent Infirmary fell in and several Sisters who were there against rule, were crushed under the ruins. It is quite certain that the Sisters ought not to go out of the Enclosure except when they travel from one house to another, or when one or two are required to accompany the children on their walk. But even those are not to go into the water or do more than is necessary. The rules of the Church respecting Religious are very clear and positive, and if they are not observed, it is necessary to enforce them by severe sanctions. Your Sisters are such good and faithful children of the Church that I am quite sure you need not do more than tell them that they are not to go beyond their own Garden, to secure full and complete obedience to your words. They have a good willing spirit, and I am quite confident that they give you many consolations . . . .[14]

On another occasion Cornelia spontaneously sent the two Cusack sisters who were both novices, to the bedside of their mortally ill father in Liverpool. She had a hard time convincing Bishop Grant that they need not lengthen the time of their noviceship because of their short stay outside its walls (not in their home but in a *convent!*) to give consolation to their suffering father.[15]

Despite constant episcopal interventions regarding enclosure it did not occur to Holy Child sisters, for the first twenty-eight years to lock their noviceship doors. When this was imposed by Bishop Danell's rule in 1874, the sisters thought this "contrary to our spirit." But Cornelia's answer was: "it is in accordance with the spirit and wish of the Church, and that's enough."[16]

One could multiply the ways in which SHCJ, as apostolic religious committed to "meet the wants of the age," to give an "education best adapted for each particular state in life,"[17] continued to try to develop a life-style reflective of a wholesome attitude to the world they were called to serve. They continued to make it clear that they accepted, from a motive of obedience, the enclosure their bishops imposed. They expressed no personal convictions as to its value. Near the end of her life, Cornelia found that even a "pony trap"—which, for Bishop Danell was an "open carriage"—violated enclosure. Her chaste spirit was magnanimous enough to let the pony trap go. She wrote to Bishop Danell:

> I heard indirectly last week that your Lordship did not like our Sisters going out in the pony trap, which we have used occasionally during the last two years. If this is correct we shall part with it immediately, —yes or no will be sufficient.[18]

The Bishop responded:

> I am pleased with your promised obedience to my strong wish that it should not be used for the future.[19]

Obedience

Obedience for Cornelia meant "doing the will of God whom I love"[20] — This was *the* pursuit of her life. More and more she came to see that it was a discerning obedience offered by mature persons who had grown up in Christ which best built up the Church for the glory of God. As she gained experience governing the community she had been inspired to found, she struggled perseveringly to make the lines of authority and obedience appropriate to the nature and end of her institute.

She had genuine faith in and love for the "One, Apostolic, Holy Roman Catholic Church." Her own constitutional statement of the Society's mission enjoined her sisters to "vividly unfold in the course of our education the beauty of the morality, charity and truth" of that beloved Church.[21] That this was no empty rhetoric was witnessed by her unfailing loyalty to the church whose hierarchy sometimes tried her sorely, even as she challenged them.[22] She had an ardent affection for the Church, writing in the midst of great sufferings: "There is but one principle to act upon—the Vicar of Christ and His flock!"; and: ". . . our cause, which is the cause of God and His Church."[23] Holy Child sisters became accustomed to the frequent exhortation in her letters: "Pray much, my dear ones, for the Church of Christ and for our Holy Father the Pope and the Cardinals."[24] To a woman contemplating conversion in 1872 she wrote with feeling of "God's beautiful Church, the One, Holy Apostolic and true Church," of "Treasures of Grace, of Faith and Hope," of "Love unrealized until sealed by the Sacraments." She exclaimed: "I have been a Catholic thirty-seven years . . . . Oh! do not resist the interior voice speaking to your heart. It is the voice of the Holy Spirit."[25]

The Spiritual Exercises had helped her to respond fully to the Paschal Mystery in her life, to respond with a love that shows itself in deeds. She had written in her spiritual notebook: "The end, the glory of God and the salvation of souls; the means, obedience."[26] The conflicting demands of ecclesiastics—conflicting among themselves, and conflicting with her inspiration from the Spirit—challenged her to find the path of a truly mature obedience. In humility, even to the Cross, she found and pointed the path to her sisters:

> I am quite certain that the new Rule [Constitutions of Bishop Danell] *cannot work* and as convinced that it will *not* be approved without change. It is for us to point out our objections and to send them to Rome, but we ought to be very sure of what we are about. And to be very submissive and docile to the decisions of Rome. The humble shall be exalted. If it were God's Will to keep us waiting thirty years longer we must still say God's Will is sweeter even than the longed-for approval of the Holy See . . . . Be full of confidence in God and in humble resignation to these crosses while we must do all that depends upon us for our safety.[27]

She would die in "humble resignation." Her sisters would practice it for eight more years until the longed-for approval of their *own* Constitutions was given. She reiterated her teaching as her death grew closer. Two years before she died, she gave a parting instruction to the Holy Child community in Neuilly, France:

> First—*Obedience.* All have to obey—the Bishop—the Pope—all superiors. There is no such thing as freedom from the yoke of authority and the self-will principle must be abolished in our conduct and in our hearts. Nothing must be done *because it is our wish to do it*, but simply because it is the will of God.[28]

Cornelia is instructing here on the process of discernment—realism regarding external situations and asceticism regarding internal motivation. That she is not counselling subservience can be seen in the forthright responses she gave to demands for ecclesiastical obedience: She will obey in what is not sinful. She makes equally clear the spiritual values, the principles of justice, the needs she sees. She informs those who command of the responsibilities. The following incident and letter will illustrate these points:

Through the 1850's and 1860's her Society had been badgered by problems in which Roman and Episcopal authorities involved themselves. Cornelia had grounded her obedience in her faith in God as the source of all authority. A member of the parish of All Souls at St. Leonards-on-Sea had tried to reclaim much of the property which the SHCJ were rightfully using for Catholic education according to the trust established by Father Jones' heir. The parishioner, Dr. Duke, had falsely misrepresented the parish claims to Propaganda Fide, and for a while in 1864, the Holy Child sisters were again threatened with the loss of St. Leonards—the convent and school Our Lady of Sorrows had saved for them in 1851. Although the owner of the St. Leonards' Trust (Father Jones' heir), had no intention of allowing a misinformed Propaganda Fide to evict Holy Child educators—nor did he—Cornelia reached a point in 1864, just before Propaganda saw the truth, when she felt she must enunciate the Society's position:

> It would be impossible to gain this end (God's greater glory) save in the usual protection of our Ecclesiastical Superiors and also in their satisfaction, and no temporal interest whatever could compensate for any want of peace and union with authority which we shall ever hold sacred. Neither could the possession were it hundredfold beyond the value of this ever repay the suffering of persecution borne only for Christ's dear sake. Pray let me assure you, dear Col. Towneley, that unless our affairs are settled by the S.C. (Sacred Congregation) with you, we shall hail the day that decides our removal from here. Though I must at the same time add that we should expect to be fully remunerated on the sale of the property for the large sums we have expended on the buildings, etc. etc.
>
> Either we must labor in peace for the extension of the Catholic Truth and for the service of God in our vocation, or we must cease our work totally. Satan is strong in his persecutions but our Blessed Lord is still stronger and will show His will and His way to those who seek His glory beyond all temporal property.[29]

Underlying all the other demands on her to discern the path of obedience was the anomaly we have described of her striving to realize her Society's mission to be pontifical in status, while governing for thirty-three years as general under diocesan authority. It would seem that she kept alive a viable doctrine of apostolic obedience through the equilibrium to which Ignatius' doctrine of creatures and of the Two Standards had brought her.[30] She held tenaciously to her ultimate goal—central government of the SHCJ responsible directly to Rome—but she gave and taught loyal obedience to the bishops who were in God's providence, the "creatures" expressing His will and giving the Church's sanction to the Society's existence. What Cornelia sought was "freedom of action" for internal unity and apostolic effectiveness in a Society which ministered in several dioceses. She took the opportunity of a new start in America to clarify the Society's vision of government for apostolic vitality:

> No Educational Order could ever flourish to any extent in unity of purpose and in effective work unless a certain bond of union exists between the branches and the parent stem nor could there be the freedom of action necessary for an Educational order were we tied down to the restrictions of cloistered nuns and obliged to seek . . . an external authority for effecting the internal details of our ordinary duties and arrangements.[31]

Cornelia was to make much the same point, but extended it to all religious orders eleven years later when the Ordinary of the diocese of Southwark declared himself Bishop-Superior of the Institute [of the Holy Child Jesus] and imposed his own rule. She wrote:

> The Government of the Order as proposed interferes with the autonomy necessary for the life of any religious order, which seems as necessary as the heart is to the life of the human body, and we beg for a Cardinal Protector.[32]

But this is moving ahead to the ultimate crises of the Society and meanwhile we have a statement from 1870 in which she continued to elaborate on the needs of apostolic congregations. In 1870, when she thought that the Society would very soon receive pontifical status, she wrote rather anxiously to her Ordinary fearing that a clause concerning the jurisdiction of the bishop had been introduced into the SHCJ Constitutions which belonged, she thought "to the old cloistered orders, and not binding upon any of the lately approved active Orders." She explained that her sisters understood "Our obedience to the Bishop as our Superior and lawful prelate is of obligation by the fourth commandment of God." But she feared that something further might be made "binding upon uncloistered religious," and she did not see the need "of bringing each poor Sister under the Canons which were made for cloistered simply contemplative nuns." She emphasized the importance of the issue: "Our vows are made according to the Constitutions . . . . We should never understand our position or even the force of the Constitutions . . . ."[33] Evidence from

Bishop Grant's reply seems to show that the clause which concerned Cornelia applied only to the ordinary jurisdiction of the Bishop. Her concern was valuable for us since it evoked a further elaboration of her views on the lines of authority and obedience for apostolic religious.

One of the enduring fruits that has come from Cornelia's long years of relating to her Ordinary as ecclesiastical superior is her demonstration of an open, adult, obediential relationship. She carried on a continuous, almost weekly, sometimes almost daily, friendly correspondence with one whom she knew as a collaborator in the work of God, whom she also called a "father" in Christ.[34] To the delight of his heart she saw that he was truly father to her community and students at St. Leonards-on-Sea. With these he spent some of his happiest hours. Together he and Cornelia struggled through many crises. In 1862 when she was beleaguered by the persecutors of both the St. Leonard's parishioners and the unfriendly training College inspector, she share her feelings with him: "I think it is my turn to cry out with President Lincoln: 'One war at a time!' "[35] It was at this time and in connection with the St. Leonard's parish dispute that the Bishop's fearfulness overcame him and he began to capitulate to the parishioners though he knew them to be wrong. He wrote that he would allow no more clothings or professions at St. Leonards. Cornelia's answer pointed to new directions for women in the Church!

> I took you letter recd by the 3 o'cl post . . . and read it to Our Lady of Sorrows asking her in her own sweet meekness to listen to it — and the interior answer I got was 'burn the letter and tell Bp to forget what he wrote & to come to tell you what more you can do than you have done.' I have burnt it, my Lord, & now will you come down & tell me what more I can do than I have done?[36]

But she had had earlier an even more difficult problem to deal with when Bishop Grant commanded the Society to pay the full amount the Bowles family demanded on a debt contracted by Sr. Emily Bowles without Cornelia's knowledge or consent. Emily had left the Society and the Bishop knew the Society had no legal responsibility. But he feared scandal, and pressed Cornelia to agree to payments beyond the Society's financial means. She responded openly on September 27, 1857:

> . . . Your charity for all parties, my Lord, would induce to every sacrifice, but I would have to effect some superhuman means to bring forth satisfaction for these claims. We have not the means to meet your wishes nor could we honestly promise to raise them.[37]

Still the fearful Bishop pressed and Cornelia responded on October 13 with a firmness and courage that must at least have summoned the Bishop to his own sense of responsibility:

> My Lord Bishop (Grant)
> . . . I have already represented the absolute impossibility on our part to meet the demand. You my Lord are our Superior and I am ready to *se-*

cond the responsibility you take to the very utmost of my power. Will you remember this my Lord, but at the same time I again repeat *that it is impossible for us to meet your last proposal.*[38]

The Society bore the heavy burden of the Bowles debt for many years, but gained experience both with regard to their internal affairs and their dealings with external authorities.

How much did Holy Child sisters imbibe of the forthright womanliness of their founder who had exhorted them to "despise the pettiness of women," who had exhorted her sister to "act like a woman with a head and a heart."[39]. We have not, of course, writings from numerous sisters by which to judge. But one letter of the superior of the mission to America, written to Cornelia a few days after the arrival in the U.S., is revealing of the maturity Cornelia tried to inculcate in women whose Constitution called them to "go wherever the greater service of God . . . may be looked for."[40] Beneath the snobbishness which breaks through in this utterly spontaneous letter, there *is* demonstrated an awareness of the responsibility of the religious woman to be her own person, to be a woman, not a child, in her dealings with ecclesiastics:

> The community we are now staying with is the third we have been introduced to since our arrival in America, oh Reverend Mother, if anyone wants an increase of devotion and love to our Society let them see other religious as we have done, it seems to me I could never have been a religious if *our* Society had not been instituted — the *extraordinary want* of education, of *mind*, of independence of *priestly* government, o dreadful! a Bishop or priest lord and master of the house!! — we can never be sufficiently grateful for our *training*. Of course we must not judge but in some cases the apparent want of religious spirit is to us startling, and in others the over-subdued looks would make me wretched.[41]

Another report of one of the American missionaries on the relationship of the SHCJ with their first American bishop indicated his approval of their attitudes and revealed further the kind of formation Cornelia had given them:

> . . . he sees we have been trained to *work for ourselves and help* ourselves without depending upon the bishops and priests to do all for us . . . . He said he saw . . . the first afternoon he spoke to us in Philadelphia that we would do *our own work*. His definition of a *lady* — "One who will put her hand to *everything*. We told him you would never let us say "can't," or if we did, that would be the very reason that would make you tell us to try.[42]

The interchange of letters between Cornelia and her American missionaries, and many, many interchanges with her sisters throughout England and in France show numerous warm and authentic friendships and a real practice of subsidiarity on her part.[43] In the ensuing pages, where we shall see a break-down in communications between the founder and a number of her sisters with resultant problems, we shall have to ask what more is needed to create an enduring corporate endeavor beyond the considerable endowments for spiritual direction and friendship, for administration, and for ministry of a generous dedicated founder.

Purification

By the end of the 1860's the spiritual and apostolic vitality of the Society of the Holy Child Jesus was manifest. By then it had three foundations in America, and Cornelia was to initiate steps toward a foundation in France in 1869. In that year Cornelia also went to Rome to work with Consultors of Propaganda Fide so as to obtain pontifical approbation of her Constitutions. It is with this initiative on her part and its far-reaching consequences that this section of Chapter VI will be concerned.

By 1869 the urgent need to obtain pontifical status was very evident to Cornelia and to many sisters who were experiencing the effects of the anomaly under which they labored: They ministered in four dioceses on both sides of the Atlantic, yet were subject to the Bishop of Southwark, England. Not only had his exercise of authority proven to be problematic but they were aware of the tendency of nineteenth-century bishops to assume that women religious were automatically under their control.[44] Cornelia enunciated the problem clearly to an SHCJ superior in America: "You know quite well that Bishops prefer diocesan orders where their power is without appeal."[45]

The Spirit was stirring the Church in the nineteenth century with an inspiration toward non-cloistered apostolic congregations for women with a missionary thrust that went beyond the bounds of local dioceses. Many women religious struggled to respond to this inspiration but Bishops were slow to allow new developments in spirituality, lifestyles and structures, while the same bishops welcomed the new effective ministries with which the Spirit was gifting the Church. By 1869 Cornelia was experiencng the full effect of the pain of giving birth to a new gift for the Church. The complexities of the Society's constitutional problems, including those to which Pierce had contributed, caused her to fear for the stability of the Institute. Besides this, Cornelia now felt the strain of the prolongation of her "personal government" — that is, of her position as appointed General only (since 1847 by Wiseman) without the assistance of General Chapters. She summarized this situation when she looked back on it in 1872:

> The *Spirit* of the Government had been carried out without ever having the power to call a General Chapter or of Electing a General and Assistants —
> An Election was repeatedly proposed without being accepted by our Bishop, Dr. Grant — the Bishop of Southwark.
> [The second general of the Society, Mother Angelica Croft, later inserted here: "If the Mother General did not force it — it was because the Bishop, Dr. Grant, did not correspond."][46]

In another account Cornelia mentioned again, "not having had the Elections or the presiding of the Bishop over a Chapter. This was only in the power of the Bishop and not in our power."[47]

It is important, in the light of ensuing events, to remember that Cornelia went to Rome with all her energies focused, as only she could focus ("what one is called to do, she is called to do with all her might,")[48] on the obtaining of pontifical approbation to preserve her Society.

She made her own succinct record of that journey to Rome, the revision of the Constitutions it entailed, and their submission to the Society:

> In 1869 the Superior and two of the elder Sisters went to Rome for the purpose of revising the Rule and they presented letters to Cardinal Barnabò [Prefect of Propaganda Fide] from their Bishop, Rt. Rev. Dr. Grant, Bishop of Southwark, Rt. Rev. Dr. Manning—now Cardinal Archbishop of Westminster—the Rt. Rev. Dr. Goss, Bishop of Liverpool and from the Rt. Rev. Dr. Wood, Bishop of Philadelphia.
> The revision of the Rule was made under the Rev. Father Anselmo Knapen [OFM] Consultor of Propaganda, and printed in the Propaganda Press. By order of the Rt. Rev. Dr. Grant, the Rule was again printed in English to be sent to all the Houses in England and America together with a translation of Cardinal Barnabò's letter. This was done [in March, 1870], and the Cardinal's letter read to all the Sisters, and the Rules were also read and left to them to make any remarks they might wish to make.[49]

Cornelia and her two companions had worked in Rome through the summer of 1869 on extensive changes Fr. Knapen demanded in the Constitutions. One would not say today, from perusal of the text, that he altered their most fundamental meaning and spirit. He developed a great esteem for Cornelia as a person and as founder and encouraged her to make the prescribed changes as much as possible herself.[50] He allowed her First Chapter to remain *in toto*. But he put the Jesuit Summary, Common Rules and Rules of Modesty, texts to which the SHCJ had given much meaning, at the very end of the book under the heading "Common Rules." He required, of course, that the full structure of government be spelled out for all the sisters to see and approve, something they were not used to seeing in their previous truncated Constitutions. And, sadly, he insisted on real distinctions to be made between House and Choir sisters, allowing only annual vows for the former, prohibiting them from voting, and requiring separate recreations.[51] Some House Sisters were among Cornelia's earliest and loyal companions. We have seen this in the reminiscence of Sr. Aloysia Walker. We have seen that, for many years there was little distinction in rank in the Society. Sisters were deeply hurt by the changes for which they held Cornelia responsible.[52]

Cornelia alone perhaps knew how urgent it was by 1870 to have approbation of SHCJ Constitutions and Institute. Only Cornelia and her two SHCJ companions had had the experience of working through the changes demanded, especially to remedy the defects in the structure of government. Only Cornelia and her two companions had had the inspiration (if also the rigors) of working in Rome with Propaganda Fide and renewing their sense of mission within the universal Church. A few months after her return from Rome, she went away again on the doctor's orders to southern France. It was from there she *sent* the revised Constitutions with the Prefect of Propaganda's accompanying letter, to all the SHCJ communities, requesting their signatures. Weary, ill and aging—she was sixty-one in January, 1870—Cornelia had lost perspective on the problems her sisters had regarding the Constitutions and her authority. This was especially true of the sisters in Preston, in the north of England. Two other sisters who were in no way alienated from her recorded her miscalculation of attitudes and the consequences of the circulation of the revised Constitutions:

> The Sisters were unexpectedly called upon to hear, (and in some cases from those who showed little prudence and less tact) that they were to accept changes in the Rule—that Rule which had become their mainstay, and for which they had been trained by their mother to make any sacrifice, and to remain faithful to death.

The record continued:

> Reverend Mother was much distressed by the dissatisfaction which this Rule caused almost universally among the Sisters. She had not calculated on the effect it would produce . . . . There is no doubt but that Reverend Mother Foundress made, unconsciously, a very great mistake in transacting this important business through different local Superiors. Had she delayed until her return to England [from France] and read it publicly in each House, her personal influence would have upheld the 'Cor unum et anima una,' but the mere perusal of it individually had no such effect. Though all signed, all were not united . . . . Letters of disapproval and protests arrived from all sides.[53]

M.M.F. Bellasis, who gave us the major part of this record, had an important insight on the nature of the crisis that was rising. She saw that a Society which had been governed for so long—twenty-four years—by personal government, that is, largely by the founder's personal influence, was not going to respond to a serious problem without that support. Gradually, through the Spring of 1870, Cornelia, who had returned to England, brought many to see that the need for approbation was paramount, and that she herself had sacrificed some of her own preferences in revising the Constitutions, especially that of general-for-life. But even with these gains, particularly with the communities in the north of England, crisis was by no means averted. Truly "she had not calculated on the effect" she would produce by asking the three SHCJ communities in Preston to send their signatures of consent to the revised Constitutions. Her own record of what transpired was as follows: ". . . all the Choir Sisters . . . were told that they were perfectly free to make their observations on the revised Constitutions, but some three or four in Preston signed their names to them and at the same time *secretly* reserved their dissatisfaction . . ." In further notes, Cornelia specified: "The Preston Cabal . . . those who made their objections to

Rome, or their complaints;" and finally she spoke of the one who "nearly created a schism in Preston."[54]

In fact the three superiors of the SHCJ communities in Preston under the leadership of one, Mother Mary Lucy Woolley, had sent substantial representations to Cardinal Barnabò, Prefect of Propaganda Fide, against the mode of government of their founder-general; at the same time they had sent to her signatures of approval of the revised Constitutions. For this course of action they had the advice of more than one Jesuit and more than one diocesan priest.[55] Cornelia was informed privately by a member of a Preston community about the representations, in time to prevent her from sending the signatures of those who had represented their difficulties to Rome.[56] She was deeply wounded by what she regarded as the perfidy of the false signatures. Meanwhile, Mother Christina Cusack, one of the Preston Superiors, was writing to the Cardinal Prefect of Propaganda Fide: "my confidence in our Mother General is shaken."[57] The Society was indeed nearly in schism; there was a break-down in communication between the founder-superior and her sisters; with a few in Preston it was nearly complete. There were faults and mistakes on both sides of the break-down—sources make this clear.

The discord, continuing well into the 1870's, generated enough correspondence now found in the archives of the Society, of the dioceses of Southwark and Liverpool, England; of Philadelphia, USA; and of Propaganda Fide, Rome, to produce a separate study.[58] Here we can only touch upon the facets which show how Cornelia with her human limitations, struggled to fulfill her responsibility to form an enduring congregation, and how her sisters struggled to obtain a form of government which was viable for them. The discord reminds us that supernatural gifts, both for foundation and for participation in the spirit of a Society, did not and do not confer impeccability on the founder or the members of her religious family.

Many details are given in the biographies of Cornelia showing the real steadfastness, dignity, forgiveness, and magnanimity with which she acted throughout the 1870's. More could be given from the sources to show many excellent examples of her practice of subsidiarity throughout her whole life in the Society. And more could be added to the biographical accounts of her practice of spiritual government, that is, missioning, and providing in other ways, for individual sisters in terms of her intimate knowledge of their capabilities, spiritual aspirations and spiritual difficulties.[59] But more could also be added to show the very real distress and concern of the many sisters for whom, by 1870, she was no longer a personal spiritual guide, and who found that there were no effective constitutional means for communicating in an objective forum, their very real concerns about fundamental constitutional defects of the Society to which they had committed themselves for life.[60] Their concerns were shared by at least one Jesuit to whom Cornelia had sent them for help, and by several other ecclesiastics, who, it must be said, involved themselves rather avidly in the SHCJ schism.⁶¹

A number of SHCJ (apparently more than Cornelia realized), no longer, in 1870, shared her absolute commitment to obtain pontifical status for the Society. As that year opened she had every hope that this approbation would finally be given for the latest revision of the Society's Constitutions. She did not realize how much these Constitutions seemed to the Preston sisters to be one more product of her arbitrary government. At first she took in stride their delay in signing approval of the Constitutions: "You must, however, make your own remarks," [on the election of the General], she wrote, adding, "You must think and act for yourselves." But as the year wore on, she grew more anxious, and wrote: "I hope this will give you a clear light upon the subject and that I shall receive your signatures in good faith by return of post."⁶² Finally, however, she seems to have lost her equilibrium. Her charismatic ardor to fulfill her mission as founder by obtaining pontifical approval and the much-needed security of Constitutions, made her lose sight, at least momentarily, of her obligation as Superior-General to receive and respect representations made "in conscience." It was a costly fault. A copy of what she wrote to at least one of the Superiors in Preston was sent by the latter to the Cardinal Prefect of Propaganda Fide where it can be read today:

> Will you therefore, have the rules signed without delay, that all may be forwarded to Rome immediately . . . . The vows stand just as they were made, and under the same conditions as received, until the last Vows. Therefore let there be no further discussion . . . If anyone should turn up whose opinionatedness or obstinacy (or soi-disant conscience) will not allow them to sign, leave them to themselves, and to do as they please, sign or not. They are perfectly free, and it will be an excellent test of how much they prefer their own will and opinions to union with the Society.

Mother Lucy Woolley, the Superior who sent the copy of this letter to Cardinal Barnabò, added: "These words were regarded by the Religious as coercion, and after taking advice on the subject, they signed the rules to prevent further troubles. At the same time we wrote to your Eminence by the advice of Monsignor Capel."⁶³

Another Preston Superior, who also cited Cornelia's references to "self-opinionatedness, or obstinacy or soi-distant consciences," represented to Cardinal Barnabò:

> This put many sisters into a dilemma. They felt that if they refused to sign they would be looked upon as obnoxious persons that their lives would be rendered very miserable, and that, in consequence they might be dismissed from the Institute.
>
> Considering the unlimited authority of Mrs. Connelly, and the arbitrary and unconstitutional manner in which, from time to time, she uses it, the Sisters are afraid to oppose her. Besides this, many feel there is a want of probity and straightforwardness in her intercourse with them.⁶⁴

These are serious charges; they can be countered by assertions not only of Cornelia, but also of bishops and priests (who, as has been said, involved themselves in the conflict), that Mother Lucy Woolley was herself a source of conflict, though not lacking in considerable apostolic and administrative gifts.[65] We would be caught entirely between two unwitting protagonists if there had not come to light recently a confidential representation of the SHCJ Superior at Blackpool who had not been associated with what Cornelia called the "Preston Cabal", and was trusted by the sisters in general, including the founder. Mother Gertrude Day, as will be seen below, shared many of the concerns of the Preston sisters. Her representation will allow us to see that, however lacking the latter had been in their deception of Cornelia, they were perceptive regarding abuses in Society government and the urgent need for remedies felt by many sisters.[66]

But to see the context of Mother Gertrude's representation and to place it chronologically, we must first trace events in the Society from the year 1870, when division and alienation became open, to 1874 when, through Cornelia's persistent efforts the Society held its first General Chapter.

By 1871, with the revised Constitutions of 1869 in abeyance—this time because of the *SHCJ* objections—Cornelia knew that the Society could wait no longer for a Chapter. She petitioned the new Ordinary, Bishop Danell, consecrated in 1871, for a General Chapter. Danell allowed Cornelia, both in 1872 and 1873 to send out circulars for voting from all the convents, only to cancel the Chapter peremptorily, to her great humiliation and anguish. With her characteristic ability to look on the positive side of things, she wrote to him in 1872: "I can truly say, my Lord, that if there were not almost unlimited elasticity and simplicity of spirit amongst us, I should look upon the faithfully loving confidence proved in our dear Community as an undeniable miracle of God and his Immaculate Mother."[67] One feels she did not use "miracle" figuratively. She had some reassurance that year. Bishop Danell, having made a visitation of St. Leonards in 1872 on the request of Propaganda Fide, and having, in Cornelia's words "expressed his admiration of the work, and his perfect satisfaction regarding the Community," declared the force of the Constitutions of 1854 (what the sisters called "our old Rule) to be restored temporarily.[68]

But Cornelia was finding that, in the absence of a General Chapter, her position was becoming more and more intolerable; she wrote to Danell in 1873:

> Religious discipline must gradually be utterly destroyed when gentleness is *forced* into weakness. At present, while the Mother House is held responsible for the Branch Houses, we are divested of the smallest authority over those in the North.[69]

She wrote to a sympathetic superior: I very often have to remember . . . not to allow one's poor heart to drop blood till it withers."[70]

Years of Purification: 1869-79 187

Finally in the summer of 1874, Bishop Danell carried through his promises to sanction a General Chapter. He sent printed instructions to the convents on the procedures and purposes of the Chapter. A total of nineteen delegates were to be elected in proportion to the numbers in each convent. All Professed Sisters had active voice, including the House sisters for this time only. There were no *ex officio* members, not even local superiors. The two-fold object of the Chapter was to hold elections, and to deliberate on the Constitutions in the presence of Bishop Danell.

The first General Chapter of the Society of the Holy Child Jesus assembled on August 17, 1874, at St. Leonards-on-Sea. The nineteen delegates from communities in England, France and the United States represented a troubled congregation. They had been unable to unite behind the Constitutional revision of 1869 which *was* acceptable to Rome, because some could not trust the founder; they regarded the revision as one more product of the arbitrary government they now saw as her characteristic mode. Yet without revision and approval of Constituions they had no juridical foundation for a constitutional government by which to develop improved forms of governing. They seem to have arrived at a moment of testing their faith in the inspiration Cornelia believed that the Spirit called her to embody.

The Chapter elections were momentous. Cornelia's charism was affirmed. She was elected General of the Society by fifteen of the nineteen votes of the Chapter. Four General Councillors were elected to assist her.[71] She would remain elected General till her death less than five years later. They would be five years of continued severe testing of the spirit of the Society. But the Holy Spirit was with those who were open to him in the midst of trials leading up to the Chapter, and in the trials which would stem from it. Gradually the sisters began to mature within themselves, to take more responsibility for the development and government of the Society by leaning less on their founder's remarkable abilities and ardent religious dedication, and more on their own communal efforts. Her strength—to sustain the Society by the sheer force of her supernatural and natural gifts—was ultimately a weakness. No single person could have resolved all the juridical problems the Society had in its relations with ecclesiastics. Not even all the sisters together could have altered ecclesiastical attitudes in their time. What became apparent was, that to endure, they must understand their problems and suffer their difficulties together, and share with their founder the responsibility for solutions.

Meanwhile their General Chapter would give them ample means to share sufferings together. The next event of the Chapter after the elections challenged them to the utmost. To the complete amazement of the founder, and most of the sisters, (though not the Preston sisters) Bishop Danell imposed on the Society completely *new Constitutions*, having no reference to the original inspiration of the Society, and naming him Bishop Superior of the Institute![72]

The profound, long-lasting negative effects of this act of Bishop Danell will be traced below. On the positive side it ultimately fostered greater unity among the sisters, and greater clarity about their true spirit. But first it is necessary to retun to Mother Gertrude's representation to understand what deep divisions the Society still faced even after their momentous affirmation of their founder as *elected* General.

Mother Gertrude had been for fifteen years a loved superior and apostolic leader in Blackpool. She was affirmed, even as Cornelia was, in the elections of the General Chapter of 1874, by being elected a General Councillor.[73] Shortly after her election, she wrote a confidential representation to her Ordinary, Bishop O'Reilly of Liverpool, demanding confidentiality because "it would be ruinous to my happiness for life if it were known to the Society that I had put matters before your Lordship."[74] Her representation confirmed what the Preston superiors had reported to Cardinal Barnabò about Cornelia's General Councillors appointed by herself previous to 1874.[75] (Cornelia had consistently begged for a Chapter for election of Councillors.) Mother Gertrude affirmed Mother Lucy Woolley's pungent report on the former appointed Councillors:

> That during the twenty-five years that the body had been in existence, M.C. [Mrs. Connelly] has had no advisors or counsellors except those of her own election, and these have not been remarkable for their practical sense, but only for their devotion to M.C. and for their facility in adapting their views to hers.[76]

Mother Gertrude gave an even more significant and surprising confirmation to a basic representation of the Preston sisters. They maintained that there were problems in the government of the Society so urgent as to demand the intervention of the Bishops. The Preston superiors had, in fact, encouraged and helped Bishop Danell while he was composing his Constitutions prior to the Chapter of 1874. In Mother Gertrude's confidential representation to her Bishop, she expressed her conviction that Bishop Danell's Constitutions should *be accepted* for the Society because "it *contains a form of government* and *limits the power of superiors*" (emphasis added).[77] In other words, even Mother Gertrude, trusted enough by the Society to be elected a General Councillor, trusted and praised by Cornelia,[78] believed that a resolution of the Society's problems concerning its government must take priority over its mission to be pontifical. Cornelia truly had not understood how far the crisis of government had caused some in the Society to lose confidence in their pontifical mission.

Mother Gertrude died suddenly after only two years in office. Her attempt and that of the Preston superiors to keep the Society under episcopal control did not succeed within the whole body. The sisters gradually became more united in their sense of Society identity. To have Danell as "Bishop-Superior of the Institute" was not a viable solution to the Society's problems. Indeed, by so proclaiming himself, Danell understandably incurred the opposition of the other bishops in whose dioceses the SHCJ ministered, and thus unwittingly helped the Holy Child Sisters to rid themselves of his Constitution thirteen years later.[79] Meanwhile at the time of the Chapter in 1874 and for the remainder of the decade, the *elected* General Councillors had to confront *with* Cornelia the mounting dilemmas caused by the assertion over the Society of three conflicting episcopal authorities—Southwark, Liverpool, and Philadelphia. They began to see the wisdom of Cornelia's vision for a pontifical Society. A General Councillor expostulated in 1876:

> . . . the forbidding us to remove *any of the sisters in his diocese . . . without his sanction*, at *any time*, clearly shows that he [Bishop O'Reilly of Liverpool] objects to the general government, and would prefer a Diocesan order over which he would have sole control . . . . If any of the Sisters in the North second the Bishop's wishes on this point, there *must* be a schism.[80]

The General Government of the Society persisted in its quest for pontifical approbation and received it after Cornelia's *and* Pierce's deaths, 1879 and 1883.[81] In her last years they came to share increasingly and to take over the burdens of the Society, as their founder, humiliated, but courageous, and hastening toward her death in serious and painful illnesses, handed over much of her responsibilities. As she did so, her spiritual influence was renewed, and in her last illness she became again a powerful exemplar, this time of dying humbled in union with her "humbled God."[82] Before we can consider this last charismatic gift to her Society, we must return to 1874 and her work with her sisters on the revision of Bishop Danell's Constitutions.

We can surely share the anguish of the Holy Child sisters as they struggled through the Chapters of 1874 and 1877 to communicate to Bishop Danell and his priest-canonist what their spirit was and how his Constitutions failed to express it, even contradicted it. Cornelia spoke for them when she said that they were dealing with ultimates—"matters of the highest importance to the Work of God and to the life or death of the order."[83] This experience of crisis provoked the founder and her first companions into elaborating more fully what was an appropriate expression of their charism in Constitutions. They were clearly identifying themselves as participants in a charismatic endeavor—"the Work of God." Their notes and constitutional endeavors enlighten us further on two points: how their "old Rule" [Constitutions] expressed the original inspiration and fostered a spirit; and what further development they gave to the inspiration and spirit by additions to the Constitutions before and just after Cornelia's death at the Chapters of 1877 and 1880.

To understand these two we must look briefly at the Danell Constitutions. It consisted of five Parts, the last of which, a sort of Appendix, headed "Common Rules," contained a truncated version of the Jesuit Summary, Common Rules and Rules of Modesty. Part I, with section 1: "The End of the Institute" omitted Cornelia's First Chapter, leaving out *all* reference to the Holy Child Jesus, to his humble and hidden life. Even the single sentence echoing faintly her First Chapter, i.e., "As it is the duty of all Christians to imitate the example of our Divine Lord, so it is more especially the duty of all religious to follow Him more closely . . ." missed Cornelia's profound insight on the duty of religious "to seek in the mysteries of the life of this Divine Lord all that can serve to their greater perfection and the good of their neighbor."[84] Cornelia and her sisters had consistently approached the Living Word, the Gospel, as the privileged *locus* where through contemplation, the human creature is transformed into the likeness of Christ in a true divine-human encounter.[85] And they had understood the urgency of the *magis*, the call to always greater perfection, greater good of their neighbor. The theological aspects of a charism of foundation seem to have completely eluded Bishop Danell and his canonist/theologian, Father Bosio. This will be illustrated below from SHCJ additions to the Constitutions.

Parts II, III and IV of the Danell Constitutions were long, detailed, and sometimes repetitive explanations and prescriptions for the administration of the Society and its temporalities through all major and minor offices. (It should be noted that Danell included some of the rules for minor offices from the SHCJ Constitutions of 1854). The sisters were rightly to question the "complication in administration."[86] From the American sisters came more than one pungent comment, e.g., "There is an immense deal of useless talk in this book . . . . The Rules must be expressed in short sentences. They are more clear and better retained;" and "The whole tone of the Rule offensive."[87] When the Chapter of 1877 opened and Bishop Danell signaled to the youngest delegate, Mother Marie Claire Hadfield, to commence commentary on the Constitutions they had lived under for three years, she said: "It seems to me that the new Rule has been drawn up to correct abuses that do not exist, and it does not lead us to love and obey our Superiors."[88]

One word at least should be said in Bishop Danell's defense: Anyone who today reads the flood of representations and complaints from SHCJ that poured into him and to the Bishop of Liverpool throughout the 1870's, concerning the arbitrary government of Cornelia and consequent confusion and insecurity in the communities, can see why Danell resorted to minute prescriptiveness to remedy "abuses" which he had heard *did* "exist."[89] Holy Child sisters were learning the hard way that difficulties such as they had were best resolved from within their body, even if it meant confronting a very forceful founder.

What is less defensible though evidently also intended to correct the alleged abuses in Cornelia's government, was Bishop Danell's constitutional provision that he be Bishop-Superior of the Institute. If anything helped to make Holy Child sisters "close ranks" behind their own elected general it was the complications that ensued from the attempt to impose diocesan authority beyond its bounds. Cornelia wrote with her usual force:

"The government of the Order as proposed [in the Danell Constitutions] interferes with the autonomy necessary for the life of any religious order, which seems as necessary as the heart is to the life of the human body, and we beg for a Cardinal Protector."[90]

Now we turn to a fundamental positive concept regarding SHCJ ideas on the total structure and content of their Constitutions which they seem to have clarified for themselves as they worked to criticize Danell's Constitutions and formulate representations to him and Propaganda Fide. They saw that their Constitutions must express the hierarchy in the means and values by which they lived, those to which they were called by Cornelia's inspiration. The order, that is the sequence of text and chapters, appears to have been very important to them (it seems also to have been important to the rejection of the ill-fated Constitutions of 1870). The sequence appropriate for them was that of the Constitutions of 1854, that is, first in order, the First Chapter—Cornelia's expression of the inspiration and mission of the Society revealed in the "humble and hidden life;" secondly, immediately following, the Jesuit Summary, Common Rules and Rules of Modesty and the rules for each one's minor office. These second items, especially the Summary, constituted a code for maintaining and developing a truly spiritual life under the Counsels, the life to which their discernment of Christ's standard—his way as opposed to the world's way—had led them. Taken as a whole, the corpus consisting of Cornelia's First Chapter, and the Jesuit Summary, Common Rules and Rules of Modesty, in its proper place at the head of their Constitutions, proclaimed for them that their life was supernaturally rather than naturally oriented, that their inspiration and motivation for action was based on a spiritual foundation, that action took place in the midst of contemplation. This seems to be what Cornelia meant when she represented against the Danell Constitutions that "The Spirit is not of the religious tone inculcated in the Old Rule of Cardinal Wiseman [Constitutions of 1850]. She represented again: "Unfortunately we find the material part of our life predominates over the Spiritual in the *New Code proposed*, and we do not think it possible to make these 'work out our perfection and salvation'."[91]

Having seen what the Holy Child sisters found highly expressive of their spirit in their Constitutions from 1854-74, what in Danell's contradicted it, we turn to what they added in 1877 and 1880 to shape Danell's alien Constitutions more to their spirit. For despite their dismay with what their Bishop had imposed on them, and despite their sometimes highly penetrating criticism of it, Danell continued to insist that they follow his Constitutions. When Cornelia died, the Society was still living under Danell's Constitutions—a great humiliation for one who had struggled during the thirty-three years she had governed the Society, and even the year before its foundation, to ensure that it would have adequate Constitutions.[92]

By 1877 the determined Holy Child sisters had won from the bishop the restoration of their First Chapter, and to first place. By 1880, with Cornelia's help before her death in 1879, they had moved the Summary, Common Rules and Rules of Modesty into a sort of second position after Part I on vows and various spiritual exercises. By then, they had adopted a new ordering of these texts influenced by a schema set up by a contemporary Jesuit, Pierre Cotel.[93] It was in this form that the Jesuit Rules remained in the Holy Child Constitutions till 1970. The schema was obviously more satisfactory to Diocesan and Propaganda authorities than the original form of the Summary because they had never seen it in relation to the total Ignatian Constitutions from which it was excerpted. In the light of the importance the Jesuit Summary has held in SHCJ constitutional development, it is worth noting we give here the headings under which its contents were distributed after 1880:

Spirit of Detachment
Spirit of Humility
Esteem of perfection and Spiritual things
Purity of Intention
Spirit of Mortification
Temptations and Delusions
Charity
Vow of Poverty
Vow of Chastity
Vow of Obedience[94]

By 1880 also the Sisters added to the head of the Summary a significant text, a small part of which they had been able to include by 1877. In slightly adapted form, they borrowed the passage with which Ignatius commenced his Constitutions. It recalled for them, that God who had raised up the Institute would provide for it; that the Holy Spirit would direct its members by his interior law of love. Within this context it asserted the necessity and value of Rules and Constitutions:

> Although in all confidence we should trust that Almighty God, who has raised up this Institute will, in His goodness, watch over, direct, and increase it in His holy service, and although the interior law of love and charity which the Holy Spirit engraves on the heart of each of its members, contributes more efficaciously to this end than all exterior laws, nevertheless, it is necessary that the sisters should have written Rules which may help them to walk more securely, according to the true Spirit of their vocation. It is therefore the duty of each Sister to endeavor, as far as possible with Divine Grace, to forward the work of God—not only by docility to the interior law of charity, but also by faithfully observing the Rules and Constitutions of the Institute.
>
> Some of the Rules contain the principles of Religious Life, and are to teach the Sisters what they ought to be, or endeavor to become, before God by His holy grace; others concern more the exterior, and prescribe the acts which should be performed on these principles to aid in establishing Religious Discipline.[95]

The addition of this paragraph with its "nevertheless, *it is necessary*

Years of Purification: 1869-79 193

that the Sisters should have written Rules . . . to help them to *walk more securely*" may indicate that both the pressures from Danell and the crisis over Cornelia's personal government was helping Holy Child sisters to clarify the scope and role of Constitutions and to utilize them soundly.

One of the few consolations the sisters had in their dealings with Danell and Bosio was that they introduced them to Cotel's schema for constitutions. Cornelia wrote with enthusiasm in her notes compiled for revision of Danell's Constitutions: "Père Cotel's remarks are excellent and you had better make use of them. The Spirit of what he has drawn out is the same as our old Rule . . . ."[96] To their joy the SHCJ found that he had defined that fundamental reality of their lives they struggled to convey to Danell yet found elusive of definition—the "Spirit of a Religious Institute." They introduced into Danell's Constitutions, following Cornelia's First Chapter, not only Cotel's definition but his elaboration of the spirit of an apostolic institute in terms of zeal. His passages which have continued to influence Holy Child Constitutions through the twentieth century, are given below. It was a tribute to the spirit of the Holy Child sisters, growing under trials to a more mature understanding of the charism of their founder, that their last edition to their Constitution before her death was in terms of zeal. In the sufferings they were experiencing they might have turned in upon themselves, but instead they committed themselves even more fully to that for which their founder was gifted, that for which the Spirit bestows all his charisms—the building up of the Church.

1. —The Spirit of a Religious Institute is that interior principle which gave it birth, and with which all its members ought to be penetrated, so that every individual in particular, and the body in general, may be maintained in its primitive fervor. The Spirit of this Institute, being that of the Holy Child Jesus, is a spirit of simplicity, humility, obedience, and charity together with a spirit of affectionate devotion to the works of zeal and charity undertaken by its Members.

2. —This Spirit embraces in a very special manner the virtue of zeal, because its chief end is our own sanctification and the salvation of souls. But it is very important that this zeal should possess those qualities which can alone render it agreeable to God and profitable to souls. Therefore it should be

A well regulated zeal, which begins by the extirpation of our own faults and the acquisition of religious virtues, and is always subject to obedience.

A humble and disinterested zeal, which seeks nothing but the honor of God.

A courageous zeal, ready to sacrifice all for the glory of God.

A gentle and insinuating zeal, to draw hearts to God.

A patient and persevering zeal, which knows how to bear with the defects and coarseness of children and the poor, and which, without being discouraged when labour is not crowned with success, continues to sow and water, waiting in patient hope for the increase that God will surely give to those who confide in Him.

Finally, a discreet zeal according to knowledge which leads us to instruct ourselves before attempting to teach others, and, in matters which regard religion, to confine ourselves to simple and approved explanations of Christian Doctrine and the duties of solid piety.

3. — The particular means by which the Sisters who are engaged in the great work of training children may acquire and preserve the true Spirit of the Institute, will be to cultivate assiduously a loving devotion to the Holy Child Jesus, and to the infancy of Mary. Thus, they will be constantly reminded to see Jesus and Mary in each of the children whom they have to train, and they will often be reminded of that which their Divine Spouse has Himself declared: "Whatsoever you do unto one of these my least brethren, you do it unto Me," and again showing His disciples a little child: "He who receives one such little child in My name, receiveth Me."

4. — With this thought ever in view, the Institute has chosen for its principal feasts, those of Christmas, the Epiphany, the Immaculate Conception, and the Presentation of Mary in the Temple at the age of three years. Moreover, it honors St. Joseph with singular devotion as the guardian of the Infancy and Childhood of Jesus, St. Anne, who watched over the infancy of Mary, and the holy Guardian Angels, whom the Sisters should regard as their protectors and models in all that concerns the charge of the children.[97]

The first two paragraphs above from Cotel were fully consonant with Holy Child Spirit. Some of paragraphs 3 and 4 were also consonant and were retained by Holy Child sisters in 1886. But they removed, as soon as they had the power, an addition to Cotel's text that was theologically defective. The addition was made by Bishop Danell and his canonist-theologian! These two clerics added to the above exhortation to "devotion to the Holy Child Jesus," devotion to "the Infancy of Mary." When Holy Child sisters were given some voice in revision of their Constitution in Rome in 1887, they wrote emphatically:

Bisogna ommetera "ed all'infanzia di Maria" "e Maria"
We wish this ommitted.
1st. Because it was never in our own Rule as written by our Foundress.
2nd. Because here is mentioned our distinctive and special Devotion, which is to the "Holy Child Jesus" and there is not and never has been any special devotion to the "infancy of Mary" in the Society.[98]

This event is significant for current efforts to recover women's contribution to nineteenth century theology. Cornelia's theology was learned from the Presbyterian and Episcopalian pastors of her youth, from her husband, from her own assiduous and discerning spiritual reading, and above all, in the school of prayer and experience especially as these were integrated and clarified for her by the Spiritual Exercises. As "theologian" Cornelia understood that what makes the childhood of Jesus an inexhaustible and efficacious mystery for all who contemplate it, is the fact that it reveals the childhood of *God*. It was the light of *God* humbled and hidden that illumined this earthly pilgrimage for Cornelia and her sisters. This all-essential point seems to have eluded the Bishop and his theologian. But the insight of the nineteenth-century Holy Child sisters into the meaning of the Infancy Narratives is once again being verified by current exegesis on this "Gospel in miniature."[99] Hopefully this exegesis will encourage renewed

Cornelia's Last Years and Death

Her final contributions to the Constitutions were not the only means by which Cornelia gave expression in her last years to the spirit of the Society. Her life itself became more and more evidently, as in the primitive years of the Society, a manifestation of the humble, hidden way of the Son of God in his first thirty years on earth. Danell's position as Bishop-Superior of the Institute was a constant source of humiliation for Cornelia, and of frustration for her and for others in authority in a congregation ministering in several dioceses, near and far. Within the Society there were also sources of humiliation and suffering, as the troubles of the 1870's "tended to estrange from her so many of those who in former years had been her most devoted children," while "with regard to others who knew her less well, the result was want of confidence, and . . . opposition to her views and wishes." One of her earliest companions who noted these reactions, was "much struck by the calm dignity with which she encountered all the opposition . . . and the many humiliations she had to undergo." It was the same as when, almost thirty years before, Pierce had humiliated her before the world—she had gone on attending "calmly and cheerfully to all the details of community life."[100]

Those who had shared with Cornelia the earlier vicissitudes of the Society and had themselves contributed in no small measure to its spirit held fast to their conviction of the charismatic nature of her role and of the Spirit's continued guidance of the Society. One wrote:

> . . . the last supreme trial had its fruit in the perfection of the Institute Mother Connelly had given up so much to commence—The last sacrifice was the most painful of all—and Mother Connelly's character underwent its last transformation—crushed and annihilated before men, she annihilated herself more profoundly before God, and in a letter she wrote to me at the time . . . she expressed herself as receiving only what she deserved, and begged me to pray for her that her pride might be forgiven by God and that He would spare the Society and accept her as its victim.[101]

And in a later recollection M.M.J. Buckle added: "She took all the humiliations she received from persons in authority as a Saint, and said, "God has permitted all as a punishment of her pride" [sic].[102]

We must not overrate the disaffection and alienation from the founder. She received confirmation of the Society's recognition of her charismatic role in 1877: Unaccountably Bishop Danell required another election for general government at the Chapter of 1877, even though Cornelia and her Council had been elected for six years in 1874; the founder, though failing in heatlh, was again elected General.[103] But she whose beauty, charm, talents and above all, spiritual gifts, had for so long given her a commanding position, felt her sufferings keenly. With that openness she had deliberately cultivated in her relations with ecclesiastics she spoke of her sufferings even to Danell, when urging that the next superior general ought to be "Head of the House in which she lives." She wrote: "I do not say that my heart has not been cut a thousand times, and when no one but God has known of it amongst my numerous imperfections and faults, but my portion lies in this by the sweet will of God."[104]

What is most moving, and lends authenticity to what Cornelia wrote to others, are her few private spiritual notes which have somehow survived from the 1870's. Their emphasis is all on humility, charity, and that center toward which her whole being was directed—the Will of God. These jottings are in continuity with her private spiritual notes from thirty years before in Grand Coteau and Rome, where her insistent prayer had been to attain to that Third Degree of Humility which would make her more like Christ.[105] In 1872, when the sting of the Preston schism was still weighing heavily upon her, she wrote: "In difficulties . . . ask . . . "Why did I become a Religious—To become perfect—To become a Saint." She continued:

> . . . thinking too much of self, weighing every little slighting word and act of others, yielding to wounded feeling and anger, compassionating myself, giving way to sadness and tears. The remedy for this is meditation on the sufferings of Our Lord and a generous desire to accept suffering for His sake—Rejecting all thoughts of self love and self compassion. The heavier the cross the more Our Lord loves you, the more constant the touches of His hand, the more He thinks of you, cares for you. Walk on steadfastly in your sorrows to meet Jesus at Jerusalem.[106]

By 1875 the imposition of Danell's Constitutions with all its consequences had brought Cornelia even closer to the Jerusalem of Christ's Passion. As was her custom she made retreat notes for that year:

1. Frequently to renew my Intention of doing all my actions for God.
1. When forgotten, passed over and neglected, to say as fervently as I can: "Deo Gratias."
3. When corrected or disapproved, even for what I had intended well—to make an offering of this to Our Lord in atonement for past sins, saying "Give me Thy Humility . . ."[107]

The following year she was still much preoccupied in prayer with acquiring his and his Mother's humility:

> . . . 2. Have I conducted myself like a Religious, cherishing interior humility, regarding myself as the last and least of all?
> 3. Have I been humble and respectful in my words and manner to my Superiors and all the Sisters?
> 4. Have I obliged myself to put away wounded feeling and vanity, and be even-tempered—not one day dull, and another bright . . . asking myself: what is God's view of this matter? How would Our Lady have me act, overcoming self generously?[108]

Accompanying these notes were her questions to herself on "Charity."

She had frequently reminded her sisters: "Perfection consists in Charity." Now she examined herself:

1. Have I allowed any feelings of dislike to grow up in my heart, to any one?
2. Whenever I have perceived such feelings, have I immediately made an act of charity, saying "O my God, I love Thee and my neighbour as myself, for the love of Thee—"Jesus most charitable," etc., or a Hail Mary for the person?
3. Have I made it an especial point to do as many acts of personal kindness as I could, either in words or actions? . . .
6. Have I been the first to apologize for any want of humility? or charity? Remembering Our Lord's word "Love one another, as I have loved you."[109]

These notes are dated April, 1876. In May she jotted: "However deeply thou mayest humble thyself, thou wilt never be more humble than Christ crucified;" and "In all the troubles and difficulties of life, one only support is left to us, 'the Will of God.' "[110] Finally, her retreat notes of 1876 reveal her spirit at peace in loving, simple union with her God:

1. To aim at loving and serving God alone, and all creatures in Him.
2. When creatures trouble or neglect me, to turn to God to whom alone I ought to give my heart: "God alone." "For Thy sake, my God."
3. To aim at simple childlike, obedience in all things, as being the will of my God whom I love . . . .[111]

". . . the will of my God whom I love." It was because she was so faithful interiorly that, in spite of illness, advancing age, and seeming failure, she could still touch the hearts of her sisters with the themes that expressed their spirit. What she wrote to the American novices in 1876 provides commentary on that "childlike obedience" she aimed at. It included "the love of all that He—the Holy Child—loved and taught." For her the will of the Father was personified in his Child, his Son:

> I wish we could pray so fervently as to obtain for all the true spirit of the Holy Child and the love of all that He loved and taught. Prayer and self-denial will obtain this if we persevere in Humility. Humiliy must be dear to us as the apple of our eye for all true charity lies founded on Humility . . . .[112]

Her last Epiphany letter in 1878, brief because she was already very ill, but strong with the themes on which she had begun the Society, read:

> A happy and joyful Epiphany to you each—and may you pass the most holy year of your lives in 1878.
> May you correspond to the advice given by Fr Balthasar in the "Hints to a Novice" given in the little Manual, especially in the practice of heroic virtue, by the hidden acts of your every day life—with only God to witness the crucifixion of the will and inclinations.
> I am sure that you pray for me . . . .[113]

Soon after that letter she became so ill she was thought in danger of death and was given the Sacrament of the Sick. Actually she still had fifteen more months of life, that life which she had long regarded as a pilgrimage toward heaven. Heaven she had often referred to as familiarly as America or even London, and now she looked forward eagerly to meeting her Lord there.[114] The many sisters who cared for her left sincere recollections of her courage, patience, peace, and her charity towards others. One who spoke of the "privilege" of helping the infirmarians said, "With all the love of her maternal heart she said to us 'May you both come nearer, and become dearer to the Sacred Heart with every breath you draw.' "[115] Another who had been close to her for many years wrote of "how great her weakness and how many her pains have been, . . . how bravely her strong and bright spirit has fought against them all, and with what saintly resignation she accepted them all because it was the will of God." This sister added an incident illustrative of a spirit "strong and bright" to the end. Though unable to walk in her last year, she managed, with help, to plant "kitchen garden plants and flowers," and,

> as she sat hour after hour in the Council room . . . she tended and watched[them] with such care because, as she said again and again, they seemed, as they shot up in all their variety, to be the very image of the beauty of God.[116]

By March of 1879 a virulent eczema, caused by the severe nephritis from which she was dying, covered her whole body, causing intense pain and irritation, and giving her the appearance of one scalded, or, as her sisters said, of a leper. She lingered on, sometimes delirious, sometimes semi-conscious, praying in her moments of consciousness. Two days before her death, April 16th, she was able to receive Holy Communion.[117] The following day a sister who was trying to ease the sufferings caused by her eczema heard what was perhaps the most significant utterance of her long passion. The sister saw Cornelia strike one hand with the other three times and say "with great decision: 'in this flesh I shall see my God.' "[118] Cornelia was indeed and had long been "Job;" was she not proclaiming, as she approached death: "I know that my Vindicator lives!"[119] Was not this the same kind of grace that had enabled her, forty years before when she had held her scalded son dying in her arms, to identify with Mary and Jesus, and to proclaim that her son, too, "was taken into the temple of the Lord on the Purification"?[120] Does not Cornelia, in the critical moments of her life, witness to a profound consciousness of her insertion into the Paschal Mystery identifying herself within the divinely revealed plan of salvation?

Her last words uttered a few hours later in the midst of intense suffering were "My Jesus, have mercy on me! Oh God! have pity upon me!" In the early hours of April 18th, Easter Friday, she gradually lost consciousness, and at noon-time she entered into the joy of her Lord, thirty-three years to the day that she had left Rome to begin her mission for the Church.[121] In life she had rarely lifted the veil on those glimpses of eternal nuptials with which we may believe the Lord now welcomed his faithful virgin. One personal spiritual note, jotted on Epiphany in 1865, reveals not only a brief foretaste of heavenly ecstasy, but also, as she moves spontaneously in her prayer from *I* to *we*, she was linked irrevocably in spirit with those she had nurtured in the Spirit: She wrote:

> "I have loved thee with an everlasting love." O God of Gods, and light of lights, and joy of joys, fill my poor soul that I, too, may love Thee with an everlasting love, that we may all be one in Thee, and live and breathe for Thee alone.[122]

Notes

1. CC 15:15.
2. Bisgood, p. 258.
3. Bisgood, pp. 146-63; 255-57.
4. CC 12:25.
5. CC 12:72.
6. CC 14:52.
7. D 44:7.
8. Bellasis D 74:446; Const 1854, *Source* 4:78.
9. D 30:135-36.
10. CC 8:86, 90.
11. CC 30:1, CC 28:1-18 passim.
12. D 42:36-37.
13. D 43:53.
14. D 43:55.
15. CC 11:21, 24.
16. D 71:38.
17. Const 1854, *Source* 4:78-79.
18. CC 17:6.
19. D 22:101.
20. CC 22:18.
21. Const 1854, *Source* 4:78.
22. J. Walsh in "Introduction," to Bisgood, pp. vii-viii; Bisgood, pp. 310-14.
23. CC 45:22; CC 13:5.
24. CC 5:126b.
25. CC 2:38-39.
26. CC 21:57.
27. CC 8:97.
28. Buckle D 67:55.
29. D 19:26-27.
30. Ex 23, 136-48.
31. D 30:135-36.
32. CC 45:19.
33. CC 15:5.
34. CC 18:3, CC 11:25.
35. CC 13:49.
36. Cited by Bisgood, p. 195.
37. CC 11:69.
38. CC 11:75.
39. CC 8:89-90; CC 1:46.
40. Const 1850, *Source* 4:26.
41. D 30:48.

42. D 30:101-02.
43. References to Cornelia's concern for and friendship with the sisters are innumerable: e.g.: CC 6:17, 28, 50; CC 7:5; CC 8:52, and throughout CC 6, 7, 8, passim; also CC 16:94; equally numerous throughout CC 6, 7, 8 (letters to sisters) and throughout her letters to bishops (CC 10-18), are clear evidences of her practice of subsidiarity: CC 6:81, 97, 102; CC 7:41; CC 8:19, 59; CC 9:7; CC 10:19; CC 11:71; CC 12:71, 75, 76, 103, 110; CC 13:66, 69, 71; CC 16:50; D 51:60.
44. Crook, Part I, *Source*, 9 (1979), 10-12; McCarthy, "Constitutions for Apostolic Religious," *Way Supp*, 14 (1971), 33-35; and "Apostolic Congregations of Women and the Ignatian Charism," *Way Supp*, 20 (1973), 10-16; J. Beyer, "Der Einfluss der Konstitutionen der Gesellschaft Jesu auf das moderne Ordensleben," *Geist und Leben*, 29 (1956), 440-54; Craisson, pp. vi-xi.
46. CC 45:1, *Source* 4:13-17.
47. CC 45:18.
48. CC 21:6; a private spiritual note of Cornelia when she was discerning her vocation in 1840 at the time Pierce asked her to cooperate with his efforts to become a Catholic priest.
49. CC 45:1-2.
50. D 51:129-37; Bisgood, pp. 262-64.
51. Const 1869-70, *Source* 4:112-34; Bisgood, pp. 262-64.
52. D 54:36, 151-53; 164-66.
53. Bellasis D 75:593; Laprimaudaye D 70:194-95.
54. CC 45:2, 13, 15.
55. Bisgood, pp. 264-71.
56. D 52:115.
57. D 52:54. The other Preston Superior, besides Mothers Lucy and Christina, was Mother Alphonsa Kaye.
58. Much of this correspondence is reproduced in the Documentation for the Cause of Cornelia, D 50-58.
59. Gompertz, passim, especially pp. 108-18, 132-39, 373-98; Bisgood, passim, especially pp. 138-48, 264-92, 314-16.
60. The Documentation volumes, especially D 52-56, contain representations of SHCJ to Bishops and to Propaganda Fide about the government of the Society. Representations of the Preston Superiors, D 52:30-39, 53-56, 74-84, 90-93, 96-103, 131, 133, 135; and of Mother Gertrude Day, D 54:188-91, 207-19, are especially relevant to further studies.
61. Bisgood, pp. 266-71.
62. D 52:46-47, 71.
63. D 52:102.
64. D 52:37.
65. D 54:184, 213.
66. D 54:207-16.
67. Bisgood, pp. 277-79.
68. CC 45:2; Gompertz, p. 413.
69. Cited by Bisgood, p. 278.
70. Cited by Bisgood, p. 281.
71. D 54:144-46; Bisgood, pp. 281-83.
72. Bisgood, pp. 283-86.
73. D 83, Part I:115.
74. D 54: 207-16; citation from p. 216.
75. D 54:214; one of the sisters in question was Mother Teresa Hanson; a priest concerned with SHCJ problems reported the same as Mother Gertrude, see D 54:202.

76. D 52:99; see also D 54:147, 202.
77. D 54:215.
78. CC 7:30; CC 8:119-21; CC 17:33.
79. Bisgood, pp. 288-89; D 54:219-56; D 31:79, 101-02, 143-44; D 58:22-24.
80. D 55:17.
81. Weinig, "The Long Desired Approval of Our Rule," pp. 5-29.
82. Const 1850, *Source* 4:51; Bisgood, pp. 303-09; Gompertz, pp. 457-71.
83. CC 45:4.
84. The Danell Constitutions are held in SHCJ Archives, Rome; Cornelia's Const 1854 are printed in *Source* 4; pp. 77 for citation; one copy of the Danell Constitutions contains an SHCJ annotation for the section "End of the Institute." which reads: "We want the spirit of the Holy Child Jesus and more unction."
85. D. Stanley, in "Contemplation of the Gospels, Ignatius Loyola, and the Contemporary Christian," *Theological Studies* (Sept. 1968), pp. 417-18, 432, and passim, 417-43, gives an excellent treatment of contemplation in the sense described above.
86. CC 45:20.
87. Annotated copy of the Danell Constitutions, pp. 12, 4, SHCJ Archives, Rome.
88. Cited by Bisgood, p. 301; Armour, *Cornelia*, p. 80.
89. Documentation (D) vols. 52-56, contain much of this correspondence, passim.
90. CC 45:19; Bisgood, p. 302.
91. CC 45:19, 3; D 56:78.
92. Bisgood, pp. 300-02.
93. SHCJ Archives, Rome contains MSS in French and in English entitled "Projet des Constitutions" and "1st Scheme of Constitutions" (for typescript of the latter, v. D 57:49-114.) From Cornelia's notes (CC 45:20) and M.M.J. Buckle's biography (D 67:128-30) it is clear that the author is Pierre Cotel, S.J. The MSS have proved to be an adaptation of the *Constitutions des Soeurs de l'Instruction Charitable du Saint-Enfant Jésus* which Cotel apparently composed for this congregation also known as Les Dames de S. Maur, by 1866 (C. Sommervogel, *Bibliothèque de la Compagnie de Jésus*, première partie: Bibliographie, par P.P. Augustin et Aloys de Backer, S.J.: Seconde partie: *Histoire*, par A. Carzyon, S.J.; *Tables*, par P. Bliard, SJ: 12 vols., Brussels and Paris, 1890-1932). Cotel's Constitutions were also published in 1872 in Paris, Bp Danell and his canonist/theologian made the Scheme available to the SHCJ by 1874.
94. *Source* 4:141-42; this schema is by no means identical, but is obviously influenced by Cotel's Scheme, D 57:86-101. The SHCJ text remains closer to the original Jesuit Summary.
95. *Source* 4:140; Const SJ, no. 13.
96. CC 45:20.
97. *Source* 4:138-39.
98. D 58:119; 135-37; cited in *Source* 4:149.
99. Brown, p. 8.
100. Buckle D 67:52; D 78:73; D 78:26.
101. Buckle D 63:36-37.
102. Buckle D 78:67.
103. Bisgood, p. 302.
104. D 56:112.
105. Ex 165-68; CC 21:14-15, 27-29, 47, 74.
106. CC 22:16-17.
107. CC 22:21-22.
108. CC 22:20; in item no. 3, "Superiors" may refer to bishops since Cornelia referred to them, especially her Ordinary, by this term in other writings.

109. CC 22:21; CC 8:95.
110. CC 22:17-18.
111. CC 22:18.
112. CC 8:118.
113. CC 8:131; Fr. Balthasar's "Hints" have not been found under his name. Cornelia is probably referring to her own *Manual for the Use of the Novices of the Holy Child Jesus* (a very "little" book in size) where are found, on pp. 96-103, "Hints to a Novice;" these are attributed to P. Lancicius; Balthasar may have translated these.
114. D 9:159; CC 1:113; D 54:7; Buckle D 64:122; Bellasis D 73:253.
115. D 76:78-79.
116. D 59:67.
117. Bisgood, p. 307; an MS report on the nature of Cornelia's last illness by A.K. Mant, Pathologist, Head, Dept of Forensic Medicine, Guy's Hospital, London, Nov. 4, 1977, may be found in SHCJ Archives, Rome. The recollections of the SHCJ call to mind Is 53:2-5.
118. D 71:57; Job 19:26.
119. Job 19:25.
120. CC 21:5; Lk 2:22, 27.
121. CC 59:94.
122. CC 27:3; Jer 31:3.

Conclusion

In God, For God, With God

The emphasis of this study has been on the person of Cornelia, on her identification with Jesus in the mysteries of his earthly life, and on the expression she gave to his way of life in the Society of the Holy Child Jesus. In its approval of her Institute and its Constitutions in 1893, the Catholic Church affirmed its belief in a "charism" of Cornelia, her supernatural gifting for the establishing of the Society. Has the emphasis of this study on the person of Cornelia, on her experience of the Spirit in the events of her life, contributed toward a better understanding of the theological notion of charism? We believe it has, in showing the significance of those elements which were emphasized in Chapter 1, that is, the understanding that a charism is not a "superstructure," a "crown" on a "head," but rather an energizing and an enabling woven into the very fabric of a person's life. Cornelia's charism can be seen "to touch the whole of human reality, individually and collectively, . . . to set free natural gifts according to the diversity of people and the human community."[1] The Spirit's gifting and her response enabled Cornelia to utilize the full richness of her life experiences as woman not only for her own ministry but also to form her sisters for ministry to the people of God. She said to them: "Of yourselves you can do nothing, but in God, for God, and with God you can do all things"[2] "In God, for God, with God" was Cornelia's experience of charism. Like other women founders and religious leaders of the nineteenth and twentieth century her experience of living "in God, for God and with God" enabled her to implement a vision for the human community that transcended, among other evils, the misogynist elements of her culture. She had been painfully oppressed by the latter but had rejected their deceptions and had found the truth of her being in God and his mission for her.

Cornelia manifested an awareness of her gifting for ministry to the concrete historical needs of God's people in her own time. This awareness was seen as much in her deeds as her words—her prayer life, her initiatives, acceptances, decisions, commitments traced in this study of her founding of the Society of the Holy Child Jesus.

And what of her words? If we exclude the explicit use of the term "charism," not common in her time, then it would seem that much of her speaking and writing witnessed clearly to an awareness of the empowering of the Spirit and her own response. She spoke of her own mission and of the Society itself in the same terms as had Father Grassi in 1846—as a "work of God."[3] This evokes images from the whole panorama of salvation history reaching back to the ancient Hebrew awareness of the great deeds of God for his people. In time of crisis when Cornelia felt the Society was threatened she gave another powerful expression to her experience of charism: "The Society of the Holy Child Jesus is not my work. I have only followed the inspirations of God in obedience to His not my will." She added, "Had it been my own work, I should long ago have given up and retired to some corner to pray."[4] When she felt that Bishop Danell's constitutions threatened the identity of her Society, she reminded him that it was a "Work of God."[5] And in a less solemn but no less heartfelt expression she counseled an ailing sister who was endeavoring to continue her teaching: "Pray and have great confidence in God who will take care of his own work and guide and govern it by His Holy Spirit."[6]

Cornelia spoke of the Holy Spirit frequently and familiarly, more so perhaps than was common in her time. She especially recommended prayers to the Holy Spirit in times of Society difficulties and great need: "go on hoping and praying . . . that the Spirit of our good God will remove it" [unjust attack];[7] "We must all pray much to the Holy Spirit to guide and enlighten us"; "Veni Creator. Do say frequently."[8] Just as often Cornelia reminded herself or those she was guiding of the abiding friend and counselor who dwells within. "Do not resist the interior voice speaking to your heart, . . . the voice of the Holy Spirit";[9] The saints tell us many things which we take hold of . . . only when the Holy Spirit gives us light to see . . . . How I wish for you that His Holy Spirit may whisper in your ear all that He wishes you to do";[10] "Be careful not to thwart in others desires for higher things. You may be thwarting the Holy Spirit."[11] "What a wonder it is that any nun can not have great devotion to the Holy Ghost!"[12] The realistic quality of Cornelia's own devotion is seen in her personal note written at a time of great suffering: "Give to the Holy Ghost many smiles, and offer each smile as . . . a co-operation with grace."[13]

Cornelia manifested a Pauline sense of call to cooperation with Christ in mission; she and her sisters were collaborators *with* Christ. In her spiritual notebook she jotted the prayer, "Give me, O Lord, a love full of action;"[14] she reminded the novice mistress: "The Society has much more need of labouring sisters than of devout statues . . ."[15]

Cornelia also spoke of cooperation with Christ in redemptive suffering. She wrote to her sisters in 1857: "Fill up what is wanting in the Passion of Christ—your cooperation."[16] Her life was filled with suffering, yet those who lived with her spoke of her "outward serenity," her "fresh, bright spirit" which "cast a sunshine round her which no other presence did or can create."[17] Cornelia herself spoke of union with God as giving "that jubilee of heart . . . not bargained for in this life of accepted suffering."[18] She seems to have accepted the betrayal of Pierce and the loss of her children as a participation in the mystery of the redemptive suffering of Christ. She spoke very little about the loss of her children. When prostrate with grief at the death of her twenty-one year old son Mercer, she told the sisters: "You do not know what it is to be a mother."[19] Once she confided to a sister: "The remembrance of my children never leaves me."[20] Though she continued to write to her children after Pierce took them, and received visits from Frank and Adeline when they were adults, she never had the joy of full reconciliation with them. She never saw Pierce again after 1847. By 1867 he had been restored to the American Episcopal ministry in Florence, Italy, where he served until his death in 1884.

Cornelia's faith encompassed the "scandal of the Cross."[21] "In God, for God and with God," she accepted this mystery and was not destroyed by it. Her ultimate answer to her oppression as a woman was to find a true affirmation of herself in God. She was not given to dissipating her energies in wrestling with humanly insoluble problems; Pierce's psychological problems seemed insoluble in her time, and the law did not support her maternal rights. One of her brief annotations to his pamphlets gives us a rare glimpse of how "in God," she could accept suffering. Pierce had complained publicly that Cornelia's natural affections for him and their children had "dried up." She noted simply: "The affections do not so easily *dry up*, but they may mount up to Him alone who is capable of filling the heart."[22]

Cornelia's deepest awareness was of her call to intimate union with God in love. From the time of her marriage she had sought and welcomed the light Christ shed on her life through the Gospel. She grasped the fullness of redemptive love he revealed in the humble, hidden life he had chosen for most of his years on earth. During her years of marriage she was already zealous to draw others to contemplative prayer; as a founder she made the call to contemplation central to her own and her sisters' vocations.[23] Through contemplation she had seen a whole way of life revealed in Bethlehem and Nazareth where God had shared the life of every ordinary man, woman, and child.

In contemplating Christ in Bethlehem and Nazareth, Cornelia and her sisters found the ministry of education integral to their vocation. This integration was expressed at the time of Vatican Council II's call to religious congregations to renew in the spirit of their founder:

> . . . This orientation [to the mysteries of the incarnation, birth, childhood and hidden life of Christ] attaches to itself the . . . dynamism of growth. It places at the service of education all that is to be learned from focusing precisely on those years of Christ which show the mysterious process of the

one perfect Childhood gradually unfolding into perfect Manhood. It is the mystery of a divinely unfolding maturity that offers such powerful "particular means" for the task of guiding young lives toward their own maturity.... It presents a model to match each age, keeping pace with the process of growth, spurring on and divinizing that process. "*Growing as He Grew*," wrote Mother Connelly in the introduction to the *Meditations for Whitsuntide*. It provides the example and dynamism for precisely that harmonious growth of which the Declaration on Christian Education [of Vatican II] speaks.[24]

The experience of her own relationshp with God led Cornelia to strive for the ideal of respecting the uniqueness of each person, students as well as sisters. She conveyed to students, and to lay persons, as well as to sisters, the reality, the worth, the joys, the challenges, even the imperative summons to a life of union with God, and she encouraged their spiritual journeys.[25]

It has become evident throughout the course of this study that two of Cornelia's early SHCJ companions had a remarkable ability to express their awareness of their founder's charism. Reflection on their writings has shown that the two earliest so-called "biographies" written by the two sisters are basically expositions of her charism, that is, testimonies of her companions to a very rich experience of the Spirit in which they were sensitive and whole-hearted participants. These testimonies are still in manuscript form in the SHCJ archives. They have been used throughout this study in conjunction with Cornelia's own writings.

Mother Maria Joseph Buckle (1822-1902) who entered the Society less than two years after its founding, composed/compiled what she called "Materials Collected for a Life of Cornelia Connelly." She did the major part of this work between 1879 and 1886, with added recollections between 1891-99. She cited at length from sources such as letters and notebooks.[26]

Mother Mary Francis Bellasis (1842-1927) who entered the Society in 1860 after attending the Holy Child School at St. Leonards-on-Sea, composed, between 1911 and 1911, "Life of the Mother Foundress of the Society of the Holy Child Jesus." It is evident that she used M.M.J. Buckle as her base, but that she also presented much of her own knowledge and insights. As her title suggests, she organized her materials much more than her predecessor.[27]

The distinctive personalities of these two sisters comes through in their writings. This is a tribute perhaps to what M.M.F. Bellasis records of Cornelia's teaching: "Be yourself but make that self just what God wants it to be."[28] With the recovery, in the last thirty years, of a large body of Cornelia's own writings, it has become possible to see where the thinking of the two sisters influences their expression of their founder's graced personality and teachings. It has also been possible to see that these two sisters are remarkably true to the portrait that Cornelia has left of herself through her own writings.

They record their experience of the consonance between her personal spiritual life and her guidance of others, between her deeds and her words. Especially when they read her private spiritual notes after her death they recognized how deep was this consonance. They are excellent witnesses to her teaching on the primacy of the spiritual, on prayer, and on the harmony of prayer and action in the lives of those whose ministry springs from its gospel inspiration. They knew and valued her as a spiritual director, and found her an authentic exponent of renunciation for the Kingdom, noting that her most frequent scriptural citation was "Unless the grain of wheat falls on the ground and dies, it remains only a single grain; but if it dies, it yields a rich harvest."[29] Both noted that she exemplified in her life the motto of the SHCJ: "Actions not words." M.M.F. Bellasis noted that "it was in meditating on the love of God in the Spiritual Exercises [Ex 230-37] that she determined to choose the motto. This insight reveals again Cornelia's awareness of God's gifting and her response in her labors for her congregation. Ignatius wrote: " I will ponder with great affection how much God our Lord has done for me . . . . Then I will reflect upon myself, and consider . . . what I ought to offer the Divine Majesty, that is, all that I possess, and myself with it."[30]

Cornelia had offered all of her gifts and experience to bring the Society of the Holy Child Jesus into existence. At the root of this offering was the offering of herself, her response to God's fundamental call to every human person to holiness. Cornelia was preoccupied with that call, and she kept clearly before her sisters their vocation to be saints. They felt that the spirit of their Society was rooted deeply in God's great plan of salvation. Students, and all to whom she ministered knew that she believed them destined to holiness. In our time we hear the Church, speaking through Vatican II to proclaim a universal call to holiness: "It is evident to everyone that all the faithful of Christ of whatever rank or status are called to the fullness of the Christian life and to the perfection of charity." Cornelia points the way to live this doctrine. One who studied her living inspiration very deeply wrote of her:

> This was the measure of her life's achievements—not the souls she had gathered together and taught the higher paths of love, not the sanctuaries she had set up and her children had tended, not the thousands of little ones whom they had taught and trained, not the higher standard to which Catholic education had been raised, but the one great fact that, in light and darkness, in storm and calm, she had known and loved and served her God, that the governing factor of her life had always been His Will, and that the precious casket of her heart had been broken at His Feet.[31]

The significance of Cornelia's life as wife, mother, religious and founder seems wonderfully to touch all vocations because of her profound affirmation of the meaning of vocation itself. In manifold joys and in agonizing sorrows, on clear paths and on impassable trails, she knew him in whom she had believed, she hoped against hope, and she loved him who had called her by name, called her to share his life. She conveyed to others that this was the meaning of their lives. It is the mission she passes on to us—, to strengthen and support one another in the mysterious vocation of every human person to the holiness of God himself.[32]

Notes

1. Laurentian, p. 7.
2. Bellasis D 74:362.
3. D 10:77.
4. Buckle D 63:27.
5. CC 45:4.
6. CC 7:6.
7. CC 13:5.
8. CC 8:66.
9. CC 2:37-38.
10. D 44:247.
11. GA, p. 47.
12. D 44:247.
13. CC 22:2.
14. CC 54:26.
15. CC 54:84-85.
16. CC 8:96.
17. D 76:25.
18. *Walking with God*, p. 4.
19. Cited by Armour, *Cornelia*, p. 50.
20. Buckle D 63:42.
21. I Cor 1:18-29; E. Brandenburger, "Cross," *New International Dictionary of New Testament Theology*, ed. C. Brown, 1 (1975), 397; J. McKenzie, *Dictionary of the Bible* (London, 1965), p. 162.
22. D 8:141.
23. CC 21:22, passim; CC 1:91, 98; Source 4:77-78.
24. M.E. Slater, *Mysteries of the Most Sublime Teaching* (Phila., 1968), p. 3; *Meditations as a Preparation for Whitsuntide* (London, 1851), "Preface;" "Declaration on Christian Education," in *Documents of Vatican II*, ed. W. Abbott (N.Y., 1966), p. 63, no. 1; also Source 4:139, for the text of the SHCJ Const of 1877 to which Slater refers.
25. See, e.g. CC 1:29, 98, 101; CC 6:66, 67, 71; CC 8:8, 94; CC 21:23; CC 2:7, 14, 34, 37-39.
26. D 63:67, 78.
27. D 72:75.
28. Bellasis D 73:174.
29. Jn 12:24; Buckle D 63:42.
30. Ex 234. Other examples of Buckle and Bellasis on the character and teachings of Cornelia are: Buckle D 63:11, 18-22, 65-67, 73-74; D 64:74, 94, 122; D 65:7; D 67:146-47; Bellasis D 72:108, 128-30; D 73:172-4; 209, 213, 285; D 74:317; D 75:566, 646. One would have to cite most of their books to cover their full exposition of their founder's charism.
31. Gompertz, p.468.
32. I Tm 1:12; Heb 6:13-0, 11:13; Is 43:1; Jn 14:20; Mt 5:48.

Appendix A

The Writings of Cornelia Connelly: Survey and Analysis

What has been said of 19th century French founders can be applied to Cornelia—that she saw her times, as they did, as a "time for doing rather than writing." In 19th century England she saw, as did the French founders, "ruins to be built up." She understood, as they did, that her service to the Church and the manifestation of her spirituality was "much more in works which were being carried out everywhere, than in books which few had time to write."[1] At no point did she compose a lengthy comprehensive formal synthesis of her spiritual teachings, although the chapter with which she opened her Constitutions is a brief and meaningful one. Nevertheless, she had left a considerable body of writings, much of it occasional in nature, reflecting her life experiences. These writings have been collected in fifty-eight volumes for the historical process for her beatification. All of these, their nature, contents, mutual relationships, were studied deeply for this book in order to give an authentic account of her spiritual pilgrimage, and within that, the manifestations of her charism for founding the Society of the Holy Child Jesus. The results of this study are shared below so that others may be encouraged to approach her through her own writings.

One can estimate that more than one-half the contents of the typed and photocopied volumes of Cornelia's writings bear directly on the spiritual life and the governing of her congregation, and from these were drawn most of the texts for this book. The remaining writings show a true contemplative in action: running schools, orphanages, convents, a farm; rebuilding a medieval ruin; introducing the latest method of teaching grammar. These latter writings—Training College journals, letters to businessmen, etc., are not unimportant in showing the energy and uprightness with which Cornelia pursued God's work in the world and "found him in all things."[2] Since she had given herself unreservedly to the service of the Church, she applied all of her educational skills and all of her inherited business acumen to insuring the excellence of the institutions for which she was responsible.

The writings which are more directly spiritual can be divided roughly into *formal, semi-formal,* and *informal writings.* These last can be subdivided into personal notes and writings for the guidance of others, although these two categories tend to overlap and the two kinds of notes are frequently mingled in her notebooks. The notebooks give clear evidence of the consistent claim throughout this entire book that Cornelia's teachings arose spontaneously out of her own experience, prayer, and action, and was verified by these.

Informal Writings

By far the largest group of her writings are Cornelia's 1261 extant letters. While many of them might be classified as semi-formal, all are characterized by the same simplicity and lack of pretention, by vigor, clarity, and frankness. It is an attractive, highly-endowed, fearless, loving, and compassionate woman who reveals herself in her letters. As has been said, they constitute a remarkably good base for a study of a contemplative in action. Although occasional citations have been used from all the categories of informal letters, certain groups proved most useful for this study: 61 to members of her family, including her husband and children (CC 1); 234 to individual members of her Society (CC 6-8); 403 to Bishop Grant, her Ordinary for nineteen years (CC 11-15). Some of Cornelia's best spiritual teachings flash forth in these letters, e.g., to a sister: ". . . *humiliations sent to you straight from his own humble heart.* Christmas will show you."[3]

The second group of writings found useful for this study consists of several notebooks and one commonplace book kept both for her own personal devotion and discernment, and as a record for her instructions and guidance of others. Informal notes also include single sheets found in books with often very meaningful notations. Especially valuable are three spiritual journals kept during the period of discerning her vocation, 1839-46, and two kept in a period of crisis in her Society, 1869-79.[4] Cornelia's practice of personal spiritual note-taking, to which she was initiated by the Jesuits in America, is so well described by their eminent predecessor, Francis Xavier, that we give his description here:

> If in meditating on Divine things, our most merciful God should favour you, as is His wont, with some heavenly illumination, do not let it escape from your mind, but note it down in some little book to assist your memory. Believe me that a great part of the real spiritual profit of God's servants consists in such observation, and in carefully recalling to mind pieces of knowledge of this sort given to them in mental prayer and meditation. And if anyone who has been from time to time favoured with these flashes of Divine light, writes down the truth revealed by them, he will read them over again after a while, with a very great increase of affec-

tion and advantage—that is to say, when he has himself experienced what he had set down in writing. He will recall to mind those beautiful thoughts, and taste again those keen feelings which had passed from his memory; or at least he will gain from their clearer consideration the salutary vigour which will enable him to labour fervently and to think wisely according to the needs of his present circumstances. Great indeed is the difference in savour and spiritual sweetness between ordinary readers of things written by saints when fresh from their conversations with God, and those who read therein the record of what they have themselves experienced or made their own.[5]

Cornelia's personal spiritual notes reveal that what she taught was consistent with what the Lord himself had taught her, what she had "experienced and made her own."

Semi-formal Writings

Over 400 letters by Cornelia or written at her direction are extant, addressed to businessmen and professionals—including educational authorities; to priests, bishops (besides Bishop Grant) and cardinals, and to the Holy See. Most of these are formal letters, classified here as semi-formal writings. As has been said, the business letters show maturity and shrewdness. Her letters to ecclesiastics show zeal, maturity, forthrightness, and loyalty to the Church. Those which occasioned clear statements on the nature and mission of the Society have been the most helpful for this thesis.[6]

The thirty-one extant general letters to her Society have been used as a prime source for understanding her charism. Of these, seven extant Epiphany letters, written at the beginning of the new year to encourage and inspire her sisters as they renewed their vows on Epiphany, are rich in content, particularly on Cornelia's teaching on the hidden and discerning life. Perhaps Cornelia wrote them every year from 1852 onwards, but, if so, only seven have survived.[7]

Another semi-formal writing which has been important for the study of Cornelia's charism is a so-called "Customal" which exists in five variant manuscript versions in SHCJ archives. It has been classified as semi-formal both because it has remained in manuscript form and because, although it is the length of a small book, its content in Cornelia's time exhibited no overall pattern of organization beyond that of notes, mundane or sublime, for the running of a religious congregation. Contents range from housekeeping directions to significant passages on the ascetical and mystical life.[8] Cornelia had begun to use such "Directories" as were common in religious congregations, but her Customal, though containing some "directory" material was more substantial. She seems to have derived the idea of it from Francis de Sales, who, finding that there were omissions in his Constitutions, supplemented them with a "Customary" or "book of advice" to his Sisters of the Visitation.[9] Cornelia's Customal is largely a set of compilations from spiritual authorities she valued. Throughout her writings Cornelia was as much a compiler as a composer—a subject which will be treated below.

In the Customal, as well as in her Commonplace Book and in a separate notebook, Cornelia gathered materials, mostly compiled, but with some of her own composing, for a "Directory for the Novice Mistress, SHCJ."[10] Since this especially highlights her efforts in formation to the spirit of the Society of the Holy Child Jesus, it is treated more fully in the appendices. The final items to be mentioned here under semi-formal writings are notations she made concerning the government of the Society, under such headings as "Notes for Council, Superiors and Mistress of Novices," "Notes Concerning the Constitutions," and "Notes on Temporalities."[11]

Formal Writings

Almost all the writings considered here as "formal" were printed or published by Cornelia. Chief among these writings, containing the single most important texts for the expression of her charism, are her Constitutions. Although they were perforce largely compilations, she wrote her own opening chapter giving powerful expression to her inspiration for her Society drawn from "contemplating the Eternal Wisdom in the lowliness of His humanity." She wrote this chapter at the expressed request of the young congregation she had guided for seven years, as they and she prepared for her journey to Rome to present her Constitutions for approval.[12] Although the Constitutions represent the most significant single effort toward a synthesis of her vision for the Society, they are not a final synthesis taken by themselves. Cornelia was, as were all religious women of her time, subject to much ecclesiastical restriction and imposition, regarding her Constitutions. And she was subjected to life-long delays over the approval of her Constitutions. She supplemented them with auxiliaries such as her Customal and Epiphany letters and above all by the living tradition of the Society. The Constitutions are treated more fully in Chapters IV, V and VI, as Cornelia's work of developing the Society is described, and in the appendices.

Her next most significant publication was her *Book of the Order of Studies in Schools of the Society of the Holy Child Jesus*. Its primary importance is its witness to her talents as an educator. This endowment was part of all that she was, that she utilized for God and for man to realize her vocation as a founder. The *Book of Studies* also shows how she directed deeply humanistic educational efforts as a means of gaining souls to God.[13]

Her formal writings also include three prefaces to spiritual books she caused to be translated by her sisters and published in 1851, 1857, and 1859.[14] They synthesize her teaching on prayer for both religious and seculars, including children. Cornelia advises method in prayer—Ignatian method clearly made her own. But she does much more—she invites all to true contemplative experience. These prefaces are among her best teachings on the hidden life, and her witness to the sure promise of continuing growth in the Spirit for all who faithfully await the coming of the Bridegroom.

Cornelia also compiled and had printed a small *Manual for Novices* (1869), and manual for *The Practice of Virtue* (1874). These, fitting into an easily identifiable genre of her time, having nothing exceptional about them. But they help to maintain her emphasis on a life of solid virtue as the ultimate expression of the spirit of the Society derived from the contemplation of the humbled, hidden God.

Cornelia as Compiler

The author of Cornelia's first published biography wrote in 1932 after years of research:

> I remember being strongly impressed with Cornelia Connelly's power of adopting and adapting the best ideas of others, rather than using her own originality. I should be inclined to say that she had very little originality, but a perfect genius for selecting the best from other people's ideas.[15]

Since 1932 a wealth of occasional writings of Cornelia have been found, indicating that she had perhaps more originality, had she chosen to write formally, than her first biographer attributed to her. But certainly all researches subsequent to 1932 confirm Mother Mary Catherine Gompertz's conclusion that Cornelia had a "perfect genius . . . for adopting and adapting the best ideas of others." Her two earliest biographers confirm M.M.C. Gompertz, and add what Cornelia herself professed—that she wished to draw from the saints. M.M. Joseph Buckle tells us that she

> made her own . . . the sentiments of the Saints . . . and then handed them on to her children. As a rule, if she could find a sentiment expressed in the words of a saint, she would adopt it as her own language . . . . It is very difficult to separate what belongs to Mother Connelly from what is the Author's; she . . . filled herself with the spirit she was drinking in from the holy writings she meditated . . . . They are so adapted that they are really her own.[16]

Cornelia compiled with the delightful freedom of biblical, medieval and early modern writers who, without inhibition, borrowed, adapted, improved or truncated the texts of leaders who had contributed to a common spiritual patrimony. Sometimes, especially in her Constitutions, she created a veritable mosaic not only by selecting well, but also by harmonizing with apt juxtaposition of texts, and by adapting borrowed texts with her own introductions and conclusions.[17]

She compiled because it suited her. She read wisely, she lived, prayed, reflected deeply. She excerpted and compiled, for personal use or for others, what corresponded to her own inner experience of God's design for her and her mission. She was conscious of the Spirit's guidance in her reading.

The Saints tell us many things which we take hold of and apply to ourselves only when the Holy Spirit gives us the light to see . . . and fidelity to practice what he shows us . . . the Spirit from whom all good comes. (*God Alone*, p. 52)

Compiling left Cornelia free for living, doing, praying. She compiled also because, in her time and circumstances, she, as woman and convert, would not have had her words accepted on her own authority. This was particularly true for her Constitutions.

The potential in her Constitutions (the full text of which was given in *Source* 4), and in many more of her writings, for yielding deep insights into and inspiration for the Society has not been exhausted. This brief guide to her writings is offered for those who desire more and more to hear Cornelia speaking for herself.

Notes

1. P. Pourrat, *Christian Spirituality*, trans. D. Attwater (Westminster, 1955), 4:409; A Rayez, "France: Spiritualité de: De la révolution au début du XXe siècle," *DS* (1963), 954.
2. Cornelia incorporated into her Constitutions of 1850 Ignatius' constitutional text No. 188, on "finding God in all things" (see *Constitutions of the Society of Jesus*, trans. G. Ganss [St. Louis, 1970]). She used this text as No. 17 of the Jesuit "Summary of the Constitutions" (No. 15 in her adaptation of the latter); see *Constitutions of the Society of the Holy Child Jesus*, 1850, *Source*, 4:28. For her Training College journals see CC 32-34; for letters to professional and businessmen, see CC 3, 4.
3. CC 7:29.
4. Spiritual notes for 1839-46 are found in CC 21 and 22; for 1869-79, and single sheets, CC 22. The Commonplace Book is found in CC 23, 24, 25. Other spiritual notes are found in CC 26, 27, 28 *passim*, and in CC 29.
5. Cited by J.H. Pollen, ed., in Introduction to J. Morris, *Journals Kept during Times of Retreat* (London, 1896), pp. vii-viii.
6. CC 3-4, 9-19 passim.
7. General letters, CC 8:80-132; Epiphany letters, 1852, pp. 80-81, 84-85; 1854, pp. 86-87; 1856, pp. 91-94; 1858, p. 100; 1870, pp. 105-06; 1870, p. 131.
8. CC 54-55 contain an amalgam of five somewhat varying editions of the evolving Customal. For commentary, especially in terms of the evolution of the Customal from the Commonplace Book, see M.A. Weinig, "The 1880 Chapter and the Customal," *Source*, 8 (1978), 92-100. Later printed customals of the SHCJ are much more limited in scope than Cornelia's.
9. See citations from Francis de Sales quoted by Jane Frances Fremyot de Chantal in her note included in *Rules of St. Augustine and Constitutions of the Sisters of the Visitation, and Spiritual Directory*, after the original MSS, and 1637 ed. of the Customary. Trans. from the French (London, 1930), pp. 231-32.
10. CC 54:84-88; CC 55:56-59.
11. CC 41, 45, 40a and b.
12. The text of the first chapter is found in *Source* 4:77-80. Citations from the SHCJ Constitutions will be given from this volume which is presently the most accurate edition of Cornelia's evolving constitutional texts. The record of the origin of the first chapter is found in Buckle D 63:45-46 and Annals D 68:64.
13. Printed at St. Leonards-on-Sea, 1863. For the ultimate end of education, see especially pp. 77-78.

The Writings of Cornelia Connelly: Survey and Analysis 215

14. *Meditations as a Preparation for Whitsuntide*, trans. M.E. Bowles (London, 1851) (author unknown); *Meditations on the Holy Childhood of Our Blessed Lord*, trans. M.M.I. Bridges (London, 1857) (author unknown); J. Rigoleuc, *Walking with God*, trans. M.M.I Bridges (London, 1859).
15. Letter of M.M. Gompertz to M.M. Amadeus Atchison, Sup. Gen., Feb. 2, 1932, SHCJ Archives, Mayfield, England; see also Gompertz, *The Life of Cornelia Connelly* (London, 1922), pp. 84-86.
16. D 64:65, 116, 126; see also Bellasis D 75:566; 72:135-36.
17. *Source* 4:4-5, 7-9.

Appendix B

Schematic Outline of SHCJ Constitutional History: 1854-1986

TEXTS USED AD EXPERIMENTUM	TEXTS GIVEN EPISCOPAL APPROBATION	TEXTS PRESENTED FOR BUT NOT GIVEN PONTIFICAL APPROBATION	TEXTS GIVEN PONTIFICAL APPROBATION
1845-6			1845-6
1. *Rules of the Society of the Holy Child Jesus* (MS)			1. This outline of Constitutions was given verbal approbation by Cardinal Fransoni, Prefect of Propaganda Fide.
	1850		
	2. *Constitutions, Society of the Holy Child Jesus* Approbation of Bp. Wiseman, Vicar, Apostolic, London, June 1. (MS)		
		1852	
		3. Revision of Const. of 1850 (approved by Bp. Wiseman) presented for CC by P. Melia, SJ. (MS)	
		1854	
		4. *Constitutions du Saint Enfant Jesus*, presented by CC. (Further revision of Const. of 1852). (MS)	
	1861		
	5. *Constitutions of the Society of the Holy Child Jesus, Abridged* (Abridgment contained Part One of Constitutions of 1850). (printed)		
5. The Abridgment of 1861 also contained borrowings from Jesuit sources, added after 1850 e.g., "Letter of St. Ignatius on Obedience," Admonitions and Decrees, Prayers. It also contained Cornelia's First Chapter which was not in the Constitutions of 1850.			
		1864	
		6. *Costituzioni e Regole dell'Istituto del Santo Bambino Gesu* (Further revision of Const. of 1852). (MS)	
		1869	
		7. Revision of Const. of 1854 and 1864. (MS)	
		1869	
		8. *Constitution of the Institute of the Holy Child Jesus*. (Thorough revision of Const. of 1854, 1864 under direction of A. Knapen, OFM, consultor of Propaganda Fide. (printed)	

Outline of SHCJ Constitutional History 217

	TEXTS GIVEN PONTIFICAL APPROBATION (Con't)
1874 9. *The Society of the Holy Child Jesus*. Constitutions imposed by the Ordinary of the SHCJ, Bp. Danell. 1877 10. *Constitutions of the Society of the Holy Child Jesus*. 1st revision by SHCJ of Bp. Danell's Constitutions. 1880 11. *Constitutions of the Society of the Holy Child Jesus*. 2nd revision of Danell's Rule.	1887 12. *Constitutions of the Society of the Holy Child Jesus*. Approbation for five years, August 7, 1887. 1893 13. *Constitutions of the Society of the Holy Child Jesus*. Final approbation May 20, 1893; Bull of ratification of Pope Leo XIII, July 18, 1893. 1922 14. *Constitutions of Rules of the Society of the Holy Child Jesus*. 2nd revision. Approved SCR,* June 20, 1922. 1953 15. *Constitutions and Rules of the Society of the Holy Child Jesus*. 3rd revision. Approved SCR,* July 16, 1953. 1964 16. *Constitutions and Rules of the Society of the Holy Child Jesus*. 4th revision. Approved SCR,* 1964. 18. *Society of the Holy Child Jesus: Foundation Texts and Constitutions*. 5th revision. Approved SCRIS,* 1983. (*Sacred Congregation for Religious . . . and Secular Institutes.)
1968-80 17. *General Chapter Documents*, 1958, 1970, 1976. (This outline is a revision of an outline by Helen Forshaw, SHCJ, 1977.)	

Sources and Select Bibliography

Sources

Archives of the Society of the Holy Child Jesus: Rome; Mayfield, England; and Rosemont, USA

The Writings of the Servant of God Cornelia Connelly, compiled in typescript and photocopy from manuscripts and printed texts for the apostolic process for her beatification and canonization (referred to as CC); 58 vols. including an index:

                                                                                                                       Vol.

Section I: Letters

Letters to Members of her Family	1
Letters to Pupils and Former Pupils and Letters to Others	2
Letters to Professional and Business Men	3
Letters to Professional and Business Men	4
Letters to Educational Authorities	5
Letters to Members of the SHCJ	6
Letters to Members of the SHCJ	7
Letters to Members of the SHCJ	8
Letters to Ecclesiastics: Priests	9
Letters to Ecclesiastics: Bishops Goss and O'Reilly	10
Letters to Ecclesiastics: Bishop Grant, 1851-58	11
Letters to Ecclesiastics: Bishop Grant, 1859-61	12
Letters to Ecclesiastics: Bishop Grant, 1862-64	13
Letters to Ecclesiastics: Bishop Grant, 1865-68	14

Sources and Select Bibliography 219

Letters to Ecclesiastics: Bishop Grant, 1869-70, and undated letters 15
Letters to Ecclesiastics: Bishop Danell, 1870-72 16
Letters to Ecclesiastics: Bishop Danell, 1873-79 17
Letters to Ecclesiastics: Cardinals, Archbishops 18
Letters to the Holy See 19
Letters Written at the Direction of the Servant of God 20

Section II: Private Notebooks and Memoranda

Spiritual Notebooks (Spiritual Notebooks 1 & 2) 21
Supplement: Spiritual Notes 22
Common Place Book (Part 1) 23
Common Place Book (Part 2) 24
Common Place Book (Part 3) 25
Community Work Book (extracts only) 26
Notes, Directives — Instructions 27
Dates of Events 28

Section III: Varia

Various Writings of the Servant of God (Part 1) 29
Various Writings of the Servant of God, including Practice of Virtue,
    printed 1874 30
Manual for Novices, printed in 1860 31
Training School Journal 1856 32
Training School Journal 1858-1862 33
Training School Journal 34
Educational Directives (Parts 1 & 2) 35
Ratio Studiorum (unofficial copy) 36
Book of Studies 1863 37
Account Books 38
Mayfield Account Book (1863-65) 39
Notes on Temporalities 40
Notes on Temporalities — Supplement 40
Notes for Council, Superiors and Mistress of Novices 41

Section IV: Legal and Personal Documents

Legal and Personal Documents 1844-78 42
Case of Reverend Pierce Connelly
    (Annotations) 43
    (N.B. The text of Cornelia Connelly's allegation in Connelly vs
    Connelly is printed in D 7)

Section V: Notes Relative to the Constitutions

Translations and Annotations (Craisson) 44
Notes Relative to the Constitutions 1874-76 45

Section VI: Constitutions and Rules, and Customal

Succeeding editions of the Constitutions of the SHCJ, 1846-80 46-53
  have been edited and incorporated in a single volume, *A Study of the
  Constitutions of the SHCJ As Developed under Cornelia Connelly*, by
  C. McCarthy. *Source* 4, 1975. See also C. McCarthy, *Studies in the
  Spirituality of the Society of the Holy Child Jesus: Key Texts from the
  Original Rule. Source* 1, 1970.
Customal 54
Customal (cont'd) 55

Section VII: Index and Supplements

Index of Writings 56
Supplementary Volume 57
Second Supplementary Volume 58

Privately Printed Works

> *Practice of Virtue*, 1874, vol. 30
> *Manual for Novices*, 1869, vol. 31.
> *Book of the Order of Studies of Schools of the SHCJ*, 1863, vol. 37.
> *Constitutions and Rules of the SHCJ*, 1861, 1864, 1869, 1877, 1880.
> *Legends of Our Lady and the Saints*, 1874, dedication only by Cornelia Connelly, reproduced in CC 30.

Published Works

The following books were translated by SHCJ and were published under the supervision of Cornelia Connelly. All but Nepveu's *Higher Paths* contain prefaces written by her.

> *Meditations as a Preparation for Whitsuntide and Other Feasts*, together with such helps in the practice of mental prayer and examination of conscience, as tend to the leading of a more spiritual life. Trans. M.E. Bowles, London: Richardson, 1851 (author unknown).
>
> *Meditations on the Holy Childhood of Our Blessed Lord*, in which we are led to abide in humility with the Holy Family of Nazareth, and thence to drink sweet encouragement and counsel for every circumstance of life. Trans. M.M.I. Bridges. London: Richardson, 1857 (author unknown).

Nepveu, F., SJ. *Higher Paths in the Spiritual Life*, being a retreat for the religious. Trans. M.M.I. Bridges, London: Richardson, 1859.

Rigoleuc, J. *Walking with God*, or dwellers in the recreation house of the Lord. Trans. M.M.I. Bridges, London: Richardson, 1859.

An anthology of the spiritual writings of Cornelia Connelly, *God Alone*, compiled and ed. by J. Walsh and C. Sullivan, was published at London, 1959 (referred to as GA).

Documentation Presented by the Historical Commission for the Beatification and Canonization of the Servant of God, Cornelia Connelly, Foundress of the Society of the Holy Child Jesus.

These vols. (referred to as D) have been used throughout, especially D 2-9, and D 63-78. They repeat many of the writings of Cornelia Connelly. They contain also some of Pierce Connelly's writings.

Title	Vol.
Biographical Conspectus	1
Family Affairs	2-9
Foundation at Derby	10
Foundation at St. Leonards	11-22
Foundations in London	23
Foundations in Liverpool	24-26
Foundations in Preston	27
Foundation in Blackpool	28
Foundations in America	29-31
Foundations at Orr and Mark Cross Orphanages	32
Foundation at Mayfield	33-34
Foundations in France	35
Training College	36-40
School Affairs	41-42
Community Affairs in General	43-44
Chaplains at St. Leonards	45
Chaplains at Mayfield	46
Inheritances	47
Defections	48-49
Affairs of Government	50-58
Last Days, Death and Burial	59
Sacristy Journals, 1849-1879	60
Diaries, 1855-1877	61
Extracts from Diaries kept by the Secretary General: 1878-1879	62

Notes Collected by Mother Maria Joseph Buckle for a Biography of the
  Servant of God 63-67
Annals SHCJ: 1846-76 .... 68-71.
Biography of the Servant of God by Mother Mary Francis Bellasis ... 72-75
Recollections and Testimonies 76-78
  (Vol. 78 is by Mother Maria Joseph Buckle)
Evidence from Letters of Fama Sanctitatis 79
Outstanding Cures 80
Favours listed According to Years 81
Introductions translated into Italian (Parts 1 & 2) 82
Biographical Dictionary (Parts 1 & 2) 83
Index and List of Archives Searched 84
Supplementary Volume—Varia 85

In 1983, in Rome, the SHCJ printed *Positio: Documentary Study for the Canonization Process of the Servant of God Cornelia Connelly (née Peacock) 1809-79*. Sacred Congregation for the Causes of Saints, Prot. No. 953, Southwark, 3 vols. These vols. contain selected documents from the sources listed above under Writings (CC) and Documentation (D), and commentary. The *Positio* is available in SHCJ Archives.

Archives of the Archdiocese of Birmingham, England: Connelly Papers.
Archives of the Archdiocese of New Orleans, La.: *L'Abeille*, Nov. 24, 1835.
Archives of the Archdiocese of St. Louis, Mo.: Letters and Papers of Non-Clerics, 1834-1840.
Archives of the Religious of the Sacred Heart:
Rome: Journal de la Trinité du Mont.
  Letters of Madeleine Sophie Barat, RSCJ, 1839-49.
  Letters of Josephine de Coriolis, RSCJ, 1839-45.
Grand Coteau, La.: Journal de la Maison du Sacré Coeur de Jésus.
Archives of the Sacred Congregation of Propaganda Fide, Rome.
Archives of the Society of Jesus, Grand Coteau, La.: Diarium Praefecti Scholae, 1838-.
  Historia Domus Collegii Sancti Caroli, 1838-.
  Journal [of the Minister], St. Charles College, 1838-.
  Liber Consultationum Collegii Sancti Caroli, 1838-.
  Registre des Enterrements de la Paroisse Saint Charles Borromée, 1838-.
MS Division, Library of Congress, Washington, DC:
Papers of Joseph Nicolas Nicollet.
Papers of Henry Schoolcraft.

Select Bibliography

Works Consulted: On Cornelia Connelly and the Society of the Holy Child Jesus

"A Bibliography of the Society of the Holy Child Jesus" was presented as a Master's dissertation to Catholic University of America in 1955 by Sr. M.D. Lynch. Her list of studies on Cornelia Connelly to 1955 will not be repeated here. Biographies before 1955 will be listed, and one drama published in 1961 when it was produced on the stage.

Biographies of Cornelia Connelly

Cornelia Connelly has not lacked biographers. None of their works, however, is definitive, nor do they trace adequately her spiritual itinerary. Gompertz, Bisgood and Armour are the most helpful and depend most directly on sources. But some recently discovered sources crucial to understanding the evolution of Cornelia's vocation prior to founding the Society were not available to Gompertz and Bisgood. The latter incorporates sources on Cornelia as Superior General not available to Gompertz. Both build upon two unpublished biographies of Cornelia Connelly written by two of her contemporaries M.M. Joseph Buckle, SHCJ and M.M. Francis Bellasis, SHCJ. Armour incorporates several new findings, but is too brief to indicate their full significance. Gompertz, Bisgood, de Maille and Armour present fundamental insights that Cornelia's holiness lay in her unreserved fidelity to God's successive calls, that the core of her teaching was self-oblation in Christ, but they did not have the sources available to trace these fully in her early years, nor to deal with the questions which arise concerning the genesis of her religious vocation. These four biographies are by members of the Society of the Holy Child Jesus. Wadham, a laywoman, wrote in a more popular style. Her biography is characterized by both misinterpretation and inadequate use of sources, and by real insights drawn from the author's own life experience as wife and mother.

One remarkable forty-two-page biographical article by F. Tourcher has been included with the list of books below. It was written in 1920 before the first published biography. The author acknowledges his debt, not only to M.M.F. Bellasis' manuscript, but also to "the recollections of living sisters who knew Mother Connelly personally."

Armour, M.A., with collaborations of M.U. Blake, A. Dawson. *Cornelia*. N.Y., 1979.

Bisgood, M.T. *Cornelia Connelly: A Study in Fidelity*. Westminster, Md., 1963.

Firtel, H. ". . . *denn mein Mann wollte Priester werden.* Freiburg, 1958.

Gompertz, M.C. *The Life of Cornelia Connelly.* London, 1922, 2nd and 3rd edition, abridged, 1924, 1938; 4th edition abridged and rev., 1950.

Kaye-Smith, S. "Cornelia Connelly," in *Quartet in Heaven*, pp. 57-124. N.Y., 1952.

Larnen, B. *Connelly vs. Connelly.* N.Y., Blackfriars Guild, 1961.

de Maillé, M.O. *Cornelia Connelly*, Paris, 1931; rev. ed. *Du Mariage au Cloître*, Paris, 1962.

Rispoli, G. *Un Dramma dell'Amor di Dio. Cornelia Connelly: 1809-79.* Naples, 1962.

Slater, M.E. *The Triumph of Trust.* Phila., 1950.

Tourcher, F.E. "Sketch of the Life of Mother Cornelia Connelly, Foundress of the Society of the Holy Child Jesus, 1809-89," *Records of the American Catholic Historical Society*, 31 (Mar., 1920), 1-42.

Wadham, J. *The Case of Cornelia Connelly*, London, 1956.

Selected Studies on Cornelia Connelly since 1955

Significant progress on the Cause for the Beatification of Cornelia since 1959, followed by Vatican II's call to religious to renew in the spirit of their founder has fostered research and writing on Cornelia Connelly. The articles and dissertations listed below are based on sources, and contain insights not found in published biographies.

Armour, A. "Apostolate Studies: The Poor Schools in Preston," *Source*, 2 (1971), 45-58.

_____. "Cornelia — at home," *Pylon*, 29, No. 3 (1968), 19-21.

_____. "Derby: The Cradle of the Society," *Source* 4 (1976), 31-44; 6 (1977), 34-43.

_____. "Two Valiant Women," *Catholic Gazette*, 52, No. 7 (1961), 183-7.

Bisgood, M.T. "Cornelia Connelly: Her Educational Principles," *Pylon*, 22, Nos. 1 and 2 (1960), 7-13, 4-14.

Blake, M.U. (pseud. L.S. Muir). "The Connellys' First Visit to Rome," *Pylon*, 23, Nos. 1 and 2 (1961), 2-7, 3-7.

_____."Cornelia Connelly Belongs to Everyone." *Pylon*, 28 (1967), 25-8.

_____. "Cornelia Connelly and the Spirit of the Liturgy," *Pylon*, 26, No. 2 (1964), 8-13.

_____. "Cornelia Connelly's Second Stay in Rome," *Pylon*, 29, No. 3 (1968), 26-38.

_____. "The Incarnation as Inspiration for the Society of the Holy Child Jesus: Cornelia and Gioacchino Ventura," *Source*, 3 (1972), 36-44.

Bowring, K.B. "Reminiscences of a St Leonard's School Girl," *Source* 7 (Autumn, 1977), 58-64.
Crook, Maureen, "Cornelia's Constitutions: Introduction." *Source*, 9 and 10 (1979), 10-20.
Cruchon, G. "The Case of Pierce Connelly," *Source*, 5 (1976), 5-19.
Dawson, A. "Cornelia Connelly: Three Characteristics," *Source*, 9 (1979), 61-85.
Flaxman, R. "Apostolate Studies," *Source*, 3 (1972), 1-21.
———. "Apostolate Studies: The Young Ladies' School at St. Leonard's," *Source*, 2 (1971), 31-44; 6 and 7 (1977), 44-59; 51-57.
Hargrove, B. "Connelly vs. Connelly," *Source*, 6 (1977), 5-9.
Lynch, M.D. "Connelly vs. Connelly: Aftermath—Trial by Press," *Source*, 6 and 7 (1977), 10-23; 30-50.
McCarthy, C. "The Connellys in the Church of the Mississippi Valley," *Pylon*, 29, No. 3 (1968), 8-18.
———. "Cornelia and Pierce Connelly, New Perspectives on Their Early Lives," *Records of the American Catholic Historical Society of Philadelphia*, 71 (1961), 93-105.
———. "Cornelia Connelly" and "Holy Child Jesus, Society of the," *NCE*, 4 (1967), 180; and 7 (1967), 160.
———. "Exploring our Spiritual Roots," *Source* 2, (1971), 1-13.
———. "The Incarnation as Inspiration for the Society of the Holy Child Jesus: The Child as 'Key'," *Source*, 3 (1972), 22-35.
———. "Introducing the Reverend James Montgomery," *Pylon*, 27, No. 2 (1965), 4-7.
———. "Penetrated by an Apostolic Spirit," *Source*, 8 (1978), 29-36.
McLaughlin, M.B. "Cornelia's Daughter," *Pylon*, 29, No. 3 (1968), 24 and 57.
Melville, A. "Connelly, Cornelia," *Notable American Women, 1607-1950*, 1 (1972), 372-5.
Molinari, P. "Commitment to Love: Reply to Cornelia Connelly's Critics," *Homiletic and Pastoral Review*, 64 (Oct. 1963), 21-9.
O'Neill, J.H. "No Support Here for Mother Connelly's Cause," *Homiletic and Pastoral Review*, 63 (June, 1963), 744-50.
Slater, M.E. "The March of Teaching and the March of Perfection: Study of the Contribution to Education of Cornelia Connelly," *Catholic Educational Review*, 60 (1962), 217-35.
Sullivan, C. "All Creation New," *Source*, 2 (1971), 15-30.
———. "The Influence of Mother Cornelia Connelly on Modern American Education." Diss. Immaculate Heart College, Los Angeles, 1959.
Wallwork, V. "Some Theological Reflections on the Title: Society of the Holy Child Jesus," *Source*, 3 (1972), 46-55.
Walsh, J. "Grand Coteau Revisited," *Pylon*, 21, No. 3 (1960), 27-30.
———. "Pilgrimage to Natchez," *Pylon*, 21, No. 2 (1959), 23-25.
———. "The Vocation of Cornelia Connelly," *Month* 20, No. 5 (1958),

261-73; 21, No. 1 (1959), 19-33; published as a pamphlet in 1959 by the Month.

———. "Why an American Foundress for England in 1846," *Pylon*, 23, No. 3 (1961-2), 3-6.

Weinig, M.A. "Cornelia Connelly and the Spirit of Suffering Obedience." *Review for Religious*, 21 (1962), 28-32.

———. "The 1880 Chapter and the Customal," *Source*, 8 (1978), 92-100.

———. "The Long Desired Approval of Our Rule: Some Relevant Texts," *Source*, 7 (1977), 5-29.

Whatmore, L.A. "Cornelia Connelly: Gold in the Fire," *Homiletic and Pastoral Review*, 63 (Feb., 1963), 400-7.

Whitten, V. "Chronology of the Life of Cornelia Connelly," *Source*, 8 (1978), 5-28.

Wilson, D. "To What Purpose?" *Source*, 9 (1979), 5-9.

Yore, M.W. "The Influence of Scripture on the Spirituality of Cornelia Connelly." Diss. Immaculate Heart College, Los Angeles, 1968.

Works Consulted: On Spirituality, Holiness, Charisms, Vocations

Adnes, P. "Mariage et vie chrétienne," *DS*, 10 (1977), 355-87.

Alfaro, J. "The Dual Aspect of Faith," *Concilium*, 21 (1967), 27-33.

Aquinas, Thomas, *Summa Theologiae*, ed. C. Ernst, 30 (1a, 2ae, 111), (1967), 125-29.

Bernard, C.A. "Famille (Affections de)" *DS*, 5 (1964), 74-83.

Brown, C., ed. *The New International Dictionary of New Testament Theology*, 3 vols. Trans. with additions and revisions from Theologisches Begriffslexikon zum Neuen Testament, ed. L. Coenen, E. Beyreuther, H. Bietenhard. Exeter, 1975-8.

Carmody, J. "Rahner's Spiritual Theology," *America*, 123 (Oct. 31, 1970), 345-8.

de Charry, J. *Histoire des Constitutions de la Société du Sacré Coeur*, Part I, *La Formation de l'Institut*. 2 vols.; Part II, *Les Constitutions Définitives et leur Approbation par le Saint-Siège*. 3 vols. Rome, 1975-79.

Cognet, I. "Esprit," *DS*, 4 (1961), 1233-46.

Congar, Y. "Laîc et Laîcat," *DS*, 9 (1976), 79-107.

———. *Lay People in the Church*. Rev. ed. Trans. D. Attwater. Westminster, 1965.

Crehan, J.H. "Charisms," *Catholic Dictionary of Theology*, 2 (1967), 19-22.

Cusson, G. "The Letter and the Spirit," *Way Supp*. 36 (1979), 82-89.

Diamond, J. "An Analogy between the Charism of the Religious Founder and the Charism of Holy Scripture." Unpublished paper, Rome, 1971.

Ducros, X. "Charismes," *DS*, 2 (1939), 504-07.
Dumeige, G, "Le Rôle de l'esprit et de la hiérarchie dans la vocation apostolique de Saint Ignace de Loyola," CIS, Rome, n.d.
———. "History of Spirituality: A Key for Self-Understanding," *Chicago Studies*, 15 (1976), 55-70.
Duquoc, C. and C. Floristan, eds. *Charisms in the Church. Concilium*, 109, N.Y., 1978.
Eichrodt, W. *Theology of the Old Testament*, Vol. I. Trans. J. Baker. Phila., 1961.
Fitz, R. and L. Cado, "The Recovery of Religious Life," *Review for Religious*, 34 (1975), 690-718.
Futtrell, J.C. "Discovering the Founder's Charism," *Way Supp*, 14 (1971), 62-70.
Gallagher, J.F. "Charism: For the Church," *NCE*, 3 (1967), 462-3.
George, A. and P. Grelot, "Charisms," *DBT* (N.Y., 1967), pp. 55-57.
Gilmont, J.F. "Paternité et médiation du Fondateur d'Ordre, *Revue d'ascétique et de mystique*, 40 (1964), 393-426.
Guillet, J. "Spirit," and "Spirit of God," *DBT* (N.Y., 1967), pp. 499-500, 500-05.
Haughton, R. *The Theology of Experience*, N.Y., 1972.
Holstein, H. "Conseils et charisme," *Christus*, 16 (1969), 172-85.
Iparraguirre, I. "Nature de la sainteté et moyens pour l'obtenir," *L'Eglise de Vatican II*, Collection Unam Sanctam, 51c (1966), 1119-35.
Jeanne d'Arc, Sr. "Les congrégations à la recherche de leur esprit." *Supplément de la Vie Spirituelle*, 20 (1967), 502-34.
Käsemann, E. "Ministry and Community in the New Testament," *Essays on New Testament Themes*. London, 1964.
Kerns, J.E. *The Theology of Marriage. The Historical Development of Christian Attitudes Toward Sex and Sanctity in Marriage*. N.Y., 1964.
Koch, R. "Charisma," *Sacramentum Verbi*, 1 (1970), 96-101.
Kyne, M.S.J. "Discernment of Spirits and Christian Growth," *Way Supp*, 6 (1968), 20-26.
Labourdette, M. "La sainteté, vocation de tous les membres de l'Eglise," *L'Eglise de Vatican II*, Collection Unam Sanctam 51c, (1966), 1105-17.
Lafont, G. "L'esprit-saint et le droit dans l'institution religieuse," *Supplément de la Vie Spirituelle*, 20 (Sept. 1967); Nov. 1967), 473-501, 594-639.
Lampe, G.W.A. *Patristic Greek Lexicon*. Oxford, 1961.
Laplace, J. *The Direction of Conscience*. Trans. of *La Direction de Conscience ou le Dialogue Spirituel*, by J.C. Guinness. N.Y., 1967. Reprinted as *Preparing for Spiritual Direction*, Chicago, 1975.
Larivière, F. "Authentication of Charisms," *Donum Dei*, 20 (1973), 49-55.
Larkin, E. "Spirituality, Christian," *NCE*, 13 (1967), 598-603.

Laurentin, R. "Charisms: Terminological Precision," *Charisms in the Church, Concilium*, 109 (1978), 3-11.
Ledochowska, T. *In Search of the Charism of the Institute*. Trans. M. Lawrence and M. Bellasis. Rome, 1976.
Lozano, J. "Founder and Community: Inspiration and Charism," *Review for Religious*, 37 (1978), 214-36.
MacAvoy, J. "Famille," *DS*, 5 (Paris 1964), 62-74.
Malatesta, E., G. Bardy et al. *Discernment of Spirits*. Trans. Sr. I. Richards. Collegeville, 1957.
Milligan, M. *That They May Have Life: A Study of the Spirit-Charism of Father Jean Gailhac, Founder*. Rome, 1975.
———. "Charism and Constitutions," *Way Supp*, 36 (1979), 45-59.
Milne Home, J. "What is Charisma?" *Source*, 8 (1978), 51-59; 9 (1979), 21-36.
Molinari, P. "Consecration for Mission," *Way Supp*, 13 (1972), 3-13.
———. "The Following of Christ in the Teaching of Vatican II, *Way Supp* 4 (1967), 92-119.
———. "Introduction and Commentary: Perfectae Caritatis," *Way Supp*, 3 (1966), 3-64.
———. "Renewal of Religious Life according to the Founder's Spirit," *Review for Religious*, 27 (1968), 796-806.
———. "Saints and Miracles," *Way*, 18 (Oct. 1978), 287-99.
———. *The Saints: Their Place in the Church*. N.Y., 1965.
Olphe-Galliard, M. "Charisme des fondateurs religieux," *Vie Consacrée*, 39 (Nov., Dec., 1967), 338-52.
P. Pourrat, "Affective Spiritualité—Piété Affective," *DS* 1 (1937), cols. 240-6.
Rahner, K. "Charism," *Encyclopedia of Theology. The Concise Sacramentum Mundi* (N.Y., 1975), pp. 184-86.
———. *The Dynamic Element in the Church*, London, 1964.
———. *Grace and Freedom*. N.Y., 1969.
———. *Nature and Grace*. N.Y., 1964.
———. *Theological Investigations*. Vols. 3 and 4, Baltimore, 1966-67; vols. 8 and 10, N.Y., 1971-3.
———. "Virtue," *SM*, 6 (1970), 337-43.
——— and H. Vorgrimler. *Theological Dictionary*. Ed. C. Ernst. Trans. R. Strachan, N.Y., 1965.
Rulla, L., J. Riddick, F. Imoda. *Entering and Leaving Vocation: Intrapsychic Dynamics*. Chicago, 1976.
———. *Depth Psychology and Vocation: A Psycho-Social Perspective*. Chicago, 1971.
Schillebeeckx, E. *Marriage, Secular Reality and Saving Mystery*. N.Y., 1965.
Schürman, H. "Les charismes spirituels," in *L'Eglise de Vatican II*, Collection Unam Sanctam, 51b, (1966), 541-74.

Sheets, J. *Toward a Theology of the Religious Life: A Sketch with Particular Reference to the Society of Jesus.* Studies SJ, 3, November, 1971.
Van Kaam, A. *In Search of Spiritual Identity.* Denville, N.J., 1975.
von Balthasar, H.V. "A Theology of the Evangelical Counsels," *Cross Currents,* 16 (1966), 213-36.
Von Rad, G. *Old Testament Theology,* vol. I. Trans. D. Stalker, N.Y., 1962.
Walsh, J. "The Difficulties of Revision," *Way Supp,* 36 (1979), 5-17.
Wright, J. *The Grace of Our Founder and the Grace of Our Vocation.* Studies SJ, 3, Feb. 1971.
Yarnold, E. "The Vows: Consecration and Sign," *Way Supp,* 3 (1966), 77-89.

Works Consulted: On the Paschal Mystery, Christocentrism, Ignatian Spirituality, the Infancy Narratives, Contemplation of the Gospels

Berrouard, M-F et al. "Enfance spirituelle," *DS,* 4 (1959), 682-714.
Botterau, G. "The 'Discreta Caridad' of Ignatius of Loyola," CIS, 18 (1975), 54-65.
Brandenburger, E. "Cross, Wood, Tree," in *New International Dictionary of New Testament Theology,* ed. C. Brown, 1 (1975), 389-404.
Broderick, J. *St. Ignatius Loyola, The Pilgrim years.* London, 1956.
Brown, R. *The Birth of the Messiah: A Commentary on the Infancy Narratives in Matthew and Luke.* N.Y., 1977.
Buckley, M. "The Contemplation to Attain Love, *Way Supp,* 24 (1975), 92-104.
———. "Rules for the Discernment of Spirits," *Way Supp,* 20 (1973), 19-38.
Coemans, A. *Commentary on the Rules of the Society of Jesus.* Trans. M. Germing. El Paso, 1942.
Conwell, J.F. SJ. *Contemplation in Action.* Spokane, 1957.
Courel, F. SJ., ed. and trans. *Exercises Spirituels.* 3rd ed. Collection Christus, 5. Textes. Paris, 1963.
———. "La fin unique de la compagnie de Jésus," *Archivum Historicum Societatis Jesu.* 35 (1966), 186-211; trans. and abridged in *Way Supp,* 14 (1971), 46-61.
———. ed. *Louis Lallemant: La vie et la doctrine.* Collection Christus, 3. Textes. Paris, 1961.
Cusson, G. *Conduis-moi sur le Chemin d'Eternité: Les exercises dans la vie courante.* Rome, 1973.
———. "Ignace de Loyola. Les Exercices Spirituels," *DS,* 7 (1967), 1306-18.
———. *Pédagogie de l'expérience spirituelle personelle.* Paris, 1968.
Danielou, J. *The Infancy Narratives.* Trans R. Sheed. N.Y., 1968.

———. "La vision Ignatienne du monde et de l'homme." *Revue d'ascétique et de mystique*, 26 (1950), 5-17.
Directory to the Spiritual Exercises of Our Holy Father Ignatius. Authorized Translation. London, 1925.
Dulles, A. "Finding God's Will," *Woodstock Letters*, 94 (1965), 139-52.
Dumeige, G. "Ignace de Loyola. Expérience et doctrine spirituelle." *DS*, 7 (1976), 1277-1306.
———. "The Progressive Discernment of God's Will in the Life of St. Ignatius," trans. for Prog. Sp. Ex. by L. Grimley from *Christus*, 7 (1955), 314-31.
Egan. H. D. *The Spiritual Exercises and the Ignatian Mystical Horizon*, St. Louis, 1976.
Futtrell, J.C. *Ignatian Discernment*. Studies SJ, 2, 1970.
Ganne, Sr. M. B., IBVM. *St. Ignatius and Mary Ward: A Striking Parallel*. Communications, 12, CIS, Rome, 1977.
Ganss, G. *The Authentic Spiritual Exercises of St. Ignatius*. Studies SJ, 1, Nov. 1969.
———. Trans. with commentary. *The Constitutions of the Society of Jesus*. St. Louis, 1970.
Guibert, J. de. *The Jesuits: Their Spiritual Doctrine and Practice*. Trans. W.J. Young. Chicago, 1964.
Guiliani, M. "Trouver Dieu en toutes choses," *Christus*, 6 (1955), 172-94.
Ignatius of Loyola. *Obras Completas*. Trans. and ed. I. Iparraguire and C. Dalmses, Madrid, 1963.
———. *Constitutions of the Society of Jesus*. Trans. G. Ganss. St. Louis, 1970.
———. *St. Ignatius' Own Story as Told to Luis Gonzales de Camara*. Trans. W. Young. Chicago, 1956.
———. *Spiritual Exercises*. Trans. L.J. Puhl. Chicago, 1951.
Iparaguirre, I. *Contemporary Trends in Studies on the Constitutions of the Society of Jesus: Annotated Bibliographical Orientations*. Trans. D. Meenan. St. Louis, 1974.
———. *The Ever-Youthful and Dynamic Character of Ignatian Spirituality*. Communications, 1, CIS. Rome, 1974.
———. "Ignace de Loyola. Vie et oeuvres." *DS*, 7 (1976), 1266-77.
———. *The Paschal Mystery and the Spiritual Exercises of St. Ignatius*: Trans. from "El Misterio Pascual y los Ejercicios de San Ignacio," *Sal Terrae* (1965), 145-54, for Prog. Sp. Ex.
———. "Spirituality: Spiritual Exercises," *SM*, 6 (1970), 162-3.
Laplace, J. *An Experience of Life in the Spirit*. Chicago, 1978.
Legasse, S. *Jésus et l'enfant*. Paris, 1969.
Leon-Dufour, X., ed. *Dictionary of Biblical Theology*, N.Y., 1967, 2nd ed. rev., trans. P.J. Cahill and E.M. Stewart. N.Y., 1973.
Lyonnet, S. "La Méditation des Deux Étendards et son fondement scripturaire," *Christus*, 12 (1956), 453-57.

McCarthy, C. "Constitutions for Apostolic Religious," *Way Supp*, 14 (1971), 33-45.

———. "Ignatian Charism in Women's Congregations," *Way Supp*, 20 (1973), 10-18.

McKenzie, Y. *Dictionary of the Bible*. London, 1965.

———. *Vital Concepts of the Bible*. London, 1968.

Molinari, P. "La sequela di Cristo nella vita consacrata," *II Cursus Internationalis Exercitiorum Spiritualium in hodierna luce ecclesiae*, II (Rome, 1969), 1-35.

Morris, J. *Journals Kept during Times of Retreat*. Selected and ed. by J.H. Pollen, 2nd ed. London, 1896.

Noye, I. "Enfance de Jésus," *DS*, 14 (1959), 652-82.

O'Leary, B. *The Discernment of Spirits in the Memorials of Blessed Peter Favre, Way Supp*, 35, 1979.

Olphe-Galliard, M. "Contemplation Ignatienne," *DS*, 2 (1939), 2023-29.

Padberg, J. *Personal Experience and the Spiritual Exercises: The Example of St. Ignatius of Loyola*. Studies SJ, 10, no. 5, St. Louis, 1978.

Peters, W. *The Spiritual Exercises of St. Ignatius: Exposition and Interpretation*. Jersey City, 1968.

Petty, M. "The Infancy Narratives and the Spiritual Exercises," trans. by C. Burton, from *Ciencia y Fe*, 20 (1964), 469-80, for Prog. Sp. Ex.

Rahner, H. "Notes on the Spiritual Exercises," *Woodstock Letters*, (1956), 281-336.

———. *Ignatius the Theologian*. Trans. M. Barry. N.Y., 1968.

Rahner, K. *Spiritual Exercises*. N.Y., 1965.

Rayez, A. "France: Spiritualité du: 19e siècle," *DS*, 5 (1963), 953-97.

Slater, Sr. M. Eleanor. *Mysteries of the Most Sublime Teaching*. Phila., 1968.

Stanley, D., "Contemplation of the Gospels, Ignatius Loyola, and the Contemporary Christian," *Theological Studies*, (Sept. 1968), 416-43.

———. "Contemplation on the Incarnation," *Theology Digest* (Winter, 1964), 275-86.

———. *A Modern Scriptural Approach to the Spiritual Exercises*. St. Louis, 1967.

von Balthasar, H.U. *Word and Redemption*. N.Y., 1965.

Yeomans, W. "The Will of God," *Way*, 18 (1978), 122-7.

Young, W., ed. and trans. *Finding God in All Things*. Chicago, 1958.

Works Consulted: History of the Church, of Theology, of Spirituality

Aubert, R. *Le pontificat de Pie IX, 1846-78, Histoire de l'Eglise*, ed. A. Fliche and V. Martin, vol. 21. Paris, 1952.

Botterau, G. "Lallemant, Louis," *DS*, 9 (1976), 126-35.

Bouyer, L. *Histoire de la spiritualité chrétienne, III La spiritualité ortho-*

doxe et la spiritualité protestante et anglicane. Paris, 1965.

———. *Introduction to Spirituality.* N.Y., 1963.

Bremond, H. *A Literary History of Religious Thought in France.* Vol. III, *The Triumph of Mysticism,* Trans. by K. Montgomery, London, 1936.

Brouillard, R. "Rigoleuc (Jean)," *DTC,* 13 (1937), 2706-08.

Cognet, L. *Histoire de la spiritualité chrétienne.* Vol., III: La spiritualité moderne, 1500-1650. Paris, 1966.

Courel, F. SJ. "Lallemant, Louis," *NCE,* 8 (1967), 335-6.

Hocedez, E. *Histoire de la théologie au xixe siècle.* 3 vols. Bruxelles, 1947-52.

Latourette, K.S. *Christianity in a Revolutionary Age*: Vol. 1, *The Nineteenth Century in Europe.* N.Y., 1958.

Leflon, J. *La crise révolutionnaire, 1789-1842. Histoire de l'Eglise,* ed. A. Fliche and V. Martin, vol. 20. Paris, 1949.

LeBrun, J. "France, Spiritualité de: Le Grand siècle de la spiritualité française." *DS,* 5 (1964), 917-53.

Nicolau, M. "Lapuente, Louis de," *DS,* 9 (1967), 265-76.

Olphe-Galliard, M. "Surin, Jean-Joseph," *DTC,* 14 (1941), 2834-42.

Poupard, P. *L'abbé Louis Bautain.* Paris, 1964.

———. "Fideism," *SM,* (1968), 335-7.

Pourrat, P. *Christian Spirituality.* 4 vols. Trans. D. Attwater. Westminster, 1955.

Schoof, T.M. *A Survey of Catholic Theology. 1800-1970*; N.Y., 1970.

Seronet, P. "François de Sales, (saint)," *DS* 5 (1964), 1058-97.

Sheppard, L. *Spiritual Writers in Modern Times,* Vol. 42 of Twentieth Century Encyclopedia of Catholicism. N.Y., 1967.

Williams, M. *St. Madeleine Sophie, Her Life and Letters.* N.Y., 1965.

———. *The Society of the Sacred Heart: History of a Spirit,* 1800-1975. London, 1978.

Works Consulted: American Background of Cornelia Connelly

Ahlstrom, S. *A Religious History of the American People.* Vol. I. New Haven, 1972. Image Book ed., 1975.

Baudier, R. *The Catholic Church in Louisiana.* New Orleans, 1939.

Billington, R.A. *The Protestant Crusade,* 1800-1860. Chicago 1938.

Blake, M.U. "Nothing if not Versatile: John Grassi, SJ" *Pylon,* 25, No. 1 (1963), 34-8.

Bray, M. "Joseph Nicolas Nicollet, Geologist," *Proceedings of the American Philosphical Society,* 114, No. 1 (1970), 37-59.

———. *Joseph Nicollet and His Map.* Phila., 1980.

———. "Joseph Nicolas Nicollet, Geographer," in *Frenchmen and French Ways in the Mississippi Valley,* ed. J. McDermott, Urbana, 1969.

Sources and Select Bibliography

Bray, M. and E. Bray, trans. and ed. *Joseph N. Nicollet on the Plains and Prairies*. St. Paul, 1976.
Bray, M. ed. and A. Fertey, trans. *The Journals of Joseph N. Nicollet*, St. Paul, 1970.
Burr, N.R. ed. *Religion in American Life*, 4 vols. Princeton, 1961.
Callan, L. *The Society of the Sacred Heart in North America*. N.Y., 1937.
Chinnici, J.P. "Organization of the Spiritual Life: American Catholic Devotional Works, 1791-1886," *Theological Studies*, 40 (June, 1979), 229-55.
Dawley, P.M. *The Episcopal Church and Its Work*. Greenwich, 1955.
_____. *The Story of the General Theological Seminary, 1817-1967*. N.Y., 1969.
Easterly, F. *The Life of Rt. Rev. Joseph Rosati, C.M.* Washington, 1942.
Farley, J. Cardinal. *The Life of John Cardinal McCloskey*, N.Y., 1918.
Garber, J.P. *The Valley of the Delaware and its Place in American History*. Phila., 1934.
Garraghan, G. *The Jesuits in the Middle United States*. 3 vols. N.Y., 1938.
_____. "John Anthony Grassi, SJ, 1775-1849," *Catholic Historical Review* 23 (1937), 273-92.
Gaustad, E. *A Religious History of America*. N.Y., 1966.
Good. H.G. *History of American Education*, N.Y., 1964.
Groome, Harry Connelly. *The Groome Family and Connections*, Phila., 1907.
Hotchkins, S. *Memoir of the Rev. James Montgomery*, D.D. Phila., 1889.
"Jean François Abbadie (1804-90)" *Woodstock Letters*, 24 (1895), 16-36.
Manross, W. *A History of the American Episcopal Church*. N.Y. 1935. 2nd ed. N.Y. 1950.
Meehan, T. "Barber Family," *Catholic Encyclopedia*, 2 (1907), 286-87.
Nye, R.B. *The Cultural Life of the New Nation*, N.Y., 1963.
Oberholtzer, E. *Philadelphia: History of the City and Its People*. Vol. 1, Phila., 1912.
Perry, W.S. *The History of the American Episcopal Church*, 2 vols. Boston, 1885.
Pillar, J. *The Catholic Church in Mississippi, 1837-65*. New Orleans, 1964.
Point, N. *Wilderness Kingdom: Indian Life in the Rocky Mountains, 1840-47*. Trans. J. Donnelly, N.Y., 1967.
Reynolds, J.A. "McCloskey, John," *NCE*, 9 (N.Y., 1967), 6-8.
Roemer, T. *The Leopoldine Foundation and the Church in the United States, 1829-39*. N.Y., 1933.
Scharff, J. and T. Wescott. *History of Philadelphia*, Vol. III. Phila., 1884.
Schauinger, J.H. *Cathedrals in the Wilderness*, Milwaukee, 1952.
Simon, A. "Gregory XVI, Pope," *NCE*, 6 (1967), 783-88.
Smith, S., R. Handy, L. Loetscher. *American Christianity: An Historical Interpretation with Representative Documents*. 2 vols. N.Y., 1963.

Spalding, M.J. *Sketches of the Life, Times and Character of the Rt. Rev. Benedict Joseph Flaget.* Louisville, 1852.

Walworth, C.E. *The Oxford Movement in America or Glimpses of Life in an Anglican Seminary.* N.Y., 1895.

Watson, W. and S.B. Dewees. *History of Westtown Boarding School, 1799-1899*, Phila.

Weigel, G. *Churches in North America*, Baltimore, 1961.

Wood, R. ed. *The Pennsylvania Germans.* Princeton, 1942.

Zenos, A. C. *Presbyterianism in America.* N.Y., 1937.

Works Consulted: American Background: Anti-Catholic Literature Available to the Connellys

Beecher, L. *A Plea for the West,* Cincinnati, 1835.

Monk, M. *Awful Disclosures of the Hotel Dieu Nunnery of Montreal.* N.Y., 1963.

Reed, Rebecca. *Six Months in a Convent.* Boston: 1835.

A Review of the Lady Superior's Reply to "Six Months in a Convent," being a Vindication of Miss Reed. Boston, 1835.

Ricci, Scipio de. *Female Converts, Secrets of Nunneries Disclosed.* N.Y., 1834.

Works consulted: English background of Cornelia Connelly

Arnstein, W. *Protestant versus Catholic in Mid-Victorian England: Mr. Newdegate and the Nuns.* Univ. of Missouri Press, 1982.

Basset, B. SJ. *The English Jesuits.* London, 1967.

Beck, G. *English Catholics, 1850-1950.* London 1950.

Briggs, A. *Victorian People.* London, 1954.

Catholic Emancipation 1829 to 1929: Essays by Various Authors, N.Y., 1929.

Chadwick, O. *The Mind of the Oxford Movement.* Los Angeles, 1960.

Digby, A. and P. Searby. *Children, School and Society in Nineteenth-Century England.* London, 1981.

Ensor, R. *England, 1870-1914.* London, 1960.

Fothergill, B. *Nicholas Wiseman.* London, 1963.

Gwynn, D. *Lord Shrewsbury, Pugin, and the Catholic Revival.* Westminster, 1946.

Harton, F.P. "Anglicane Spiritualité" *DS*, 1 (1937), 660-670.

Newman, J.H. *Selections from Prose Writings*, N.Y., 1906.

Trappes-Lomax, E. *Pugin: A Medieval Victorian.* London, 1932.

Vernet, F. "Anglaise, Ecossaise, Irlandaise (Spiritualité)" *DS*, 1 (1937), 625-60.

Ward, W. *The Life and Times of Cardinal Wiseman.* 2 vols. London, 1900.
Young, U. *Life of Father Ignatius Spencer.* London, 1933.

Works Consulted: Women's Studies

Barnhouse, R.T. *Identity.* Phila., 1984.
Biddle, G. and S. Lowrie. *Notable Women of Pennsylvania.* Univ. of Pennsylvania Press, 1942.
Burghardt, W. ed. *Woman: New Dimensions*, N.Y., 1979.
Christ, C.P. and J. Plaskow. *Womanspirit Rising.* N.Y., 1979.
Clark, E. and H. Richardson, eds. *Women and Religion.* N.Y., 1977.
Conn, J.W. "Women's Spirituality: Restriction and Reconstruction," *Cross Currents*, (Fall, 1980), 293-307.
Cott, N.F. and E.H. Pleck, eds. *A Heritage of Her Own.* N.Y., 1979.
Donnelly, D. "Women and Prayer," *Publishers Weekly*, 221, no. 7 (Feb. 12, 1982), 62-63.
Ewens, M. OP. *The Role of Nun in the Nineteenth-Century America: Variations on the International Theme.* (A microfilm xerography). Ann Arbor, Mich., UMI, 1972.
Gerstenberger, D. and C. Allen. "Women Studies/American Studies, 1970/75" *American Quarterly*, 29, no. 3 (1977), 263-79.
Holcombe, L. *Wives and Property: Reform of the Married Women's Property Law in Nineteenth Century England.* Univ. of Toronto Press, 1982.
James, J., ed. *Women in American Religion.* Univ. of Pennsylvania Press, 1980.
Kimball, G. "From Motherhood to Sisterhood: The Search for Female Religious Imagery in Nineteenth and Twentieth Century Theology." *Beyond Androcentrism*, ed. R. Gross (Missoula, Montana, 1977) pp. 259-68.
Norton, The Hon. Mrs. Caroline. *English Laws for Women in the Nineteenth Century.* London, 1854. Reprinted as *Caroline Norton's Defense*, with introd. by J. Huddleston. Chicago, 1982.
_____. *A Letter to the Queen on Lord Chancellor Cranworth's Marriage and Divorce Bill.* Third Edition. London, 1855.
Reuther, R. and R. Keller. *Women and Religion in America.* Vol. I. *The Nineteenth Century, A Documentary History.* N.Y., 1981.
Ruether, R. and E. McLaughlin. *Women of Spirit*, N.Y., 1979.
Turner, P. and B. Cooke, "Feminist Thought and Sytcmatic Thcology," *Horizons*, 11 (Spring, 1984) 125-35.

The Spirituality of Cornelia Connelly

Bibliography of the Spiritual Tradition from Which Cornelia Drew[1]

Below are listed works known to have been used by Cornelia and the SHCJ during her lifetime, besides the works she herself composed/compiled, or caused to be translated. The Bibliography has been compiled on the basis of references to, and/or citations from the works, by Cornelia and/or her SHCJ contemporaries, or from identifications within the books. The works fall into the following classifications: 1) Catechisms and Compendiums or Manuals of Christian Doctrine; 2) Church Histories and Lives of the Saints; 3) the literature of spirituality proper, i.e., ascetical and/or mystical treatises and manuals: daily, seasonal and topical meditations on the gospel mysteries, scriptural themes, the truths of faith, the virtues of the saints; 4) Liturgical books; 5) Scripture Commentaries; 6) Constitutional writings and works on canon law and the government of religious; 7) Apologetic and polemical works.

This Bibliography should be used in connection with the Outline of the Spiritual Tradition from which Cornelia drew given in the Appendices.

An Abridgement of Christian Doctrine. Derby: Richardson, n.d.

An Abstract of the Douay Catechism, revised and improved for the use of the faithful. London: Richardson. n.d.

Aquaviva, C. SJ. *Directorium in Exercitia, Industriae ad Curando Animae Morbos* in vol. 6 (1829), of Jesuit Constitutional documents published at Avignon 1827-1838, 7 vols. Vol. 6 also contains Exercitia Spiritualia S.P. Ignatii Loyolae.

Augustine of Hippo, St. *Règle de S. Augustin*, printed with *Constitutions et Directoire pour les soeurs religieuses de la Visitation*. Paris, 1818.

Bagshawe. *Catechism Illustrated* by Passages from the Holy Scriptures. London: R. Washbourne, 1870.

Bail, L. *La Théologie affective ou Saint Thomas en méditation*. 5 vols. rev. & corr. by Abbé Chevereau. Paris: Lecoffre, 1857.

Baker, T., OFM. *The Devout Communicant*: or Pious Meditations and Aspirations for Three Days before and after Receiving the Holy Eucharist. Dublin: James Duffy, 1862.

Baldassari, M. *Histoire de l'Enlèvement et de la Captivité de Pie IV*. Paris: Adrien le Clere, 1839.

Barat, M.S. RSCJ, *Règles des Dames du Sacré Coeur de Jésus*. Première partie, Paris, 1828.

Bartoli, D, SJ. *History of the Life and Institute of St. Ignatius de Loyola, Founder of the Society of Jesus*. 2 vols. N.Y., E. Dunigan, 1855.

Baudrand, B. SJ. *L'ame fidèle animée de l'esprit de Jésus Christ*, par le considération sur les divins mystères. Avec des considérations sur les mystères de la Sainte Vierge. Lyon, Gautier, 1829.

_____. *L'ame intérieure, ou conduit spirituelle dans les voies de Dieu*. Paris: Perisse, 1857.

_____. L'âme éclairée par les oracles et les conseils de la sagesse. Lyon, 1776.

_____. *The Soul Contemplating the Grandeurs of God.* Lyon, 1775.

Baudry, F. *The Life of Henry Dorié.* Trans. by Lady M.E. Herbert. London: Robson, c. 1869.

Beaufils, SJ. *The Treasure of Superiors*, or letters upon the manner of governing religious houses. Dublin: J. Fowler, 1867.

Beckx, P. SJ. *Month of Mary.* First published in German, Vienna, 1838. Eng. Trans. 2nd ed. Mrs. E. Hazeland, London: Burns & Oates, 1884.

Beda Venerabilis. *The Ecclesiastical History of the English Nation* London: J.M. Dent, 1910.

Bellarmine, R. Cardinal. SJ. *A Commentary on the Book of Psalms.* Trans. J. O'Sullivan. Dublin: J. Duffy, 1886. [Given to SHCJ by Rev. C.I.H. Carter.]

Bellecius, A., SJ. *Spiritual Exercises according to the Method of St. Ignatius of Loyola.* Augsburg, 1757. 5th ed. trans. W. Hutch. London: Burns & Oates, 1876.

Bona Mors. London, Keating, 1837.

Bonaventure, St. OFM. *Life of St. Francis of Assisi.* Eng. trans. by a Religious of the Order of St. Francis. Ed. by Cardinal Manning. London: Burns & Oates, 1867.

Bonilla, John of, OFM. *Peace of Soul.* First published in Spanish in 1580. Since 1665, published with L. Scupoli's *Spiritual Combat* and ascribed to him. See *Spiritual Combat.* Dublin: 1837.

Borgo, C. SJ. *Novena Preparatory to the Festival of the Sacred Heart of Jesus.* Trans. from Fr., ed. by the Ladies of the Sacred Heart of Jesus. Bound with *Month of the Sacred Heart.* Phila., Cunningham, 1859.

Bossuet, J.B. *Discours sur l'histoire universelle.* Paris. Guegnard, 1846.

_____. *Méditations sur l'Evangile.*

_____. *Elévations à Dieu sur tous les mystères de la religion chrétienne.* Tours, Mame, 1847.

Boudon, H.M. *Devotion to the Nine Choirs of Holy Angels*, and especially to the angel guardians. Trans. E. Thompson. London: Burns & Oates, n.d. [before 1876].

Bouhours, D. SJ. *Vie de Saint François Xavier, apôtre des Indes et du Japon.* Nouv. ed. rev. Tours: Mame, 1858.

Bowles, E. *The Life of St. Jane Frances Fremyot de Chantal.* London: Burns & Oates, c. 1870.

Boylesve, M. de. SJ. *Little Month of Saint Joseph.* Saint Joseph according to the Gospel. Meditations and anecdotes for each day of the month of Saint Joseph. Trans. Mrs. E. Hazeland. London: Burns & Oates, 1900.

Breviarum Romanum. 4 vols. Mechlinae, 1861.

Butler, A. *The Lives of the Fathers, Martyrs and Other Principal Saints,* compiled from Original Monuments and Other Authetic Records. Dublin: R. Coyne, 1833.

———. *Moral Discourses on the Sublime Truths and Important Duties of Christianity.* Dublin: c. 1800.

———. *The Movable Feasts, Fasts, and Other Annual Observances of the Catholic Church.* N.Y.: J. Doyle, 1836.

Camus, J. Bp. *L'Esprit de S. François de Sales.* Ed. Abbe C. Busson. Besancon, 1853.

Catherine of Siena. *Letters.* Trans. and ed. V.D. Scudder. London: Dent, 1927.

Catholic Legends and Traditions. A new selection. London: Burns & Lambert, n.d.

The Catholic Vade Mecum. A select manual of prayers for daily use. Baltimore: Kelly & Piel, 1865.

Caussade, J.P. de, SJ. *Abandon a la Providence divine envisage comme le moyen le plus facile de sanctification.* 2nd ed. rev. & corr. by H. Ramiere SJ. Paris, 1867. Eng. trans. of 8th ed. by E. McMahon. N.Y.: Benziger, 1887.

Chalippe, C., OFM. *Vie de St. François d'Assise.* 2 vols. Torino, 1787.

Chateaubriand, F.R. *Génie du Christianisme.* Paris, 1802.

Cotel, P. SJ. *A Catechism of the Vows.* Trans. from the 6th French ed. Phila.: Kilner, 1868.

———. *Les principes de la vie réligieuse ou l'explication du catéchisme des voeux.* Poitiers: Henry Oudin, 1869.

Craisson, Abbé. *Des communautés religieuses à voeux simples: législation canonique et civile,* Paris: Poussielgue, 1869.

Cumplido, F. SJ. *Coadjutor Perfecto.* Trans.: *The Perfect Lay-Brother* by J. McLeod, SJ, London: Burns & Oates, 1874.

Deharbe, J. SJ. *Large Catechism.* Trans. J. Fander, SJ. N.Y.: Benziger, 1862.

Délices des âmes pieuses. Paris, 1840.

Dirckink, J. SJ. *Exhortationes ad religiosos.* Cologne, 1704. Rpt. Rome, 1826.

Emery. *L'esprit de Ste. Thérèse recueilli de ses oeuvres et de ses lettres.* [Used by C. Connelly: no further bibliographical data available.]

Faber, F.W., ed. *Lives of the Canonized Saints and the Servants of God Beatified or Declared Venerable by Authority.* Derby: Richardson, 1847 ff.

Fastré, J.A. SJ. *Acts of the Early Martyrs.* "Messenger Series," No. 3. Phila.: Cunningham, 1871.

Fénélon, F. de S. de la M. *L'éducation des Filles.* Paris: Pinard, 1824.

Fifty Reasons Why the Roman Catholic Religion Ought to be Preferred to Others. Baltimore: Fielding Lucas, Jr.

Figuera, G. de la, SJ. *A Spiritual Compendium in Which the Principal Difficulties in the Way of Perfection are Explained.* Trans. Mrs. R.

Bennet. London: Burns & Oates, 1873.
Formby, J. *Scripture*.
_____. *Hymn Book*.
_____. *Church History*.
_____. *Bible History*.
Francis de Sales, *Règle de S. Augustin, Constitutions et Directoire pour les soeurs religieuses de la Visitation*. Paris, 1818.
_____. *Lettres*. 2 vols. Paris: Palme, 1865.
_____. *Practical Piety*, n.d.
Frassinetti, J. *Dogmatic Catechism*. Trans. Lady G. Chatterton, London: Burns & Oates, 1876.
Il Frutto degli Esercizi Spirituali. Rome, 1844.
Guame, J. *The Catechism of Perseverance* or An Historical, Dogmatical, Moral Liturgical, Apologetical, Philosophical and Social Exposition of Religion, from the Beginning of the World down to Our Own Days. Trans. from the 10th French ed. in 4 vols. N.Y.: Benziger, 1893.
Gautrelet, F.X., SJ. *Nouveau mois du Sacré Coeur de Jésus*, ou les trente-trois années de la vie du divin Sauveur honorées pendant le mois de Juin: Paris, 1850; Trans. G. Tickell, SJ, Month of the Sacred Heart, London: Richardson & Son, 1858; Phila.: P. Cunningham, 1859.
_____. *Traité de l'état religieux*. 2 vols. Lyons, 1847.
Gentilucci, R. *Life of the Blessed Virgin Mary*, Mother of God, of Her Spouse, St. Joseph, and Holy Parents, St. Joachim and St. Anne. N.Y.: E. Dunigan, 1858.
Gertrude, St. *Life and Revelations*, Ed. by Sr. M. Francis Clare. London: Burns & Oates, 1870.
_____. *Exercises*. Trans. P. Guéranger, Angers, 1862. Exercises. Trans. T.A. Pope, London, 1863.
_____. *Preces Gertrudianae: Prayers of St. Gertrude and St. Mechtilde*, of the Order of St. Benedict. Trans. T.A. Pope. London: Burns & Oates, 1861.
Gibson's. *Catechism Made Easy*: being a familiar explanation of the catechism of Christian doctrine. London: Burns, Oates & Washbourne, 1934.
Granada, L. de, OP. *The Sinner's Guide*. Trans. & rev. by a father of the same Order. Boston: T.B. Norman & Co., 1884.
Grou, J.N. *The School of Jesus Chist*. Trans. A. Clinton SJ, from an Original Manuscript of L'Abbé Grou. Dublin: Fitzpatrick, 1801.
_____. *The Interior of Jesus and Mary*. 2 vols. London, 1854.
_____. *Meditations in the Form of a Retreat on the Love of God*. London: Coghlan, 1796.
The Grounds of the Catholic Doctrine. Contained in the Profession of Faith published by Pope Pius IV, and now in use for the reception of converts into the Church. By way of question and answer. 13th ed. Baltimore: Fielding Lucas, Jr. n.d. [before 1844.]

Hahn-Hahn. *Select Lives of the Fathers of the Desert.* Trans. from the German. 2 vols, n.d.

Hay, Bishop. *The Sincere Christian Instructed in the Faith of Christ from the Written Word.* Edinburgh, 1911.

———. *The Devout Christian.* Edinburgh, n.d.

Hedley, J.C. OSB. *A Retreat.* London: Burns & Oates. 1894.

Hoerner, J. *Manual of Catholic Melodies.* Baltimore: John Murphy, 1843.

Horae Diurnae. London: Burns & Oates, n.d.

Hortus Animae or the Garden of the soul. London: John Philip, n.d.

Imitation de la très-sainte vierge sur le modèle de l'Imitation de Jésus Christ. Tours: Mame, 1859.

Instructor's Assistant, or short and familiar instructions on the Blessed Trinity and Incarnation, the Seven Sacraments and the Sacrifice of the Mass; to which is added a Rule of Life. Derby: Richardson, n.d.

John Eudes, St. and St. M. Euphrasia Pelletier. *Règle de S. Augustin et Constitutions pour les Religieuses de la Congrégation de Notre Dame de Charité du Bon Pasteur d'Angers.* Rome, 1856.

Judde, C. SJ. *Retraite spirituelle appelée Grand Retraite de trente jours.* 9th ed. Vols. 1 & 2 of *Oeuvres spirituelles* du P. Judde. Lyon: Perisse, 1853.

Kempis, Thomas A. *The Following* [also *Imitation*] *of Christ.* New ed. T. Jones, 1853. Bound with Scupoli's *Spiritual Combat.*

Lallemant, L. SJ. *Doctrine Spirituelle.* Compiled by P. Champion SJ. from ms. notes of J. Rigoleuc SJ, and J. Surin SJ. Paris, 1694. Eng. trans. at the suggestion of F.W. Faber, London, 1855.

Lancicius, M. SJ. *Pious Affections towards God and the Saints*: Meditations for every day in the year and for the principal festivals. London: Burns & Oates, 1874.

La Palma, L. de SJ. *The History of the Sacred Passion.* Trans. & ed. H.J. Coleridge SJ. London: Burns & Oates, 1872.

———. *A Treatise on the Particular Examen of Conscience.* London: Burns & Oates, 1873.

La Puente, L. SJ. [also known as Da Ponte]. *Meditations on the Mysteries of Our Holy Faith.* Trans. J. Heigham. 6 vols. London: Richardson, 1852.

Leonard of Port-Maurice, Bl. *The Hidden Treasure*, or the value and excellence of the Holy Mass. Trans. from Italian. Derby: Richardson, n.d.

The Life of Lady Warner. 3rd ed. with Abridgement of the Life of her Sister-in-law. By a Catholic Gentleman. London: Thomas Hales, 1696.

Little Flowers of St. Francis and of His Friars. Anon. Trans. of Actus Beati Francisci et Sociorum Ejus, ed. A. Cesari, 1822.

Ligouri, Alphonsus. *Glories of Mary.* Dublin: J. Coyne, 1837. N.Y.: E. Dunigan, 1852.

———. *Practica de Amor Gesù Christo; e Le Considerazioni sulla Passione di G.C. ed altri esercizi*. Bassano: Giuseppe Remondini, 1838.
———. *Preparation for Death*. N.Y., 1887.
———. *The True Spouse of Jesus Christ*. N.Y., 1887.
Loyola, Ignatius SJ. (Cornelia used the corpus of Jesuit documents published by the restored Society at Avignon, 1827-38, in 7 vols.:)
Constitutiones Societatis Jesu cum earum declarationibus, Vol. 1. Avignon, 1827.
Regulae Societatis Jesu, Vol. 2 [contains "Letter on Obedience"]. Avignon, 1827.
Decreta Canones, Censurae et Praecepta Congregationum Generalium Societatis Jesu. Vol. 3: Decreta 1 AD VI Congr. Incl. Vol. 4; Decreta VII AD XII Congr. Incl. Avignon, 1830.
Canones, Indiculum Decretorum, Censuras et Praecepta, Formulas, et Quorundam Officiorum Regulas. Vol. 5, Avignon, 1830.
Exercitia Spiritualia S.P. Ignatii Loyolae, Directorium in Exercitia, Industriae ad Curando Animae Morbos. Vol. 6, Avignon, 1829.
Ordinationes Praepositiorum Generalium et Instructiones ad Provinciales et Superiores Societatis. Vol. 7, Avignon, 1838.
(Cornelia also borrowed from J.H. Newman, the following) *Constitutiones Societatis Jesu*. Anno 1858. Reprinted from the original edition with an Appendix containing a translation and several important documents. London: Rivington, 1838. [A Protestant translation accompanied by hostile criticism].
(She also used:)
Les Constitutions des Jésuites avec les déclarations. Texte latin d'après l'édition de Prague. Traduction nouvelle. Paris, 1843. [Appendices criticize the Jesuits.]
Regole della Compagnie de Gesù. [contains "Letter on Obedience"] Rome, 1834.
The Spiritual Exercises of St. Ignatius of Loyola. Trans. into English. Dublin: R. Grace & Sons, 1846.
Exercises spirituels de S. Ignace de Loyola. Ed. J. Roothan. Trans. from Spanish by P. Jennesseaux SJ. Paris, 1854.
Manresa: or the Spiritual Exercises of St. Ignatius for General Use. London: Burnes & Oates, n.d.
Ratio atque Institutio Studiorum Societatis Jesu. Rome, 1599. Rpt. Paris: Didot, 1850.
Manual for Christians & an Abridged Catechism. Vienna: printed by Strauss' widow, 1838.
Manual for Use of the Novices of the Holy Child Jesus. Printed for private use, at the Convent, St. Leonards-on-Sea, 1869.
Manuel de Piété. A l'usages des élèves du Sacré Coeur. Paris: J. Lecoffre, 1862.

Médaille, P. SJ. *Méditations sur les Evangiles de l'année, et pour les fêtes de Notre-Seigneur, de la Ste Vierge et des saints.* Lyons: Perisse, 1860.

Meditations as a Preparation for Whitsuntide and Other Feasts: together with such helps in the practice of mental prayer and examination of conscience, as tend to the leading of a more spiritual life. Trans. M.E. Bowles, SHCJ: preface by Cornelia Connelly SHCJ. London: Richardson, 1851.

Meditations on the Holy Childhood of Our Blessed Lord, in which we are led to abide in humility with the Holy Family of Nazareth, and thence to drink sweet encouragement and counsel for every circumstance of life. Trans. M.M. Ignatia Bridges SHCJ; Preface by Cornelia Connelly SHCJ. London: Richardson, 1857.

Milner, J. Bp. *The End of Religious Controversy.* London, 1818.

Missale Romanum S. Pii Quinti. Malines, 1840.

Montalembert, Comte de. *Histoire de Sainte Elizabeth de Hongrie.* Paris: E.J. Bailly, 1836.

Mores Catholici, or Ages of Faith. London: Dolman, 1846.

Morris, J. SJ. *The Heroic Act of Charity*: Appendix to Mumford's A Remembrance . . . London: Burns & Oates, 1871. Rpt. Separately, London: Catholic Truth Society, 1893.

Mumford, J. SJ. *A Remembrance for the Living to Pray for the Dead.* Rpt. from ed. of 1661, with an appendix on the Heroic Act by J. Morris SJ. St. Joseph's Ascetical Library, 11. London: Burns & Oates, 1871.

Nepveu, F. SJ. *Higher Paths in the Spiritual Life*, Being a Retreat for Religious. Trans. M.M. Joseph Buckle SHCJ; dedication by Cornelia Connelly SHCJ. London: Richardson, 1851.

Newman, J.H., ed. *The Lives of English Saints.* 5 vols. London: 1844.

———. *Verses on Religious Subjects.* Dublin: James Duffy, 1853.

Neumayr, F. SJ. *The Science of the Spiritual Life.* London: Burns & Oates, 1876.

New Glories of the Catholic Church. Trans. from the Italian by the Fathers of the London Oratory. 4th ed. Baltimore: J. Murphy, 1873.

Nouet, J. SJ. *L'homme d'oraison, sa conduite dans les voies de Dieu.* 2 vols. Paris: Perisse, 1852.

Office de la Sainte Vierge. Paris: Poussielgue, 1877.

Paolo, F. di. *Compendia della vita del gran taumaturgo.* S. Pesaro, 1845.

Parsons, Rev. R. *A Christian Directory, Guiding Men to Their Eternal Salvation.* (in two parts). The First Part where of Appertains to Resolution; the Second treats of the Obstacles and Impediments which Hinder it, and how they may be removed. Now set forth with many corrections and additions. To this edition are prefixed the life of the author, and a method for the use of All, with two tables. Dublin: J. Duffy & Sons, n.d. N.Y.: D. Murphy, No. 384 Pearl St., 1851.

Patrignani, G.A. *Delizie della quotidiana conversazione col divino Infante Gesù*. Diario Dacro-istorico di Giuseppe Antonio Patrignani della Compagnia de Gesù. Venezia: Nicolo Pezzana, 1732.
Penny, W.G. *The Exercise of Faith Impossible except in the Catholic Church*. London: Baker, n.d.
Plowden, C. SJ. *Lectures on Spiritual Subjects*, from exhortations on the Rules of the Society of Jesus given to the Novices at Stonyhurst. London: Richardson, 1859.
Pergmayr, J. SJ. *Sämmtliche ascetische Schriften*. 5 vols. Augsburg, 1778-9. [Cornelia used an English or French trans. of vol. 1, a retreat according to the Spiritual Exercises and "Maximes Spirituelles."].
Perry's Full Course of Instruction for the Use of Catechists. Dublin: J. Duffy, n.d.
Pinelli, L. SJ. *Meditazioni sopra alcuni Misteri della Passione de Gesù Cristo*. Roma: Alessandro Monaldi, 1839.
Power, P. *Catechism: Doctrinal, Moral, Historical and Liturgical*, with answers to the objections drawn from the sciences against religion. 3rd ed. Dublin: J. Duffy, 1873.
Practical Methods of Performing the Ordinary Actions of a Christian Life. Dublin: J. Coyne, 1838.
Ratisbonne, T., *Règle de la Congrégation des Religieuses de Notre-Dame de Sion*. Paris: J. Claye, 1863.
Recueil de Cantiques à l'usage des élèves du Sacré Coeur de Jésus. Lyon, 1836.
Reeves' History of the Christian Church from its earliest establishment to the present century. Dublin: J. Duffy, n.d.
———. *History of the Holy Bible*. Rev. ed. by W. Gahan. Dublin: J. Duffy, n.d.
Règles et Constitutions des Soeurs de Notre-Dame. Namur, 1844.
Ricard, A. *Month of the Holy Angels*: or the month of October consecrated to the Holy Angels, and more especially to the good Guardian Angel. Trans. Rev. W. F. Cook. Phila.: Cummiskey, 1869.
Rigoleuc, J. SJ. *Oeuvres Spirituelles*. Nouvelle édition. Avignon, 1843.
———. *Walking with God: or Dwellers in the Recreation House of the Lord*. Trans. M.M. Ignatia Bridges, SHCJ; Preface by Cornelia Connelly SHCJ. London: Richardson, 1859.
Rodriguez, A. SJ. *The Practice of Perfection and Christian Virtues*. 3 vols. N.Y.: 1839. Also vol. 2 in French trans. by Abbé Regnier des Marais. Paris: Librairie Catholique, 1845.
Rohrbacher, Abbé. *Histoire universelle de l'église catholique*, continuée jusqu'en 1860 par J. Chantrel. 4th ed. 14 vols. Paris: Gaume & Duprey, 1864-7.
Roothan, J. SJ. *The Method of Meditation*. N.Y.: Sadlier, 1858.
Rules of the Congregation of the Holy Angels and of St. Aloysius. Little Offices of the Holy Angels and of St. Aloysius. Preston: Thomson, c.

1870. The Offices also printed separately for the use of the pupils of the Sodalities of the Society of the Holy Child Jesus.

Saint-Jure, J.B. SJ. *L'homme religieux.* 2 vols. Rev. ed. Abbé J.L. Tarpin, Lyon: Perisse, 1885.

_____. *L'homme spirituel.* 2 vols. Paris: Perisee, 1851. Trans. as *The Spiritual Man,* or *The Spiritual Life* reduced to its first principles. N.Y.: O'Shea, 1878.

_____. *The Life of Baron de Renty.* London: Burns & Oates, 1873.

Scupoli, L. *The Spiritual Combat.* Dublin, 1837.

Secker, T. *Works.* To which is prefixed a review of his Grace's life and character by B. Porteus, 6 vols. New ed. London: Rivington, 1811.

Sodality Manual For use in the Sodalities of Our Lady Prima Primaria-established in the Schools of the Society of the Holy Child Jesus. London: Burns & Oates, n.d.

Stone, M. SJ. *Retreat,* n.d.

Surin, J. SJ. *Science experimentale des choses de l'autre vie* acquise en la possession des Ursulines de Loudun. Paris, 1663, Rpt. 1828, 1830.

Teresa of Avila, St. *Book of Foundations.* Trans. A. Woodhead & Fr. Bede of S. Simon Stock, 1669. Trans. J. Dalton, London, 1853.

_____. *The Interior Castle,* or *Mansions.* Trans. A. Woodhead, 1675; J. Dalton, London, 1852.

_____. *Life.* Trans. A. Woodhead, 1671; J. Dalton, London, 1851.

_____. *Way of Perfection.* Trans. A. Woodhead, 1875; J. Dalton, London, 1852.

Thomas of Jesus OSA (Thomas de Andrada). *The Sufferings of Our Lord Jesus Christ.* 2 vols. Trans. from the Portugese. Rev. & corr. Dublin: J. Mullany, 1873.

Thomas of Jesus, Disc. Car. *Sermons for Every Sunday in the Year* in 4 vols. Vol. II & III. Dublin: B. Corcoran, 1763.

Tickell, G. SJ. *The Life of Blessed Margaret Mary,* with Some Account of Devotion to the Sacred Heart. London: Burns & Oates, 1869.

Urquhart's *Reflections, Moral, Religious, Political.* Rome, 1844.

Vaubert, SJ. *Le saint exercice de la présence de Dieu.* New ed. Tournai: Casterman, 1847.

Ventura de Raulica, G. *Le Bellezze della Fede.* Roma: Ospizio de S. Maria degli Angeli, 1838.

Verzeri, T. & G. Benaglio. *Costituzioni delle Figlie del Sacro Cuore di Gesù.* Rome, 1847.

Viard, S.M. *Marie, ses gloires et ses souffrances.* Vol. I. Paris: Lecoffre, 1850.

_____. *Pardon! Misericorde!* ou le cri du repentir à la voix de Notre-Dame. Paris: Lecoffre, 1855.

Weninger, F.X. SJ. *Manual of Instruction* c. 1855.

Wiseman, N. Card. *Fabiola.* London, 1854.

_____. *A Few Flowers from the Roman Campagna* offered to the Im-

maculate Conception Charity. London: John Philip, 1861.
———. Lectures on the Principal Doctrines and Practices of the Catholic Church. 3rd ed. London: Baker, 1888.
———. Recollections of the Last Four Popes and of Rome in Their Times. London, 1858.
———. Sermons on Our Lord and the Virgin. Dublin: J. Duffy, 1864.
———. Sermons on Moral Subjects. Dublin: J. Duffy, 1864.
———. The Real Presence of the Body and Blood of Our Lord Jesus Christ in the Blessed Eucharist, proved from Scripture. Dublin: J. Duffy, 1836.

Index

Abbadie, John Francis, SJ, CC's spiritual director, 55
Academy of the Sacred Heart, Grand Coteau, LA, 51, 52, 57
All Souls Parish, St. Leonards-on-Sea, 177, 179
Aquaviva, Claudio, SJ, 129, 136
Aquinas, Thomas, St. 7, 144
Armour, M. Andrew, SHCJ, 223
Assumption Parish, Philadelphia, PA, 164
Austin, Sr. SHCJ, 103
Authors used by CC, 143-148, 236-245

Balthasar, Fr., 197
Baltimore, MD, 78, 153
Barat, Madeleine Sophie, St., 111, 134, 145
Barber, Virgil and Jerusha, 63
Barnabò, Alessandro, Card. Prefect, SC Propaganda Fide, 123, 149-50, 182, 183, 184, 185
Bartoli, D. SJ, 138, 145
Baudrand, B. SJ, 138, 145
Bellasis, M. M. F. SHCJ, 122, 123, 183, 206-207, 223
Bisgood, M. T. SHCJ, 223
Blackpool, Lancs, England, 124
Blake, Ursula, SHCJ, 224
Blanc, Anthony, Bp of New Orleans, LA, 46, 47, 53, 74
Book of the Order of Studies, 155-158
Borgo, C, SJ, 138, 145
Bosio, Fr. 190, 193, 194
Bowen, John, Jr, 26, 30
Bowen, John, Sr, 25
Bowles, Emily, 68, 69, 93, 98, 108, 126, 155, 179-180
Bromby's Grammar, 161
Buckle, M. M. J. SHCJ, 81, 105, 112, 123, 130, 134, 136-137, 141, 195, 206-207, 213, 223

"Cabal". See Preston
Capel, Msgr., 185
Cardinal Protector, 178
Cardinal Vicar of Rome, 48, 65
Carter, Charles I. H. Rev. Vicar-General of Philadelphia, 163, 164, 174
Catechism of Perseverance, 147
Catholic Poor School Committee, 96, 97-98, 154-155
Catholic Revival, England, xiii, 35, 59, 68, 92, 94, 161
Charism of founder, theology of: Vatican II, 8-9; Milligan, 9-23; Laurentin, xii-xiii, 11, 208, n.1; Lafont, 14; Olphe-Galliard, 14; Gilmont, 15; spirit of founder: Milligan, 16-17, Cognet, 17; and CC, 4, 11-23, 99-101, 206-207; institutionalization: 14-20, also Part Two, 89-208
Charisms, theology of: 3-23; gifts of the Holy Spirit, xiii-xiv, 1, 5-13, 73, 203-204; Pauline, xii, 5-7; Patristic, 7; Thomistic, 7-8; Sohm vs Rome, 5; Pius XII, 8; Vatican II and after, xii-xiii, 8-9, 203; Rahner, 3-5; source of religious institutes, 8-9
Christ Church (Episcopalian), Philadelphia, PA, 28, 30
Cognet, Louis, 17
Connelly, Adeline, 36, 44, 57, 58, 62, 63, 68, 69, 70, 73, 74, 105, 205
Connelly, Cornelia Augusta Peacock, Life: German (Jewish?)/English ancestry, 25, 33, n. 3; American roots, 25; good family and education, 27-28; Presbyterian, 28-29; Episcopalian, 29-31; Baptism: adult, 30; infant?, 29; anti-catholicism, 29; marriage, love for Pierce, 30-32, 36-37, 47-49, 50, 72; births of Mercer and Adeline, 36; of John Henry, 50; of Mary Magdalen, 52; of Pierce Francis (Frank), 55; love

246

of, care for children, xi, 36, 44, 50-52, 55, 62-64, 69-70, 73-75, 105, 205; influenced toward Catholicism, 38-42; reception into Catholic Church, 46-47; preserving marriage, 45-46; in Rome, 47-49; in Grand Coteau, 51-58; deaths of Mary Magdalen, 52; of John Henry, 54; of Mercer, 97, 205; conversion of Mary Peacock, 53; discernment re Pierce's and her vocations, 55-58, 65-68, 82; at Trinità dei Monti, 59-64; separation, vow of chastity, 63; offer to resume married life, 64; plan for American foundation, 68, 93; foundation of SHCJ in England, 68, 92-96, 98-101; children kidnapped, efforts to regain, 69-70, 73-74; response to Pierce's betrayal, 69-73, Connelly vs Connelly, 72; recognition of charism by SHCJ, 99-101, 187, 195, 206-207; limitations and faults, 130-133, 184-186, 188, 195-197; criticisms of, opposition to, 183-186, 188, 195-197; last illness and death, 198-199; Cause for Canonization, xiv; for Development of SHCJ, see below, Roles, Spirituality. See also Charism of Founder, Const SHCJ, Society of the Holy Child Jesus, Misogyny. Roles: wife, 31-32, 35-40, 44-49, 70, 73-75; mother, xi, 44-46, 50-52, 55, 62-64, 69-70, 73-75, 105; convert, 39-41, 46-47; lay teacher, 27, 51; founder SHCJ, xi-xiii, 3-5, 11-13, 16-18, 65-67, 92, 123-124; Superior General, 103-104, 107, 128, 132-133, 181, 186-187; Director of SHCJ formation/exemplar, 98-117, 121-128, 136-143, 195-199; guide for converts, 92-93; educator, 27, 56, 94-97, 151-161; author/compiler, 27, 107-117, 131-132, 209-214; missionary from New to Old World, xiv, 24. Spirituality: Christ/Gospel-centered, 11-12, 18, 58, 108-117, 121, 127, 142-143, 189-190, 205; use of Scripture, 140, 147, 157-158, 207. Incarnation/kenosis: entrance to Paschal and Trinitarian mysteries, 4, 45-46, 58, 102, 109-110, 123, 127, 134, 139-40, 198; Holy Child, "humble, hidden life," 54, 66-67, 109-110, 112-114, 124, 138-139, 143, 193, 197, 205-206; Sacred Heart, 127, 134, 139, 145-146, 153, 198; Christ suffering, 40, 54, 57, 140-141, 196-197, 205; "scandal" of the Cross, 4, 132-133, 205; King, Kingdom, 124, 138, 140-141; Eucharist, liturgy, 49, 100, 124, 127, 142, 146; "In Christ," 140-141; God, Father, 39, 158; devotion to Will of God, 52, 60-61, 70, 72, 104, 106, 125, 176, 197-199; Work of God, 106, 149, 189, 204; Glory of God, "greater glory," 15, 60, 70, 116, 150, 190; Holy Spirit: devotion to: 9, 56, 82, 142, 145, 165, 204; Call to holiness, xiv, 13, 124-125, 207-208; integration of prayer with life, deeds, 11, 12, 46, 56, 61, 100, 103, 124, 137, 140-141, 146-151, 205, 207; holiness in married life, 35, 46, 51, 58, 69, 77, 79, 203; prayer, contemplative, mystical/unitive, affective, 12, 17, 59, 112-115, 123-125, 141, 199, 205; familiarity with God, 46, 57, 141; discernment, xi, 46, 52, 55, 56-58, 61-62, 65-68, 79-80, 82, 138, 145, 160; vigilance, fidelity, 124-127; uniqueness of each in spiritual life, 52, 127-128, 206; collaboration with, imitation of Christ, 110, 112-115, 125-127, 140-143, 204-205; evangelical counsels, vows, 14, 61, 104, 109, 114, 123-126, 172-181; chastity as "suffering," 77, 109, renunciation, 48, 54, 60-62, 65, 70, 105, 137, 207; sacrifice, suffering, 4, 13, 48, 54, 60-61, 65, 68-69, 123-125, 140-141, 195-199, 205; joy, peace, 50-52, 55-56, 57, 63, 65, 66, 71, 100, 106, 124, 141, 159-160, 199; eschatological orientation, 14-15, 60, 65, 104, 123-125, 198; growth in psycho-spiritual maturity as woman, xi, 24-25, 27-28, 30-32, 46-47, 55, 70-71, 96-98, 140-144, 147, 172-180, 195-197, 205-206; fostering women's development, 158-161, 164-165, 172-180, 181, 187; see also Misogyny; consonance of life with teachings, 206-207; practice of virtue, 127-128, 153; devotion to Church, loyalty to hierarchy, 45, 50, 113-115, 131, 133, 158, 176-180, 181-195; devoto Mary, especially Our Lady of Sorrows, 54, 57-58, 101, 103, 127, 129, 153, 179; devotion to St. Joseph, 56, 58; see also Charism of founder, Const SHCJ, Spiritual Exercises, Spirit of SHCJ.

Connelly, Frank (Pierce Francis), 55-56, 57, 58, 62, 63, 68, 69, 70, 73, 74, 105, 205
Connelly, George, 32
Connelly, Henry, 32
Connelly, John, 50, 74
Connelly, John Henry, 50, 54
Connelly, Mary Magdalen, 52
Connelly, Mercer, 36, 44, 51-52, 57, 58 68, 70, 73, 74, 97, 205
Connelly, Pierce, Philadelphia family background, 30, 32; Presbyterian, 32; Episcopalian affiliation and ordination, 30-32; curacies in Wilmington and Phila., rectorship in Natchez, 32, 35-43; mar-

riage to, love for CC, 30, 68; High Church, 36; reaction to Nativism, difficulties with Protestantism, 37-43; resignation of rectorship, 37-40; conviction re his priesthood, 44-45, 65, 76; influenced by Nicollet and Rosati, 40-44; reception into Catholic Church in Rome, 47-48; request for Catholic ordination, 47-49; financial losses, 50; teacher, St. Charles College, Grand Coteau, 51; distorted doctrine of perfection, 76-79; renewal of request for priesthood, 55, 57, support of Pope Gregory XVI, Roman hierarchy and aristocracy, 59, 80-82; rejected by Jesuits, 59; ordination to Catholic priesthood, ministry in England, 65; collaboration on outline of SHCJ Constitutions, 67-68; psycho-pathology, 49, 69, 72-73; conflict with Wiseman, 71; interference in SHCJ, 69; kidnapping of children, 69-70; suit to regain CC and her property, 71-75; apostasy, pamphleteering, 71-72; return to Episcopalian ministry, Florence Italy, 205; death, 188, 205

Connelly vs Connelly, 71-72, 73

Constitutions and Rules of the Society of the Holy Child Jesus ("the Rule"): Schematic Outline of Texts and Approbations, 216-217; compiled/composed by CC 1845-79, 106-120, 128-143, 182-195; first sketch of, 1845-46, 67-68; contents, 106-117, 128-131; CC's expression of original inspiration, 108-120, 212; Abridgement/First Chapter, 111-117; sources: Const of the Congregation of Our Lady of Sion, 134; Const of the Figlie del Sacro Cuore di Gesù, 128, 133-134; Const of the Religious of our Lady of Charity of the Good Shepherd (Angers), 131-132, 134; Const of the Religious Sisters of the Visitation, 67, 108, 109, 129, 132, 133, 136; Const of Sisters of Notre Dame de Namur, 134-135; Const SJ, 103-104, 135-136; Summary of Const SJ 136-137; Const of the Society of the Sacred Heart, 111-112, 133; Abrégé of, 111-112, 129, 133; Gautrelet and Aquaviva, 129; role in SHCJ life, 98, 103, 106-108, 121-122, 193; truncated editions used, 128-130, 137: "spirit of the Constitutions," 191-194; approbation: of Wiseman, 107, 216-217; difficulties with Rome, 111, 130-133, 181-183, 188-189, 216-217; difficulties with SHCJ: 183-189, 216-217; Danell edition, 187-195; auxiliaries, 108, 122-128, 212; spurious const of Pierce, 70

Cotel, Pierre, SJ, 19, 108, 145, 192, 193, 194
Craisson, l'Abbé, n. 45, 166, 238
Croft, M. M. A. SHCJ, 106, 181
Cruchon, George, SJ, 72
Cusack, M. F. X. SHCJ, 175
Cusack, M. M. C. SHCJ, 175, 184
Customal, 108, 122, 127-128, 145, 150, 211, 212

Danell, James, Bp of Southwark, 18-19, 152, 173, 174, 176, 178, 186, 187-189, 190-191, 193, 194, 195, 196, 197
DaPonte, Luis, SJ. See Lapuente, Luis de, SJ
Dawson, Annette, SHCJ, vii, 225
Day, M. M. G., SHCJ, 186, 188
Derby, England. See St. Mary's convent and school
Dower, 172-173, 174
Drummond, Henry, MP, 71
Dublin Review, 42, 76
Duke, William, Dr, 177
Dumeige, Gervais, SJ, xiii, 11
Duval, Adeline Peacock, 26, 29, 30, 31, 37, 39, 66
Duval, Lewis, 29

English College, Rome, 132
Epiphany, Feast of, and Letters, 103, 122-127, 197, 199, 211, 212

Faber, Frederick William, CO, 92
Fairlight, Sussex, England, 174
Fénelon, Francois de Salignac de la Mothe, 145, 147
Figlie del Sacro Cuore di Gesù, See Verzeri, Teresa
Flaget, Benedict Joseph, Bp of Bardstown, KY, 82
Flaxman, Radegunde, SHCJ, 225
Francis of Assisi, St, 134, 145
Francis de Sales, St, 93, 108, 125, 133, 145, 211
Fransoni, Giacomo Fillipo, Card. Prefect, SC Propaganda Fide, 63, 70, 92-93, 132
Futtrell, J. C., 10

Gailhac, Jean, 10, 17, 19-20
Gallwey (also Gallway), Peter, SJ, 136
Gautrelet, F. X., SJ, 129, 138, 145-146
German Reformed Church (Old First Reformed), 25, 28, 29
Gertrude of Helphta, St, 124, 145
Gilmont, J. F., 15-16

Gompertz, M. M. C., SHCJ, 213, 223
Goss, Alexander, Bp of Liverpool, 182
Gough (Goff), Sally, 57
Grace. See Charisms
Gracemere (Connelly home in Grand Coteau, LA), 51, 69
Grand Coteau, LA, 27, 51-58, 63, 145
Grant, Thomas, Bp of Southwark, 122, 131, 132, 151, 154, 160, 172-173, 174-175, 179-180, 181, 182, 210
Grassi, John Anthony, SJ, 65, 67, 68, 98, 106, 128, 133, 135, 204
Greek Rite, 48, 76
Gregory XVI, Pope, 59, 63, 65, 80, 81, 92-93, 111, 132
Guéranger, Dom, 146
Guerra, Mary Ann (née Noonan), 32-33, n. 3

Hadfield, M. M. C., SHCJ, 190
Hadham, Herts, England, 151
Hargrove, Bernard, 73-74, 75
Haughton, Rosemary, 165, 171, n. 106
Hobart, William Henry, Episcopalian Bp of New York, 30
Holy Trinity Church, Natchez, MS, 31, 32, 36-38, 39, 44

Ignatius of Loyola, St., see Const SHCJ; Spiritual Exercises
Ignatian influence, 67, 103, 133, 134; see Const SHCJ, Spiritual Exercises
Infancy Narratives, 58, 110, 122-123

Jesuits, 51, 55, 59, 63, 98; see Ignatian influence
John, St (Apostle), 125
John the Baptist, St, 126
Jones, John, Rev, 101-102, 148

Kasemann, E, 6, 7,
Kay-Shuttleworth, Sir James, 96
à Kempis, Thomas, 145
Knapen, Anselmo, OFM, 134, 182
Kohlmann, Anthony, SJ, 47

Lallemant, Louis, SJ, 116, 138, 145, 146
Lapuente, Luis de, SJ, (LaPuente, Da Ponte), 105, 124, 138, 142, 145, 146, 165, n. 16
Laurenza, Sr., SHCJ, 160
Ledochowska, Teresa, 4
Leeds, Louisa Catherine, Duchess of, (née Caton), 162
Leopoldine Association of Vienna, 50, 81

Liturgical and Para-liturgical devotions, 146, 158
Liverpool, 97, 126, 184
Logan, Helen, SHCJ, vii
London, England, 97, 102, 155
Louisiana, USA, 35
Lynch, M. Dennis, SHCJ, 223
Lythgoe, Fr. SJ, (English Provincial), 78

McCarthy, Elinor, 3, n. 33
McCloskey, John Cardinal, 48, 81-82
McSorley, Therese, SHCJ, vii
Mack, Adeline Duval, 30, 31, 81
de Maille, M. O., SHCJ, 223
Manning, Henry Edward Cardinal, Archbp of Westminster, 182
Marriage, theology/spirituality of, 9, 35, 46, 58, 69, 75-80, 203
Martyrdom of early Christians, 40; of 19th century Christians, 40
Mason, Henry, 79
Matrimonial law, English, 71-75
Mayfield, Sussex, England, 124, 161-162
Merici, Angela, 4
Metternich, Clemens Lother Wenzel, Pr, 50, 81
Milleret de Brou, Mére Eugenie, Bl, 68
Milligan, Mary, RSHM, 10-11, 12-13, 14, 16, 17, 19-20
Milne-Home, Janey, SHCJ, 6-7
Misogyny, xii, 73-75; experienced by CC, 63-64, 69, 73-80, 132-133, 147-148, 212
Molinari, Paolo, SJ, 18
Montgomery, Austin, 26
Montgomery, Isabel (Isabella) Bowen, 25 26, 28, 29, 30, 31
Montgomery, James, Rev, 30

Natchez, MS, 31, 35, 36-46, 50, 51
Nativism, 37-38, 41, 72
Nepveu, F., SJ, 105
Neuilly-sur-Seine, Paris, France, 121, 151, 177
Newman, John Henry Cardinal, 78, 92, 135
New Orleans, LA, 46, 50
Nicollet, Joseph ., 40-43
Norton, Caroline, 73, 75

Odescalchi, Carlo, Cardinal Vicar of Rome, 47, 48, 76
Ore, Sussex, England, 152
O'Reilly, Bernard, Bp of Liverpool, 189
Otey, James Hervey, Episcopal Bp of Tennessee, 38, 44-45
Oxford Movement, 30

Palatinate, Germany, 25
Paris, France, 68
Parsons, Robert, SJ, 105, 242
Pascal, Blaise, 79
Paul, St, xii, 5-7, 9, 140
Peacock, Adeline. See Duval
Peacock, Mary, RSCJ, 26, 27, 49, 53
Peacock, Mary Swope (Bowen), 25-29
Peacock, Ralph, Jr., (changed name to John Bowen), 66
Peacock, Ralph, Sr., 25-27, 28-29
Pelletier, Mary Euphrasia, 134
Pergmayr, J., SJ, 105, 144, 243
Philadelphia, PA, 25-32, 163-164
Pius IX, 70
Point, Nicholas, SJ, 52-53
Poor Schools, 94, 96, 102, 151-153, 161
Portier, Michael, Bp of Mobile, AL, 46
Presbyterian Church, Philadelphia, PA: First, 32; Second, 27
Preston, Lancs, England, 97, 155, 183-184, 185, 187, 188, 196
Propaganda Fide, Sacred Congregation of, 111, 132-133, 181, 182, 186, 191
Propagation of the Faith, Society of the, 81
Pugin, Edward Welby, 162

Rahner, Karl, SJ, 3, 4-5, 8, 13-14, 61-62, 73, 80
Ranger, Clare, SHCJ, 127
von Reisach, Karl August Cardinal, Bp of Eichstatt, 49
Reze, John Frederic, Bp of Detroit, 81, 88, n. 217
Rigoleuc, Jean, SJ, 105, 124, 138, 145
Rodriguez, A., SJ, 145
Rome, 35, 47-50, 58-68
Roothan, John Philip, SJ, 59
Rosati, Joseph, Bp of St. Louis, MO, 38, 41, 42-43, 44, 46-47
Rule. See Constitutions SHCJ
Rule of St. Augustine, 67

St Charles College, Grand Coteau, LA, 51, 52, 54, 57
St James, Episcopalian church, Kingsessing, Philadelphia, PA, 31, 32
St Leonards-on-Sea, Sussex, England, 96, 101, 125, 152, 154, 155, 158, 160, 161, 174, 177, 179
St. Mary's convent and school, Derby, England, 70, 92, 93, 94, 96, 98, 99, 106
St. Stephen's Church (Episcopalian), Philadelphia, PA, 29, 30
Schryer, Anna Maria, 25
Schurmann, H., 6
Scupoli, L., 145
Second Vatican Council, 3, 8-9, 16, 80, 205, 206, 207, 224
Seton, Elizabeth Ann, St, xi, 24
Sharon Hill, PA, 163
Shrewsbury, John Talbot, 16th Earl of, 48, 49, 57, 58, 68, 69, 71, 76, 77, 92, 93, 94
Society of the Holy Child Jesus: original inspiration, 4-5, 10-20, 65-68; spirituality and institutionalization, 89-208; Foundations, see place names; approbation: diocesan, 111, 178-179, 181-182, 188-189; pontifical, 111, 131-133, 182-189; community life, 99-107, 122-127, 180-181, 184, 186, 190; ranks of sisters imposed, 102-103, 182-183; internal dissension, 181-191; government: general chapters, 90, 129-130, 181-190; see Cornelia Connelly; Const SHCJ; apostolic character of SHCJ vs cloister rules, 90, 172-179, 181; motto, 61, 103, 207; mission and ministry: spiritual works of mercy, 93-95, 151-153; education: integral to SHCJ mission, 15, 115, 123, 205-206; theology/philosophy, methods, Book of Studies, 97, 151-161, 212; teacher training, 97, 125, 151, 153-156; schools, 94, 155-162; excellence, relevance, 97, 151, 161; expansion: in CC's lifetime, 95, 121, 151, 173; after 1879, 163-164; see also Catholic Revival; Charism of founder; Spirit of SHCJ
Society of Jesus, influence of. See Spiritual Tradition from which CC drew; Const SHCJ; Spiritual Exercises
Society of the Sacred Heart, 28, 51, 55, 63, 65-66, 68, 96, 98, 108, 135
Sodalities, 159
Spirit: use in spiritual literature, 17; of a religious founder, 16-17; of a religious institute, 16-17, 19-20, 193; of the mysteries of Christ (Bérulle), 23, n. 82; "of Mother Connelly," 121-122; CC's usage: of the Holy Child, 66, 124, 138, 193; of the SHCJ, 17-19, 113, 114, 121, 134, 193; of the Const SHCJ, 138; of the SHCJ government, 181; of St. Ignatius, 135
Spiritual Exercises of Ignatius of Loyola: fundamental formative instrument for CC, 12, 52-53, 103-105, 137-143; a way of living the Paschal Mystery, 105, 139-140; references to individual Exercises, 57, 60, 126, 137-138, 207; CC's expression of dynamics and themes, 103-105; CC's adaptations for women, 142-143
Steinmetz, Daniel, 25
Stokes, Mr, 155, 179
Sullivan, Claire, SHCJ, 225
Swope, Suzanna Steinmetz, 25, 26

Index

Teacher Training Colleges, 97, 125, 151, 153-155, 156
Teresa of Avila, St, 142, 145
Tourcher, F., 223
Towanda, PA, 121, 162-163, 164, 165
Towneley, Charles, Col, 177
Trinità dei Monti, 27, 59, 62
Trinity (Old) Church, Wilmington, DE, 32

Ullathorne, Bernard, Bishop, 99

Varin, Louis, Rev, 111
Ventura, G, Theatine, 145
Verhaegen, Peter John, SJ, 41
Verzeri, Teresa, Bl, 128, 133-134, 135, 145
Vienna, Austria, 50
de Villefort, Fr, SJ, 63

Wadham, Juliana, 223
Walker, Sr Aloysia, SHCJ, 99-101, 103, 105, 182

Walking with God, 124, 221, 243
Warner, Lady, 79
Weinig, M. Anthony, SHCJ, 127-128
Weyburg, Caspar, 25
White Cottage (Twin Oaks), Natchez, MS, 46
White, William, Episcopalian Bp of Philadelphia, PA, 30, 32
Whitty, Robert, SJ, 137
Wiseman, Nicholas Cardinal, Archbp of Westminster, 68, 69, 70, 92, 93, 94-96, 97, 99, 102, 107, 111, 129, 130, 148, 181, 191
Wood, James Frederick, Bp of Philadelphia, PA, 163, 180, 182
Woolley (also spelled Wholley), M. M. L., SHCJ, 184, 185, 186, 188

Xavier, Francis, St, SJ, 210-211

Yore, M. Wilfrid, SHCJ, 169, n. 121, 226

STUDIES IN WOMEN AND RELIGION

1. Joyce L. Irwin, **Womanhood in Radical Protestantism: 1525-1675**
2. Elizabeth A. Clark, **Jerome, Chrysostom and Friends: Essays and Translations**
3. Maureen Muldoon, **Abortion: An Annotated Indexed Bibliography**
4. **Lucretia Mott: Her Complete Speeches and Sermons**, edited by Dana Greene
5. Lorine M. Getz, **Flannery O'Connor: Her Life, Library and Book Reviews**
6. Ben Kimpel, **Emily Dickinson as Philosopher**
7. Jean LaPorte, **The Role of Women in Early Christianity**
8. Gayle Kimball, **The Religious Ideas of Harriet Beecher Stowe: Her Gospel of Womenhood**
9. **John Chrysostom: On Virginity; Against Remarriage**, translated by Sally Rieger Shore
10. Dale A. Johnson, **Women in English Religion: 1700-1925**
11. Earl Kent Brown, **Women of Mr. Wesley's Methodism**
12. Ellen M. Umansky, **Lily Montagu and the Advancement of Liberal Judaism: From Vision to Vocation**
13. Ellen NicKenzie Lawson, **The Three Sarahs: Documents of Antebellum Black College Women**
14. Elizabeth A. Clark, **The Life of Melania the Younger: Introduction, Translation and Commentary**
15. **Lily Montagu: Sermons, Addresses, Letters and Prayers**, edited by Ellen M. Umansky
16. Marjorie Procter-Smith, **Women in Shaker Community and Worship: A Feminist Analysis of the Uses of Religious Symbolism**
17. Anne Barstow, **Joan of Arc: Heretic, Mystic, Shaman**
18. Marta Powell Harley, **A Revelation of Purgatory by an Unknown Fifteenth Century Woman Visionary: Introduction, Critical Text, and Translation**
19. Sr. Caritas McCarthy, **The Spirituality of Cornelia Connelly: In God, For God, With God**
20. Elizabeth A. Clark, **Ascetic Piety and Women's Faith: Essays in Late Ancient Christianity**
21. John and Carol Stoneburner (eds.), **The Influence of Quaker Women on American History: Biographical Studies**